Drawing and Detailing using SolidWorks 2010

David C. Planchard & Marie P. Planchard CSWP

ISBN: 978-1-58503-571-7

PUBLICATIONS

Schroff Development Corporation

www.SDCpublications.com

SDC Publications

P.O. Box 1334

Mission KS 66222

(913) 262-2664

www.SDCpublications.com

Publisher: Stephen Schroff

Trademarks and Disclaimer

SolidWorks® Corp. is a Dassault Systèmes S.A. (Nasdaq: DASTY) company that develops and markets software for design, analysis, and product data management applications. Microsoft® Windows, Microsoft Office® and its family of products are registered trademarks of the Microsoft Corporation. Other software applications and parts described in this book are trademarks or registered trademarks of their respective owners.

Dimensions of parts are modified for illustration purposes. Every effort is made to provide an accurate text. The authors and the manufacturers shall not be held liable for any parts or drawings developed or designed with this book or any responsibility for inaccuracies that appear in the book. Web and company information was valid at the time of the printing.

Copyright© 2010 by D & M Education LLC

Examination Copies

Teacher evaluation copies for 2010, 2009, 2008, 2007, and 2006 SolidWorks books are available with classroom support materials and initial and final SolidWorks models. Books received as examination copies are for review purposes only. Examination copies are not intended for student use. Resale of examination copies is prohibited.

Learn by doing, not just by reading! Drawing and Detailing with SolidWorks 2010 is target toward a beginner or intermediate user who is looking for a step-by-step project based approach. This is NOT a drawing and detailing Engineering reference book.

Electronic Files

INTRODUCTION

Drawing and Detailing with SolidWorks 2010 is written to educate and assist students, designers, engineers, and professionals in the drawing and detailing tools of SolidWorks. Explore the learning process through a series of design situations, industry scenarios, projects, and objectives target towards the beginning to intermediate SolidWorks user.

Work through numerous activities to create multiple-view, multiple-sheet, detailed drawings, and assembly drawings. Develop Drawing templates, Sheet formats, and Custom Properties. Construct drawings that incorporate part configurations, assembly configurations, and design tables with equations. Manipulate annotations in parts, drawings, assemblies, Revision tables, Bills of Materials and more.

Apply your drawing and detailing knowledge to over thirty exercises. The exercises test your usage competency as well as explore additional topics with industry examples. Advanced exercises require the ability to create parts and assemblies.

Drawing and Detailing with SolidWorks 2010 *is not a reference book* for all drafting and drawing techniques. The book provides examples to:

- Start a SolidWorks 2010 session and to understand the following interfaces: Menu bar toolbar, Menu bar menu, Drop-down menus, Context toolbars, Consolidated drop-down toolbars, System feedback icons, Confirmation Corner, Heads-up View toolbar, Document Properties and more.

- Apply Document Properties to reflect the ASME Y14 Engineering Drawing and related Drawing Practices.

- Import an AutoCAD file as a Sheet format. Insert SolidWorks System Properties and Custom Properties.

- Create new SolidWorks Document tabs.

- Create multi-sheet drawings from various part configurations and develop the following drawing views: Standard, Isometric, Auxiliary, Section, Broken Section, Detail, Half Section (Cut-away), Crop, Projected Back, with a Bill of Materials and a Revision Table and Revisions.

- Insert and edit: Dimensions, Feature Control Frames, Datums, Geometric Tolerancing, Surface Finishes, and Weld Symbols using DimXpert and manual techniques.

- Create, apply, and save Blocks and Parametric Notes in a drawing.

Chapter 7 provides a bonus section on the *Certified SolidWorks Associate CSWA program* with sample exam questions and initial and final SolidWorks models.

The book is designed to compliment the SolidWorks Users Guide, SolidWorks Reference Guide, Standards, Engineering Drawing/Design and Graphics Communications reference books.

The authors recognize that companies utilize additional drawing standards. The authors developed the industry scenarios by combining industry experience with their knowledge of engineers, sales, vendors and manufacturers. These professionals are directly involved with SolidWorks everyday. Their work goes far beyond a simple drawing with a few dimensions. They create detailed drawings, assembly drawings, marketing drawings and customer drawings. SolidWorks users work between drawings, parts, assemblies and many other documents to complete a project on time.

Note to Instructors

Please contact the publisher: http://www.schroff.com for additional materials that will support the usage of this text in your classroom.

Trademarks, Disclaimer, and Copyrighted Material

SolidWorks® Corp. is a Dassault Systèmes S.A. (Nasdaq: DASTY) company that develops and markets software for design, analysis, and product data management applications Microsoft Windows®, Microsoft Office® and its family of products are registered trademarks of the Microsoft Corporation. Other software applications and parts described in this book are trademarks or registered trademarks of their respective owners.

Dimensions of parts and model views are modified for illustration purposes. Every effort is made to provide an accurate text. The authors and the manufacturers shall not be held liable for any parts or drawings developed or designed with this book or any responsibility for inaccuracies that appear in the book. Web and company information was valid at the time of this printing.

The Y14 ASME Engineering Drawing and Related Documentation Publications utilized in this text are as follows: ASME Y14.1 1995, ASME Y14.2M-1992 (R1998), ASME Y14.3M-1994 (R1999), ASME Y14.41-2003, ASME Y14.5-1982, ASME Y14.5M-1994, ASME B4.2

Note: By permission of The American Society of Mechanical Engineers, Codes and Standards, New York, NY, USA. All rights reserved.

Additional information references the American Welding Society, AWS 2.4:1997 Standard Symbols for Welding, Braising and Non-Destructive Examinations, Miami, Florida, USA.

About the Authors

David and Marie Planchard are co-authors of the following books:

- **A Commands Guide for SolidWorks® 2010**, 2009, 2008 and 2007

- **Assembly Modeling with SolidWorks® 2010**, 2008, 2006, 2005-2004, 2003 and 2001Plus

- **Drawing and Detailing with SolidWorks® 2010**, 2009, 2008, 2007, 2006, 2005, 2004, 2003, 2002 and 2001/2001Plus

- **Engineering Design with SolidWorks® 2010**, 2009, 2008, 2007, 2006, 2005, 2004, 2003, 2001Plus, 2001 and 1999

- **Engineering Graphics with SolidWorks 2010 with Multi-media CD**.

- **SolidWorks® The Basics, with Multi-media CD 2009**, 2008, 2007, 2006, 2005, 2004 and 2003.

- **SolidWorks® Tutorial with Multi-media CD 2010**, 2009, 2008, 2007, 2006, 2005, 2004, 2003 and 2001/2001Plus

- **The Fundamentals of SolidWorks®: Featuring the VEXplorer robot, 2008** and 2007

- **Official Certified SolidWorks® Associate (CSWA) Examination Guide** Version 2 and Version 1

- **Applications in Sheet Metal Using Pro/SHEETMETAL & Pro/ENGINEER**

Dedication

Writing this book was a substantial effort that would not have been possible without the help and support of my loving family and of my professional colleagues. I would like to thank Professor Holly Keyes Ault and the community of scholars at Worcester Polytechnic Institute who have enhanced my life and knowledge and helped to shape the approach and content to this book.

A special acknowledgment goes to my wife for her support and encouragement and to our loving daughter Stephanie Planchard who supported us during this intense and lengthy project.

Contact the Authors

This is the 8th edition of the book. We realize that keeping software application books current is imperative to our customers. We value the hundreds of professors, students, designers, and engineers that have provided us input to enhance our book. We value your suggestions and comments. Please contact us or visit our website www.dmeducation.net with any comments, questions or suggestions on this book or any of our other SolidWorks books. David Planchard, D & M Education, LLC, dplanchard@msn.com. or visit our website at **www.dmeducation.net**.

References

- <u>SolidWorks Users Guide</u>, SolidWorks Corporation, 2010.

- <u>SolidWorks Reference Guide</u>, SolidWorks Corporation, 2010.

- <u>ASME Y14 Engineering Drawing and Related Documentation Practices,</u> ASME, NY[1].

- <u>ASME B4.2 Dimensions Preferred Metric Limits and Fits</u>, ASME, NY[1].

- <u>AWS 2.4: 1997 Standard Symbols for Welding, Braising and Non-Destructive Examinations</u>, American Weld Society, Miami, Florida[4].

- Betoline, Wiebe, Miller, <u>Fundamentals of Graphics Communication</u>, Irwin, 1995.

- Earle, James, <u>Engineering Design Graphics</u>, Addison Wesley, 1999.

- Giesecke et al. <u>Modern Graphics Communication</u>, Prentice Hall, 1998.

- Hoelscher, Springer, Dobrovolny, <u>Graphics for Engineers</u>, John Wiley, 1968.

- Jensel & Helsel, <u>Engineering Drawing and Design</u>, Glencoe, 1990.

- Jensen, Cecil, <u>Interpreting Engineering Drawings</u>, Delmar-Thomson Learning, 2002.

- Lockhart & Johnson, <u>Engineering Design Communications</u>, Addison Wesley, 1999.

- Madsen, David et al. <u>Engineering Drawing and Design</u>, Delmar Thomson Learning, 2002.

- SMC Corporation, Compact Guide Cylinder Product Manual, SMC Corporation.[2]

- Emerson-EPT Corporation, Shaft Mount Reducer Product Manual, Emerson-EPT Corporation, a division of Emerson[3].

- Walker, James, <u>Machining Fundamentals</u>, Goodheart Wilcox, 1999.

[1] An on-line catalog of ASME Codes and Standards is available on their web site www.asme.org.

[2.] An on-line catalog of SMC parts and documents is available on their web site www.smcusa.com. Instructions to down load additional SMC components are available in the Appendix.

[3.] An on-line catalog of Emerson-EPT parts and documents is available on their web site www.emerson-ept.com.

[4.] An on-line catalog of AWS Standards is available on their web site www.aws.org.

There are over 200 enhancements in SolidWorks 2010. Over 90% of these enhancements, were requested directly by customers.

Every license of SolidWorks 2010 contains a copy of SolidWorks SustainabilityXpress. SustainabilityXpress calculates environmental impact on a model in four key areas: *Carbon Footprint, Energy Consumption, Air Acidification and Water Eutrophication*. Material and Manufacturing process region and Transportation Usage region are used as input variables.

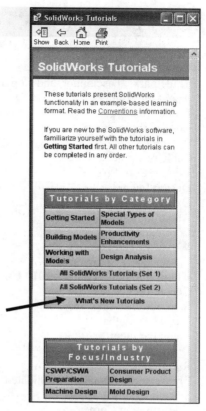

New in SolidWorks 2010 is the What's New Tutorials.

All *templates*, *logos* and needed *models* for this book are included on the enclosed CD. Copy the information from the CD to your local hard drive. Work from your local hard drive.

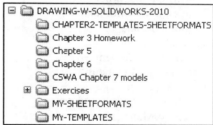

Table of Contents

Introduction   **I-1**
Notes to Instructors   I-2
Trademarks, Disclaimer, and Copyrighted Material   I-2
About the Authors   I-3
Dedication   I-3
Contact the Authors   I-3
Reference   I-4
Table of Contents   I-6
What is SolidWorks?   I-12
Design Intent   I-17
Overview of Chapters   I-21
About the Book   I-24
Command Syntax   I-24
Windows Terminology   I-26

Chapter 1 - SolidWorks 2010 User Interface   **1-1**
Chapter Objective   1-3
Start a SolidWorks Session   1-3
Menu bar toolbar   1-4
Menu bar menu   1-5
Drop-down menus   1-5
Right-click Context toolbar   1-6
Fly-out tool buttons / Consolidated menus   1-7
System feedback icons   1-7
Confirmation Corner   1-7
Heads-up View toolbar   1-8
CommandManager   1-10
  Part Document   1-10
  Drawing Document   1-11
  Assembly Document   1-12
FeatureManager   1-13
  FeatureManager design tree   1-13
  PropertyManager   1-13
  ConfigurationManager   1-13
  DimXpertManager   1-13
Fly-out FeatureManager   1-15
Task Pane   1-16
SolidWorks Resources   1-16
Design Library   1-16
File Explorer   1-17
Search   1-17
View Palette   1-17
Appearances/Scenes   1-18
Custom Properties   1-18
Document Recovery   1-18
Motion Study   1-19
Chapter Terminology   1-27

Chapter 2 - Drawing Templates and Sheet Formats   **2-1**
Chapter Objective   2-3
Chapter Overview   2-4
Engineering Drawing and Related Documentation Practices   2-5
File Management   2-6

Default Drawing Template, Sheet Format, and Sheet Size 2-7
 New SolidWorks Document 2-8
  Sheet Format/Size 2-9
  ASME Y14.1 Drawing Sheet Size and Format 2-10
Cursor Feedback 2-15
Sheet Properties 2-16
Glass Box Method 2-17
Six Principal views 2-17
Display Styles / modes 2-20
Sheet Options 2-21
 File Locations 2-21
Document Properties 2-22
 Font 2-23
 Arrowheads 2-24
 Line Widths 2-25
 Line Font 2-26
 Document Properties-Dimensions 2-27
 Drafting (Dimensioning) Standard 2-28
 Dual dimensions Display Option 2-28
 Fixed Size Weld Symbols Option 2-28
 Display Datums per 1982 Option 2-29
 Leading Zeros and Trailing Zeros Option 2-29
 Alternative Section Display Option 2-29
 Centerline Extension and Center Marks Option 2-29
 Auto Insert on View Creation Option 2-30
 Extension Lines Option 2-30
 Datum Feature Option 2-31
 Surface Finish Symbols 2-31
 Break Line Option 2-31
 Automatic Update on BOM Option 2-31
 Cosmetic Thread Display Option 2-31
 Document Properties, Annotations Font 2-34
 Note Font 2-34
 Dimension Font 2-34
 Auxiliary View / Auxiliary View Label Font 2-35
 Detail View / Detail View Label Font 2-35
 Section View / Section View Label Font 2-36
 View Arrow Font 2-36
 Surface Finish, Weld Symbol, and Balloon Font 2-36
 Tables Font 2-37
 Offset Distances Option 2-37
 Arrows Option 2-38
 Break Dimension/Extension Option 2-39
 Bent Leader Length Option 2-40
Document Properties-Notes and Balloons Option 2-41
Document Properties-Arrows 2-42
Document Properties-Line Font 2-43
Predefined and Projected Views 2-44
Save As 2-46
Sheet Format 2-49
Title Block Notes and Properties 2-56
System Properties 2-56
User Defined Properties 2-58
Linked Notes 2-58
Size, Sheet and Scale Properties 2-61
Custom Property and Logo Picture 2-63

User Defined Custom Property							2-65
Copy/Paste Custom Properties							2-65
Custom Properties in Parts and Assemblies					2-67
General Notes								2-69
Tables									2-70
Save Sheet Format and Save Drawing Template					2-74
A ANSI Size Drawing Template							2-76
Chapter Summary								2-77
Chapter Terminology								2-78
Questions and Exercises							2-81

Chapter 3 - Drawings and Various Drawing Views				**3-1**
Chapter Objective								3-3
Chapter Overview								3-4
Fundamentals of Orthographic Projection					3-8
Review the ROD Part and Configurations					3-11
ROD Drawing: Sheet1 Short Rod Configurations					3-16
View Boundary Properties and Lock View Options				3-20
ROD Drawing: Sheet2 Long Rod Configuration					3-21
ROD Drawing: Sheet3 Long Rod Configuration					3-25
ROD Drawing-Revolved Section							3-29
ROD Drawing-Broken Isometric View						3-32
Review the TUBE Part							3-36
TUBE Drawing								3-40
TUBE Drawing-Section View and Detail View					3-43
TUBE Drawing-Broken-out Section View, Auxiliary View and Crop View		3-45
TUBE Drawing-Half Section Isometric (Cut-Away)				3-50
COVERPLATE Drawing							3-56
COVERPLATE Drawing-Offset Section View and Aligned Section View		3-60
Additional View Options and View Properties					3-65
Multi-view Drawings								3-67
 Auxiliary View								3-69
 Rotate View								3-70
 Perspective View								3-72
 Alternative Position View							3-73
 Empty View								3-73
 Relative To Model View							3-74
Chapter Summary								3-75
Chapter Terminology								3-75
Questions and Exercises							3-79

Chapter 4 - Fundamentals of Detailing					**4-1**
Chapter Objective								4-3
Chapter Overview								4-4
Tolerance Type								4-10
TUBE Drawing-Detailing							4-11
Hide Dimensions								4-16
Show Dimensions								4-16
TUBE Drawing-Detailing Section View, Top View and Detail View			4-17
TUBE Drawing-Detailing Detail View and Front View				4-25
TUBE Drawing-Detailing Right View, Back View and Holes			4-29
TUBE Drawing-Adding Dimensions						4-38
Detailing Tips								4-43
COVERPLATE Drawing-Detailing							4-46
COVERPLATE Drawing-Modifying Features					4-54
Modifying Features								4-58

Additional Information-Dimension PropertyManager and Dimensioning Features   4-58
Dimension Value PropertyManager   4-60
  Style   4-60
  Tolerance/Precision   4-61
  Primary Value   4-62
  Text Dimension   4-63
  Dual Dimension   4-63
Dimension Leader PropertyManager   4-64
  Witness/Leader Display   4-64
  Break Lines   4-65
  Custom Text Position   4-65
  Arc Condition   4-65
Dimension Other PropertyManager   4-66
  Override Units   4-66
  Text Fonts   4-66
  Options   4-66
  Layers   4-67
  Dimension Properties Dialog box   4-67
  Hide Dimension Line, Hide Extension Line and Driven   4-68
  Dimension Schemes   4-69
  Foreshortened Radii   4-69
  Partially Rounded Ends, Center/Min/Max Arc Condition   4-70
  Display Option, Offset Text   4-71
  Slotted Holes   4-71
  Grid/Snap   4-73
  Location of Features   4-73
  Base Line Dimensioning   4-73
  Ordinate Dimension   4-74
View Layout Toolbar   4-75
Annotation Toolbar   4-75
Chapter Summary   4-76
Chapter Terminology   4-77
Questions and Exercises   4-81

Chapter 5 - Assembly Drawings   **5-1**
Chapter Objective   5-3
Chapter Overview   5-4
CYLINDER Assembly-Exploded View   5-7
CYLINDER Assembly Drawing-Insert Balloons   5-11
CYLINDER Assembly-Bill of Materials   5-17
Materials Editor and Mass Properties   5-20
Configuration Properties   5-24
Design Table   5-31
Bill of Materials - Part 2   5-37
  Editing Cells   5-37
  Editing Tables   5-37
  Insert Columns   5-39
  Modify Header   5-39
  Insert Equation   5-42
CYLINDER Assembly-Design Table   5-42
CYLINDER Drawing-Multiple Configurations   5-50
Revision Table   5-59
CYLINDER Assembly-Section View and Broken-out Section   5-65
Hide Behind Plane   5-66
Large Assembly Drawing Performance   5-67
eDrawing 2010   5-69

Export   5-69
Chapter Summary   5-69
Chapter Terminology   5-70
Questions and Exercises   5-74

Chapter 6 - Applied Geometric Tolerancing and Other Symbols   **6-1**
Chapter Objective   6-3
Chapter Overview   6-4
Drawing Template   6-7
VALVEPLATE1 Part - DimXpert: Plus and Minus Option   6-8
Tolerance Types and Features   6-9
Setting for DimXpert   6-9
Block Tolerance vs. General Tolerance   6-9
DimXpert Toolbar   6-16
DimXpert Annotations and Drawings   6-17
Using DimXpert Manually in a Part   6-21
Vise Assembly - DimXpert   6-21
VALVEPLATE1 - GDT Part: Datums, Feature Control Frames, Geometric   6-26
Tolerances, and Surface Finish
VALVEPLATE1 - GDT Part - DimXpert: Geometric Option   6-26
VALVEPLATE1 - GDT Drawing - View Palette   6-28
VALVEPLATE1 - GDT Drawing - Surface Finish   6-29
VALVEPLATE1 - GDT eDrawing   6-33
ASME Y14.41 Digital Product Definition Data Practices   6-34
Modify the ASME14-41 Drawing   6-36
PLATE-TUBE Assembly Drawing and Weld Symbols   6-43
PLATE-CATALOG Drawing, Design Table and EXCEL Formatting   6-50
Blocks   6-66
Additional Information   6-72
  Blocks   6-72
  DWGEditor   6-72
  DXF/DWG Import   6-73
  Geometric Tolerance Symbols   6-74
  Types of Fits   6-74
Chapter Summary   6-75
Chapter Terminology   6-76
Questions and Exercises   6-79

Chapter 7 - Introduction to the Certified SolidWorks Associated CSWA Exam **7-1**
Chapter Objective   7-3
Introduction   7-3
Intended Audience   7-3
CSWA Exam Content   7-5
About the CSWA Exam   7-7
CSWA Certification   7-7
Exam day   7-7
When I pass   7-14
Basic Theory and Drawing Theory   7-16
Part Modeling   7-21
Advanced Part Modeling   7-25
Assembly Modeling   7-34
Advanced Modeling Theory and Analysis   7-39
Definition review   7-42

Appendix   **A-1**
ECO Form   A-1
Types of Decimal Dimensions (ASME Y14.5M)   A-2
Tolerance Display for Inch and Metric Dimensions (ASME Y14.5M)   A-2
SolidWorks Keyboards Shortcuts   A-3
Windows Shortcuts   A-4
Helpful On-Line Information   A-5

Index   **Index-1**

What is SolidWorks?

SolidWorks® is a mechanical design automation software package used to build parts, assemblies and drawings that takes advantage of the familiar Microsoft® Windows graphical user interface.

SolidWorks is an easy to learn design and analysis tool, (SolidWorks SimulationXpress, SolidWorks Motion, SolidWorks Flow Simulation, etc.) which makes it possible for designers to quickly sketch 2D and 3D concepts, create 3D parts and assemblies and detail 2D drawings.

In SolidWorks, you create 2D and 3D sketches, 3D parts, 3D assemblies and 2D drawings. The part, assembly and drawing documents are related. Additional information on SolidWorks and its family of products can be obtained at their URL, www.SolidWorks.com.

Drawing refers to the SolidWorks module used to insert, add, and modify views in an engineering drawing. Detailing refers to the dimensions, notes, symbols, and Bill of Materials used to document the drawing.

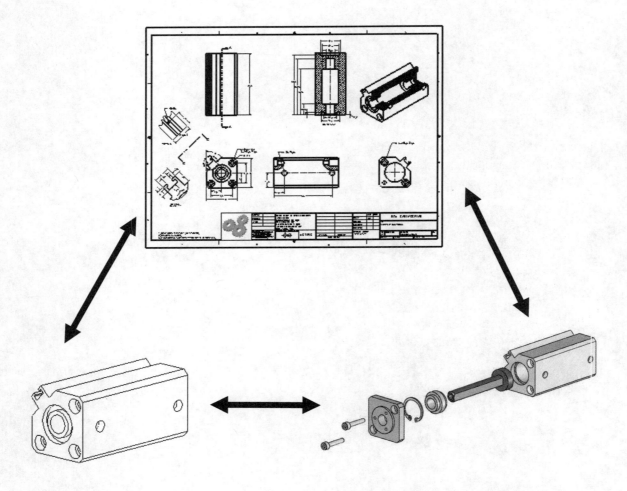

Features are the building blocks of parts. Use feature tools such as: Extruded Boss/Base, Extruded Cut, Fillet, etc. from the Features tab in the CommandManager to create 3D parts.

Extruded features begin with a 2D sketch created on a Sketch plane.

The 2D sketch is a profile or cross section. Use sketch tools such as: Line, Center Rectangle, Slot, Circle, etc. from the Sketch tab in the CommandManager to create a 2D sketch. Sketch the general shape of the profile. Add geometric relationships and dimensions to control the exact size of the geometry and your Design Intent. Design for change!

Create features by selecting edges or faces of existing features, such as a Fillet. The Fillet feature rounds sharp corners.

Dimensions drive features. Change a dimension, and you change the size of the part.

Use Geometric relationships: Vertical, Horizontal, Parallel, etc. and various End Conditions to maintain the Design Intent.

Create a hole that penetrates through a part (Through All). SolidWorks maintains relationships through the change.

The step-by-step approach used in this text allows you to create, edit and modify parts, assemblies and drawings. Change is an integral part of design!

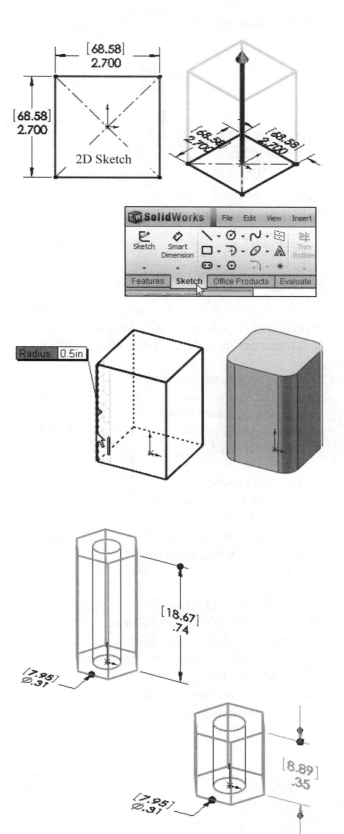

The drawing reflects the changes of the part.

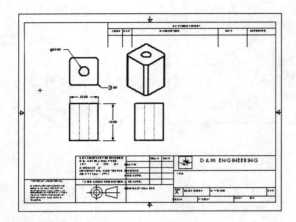
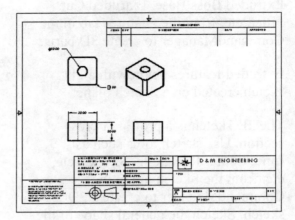

A Drawing template is the foundation for drawing information. Specified drawing standards and size, company information, manufacturing and or assembly requirements and more are included in a drawing template.

Drawing templates contain Document Properties settings such as millimeter or inch units and ANSI or ISO drawing standards.

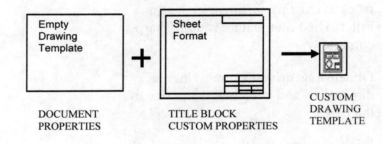

Drawing templates also contain information included in the sheet format such as a Title block, company name, company logo, and custom properties.

A drawing is a 2D representation of a 3D part or assembly. SolidWorks utilizes various Orthographic views (Third Angle Projection or First Angle Projection) to display the 3D model on the 2D drawing. Note: All drawings in this book are displayed in Third Angle Projection.

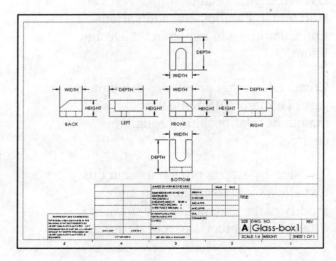

Additional views represent a 3D model or assembly. Insert views from the Drawing tools in SolidWorks such as a Section view, Auxiliary view, or Detail view. Create additional views by combining Drawing tools with different part configurations. The Half Section Isometric view utilizes second configuration that controls the state of an Extruded Cut feature.

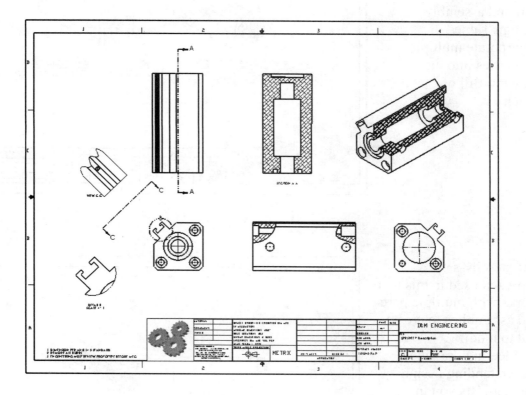

Annotations represent a text note or symbol that documents a part, assembly, or drawing.

Insert feature dimensions and annotations from the part or assembly into the drawing. Create additional reference dimensions and annotations in the drawing.

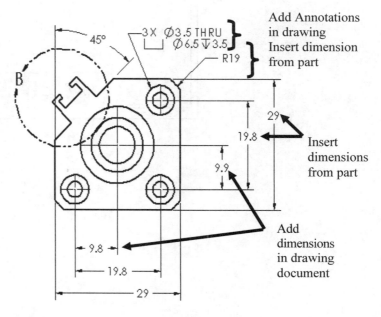

Apply different
configurations in a
drawing. Assign
properties such as
material, mass, and cost
to individual parts in
part and assembly
Design Tables.
Incorporate multiple
properties into the
drawing Bill of
Materials.

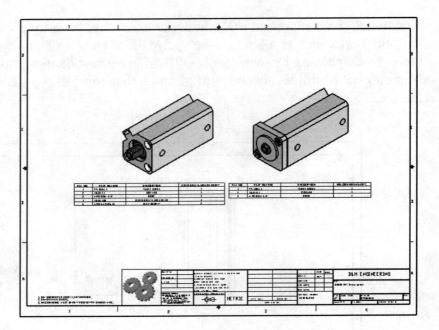

The step-by-step
approach used in this text
works with multiple parts
and assemblies to create
and to modify
engineering drawings.
Understanding design
intent assists you in
implementing changes.

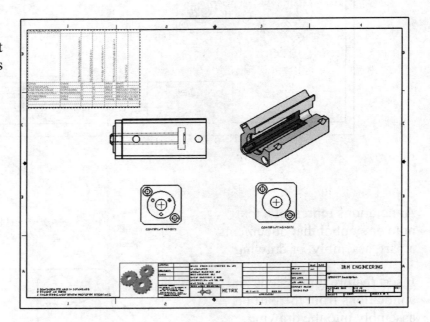

Design Intent

The SolidWorks definition of design intent is the process in which the model is developed to accept future changes.

Models behave differently when design changes occur. Design for change. Utilize geometry for symmetry, reuse common features and reuse common parts.

Build change into the following areas:

1. Sketch

2. Feature

3. Part

4. Assembly

5. Drawing

1. Design Intent in the Sketch

Build design intent in a sketch as the profile is created. A profile is determined from the selected Sketch Entity. Example: Corner Rectangle, Circle, Arc, Point, etc.

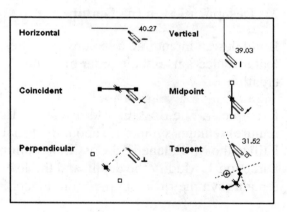

Apply symmetry into a profile through a sketch centerline, mirror entity and position about the reference planes and Origin.

Build design intent as you sketch with automatic Geometric relations. Document the decisions made during the up-front design process. This is very valuable when you modify the design later.

A rectangle contains Horizontal, Vertical, and Perpendicular automatic Geometric relations. Apply design intent using added Geometric relations. Example: Horizontal, Vertical, Collinear, Perpendicular, Parallel etc.

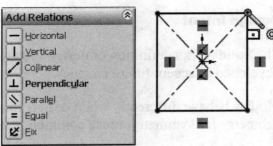

Example A: Apply design intent to create a square profile. Sketch a rectangle. Apply the Center Rectangle tool. Note: No construction reference centerline or Midpoint relation is required with the Center Rectangle tool. Insert dimensions to define the square.

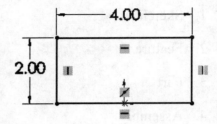

Example B: Develop a rectangular profile. Apply the Corner Rectangle tool. The bottom horizontal midpoint of the rectangular profile is located at the Origin. Add a Midpoint relation between the horizontal edge of the rectangle and the Origin. Insert two dimensions to define the width and height of the rectangle as illustrated.

2. Design Intent in the Feature

Build design intent into a feature by addressing symmetry, feature selection, and the order of feature creation.

Example A: The Boss-Extrude1 feature (Base feature) remains symmetric about the Front Plane. Utilize the Mid Plane End Condition option in Direction 1. Modify the depth, and the feature remains symmetric about the Front Plane.

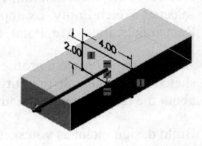

Example B: Do you create each tooth separate using the Extruded Cut feature? No. Create a single tooth and then apply the Circular Pattern feature. Create 34 teeth for a Circular Pattern feature. Modify the number of teeth from 32 to 24.

3. Design Intent in the Part

Utilize symmetry, feature order and reusing common features to build design intent into the part.

Example A: Feature order. Is the entire part symmetric? Feature order affects the part. Apply the Shell feature before the Fillet feature and the inside corners remain perpendicular.

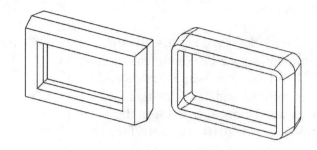

4. Design Intent in the Assembly

Utilizing symmetry, reusing common parts and using the Mate relation between parts builds the design intent into an assembly.

Example A: Reuse geometry in an assembly. The assembly contains a linear pattern of holes. Insert one screw into the first hole. Utilize the Component Pattern feature to copy the machine screw to the other holes.

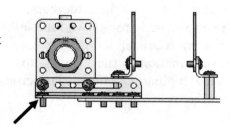

5. Design Intent in the Drawing

Utilize dimensions, tolerance and notes in parts and assemblies to build the design intent into the Drawing.

Example A: Tolerance and material in the drawing.

Insert an outside diameter tolerance +.000/-.002 into the TUBE part. The tolerance propagates to the drawing.

Define the Custom Property MATERIAL in the part. The MATERIAL Custom Property propagates to the drawing.

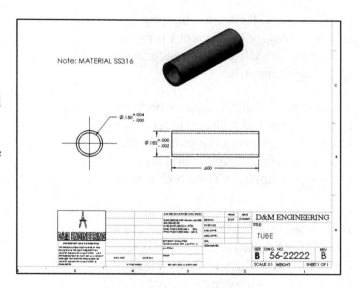

Overview of Chapters

Chapter 1: SolidWorks 2010 User Interface

SolidWorks is a design software application used to model and create 2D and 3D sketches, 3D parts and assemblies, and 2D drawings. Chapter 1 introduces you to the SolidWorks 2010 User Interface and CommandManager: Menu bar toolbar, Menu bar menu, Drop-down menus, Context toolbars, Consolidated drop-down toolbars, System feedback icons, Confirmation Corner, Heads-up View toolbar, Document Properties and more.

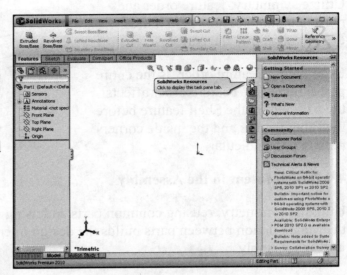

Chapter 2: Drawing Templates and Sheet Formats

Explore the SolidWorks drawing template. Apply Document Properties to reflect the ASME Y14 Engineering Drawing Standards.

Investigate the differences between a Sheet format and a Drawing template. Create two Drawing templates. Create a C-size Drawing template and an A-size Drawing template. Create a C-size Sheet format.

Import an AutoCAD drawing to create a new Sheet format. Apply SolidWorks Properties and Custom Properties in the Sheet format. Combine the Sheet format with an empty drawing template to create a custom Drawing template.

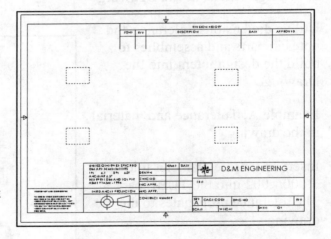

Chapter 3: Drawings and Various Drawing Views

Create three drawings: TUBE, ROD, and COVERPLATE. Insert the following drawing views: *Front Top, Right, Isometric, Auxiliary, Detail, Section, Crop, Broken Section, Half Section, Revolved Section, Offset Section, Removed, Projected, Aligned Section, and more.*

Insert, modify, suppress, unsuppressed, and delete drawing views and dimensions. Create multi-sheet drawings from various part configurations.

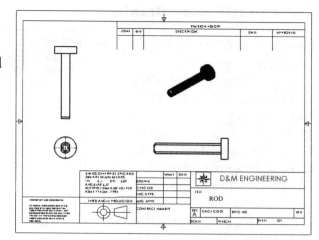

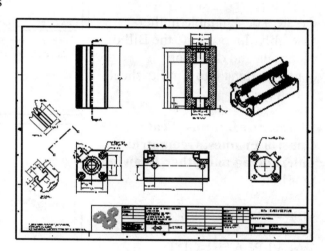

Chapter 4: Fundamentals of Detailing

Insert dimensions and annotations required to detail the TUBE and COVERPLATE drawings.

Insert, add, and modify dimensions for part features. Insert and add notes to the drawing.

Incorporate drawing standards to document specific features.

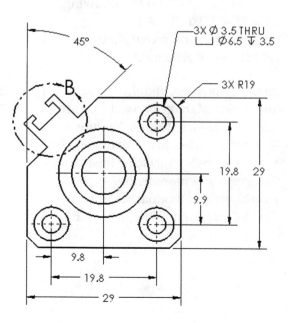

Chapter 5: Assembly Drawings

Develop the CYLINDER assembly. Combine configurations of the TUBE, ROD and COVERPLATE components.

Obtain an understanding of Custom Properties and SolidWorks Properties.

Combine Properties in a Bill of Materials.

Create a design table in the assembly. Incorporate the Bill of Materials and different configurations into a multi-sheet drawing.

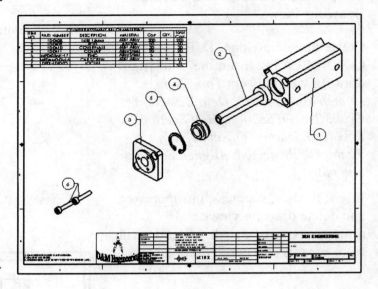

Chapter 6: Datums, Feature Control Frames, Geometric Tolerancing and other Drawing Symbols

Create five drawings: VALVEPLATE1, VALVEPLATE1-GDT, VALVEPLATE1-GDT eDrawing, PLATE-TUBE, PLATE-CATALOG, and modify the ASME14-41 drawing.

Apply DimXpert and the DimXpert Manager. Insert Feature Control Frames, Datum Feature Symbols, Geometric Tolerance, Weld Symbols, Surface Finish Symbols, and more using DimXpert and manual techniques. Format a Design Table in EXCEL.

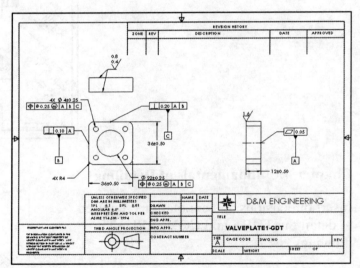

Chapter 7: Introduction to the Certified SolidWorks Associated CSWA exam

Chapter 7 provides a basic introduction into the curriculum and exam categories for the Certified SolidWorks Associated CSWA Certification program. Review the exam procedure, process and required model knowledge needed to take and pass the exam.

Review the five exam categories: *Basic Theory and Drawing Theory, Part Modeling, Advanced Part Modeling, Assembly Modeling, and Advanced Modeling Theory and Analysis.*

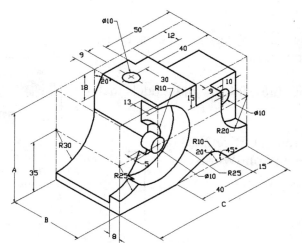

Given:
A = 63, B = 50, C = 100
Material: Copper
Units: MMGS
Density: .0089 g/mm^3
All HOLES THROUGH ALL

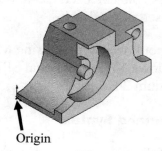

Origin

About the Book

The following conventions are used throughout this book:

- The term document is used to refer a SolidWorks part, drawing, or assembly file.

- The list of items across the top of the SolidWorks interface is the Menu bar menu or the Menu bar toolbar. Each item in the Menu bar has a pull-down menu. When you need to select a series of commands from these menus, the following format is used: Click **View**, check **Origins** from the Menu bar menu. The Origins are displayed in the Graphics window.

- The book is organized into seven Chapters. Each Chapter is focused on a specific subject or feature.

- Use the enclosed CD to obtain files, folders and models that are used in this book.

The book was written using Microsoft Office 2003 on Windows XP Professional SP2 with SolidWorks Premium 2010 SP1.

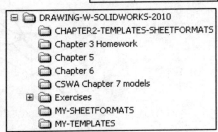

Command Syntax

The following command syntax is utilized throughout the text. Commands that require you to perform an action are displayed in **Bold** text.

Format:	Convention:	Example:
Bold	All commands actions. Selected icon button. Selected geometry: line, circle. Value entries.	Click **Options** from the Menu bar toolbar. Click **Corner Rectangle** from the Sketch toolbar. Select the **center point**. Enter **3.0** for Radius.
Capitalized	Filenames. First letter in a feature name.	**Save** the FLASHLIGHT assembly. Click the **Extruded Base** feature.

Windows Terminology

The mouse buttons provide an integral role in executing SolidWorks commands. The mouse buttons execute commands, select geometry, display Shortcut menus and provide information feedback. The table below contains a summary of mouse button terminology:

Item:	Description:
Click	Press and release the left mouse button.
Double-click	Double press and release the left mouse button.
Click inside	Press the left mouse button. Wait a second, and then press the left mouse button inside the text box. Use this technique to modify Feature names in the FeatureManager design tree.
Drag	Point to an object, press and hold the left mouse button down. Move the mouse pointer to a new location. Release the left mouse button.
Right-click	Press and release the right mouse button. A Shortcut menu is displayed. Use the left mouse button to select a menu command.
ToolTip	Position the mouse pointer over an Icon (button). The tool name is displayed below the mouse pointer.
Large ToolTip	Position the mouse pointer over an Icon (button). The mouse pointer displays the tool name and a description of its functionality below the Icon.
Mouse pointer feedback	Position the mouse pointer over various areas of the sketch, part, assembly or drawing. The cursor provides feedback depending on the geometry.
Window-select	To select multiple items, position the mouse pointer in an upper corner location. Drag the mouse pointer to the opposite corner. Release the mouse pointer. The bounding box contains the selected items.

A mouse with a center wheel provides additional functionality in SolidWorks. Roll the center wheel downward to enlarge the model in the Graphics window. Hold the center wheel down. Drag the mouse in the Graphics window to rotate the model. Review various Windows terminology that describes: menus, toolbars, and commands that constitute the graphical user interface in SolidWorks.

SolidWorks System requirements for Microsoft Windows Operating Systems and hardware are as illustrated.

⚡ SolidWorks System requirements for Microsoft Windows Operating Systems and hardware are as illustrated.

Supported Microsoft Windows® Operating Systems (9)			
	SolidWorks 2008	SolidWorks 2009	SolidWorks 2010
Windows 7 32-bit (2)(10)	No	No	Yes
Windows 7 64-bit (2)(10)	No	No	Yes
Vista 32-bit (3)	Yes	Yes	Yes
Vista 64-bit (3)(4)	Yes	Yes	Yes
XP Professional 32-bit (5)(1)	Yes	Yes	Yes
XP Professional 64-bit (4)(1)	Yes	Yes	Yes

Computer and Software Requirements:
RAM
- **Minimum:** 1GB RAM
- **Recommended:** 2GB RAM
- **Very large models:** X64 processor and Operating System with 6GB or more of RAM when system resources exceed the 2GB limit of a 32-bit OS architecture.

⚡ The book does not cover installing SolidWorks for the first time. A default SolidWorks installation presents you with several options. For additional information for an Education Edition, visit the following site: http://www.solidworks.com/sw/docs/EDU_2009_Inst allation_Instructions.pdf

⚡ There are slight screen and toolbar variations between the various versions and products of SolidWorks: *Student Edition*, *SolidWorks*, *SolidWorks Professional*, and *SolidWorks Premium*. The book was written using SolidWorks Office Premium with version SP1.0

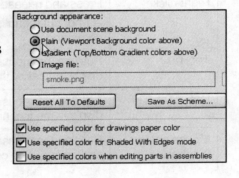

⚡ For improved drawing visibility, the default Drawing Sheet background color is modified to White in this book.

Chapter 1

SolidWorks 2010 User Interface

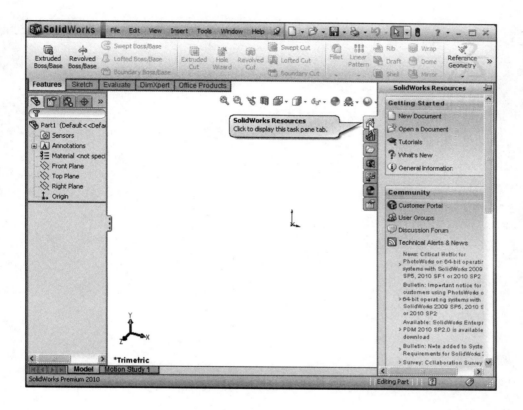

Below are the desired outcomes and usage competencies based on the completion of Chapter 1.

Desired Outcomes:	Usage Competencies:
• A comprehensive understanding of the SolidWorks 2010 User Interface and CommandManager.	• Ability to establish a SolidWorks session. • Aptitude to apply and use the following: *Menu bar toolbar, Menu bar menu, Drop-down menus, Context toolbars, Consolidated drop-down toolbars, System feedback icons, Confirmation Corner, Heads-up View toolbar, Document Properties and more.*

Notes:

Chapter 1 - SolidWorks 2010 User Interface

Chapter Objective

Provide a comprehensive understanding of the SolidWorks default User Interface and CommandManager: *Menu bar toolbar, Menu bar menu, Drop-down menu, Right-click Pop-up menus, Context toolbars / menus, Fly-out tool button, System feedback icons, Confirmation Corner, Heads-up View toolbar and an understanding of System Options, Document Properties, Part templates, File management and more.*

On the completion of this chapter, you will be able to:

- Establish a SolidWorks 2010 session.

- Comprehend the SolidWorks 2010 User Interface.

- Recognize the default Reference Planes in the FeatureManager.

- Understand and apply the Task Pane.

- Recognize the default CommandManager for a Part, Assembly, and Drawing document.

- Apply the Motion Study tool.

Start a SolidWorks Session

The SolidWorks application is located in the Programs folder. SolidWorks displays the Tip of the Day box. Read the Tip of the Day every day to obtain additional information on SolidWorks.

Create a new part. Click **File**, **New** from the Menu bar menu or click **New** □ from the Menu bar toolbar. There are two options for a new document: *Novice* and *Advanced*. Select the Advanced option. Select the Part document.

Activity: Start a SolidWorks Session

Start a SolidWorks 2010 session.

1)   Click **Start** on the Windows Taskbar.

2)   Click **All Programs**.

3)   Click the **SolidWorks 2010** folder.

4)   Click **SolidWorks 2010** application. The SolidWorks program window opens. Note: Do not open a document at this time.

☼ If available, double-click the SolidWorks 2010 icon on the Windows Desktop to start a SolidWorks session.

Screen shots and illustrations in the book display the SolidWorks user default setup.

 All models were created using SolidWorks 2010 SP1.

Read the Tip of the Day dialog box.

5)   If you do not see this screen, click the SolidWorks **Resources** 🏠 icon on the right side of the Graphics window located in the Task Pane as illustrated.

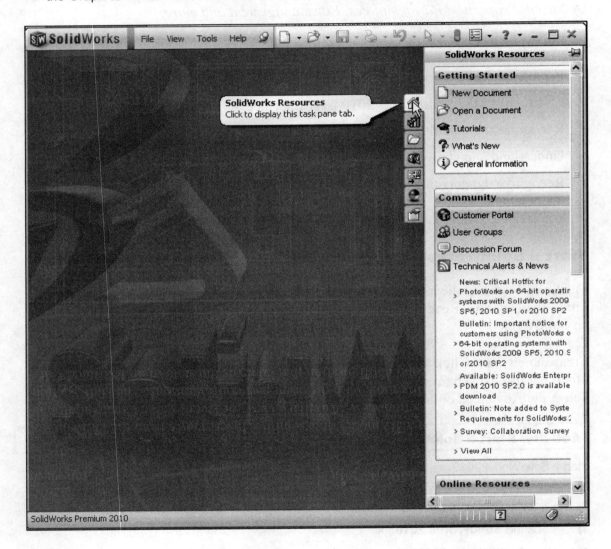

Activity: Understanding the SolidWorks UI and CommandManager

The SolidWorks 2010 (UI) is design to make maximum use of the Graphics window. The Menu Bar toolbar contains a set of the most frequently used tool buttons from the Standard toolbar. The available default tools are:

- **New** - Creates a new document.

- **Open** - Opens an existing document.

- **Save** - Saves an active document.

- **Print** - Prints an active document.

- **Undo** - Reverses the last action.

- **Select** - Selects Sketch entities, components and more.

- **Rebuild** - Rebuilds the active part, assembly or drawing.

- **Options** - Changes system options and Add-Ins for SolidWorks.

Expand the drop-down menu to display additional options and tools.

Until a file is converted to the current version of SolidWorks and saved, a warning icon is displayed on the Save tool as illustrated.

Menu bar menu

Click SolidWorks in the Menu bar toolbar to display the Menu bar menu. SolidWorks provides a context-sensitive menu structure. The menu titles remain the same for all three types of documents, but the menu items change depending on which type of document is active.

Example: The Insert menu includes features in part documents, mates in assembly documents, and drawing views in drawing documents. The display of the menu is also dependent on the work flow customization that you have selected. The default menu items for an active document are: *File*, *Edit*, *View*, *Insert*, *Tools*, *Window*, *Help* and *Pin*.

The Pin 📌 option displays the Menu bar toolbar and the Menu bar menu as illustrated. Throughout the book, the Menu bar menu and the Menu bar toolbar is referred to as the Menu bar.

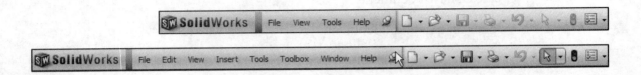

Drop-down menu

SolidWorks takes advantage of the familiar Microsoft® Windows user interface. Communicate with SolidWorks through drop-down menus, Context sensitive toolbars, Consolidated toolbars or the CommandManager tabs.

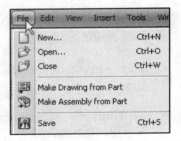

A command is an instruction that informs SolidWorks to perform a task.

To close a SolidWorks drop-down menu, press the Esc key. You can also click any other part of the SolidWorks Graphics window or click another drop-down menu.

Right-click

Right-click in the Graphics window on a model, or in the FeatureManager on a feature or sketch, to display the Context-sensitive toolbar. If you are in the middle of a command, this toolbar displays a list of options specifically related to that command.

The most commonly used tools are located in the Pop-up Context toolbar and CommandManager.

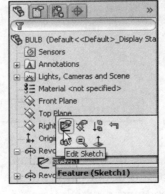
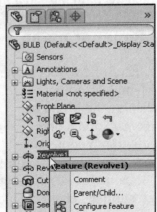

🔆 Press the **s** key to view/access previous command tools in the Graphics window.

Consolidated toolbar

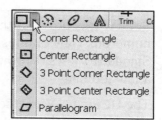

Similar commands are grouped together in the CommandManager. Example: Variations of the Rectangle sketch tool are grouped in a single fly-out button as illustrated.

If you select the Consolidated toolbar button without expanding:

- For some commands such as Sketch, the most commonly used command is performed. This command is the first listed and the command shown on the button.

- For commands such as rectangle, where you may want to repeatedly create the same variant of the rectangle, the last used command is performed. This is the highlighted command when the Consolidated toolbar is expanded.

System feedback

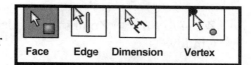

SolidWorks provides system feedback by attaching a symbol to the mouse pointer cursor. The system feedback symbol indicates what you are selecting or what the system is expecting you to select.

As you move the mouse pointer across your model, system feedback is displayed in the form of a symbol, riding next to the cursor as illustrated. This is a valuable feature in SolidWorks.

Confirmation corner

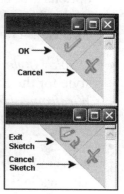

When numerous SolidWorks commands are active, a symbol or a set of symbols are displayed in the upper right hand corner of the Graphics window. This area is called the Confirmation Corner.

When a sketch is active, the confirmation corner box displays two symbols. The first symbol is the sketch tool icon. The second symbol is a large red X. These two symbols supply a visual reminder that you are in an active sketch. Click the sketch symbol icon to exit the sketch and to saves any changes that you made.

When other commands are active, the confirmation corner box provides a green check mark and a large red X.

Use the green check mark to execute the current command. Use the large red X to cancel the command.

Heads-up View toolbar

SolidWorks provides the user with numerous view options from the Standard Views, View and Heads-up View toolbar.

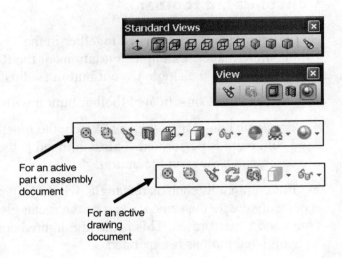

The Heads-up View toolbar is a transparent toolbar that is displayed in the Graphics window when a document is active.

For an active part or assembly document

For an active drawing document

You can hide, move or modify the Heads-up View toolbar. To modify the Heads-up View toolbar: right-click on a tool and select or deselect the tools that you want to display.

The following views are available: Note: Views are document dependent.

- *Zoom to Fit* : Zooms the model to fit the Graphics window.

- *Zoom to Area* : Zooms to the areas you select with a bounding box.

- *Previous View* : Displays the previous view.

- *Section View* : Displays a cutaway of a part or assembly, using one or more cross section planes.

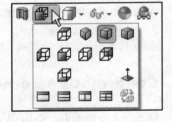

- *View Orientation* : Provides the ability to select a view orientation or the number of viewports. The available options are: *Top, Isometric, Trimetric, Dimetric, Left, Front, Right, Back, Bottom, Single view, Two view - Horizontal, Two view - Vertical, Four view.*

- *Display Style* : Provides the ability to display the style for the active view. The available options are: *Wireframe, Hidden Lines Visible, Hidden Lines Removed, Shaded, Shaded With Edges.*

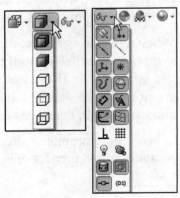

- *Hide/Show Items* : Provides the ability to select items to hide or show in the Graphics window. Note: The available items are document dependent.

- *Edit Appearance* 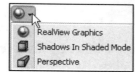 : Provides the ability to apply appearances from the Appearances PropertyManager.

- *Apply Scene* : Provides the ability to apply a scene to an active part or assembly document. View the available options.

- *View Setting* : Provides the ability to select the following: *RealView Graphics*, *Shadows in Shaded Mode* and *Perspective*.

- *Rotate* : Provides the ability to rotate a drawing view.

- *3D Drawing View* : Provides the ability to dynamically manipulate the drawing view to make a selection.

The default part and document setting displays the grid. To deactivate the grid, click **Options** , **Document Properties** tab. Click **Grid/Snaps**; uncheck the **Display grid** box.

Adding a custom view to the Heads-up View toolbar: Press the **space** key. The Orientation dialog box is display. Click the **New View** tool. The Name View dialog box is displayed. Enter a new **named** view. Click **OK**. The new view is displayed in the Heads-up View toolbar.

Press the **g** key to activate the Magnifying glass tool. Use the Magnifying glass tool to inspect a model and make selections without changing the overall view. This is a valuable tool when applying mates to an assembly.

This book does not cover starting a SolidWorks session in detail for the first time. A default SolidWorks installation presents you with several options. For additional information for an Education Edition, visit the following sites: http://www.solidworks.com/goedu and http://www.solidworks.com/sw/docs/EDU_2009_Installation_Instructions.pdf.

CommandManager

The CommandManager is a Context-sensitive toolbar that automatically updates based on the toolbar you want to access. By default, it has toolbars embedded based on your active document type. When you click a tab below the CommandManager, it updates to display that toolbar. Example, if you click the Sketch tab, the Sketch toolbar is displayed. The default Part tabs are: *Features, Sketch, Evaluate, DimXpert* and *Office Products*.

Below is an illustrated CommandManager for a default Part document.

If you have SolidWorks, SolidWorks Professional or SolidWorks Premium, the Office Products tab appears on the CommandManager.

The Office Products toolbar display is dependent on the activated Add-Ins during a SolidWorks session.

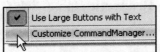

SustainabilityXpress under the Evaluate tab is new in 2010.

To customize the CommandManager, right-click on a tab and select Customize CommandManager.

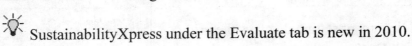

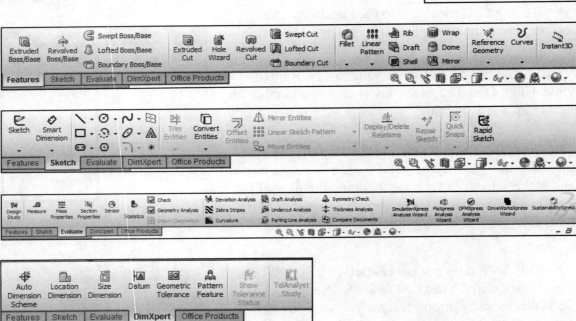

Below is an illustrated CommandManager for a default Drawing document. The default drawing tabs are: *View Layout*, *Annotation*, *Sketch*, *Evaluate* and *Office Products*.

The Office Products toolbar display is dependent on the activated Add-Ins. during a SolidWorks session.

If you have SolidWorks, SolidWorks Professional, or SolidWorks Premium, the Office Products tab is displayed in the CommandManager.

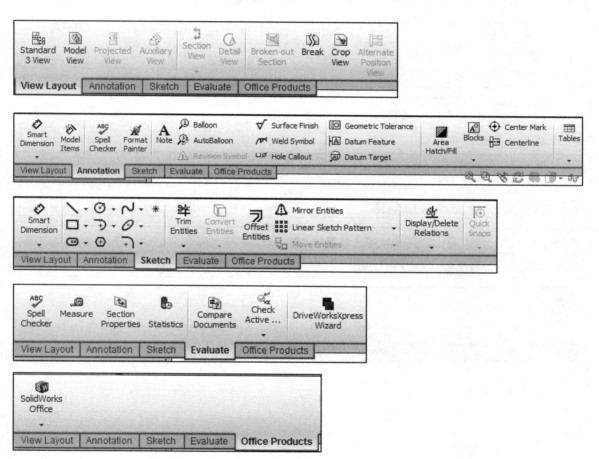

Below is an illustrated CommandManager for a default Assembly document. The default assembly tabs are: *Assembly*, *Layout*, *Sketch*, *Evaluate* and *Office Products*.

The Office Products toolbar display is dependent on the activated Add-Ins.. during a SolidWorks session.

If you have SolidWorks, SolidWorks Professional, or SolidWorks Premium, the Office Products tab is displayed in the CommandManager.

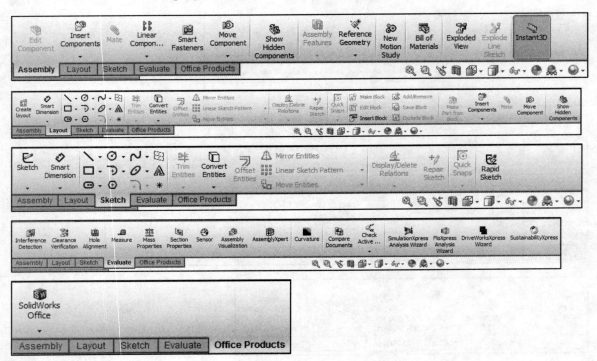

To save space in the CommandManager, right-click in the CommandManager and uncheck the Use Large Buttons with Text box. This will eliminate the text associated with the tool.

If you want to add a custom tab to your CommandManager, right-click on a tab and select the toolbar you want to insert. You can also select to add a blank tab as illustrated and populate it with custom tools from the Customize dialog box.

FeatureManager Design Tree

The FeatureManager design tree is located on the left side of the SolidWorks Graphics window. The design tree provides a summarize view of the active part, assembly or drawing document. The tree displays the details on how the part, assembly or drawing document was created.

Understand the FeatureManager design tree to troubleshoot your model. The FeatureManager is use extensively throughout this book.

The FeatureManager consist of four default tabs:

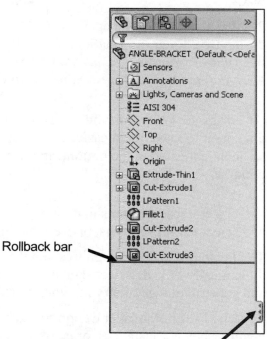

Rollback bar

- *FeatureManager design tree*
- *PropertyManager*
- *ConfigurationManager*
- *DimXpertManager*

Select the Hide FeatureManager Tree Area arrows tab from the FeatureManager to enlarge the Graphics window for modeling.

The Sensors tool Sensors located in the FeatureManager monitors selected properties in a part or assembly and alerts you when values deviate from the specified limits. There are four sensor types: *Mass properties*, *Measurement*, *Interference Detection* and *Simulation data*. See SolidWorks Help for additional information.

Various commands provide the ability to control what is displayed in the FeatureManager design tree. They are:

1. Show or Hide
FeatureManager items.

Click **Options** 📄 from the
Menu bar. Click
FeatureManager from the
System Options tab. **Customize**
your FeatureManager from the
Hide/Show Tree Items dialog
box.

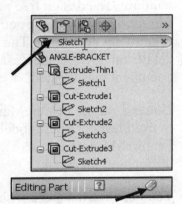

2. Filter the FeatureManager
design tree. Enter information in the filter field. You can filter
by: *Type of features, Feature names, Sketches, Folders, Mates,
User-defined tags* and *Custom properties*.

Tags are keywords you can add to a SolidWorks
document to make them easier to filter and to search. The Tags
✏ icon is located in the bottom right corner of the Graphics
window.

To collapse all items in the FeatureManager, **right-click**
and select **Collapse items**, or press the **Shift +C** keys.

The FeatureManager design tree and the Graphics window are
dynamically linked. Select sketches, features, drawing views,
and construction geometry in either pane.

Split the FeatureManager design tree and either display two
FeatureManager instances, or combine the FeatureManager
design tree with the ConfigurationManager or
PropertyManager.

Move between the FeatureManager design tree,
PropertyManager, ConfigurationManager, and
DimXpertManager by selecting the tabs at the
top of the menu.

New in 2010 is the mouse gesture wheel.
Right-click and drag in the Graphics area to
display the wheel. You can customize the
default commands for a sketch, part, assembly
or drawing.

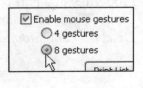

The ConfigurationManager is located to the right of the FeatureManager. Use the ConfigurationManager to create, select and view multiple configurations of parts and assemblies.

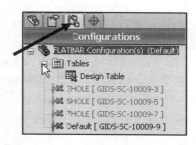

The icons in the ConfigurationManager denote whether the configuration was created manually or with a design table.

The DimXpertManager tab provides the ability to insert dimensions and tolerances manually or automatically. The DimXpertManager provides the following selections: *Auto Dimension Scheme* ⊕, *Show Tolerance Status* ⁶⁸, *Copy Scheme* ⊕ and *TolAnalyst Study* ⬚.

 TolAnalyst is available in SolidWorks Premium.

Fly-out FeatureManager

The fly-out FeatureManager design tree provides the ability to view and select items in the PropertyManager and the FeatureManager design tree at the same time.

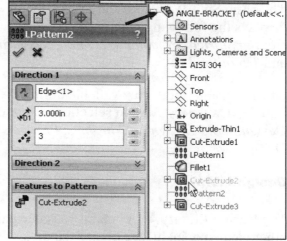

Throughout the book, you will select commands and command options from the drop-down menu, fly-out FeatureManager, Context toolbar or from a SolidWorks toolbar.

Another method for accessing a command is to use the accelerator key. Accelerator keys are special key strokes which activate the drop-down menu options. Some commands in the menu bar and items in the drop-down menus have an underlined character.

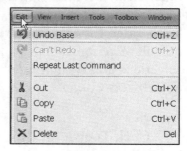

Press the Alt key followed by the corresponding key to the underlined character activates that command or option.

Illustrations may vary slightly depending on your SolidWorks version.

There are over 200 enhancements in SolidWorks 2010. Over 90% of these enhancements were requested directly by customers.

Task Pane

The Task Pane is displayed when a SolidWorks session starts. The Task Pane can be displayed in the following states: *visible or hidden*, *expanded or collapsed*, *pinned or unpinned*, *docked or floating*. The Task Pane contains the following default tabs: *SolidWorks Resources* , *Design Library* , *File Explorer* , *SolidWorks Search* , *View Palette* , *Appearances/Scenes* and *Custom Properties* .

The Document Recovery tab is displayed in the Task Pane if your system terminates unexpectedly with an active document and if auto-recovery is enabled in the System Options section.

SolidWorks Resources

The basic SolidWorks Resources menu displays the following default selections: *Getting Started*, *Community*, *Online Resources* and *Tip of the Day*.

Other user interfaces are available during the initial software installation selection: *Machine Design*, *Mold Design* or *Consumer Products Design*.

Design Library

The Design Library contains reusable parts, assemblies, and other elements, including library features.

The Design Library tab contains four default selections. Each default selection contains additional sub categories. The default selections are: *Design Library*, *Toolbox*, *3D ContentCentral* and *SolidWorks Content*.

Click **Tools**, **Add-Ins**, **SolidWorks Toolbox** and **SolidWorks Toolbox Browser** to active the SolidWorks Toolbox.

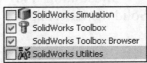

To access the Design Library folders in a non network environment for a new installation, click **Add File Location** , enter: **C:\Documents and Settings\All Users\Application Data\SolidWorks\SolidWorks 2010\design library**. Click **OK**.

In a network environment, contact your IT department for system details.

File Explorer

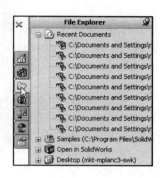

File Explorer 🗁 duplicates Windows Explorer from your local computer and displays *Recent Documents*, *directories*, and the *Open in SolidWorks* and *Desktop* folders.

Search

SolidWorks Search 🔍 is installed with Microsoft Windows Search and indexes the resources once before searching begins, either after installation or when you initiate the first search.

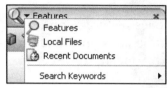

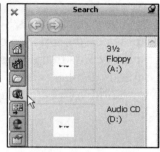

The SolidWorks Search box is displayed in the upper right corner of the SolidWorks Graphics window. Enter the text or key words to search. Click the drop-down arrow to view the last 10 recent searches.

The Search tool 🔍 in the Task Pane searches the following default locations: *All Locations*, *Local Files*, *Design Library*, *SolidWorks Toolbox* and *3D ContentCentral*.

🔆 Select any or all of the above locations. If you do not select a file location, all locations are searched.

View Palette

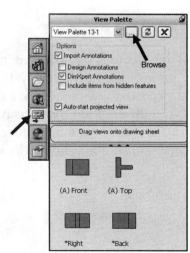

The View Palette 🔲 tab located in the Task Pane provides the ability to insert drawing views of an active document, or click the Browse button to locate the desired document.

Click and drag the view from the View Palette into an active drawing sheet to create a drawing view.

🔆 The selected model is View Palette 13-1 in the illustration. The **(A) Front** and **(A) Top** drawing views are displayed with DimXpert Annotations which was applied at the part level.

Appearances/Scenes

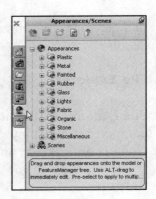

Appearances/Scenes provide a simplified way to display models in a photo-realistic setting using a library of Appearances and Scenes.

On Appearances/Scenes compatible systems, you can select Appearances and Scenes to display your model in the Graphics window. Drag and drop a selected appearance onto the model or FeatureManager. View the results in the Graphics window.

The Appearances/Scenes feature requires graphics card support. For the latest information on graphics cards that support Appearances/Scenes Graphics display, visit: www.solidworks.com/pages/services/videocardtestin g.html.

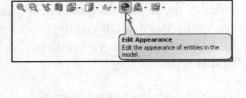

Click the Edit Appearances icon in the Heads-up View toolbar to edit an appearance.

Custom Properties

The Custom Properties tool provides the ability to enter custom and configuration specific properties directly into SolidWorks files. See SolidWorks Help for additional information.

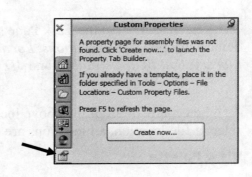

Document Recovery

If auto recovery is initiated in the System Options section and the system terminates unexpectedly with an active document, the saved information files are available on the Task Pane Document Recovery tab the next time you start a SolidWorks session.

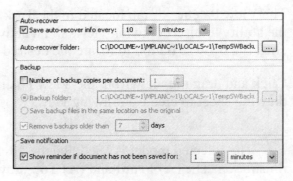

Motion Study tab

Motion Studies are graphical simulations of motion for an assembly. Access MotionManager from the Motion Study tab as illustrated. The Motion Study tab is located in the bottom left corner of the Graphics window.

Incorporate visual properties such as lighting and camera perspective. Click the Motion Study tab to view the MotionManager. Click the Model tab to return to the FeatureManager design tree.

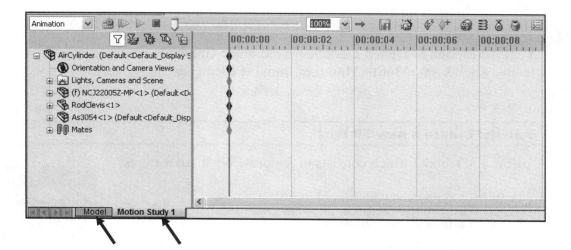

The MotionManager display a timeline-based interface, and provide the following selections from the drop-down menu as illustrated:

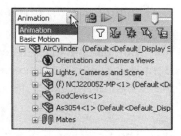

- *Animation:* Apply Animation to animate the motion of an assembly. Add a motor and insert positions of assembly components at various times using set key points. Use the Animation option to create animations for motion that do **not** require accounting for mass or gravity.

- *Basic Motion:* Apply Basic Motion for approximating the effects of motors, springs, collisions and gravity on assemblies. Basic Motion takes mass into account in calculating motion. Basic Motion computation is relatively fast, so you can use this for creating presentation animations using physics-based simulations. Use the Basic Motion option to create simulations of motion that account for mass, collisions or gravity.

☼ If the Motion Study tab is not displayed in the Graphics window, click **View**, **MotionManager** from the Menu bar.

For older assemblies created before 2008, the Animation1 tab maybe displayed. View the Assembly Chapter for additional information.

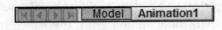

To create a new Motion Study, click **Insert, New Motion Study** from the Menu bar.

View SolidWorks Help for additional information on Motion Study.

If the Motion Study tab is not displayed in the Graphics window, click **View, MotionManager** from the Menu bar.

Activity: Create a new 3D Part

A part is a 3D model which consists of features. What are features?

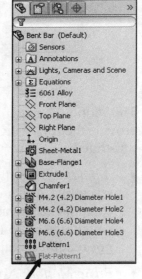

- Features are *geometry* building blocks.

- Features *add* or *remove* material.

- Features are created from *2D* or *3D sketched profiles* or from edges and faces of existing geometry.

- Features are *displayed* in the FeatureManager as illustrated.

You can suppress a feature as illustrated: Flat-Pattern1 in the Bent Bar FeatureManager. A suppress feature is display in light gray in the FeatureManager.

The first sketch of a part is called the Base Sketch. The Base sketch is the foundation for the 3D model. In this book, we focus on 2D sketches with 3D features. We do not address 3D Sketches.

SolidWorks 2010 provides additional default Templates for various Overall drafting standards.

In the book, Reference planes and Grid/Snaps are deactivated in the Graphics window to improve model clarity.

There are two modes in the New SolidWorks Document dialog box: *Novice* and *Advanced*. The *Novice* option is the default option with three templates. The *Advanced* option contains access to additional created templates. In this book, use the *Advanced* Mode.

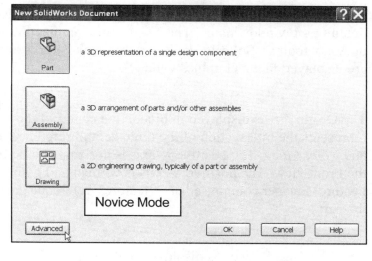

Create a New part.

6)   Click **New** ⬜ from the Menu bar. The New SolidWorks Document dialog box is displayed.

Select Advanced Mode.

7)   Click the **Advanced** button to display the New SolidWorks Document dialog box in Advance mode.

8)   The Templates tab is the default tab. Part is the default template from the New SolidWorks Document dialog box. Click **OK**.

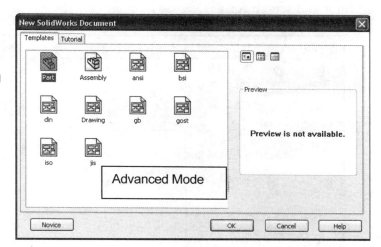

SolidWorks Web Help is active by default under Help in the Main Menu bar.

The Advanced mode remains selected for all new documents in the current SolidWorks session. When you exit SolidWorks, the Advanced mode setting is saved. The default SolidWorks installation contains two tabs in the New SolidWorks Document dialog box: Templates and Tutorial. The Templates tab corresponds to the default SolidWorks templates.

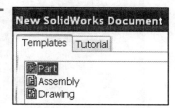

The Tutorial tab corresponds to the templates utilized in the SolidWorks Tutorials.

During the initial SolidWorks installation, you are request to select either the ISO or ANSI drafting standard. ISO is typically a European drafting standard and uses First Angle Projection. The book is written using the ANSI (U.S.) overall drafting standard and Third Angle Projection for all drawing documents.

Part1 is displayed in the FeatureManager and is the name of the document. Part1 is the default part window name. The Menu bar, CommandManager, FeatureManager, Heads-up View toolbar, SolidWorks Resources, SolidWorks Search, Task Pane, and the Origin are displayed in the Graphics window.

The Origin ↓ is displayed in blue in the center of the Graphics window. The Origin represents the intersection of the three default reference planes: *Front Plane*, *Top Plane* and *Right Plane*. The positive X-axis is horizontal and points to the right of the Origin in the Front view. The positive Y-axis is vertical and point upward in the Front view. The FeatureManager contains a list of features, reference geometry, and settings utilized in the part.

The Tags ⬦ icon is displayed in the bottom right corner of the Graphics window. Tags are keywords you add to SolidWorks documents and features to make them easier to filter and search for.

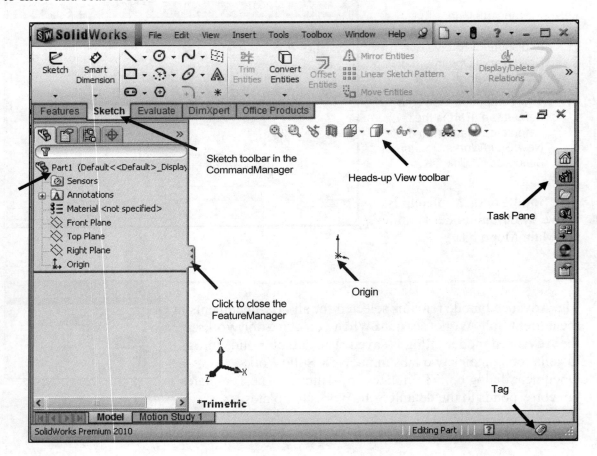

🔅 In the book, Reference planes and Grid/Snaps are de-activated in the Graphics window to improve model clarity.

The CommandManager is document dependent. The tabs are located on the bottom left side of the CommandManager and display the available toolbars and features for each corresponding tab. The default tabs for a Part are: *Features*, *Sketch*, *Evaluate*, *DimXpert* and *Office Products*.

🔅 The Features icon and Features toolbar should be selected by default in Part mode.

The CommandManager is utilized in this text. Control the CommandManager display.

Right-click in the gray area to the right of the Options 📋 ▾ icon in the Menu bar toolbar. A complete list of toolbars is displayed. Check CommandManager if required.

🔅 Another way to display a toolbar, click **View, Toolbars** from the Menu bar menu. Select the required toolbar.

Select individual toolbars from the View, Toolbars list to display in the Graphics window. Reposition toolbars by clicking and dragging.

🔅 Click **View**, **Origins** from the Menu bar menu to display the Origin in the Graphics window.

🔅 Screen shots and illustrations in the book display the SolidWorks user default setup.

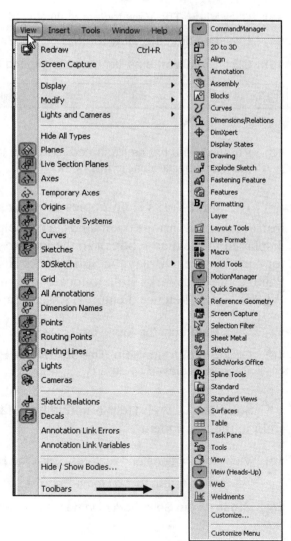

In this book, Reference planes and Grid/Snaps are deactivated in the Graphics window for improved model clarity.

Activity: Menu Bar toolbar, Menu Bar menu, Heads-up View toolbar

---

Display tools and tool tips.

9) Position the **mouse pointer** over the Heads-up View toolbar and view the tool tips.

10) **Read** the large tool tip.

11) Select the **drop-down arrow** ▼ to view the available view tools.

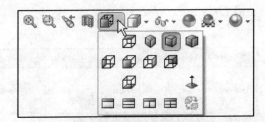

Display the View toolbar and the Menu bar.

12) Right-click in the **gray area** of the Menu bar.

13) Click **View**. The View toolbar is displayed.

14) Click and drag the **View toolbar** off the Graphics window.

15) Click **SolidWorks** as illustrated to expand the Menu bar menu.

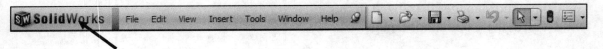

16) **Pin** the Menu bar as illustrated. Use both the Menu bar menu and the Menu bar toolbar in this book.

The SolidWorks Help Topics contains step-by-step instructions for various commands. The Help ⑨ icon is displayed in the dialog box or in the PropertyManager for each feature. Display the SolidWorks Help Home Page. Use SolidWorks Help to locate information on What's New, Sketches, Features, Assemblies and more.

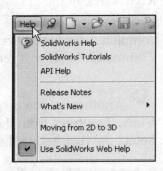

17) Click **Help** from the Menu bar.

18) Click **SolidWorks Help**. The SolidWorks Help Home Page is displayed by default.

SolidWorks Web Help is active by default under Help in the Main menu.

19) View your options and features. Click the **Home Page** 🏠 icon to return to the Home Page.

20) **Close** ☒ the SolidWorks Home Page dialog box.

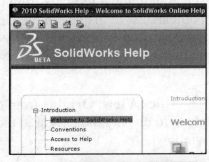

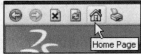

Display and explore the SolidWorks tutorials.

21) Click **Help** from the Menu bar.

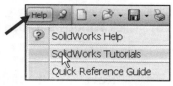

22) Click **SolidWorks Tutorials**. The SolidWorks Tutorials are displayed. The SolidWorks Tutorials are presented by category.

23) Click the **Getting Started** category. The Getting Started category provides three 30 minute lessons on parts, assemblies, and drawings. This section also provides information for users who are switching from AutoCAD to SolidWorks. The tutorials also provide links to the CSWP and CSWA Certification programs and a new What's New Tutorials for 2010.

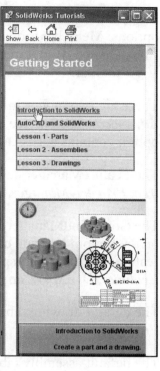

SolidWorks Corporation offers various levels of certification representing increasing levels of expertise in 3D CAD design as it applies to engineering.

The *Certified SolidWorks Associate* CSWA certification indicates a foundation in and apprentice knowledge of 3D CAD design and engineering practices and principles.

The main requirement for obtaining the CSWA certification is to take and pass the three hour, seven question on-line proctored exam at a Certified SolidWorks CSWA Provider, "university, college, technical, vocational or secondary educational institution" and to sign the SolidWorks Confidentiality Agreement.

Passing this exam provides students the chance to prove their working knowledge and expertise and to be part of a worldwide industry certification standard.

24) **Close** the ☒ Online Tutorial dialog box. Return to the SolidWorks Graphics window.

A goal of this book is to expose various SolidWorks design tools and features. The most direct way may not be shown.

Close all models.
25) Click **Windows**, **Close All** from the Menu bar menu.

 Review of the SolidWorks User Interface and CommandManager

The SolidWorks 2010 User Interface and CommandManager consist of the following options: Menu bar toolbar, Menu bar menu, Drop-down menus, Context toolbars, Consolidated fly-out menus, System feedback icons, Confirmation Corner, and Heads-up View toolbar.

There are two modes in the New SolidWorks Document dialog box: *Novice* and *Advanced*. The Novice option is the default option with three templates. The Advanced option contains access to more templates

The FeatureManager design tree consist of four default tabs: *FeatureManager design tree, PropertyManager, ConfigurationManager, and DimXertManager.*

The CommandManager is document dependent. The CommandManager tabs are located on the bottom left side of the CommandManager and display the available toolbars and features for each corresponding tab. The default part tabs are: *Features, Sketch, Evaluate, DimXpert,* and *Office Products.*

The default drawing tabs are: *View Layout, Annotation, Sketch, Evaluate,* and *Office Products*.

The default assembly tabs are: *Assembly, Layout, Sketch, Evaluate,* and *Office Products*. The Office Products toolbar display is dependent on the activated Add-Ins during a SolidWorks session.

The Task Pane is displayed when a SolidWorks session starts. The Task Pane contains the following default tabs: *SolidWorks Resources* , *Design Library* , *File Explorer* , *SolidWorks Search* , *View Palette* , *Appearances/Scenes* and *Custom Properties* .

Chapter Terminology

Assembly: An assembly is a document in which parts, features, and other assemblies (sub-assemblies) are put together. A part in an assembly is called a component. Adding a component to an assembly creates a link between the assembly and the component. When SolidWorks opens the assembly, it finds the component file to show it in the assembly. Changes in the component are automatically reflected in the assembly. The filename extension for a SolidWorks assembly file name is *.sldasm.

CommandManager: The CommandManager is a Context-sensitive toolbar that dynamically updates based on the toolbar you want to access. By default, it has toolbars embedded in it based on the document type. When you click a tab below the Command Manager, it updates to display that toolbar. For example, if you click the **Sketches** tab, the Sketch toolbar is displayed.

ConfigurationManager: The ConfigurationManager is located on the left side of the SolidWorks window and provides the means to create, select, and view multiple configurations of parts and assemblies in an active document. You can split the ConfigurationManager and either display two ConfigurationManager instances, or combine the ConfigurationManager with the FeatureManager design tree, PropertyManager, or third party applications that use the panel.

Coordinate System: SolidWorks uses a coordinate system with origins. A part document contains an original Origin. Whenever you select a plane or face and open a sketch, an Origin is created in alignment with the plane or face. An Origin can be used as an anchor for the sketch entities, and it helps orient perspective of the axes. A three-dimensional reference triad orients you to the X, Y, and Z directions in part and assembly documents.

Cursor Feedback: The system feedback symbol indicates what you are selecting or what the system is expecting you to select. As you move the mouse pointer across your model, system feedback is provided.

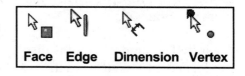

Dimension: A value indicating the size of the 2D sketch entity or 3D feature. Dimensions in a SolidWorks drawing are associated with the model, and changes in the model are reflected in the drawing, if you DO NOT USE DimXpert.

DimXpertManager: The DimXpertManager lists the tolerance features defined by DimXpert for a part. It also displays DimXpert tools that you use to insert dimensions and tolerances into a part. You can import these dimensions and tolerances into drawings. DimXpert is not associative.

Document: In SolidWorks, each part, assembly, and drawing is referred to as a document, and each document is displayed in a separate window.

Drawing: A 2D representation of a 3D part or assembly. The extension for a SolidWorks drawing file name is .SLDDRW. Drawing refers to the SolidWorks module used to insert, add, and modify views in an engineering drawing.

Feature: Features are geometry building blocks. Features add or remove material. Features are created from 2D or 3D sketched profiles or from edges and faces of existing geometry.

FeatureManager: The FeatureManager design tree located on the left side of the SolidWorks window provides an outline view of the active part, assembly, or drawing. This makes it easy to see how the model or assembly was constructed or to examine the various sheets and views in a drawing. The FeatureManager and the Graphics window are dynamically linked. You can select features, sketches, drawing views, and construction geometry in either pane.

Graphics window: The area in the SolidWorks window where the part, assembly, or drawing is displayed.

Heads-up View toolbar: A transparent toolbar located at the top of the Graphic window.

Model: 3D solid geometry in a part or assembly document. If a part or assembly document contains multiple configurations, each configuration is a separate model.

Motion Studies: Graphical simulations of motion and visual properties with assembly models. Analogous to a configuration, they do not actually change the original assembly model or its properties. They display the model as it changes based on simulation elements you add.

Origin: The model origin is displayed in blue and represents the (0,0,0) coordinate of the model. When a sketch is active, a sketch origin is displayed in red and represents the (0,0,0) coordinate of the sketch. Dimensions and relations can be added to the model origin, but not to a sketch origin.

Part: A 3D object that consist of one or more features. A part inserted into an assembly is called a component. Insert part views, feature dimensions and annotations into 2D drawing. The extension for a SolidWorks part filename is .SLDPRT.

Plane: Planes are flat and infinite. Planes are represented on the screen with visible edges.

PropertyManager: Most sketch, feature, and drawing tools in SolidWorks open a PropertyManager located on the left side of the SolidWorks window. The PropertyManager displays the properties of the entity or feature so you specify the properties without a dialog box covering the Graphics window.

RealView: Provides a simplified way to display models in a photo-realistic setting using a library of appearances and scenes. RealView requires graphics card support and is memory intensive.

Rebuild: A tool that updates (or regenerates) the document with any changes made since the last time the model was rebuilt. Rebuild is typically used after changing a model dimension.

Relation: A relation is a geometric constraint between sketch entities or between a sketch entity and a plane, axis, edge or vertex.

Rollback: Suppresses all items below the rollback bar.

Sketch: The name to describe a 2D profile is called a sketch. 2D sketches are created on flat faces and planes within the model. Typical geometry types are lines, arcs, corner rectangles, circles, polygons, and ellipses.

Task Pane: The Task Pane is displayed when you open the SolidWorks software. It contains the following tabs: SolidWorks Resources, Design Library, File Explorer, Search, View Palette, Document Recovery and RealView/PhotoWorks.

Toolbars: The toolbars provide shortcuts enabling you to access the most frequently used commands. When you enable add-in applications in SolidWorks, you can also display their associated toolbars.

Units: Used in the measurement of physical quantities. Decimal inch dimensioning and Millimeter dimensioning are the two types of common units specified for engineering parts and drawings.

Notes:

Chapter 2

Drawing Templates and Sheet Formats

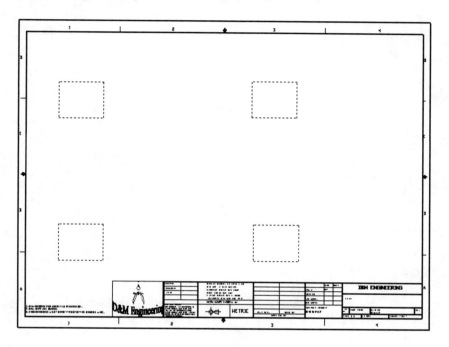

Below are the desired outcomes and usage competencies based on the completion of Chapter 2.

Desired Outcomes:	Usage Competencies:

• Two Drawing Templates:
   ○ C (ANSI) size Drawing template
   ○ A (ANSI) size Drawing template
	• Ability to apply Document Properties to reflect the ASME Y14 Engineering Drawing and Related Drawing Practices.
	
	• Understand System Options and Document Properties, which influence the drawing and Drawing template.

• One C size Sheet format.	• Import an AutoCAD file as a Sheet format. Insert SolidWorks System Properties and Custom Properties.
• New file location for Drawing templates and Sheet format.	• Ability to create new SolidWorks Document tabs.

Notes:

Chapter 2 - Drawing Templates and Sheet Formats

Chapter Objective

Create two Drawing templates. Create a C (ANSI) size Drawing template and an A (ANSI) size Drawing template. Create a C (ANSI) size Sheet format.

On the completion of this chapter, you will be able to:

- Establish a SolidWorks drawing document session.

- Distinguish between System Options and Document Properties as they relate to drawings and templates.

- Create a new SolidWorks File Location for a Drawing template.

- Set Reference Document Properties in a Drawing template.

- Create an empty C-size Drawing template. Propagate the settings to the drawing sizes.

- Import an AutoCAD drawing as a SolidWorks C-size Sheet format.

- Combine an empty Drawing template and Sheet format to create a C-ANSI-MM Drawing template.

- Develop Linked Notes to SolidWorks Properties and Custom Properties in the Sheet format.

- Insert a company logo with a relation in the Title block.

- Create an A-ANSI-MM Drawing template by combining information from the C-size Drawing template and A-size Sheet format.

Templates are part, drawing, and assembly documents that include user-defined parameters and are the basis for new documents. You can maintain many different document templates. For example, you can create:

- A Document template using millimeters and another document template using inches.

- A Document template using ANSI and another document template using ISO dimensioning standard.

- A Document template for a Detached drawing.

A *Detached drawing* is design so you can open and work in drawing files without the model files being loaded into memory or even being present.

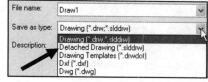

When opening a Detached drawing, SolidWorks checks all sheets in the drawing to be sure that they are synchronized with the model. If not, you are warned. To save a standard drawing to a Detached Drawing, click **File**, **Save As**, select the Save as type: **Detached Drawing (*slddrw)**.

Chapter Overview

Your responsibilities as the designer include developing drawings that adhere to the ASME Y14 American National Standard for Engineering Drawing and Related Documentation Practices. The foundation for a SolidWorks drawing is the Drawing template. Drawing size, drawing standards, units and other properties are defined in the Drawing template.

Sheet formats contain the following: *Border*, *Title block*, *Revision block*, *Company name*, *logo*, *SolidWorks Properties* and *Custom Properties*. You are under time constraints to complete the project. Conserve drawing time. Create a custom Drawing template and Sheet format.

Perform the following tasks in this Chapter:

- Modify Document Properties and create an empty C (ANSI) size Drawing template.

- Import an AutoCAD drawing and save the drawing as a C-size Sheet format.

- Add System Properties and Custom Properties to the Sheet format.

- Create an A-ANSI-MM Drawing template.

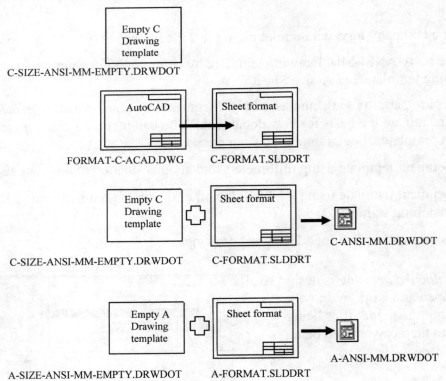

- Combine the empty drawing template and imported the Sheet format to create the C-ANSI-MM Drawing template.

- Generate an empty A (ANSI) size Drawing template.

- Modify an existing SolidWorks A-size Sheet format.

Engineering Drawing and Related Documentation Practices

Drawing templates in this section are based on the American Society of Mechanical Engineers ASME Y14 American National Standard for Engineering Drawing and Related Documentation Practices.

These standards represent the drawing practices used by U.S. industry. The ASME Y14 practices supersede the American National Standards Institute ANSI standards.

The ASME Y14 Engineering Drawing and Related Documentation Practices are published by The American Society of Mechanical Engineers, New York, NY. References to the current ASME Y14 standards are used with permission.

ASME Y14 Standard Name:	American National Standard Engineering Drawing and Related Documentation:	Revision of the Standard:
ASME Y14.100M-1998	Engineering Drawing Practices	DOD-STD-100
ASME Y14.1-1995	Decimal Inch Drawing Sheet Size and Format	ANSI Y14.1
ASME Y14.1M-1995	Metric Drawing Sheet Size and Format	ANSI Y14.1M
ASME Y14.24M	Types and Applications of Engineering Drawings	ANSI Y14.24M
ASME Y14.2M(Reaffirmed 1998)	Line Conventions and Lettering	ANSI Y14.2M
ASME Y14.3M-1994	Multi-view and Sectional View Drawings	ANSI Y14.3
ASME Y14.41-2003	Digital Product Definition Data Practices	N/A
ASME Y14.5M –1994 (Reaffirmed 1999)	Dimensioning and Tolerancing	ANSI Y14.5-1982 (R1988)

This book presents a portion of the ASME Y14 American National Standard for Engineering Drawing and Related Documentation Practices. Information presented in Chapters 2 - 6 represents sample illustrations of drawings, various drawing views, and or dimension types.

The ASME Y14 Standards committee develops and maintains additional Drawing Standards. Members of these committees are from Industry, Department of Defense, and Academia.

Companies create their own drawing standards based on one or more of the following:

- ASME Y14

- ISO or other International drawing standards

- Older ANSI standards

- Military standards

🔆 There is also the "We've always done it this way" drawing standard or "Go ask the Drafting supervisor" drawing standard.

File Management

File management organizes parts, assemblies and drawings. Why do you need file management? A large assembly or drawing can contain hundreds or even thousands of parts.

Parts and assemblies are distributed between team members to save time. Design changes occur frequently in the development process. How do you manage and control changes? Answer: Through file management. File management is a very important tool in the development process.

Utilize file folders to organize projects, vendor parts and assemblies, templates and various libraries.

Folders exist on the local hard drive, example C:\. Folders also exist on a network drive, example Z:\. The letters C:\ and Z:\ are used as examples for a local drive and a network drive respectfully. The files and folders required to complete the projects in this book are located on the enclosed CD.

Activity: File Management

Create a new folder in Windows to down load files.

1)   Click **Start** from the Windows Taskbar.

2)   Click **My Documents** in Windows.

3)   Click **File**, **New**, **Folder** from the Main menu.

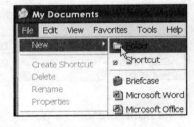

Enter the new folder name.

4)   Enter **DRAWING-W-SOLIDWORKS-2010**.

🔆 Select the Microsoft Windows commands either from the Main menu, toolbar icons or with the right mouse button. Windows XP is used in this section.

Return to the DRAWING-W-SOLIDWORKS-2010 folder.

5)   Click the **DRAWING-W-SOLIDWORKS-2010** folder.

Copy the files from the enclosed CD in the book to the new folder.

6)   **Insert** the enclosed CD. Select your **CD drive**.

7)   Right-click **Explore**. View the available files and folders.

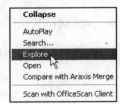

8)   **Copy** the files and folders to the DRAWING-W-SOLIDWORKS-2010 folder. The DRAWING-W-SOLIDWORKS-2010 folder is the working folder for this book.

Store chapter Drawing templates in the MY-TEMPLATES file folder. Store Chapter Sheet formats in the MY-SHEETFORMATS folder.

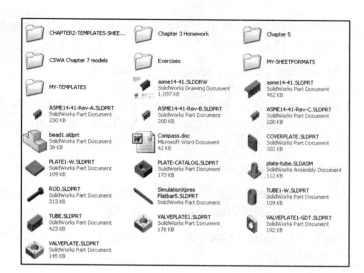

MY-TEMPLATES

MY-SHEETFORMATS

Drawing templates and Sheet formats that are created in this chapter, are located in the CHAPTER 2-TEMPLATES-SHEETFORMTS folder on the CD. Check for proper path location on your system for created Sheet formats and Drawing templates.

Default Drawing Template, Sheet Format and Sheet Size

The foundation of a SolidWorks drawing is the Drawing template. Drawing sheet size, drawing standards, company information, manufacturing and or assembly requirements: units, layers, line styles and other properties are defined in the Drawing template.

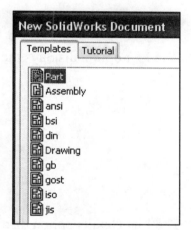

SolidWorks 2010 provides additional Drawing Templates for various Overall drafting standards.

A Sheet format is incorporated into the Drawing template. The Sheet format contains the following items:

- Sheet border
- Title block
- Revision block information
- Company name and or logo information
- Custom Properties
- SolidWorks Properties
- And more

SolidWorks starts with a default Drawing template, (*.drwdot).

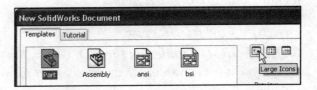

The default Drawing template is located in the C:\Documents and Settings\All Users\Application Data\SolidWorks\SolidWorks 2010\templates folder on a non-network system. SolidWorks is the name of the installation folder.

New SolidWorks Document

The Templates folder corresponds to the Templates tab displayed in the New SolidWorks Document dialog box.

The Large Icons option displays the full name, and a large document icon.

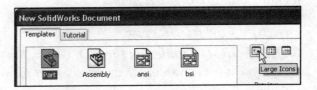

The List option displays the document icons in a list format.

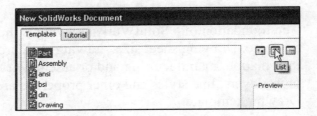

The List Details option displays the document name, size and last modified date.

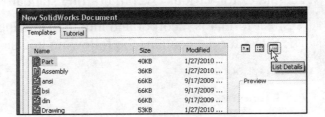

💡 **SolidWorks Design Checker** is a set of tools used to check parts, assemblies and especially drawing files against a checklist of company specified standards. The **Build Checks** tool is used to create a checklist and the **Check Active Document** tool to apply it to a SolidWorks document. The checker generates a list of failed checks and detailed information about each. The results can be sent to a report.

Sheet Format/Size

The Sheet Format/Size dialog box defines the Sheet format and the paper size. The U.S. default Standard Sheet Format is A (ANSI) Landscape. The Display sheet format box toggles the Sheet format display on/off.

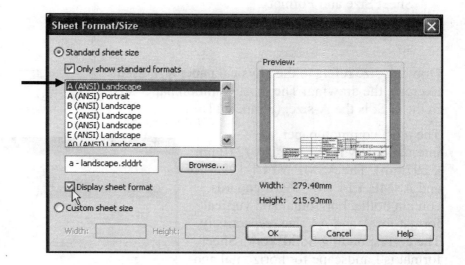

The Standard Sheet formats are located in the C:\Documents and Settings\All Users\Application Data\SolidWorks\SolidWorks 2010\lang\english\sheetformat in a non-network system.

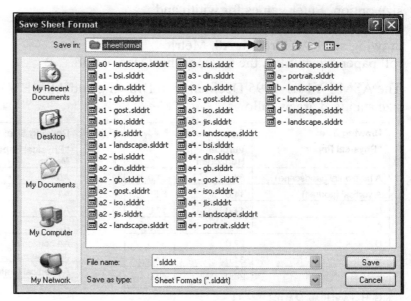

ASME Y14.1 Drawing Sheet Size and Format

There are two ASME standards that define sheet size and format. They are:

1. ASME Y14.1-1995 Decimal Inch Drawing Sheet Size and Format

2. ASME Y14.1M-1995 Metric Drawing Sheet size

Drawing size refers to the physical paper size used to create the drawing. The most common paper size in the U.S. is the A-size: (8.5in. x 11in.).

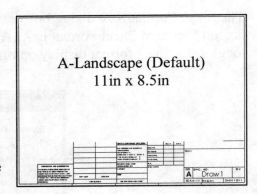

The most common paper size internationally is the A4 size: (210mm x 297mm). The ASME Y14.1-1995 and ASME Y14.1M-1995 standards contain both a horizontal and vertical format for A and A4 size respectively. The corresponding SolidWorks Sheet format is Landscape for horizontal and Portrait for vertical.

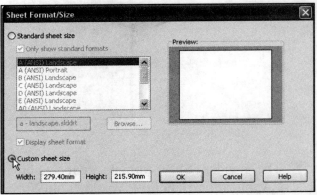

SolidWorks predefines U.S. drawing sizes A through E. Drawing sizes: F, G, H, J, & K utilize the Custom sheet size option. Enter values for width and height. SolidWorks predefines metric drawing sizes A4 through A0. Metric roll paper sizes utilize the Custom sheet size option.

The ASME Y14.1-1995 Decimal Inch Drawing and ASME Y14.1M-1995 Metric Sheet size standard are as follows:

Drawing Size: "Physical Paper"	Size in inches: Vertical	Horizontal
A horizontal (landscape)	8.5	11.0
A vertical (portrait)	11.0	8.5
B	11.0	17.0
C	17.0	22.0
D	22.0	34.0
E	34.0	44.0
F	28.0	40.0
G, H, J and K apply to roll sizes, User Defined		

Drawing Size: "Physical Paper" Metric	Size in Millimeters: Vertical	Horizontal
A0	841	1189
A1	594	841
A2	420	594
A3	297	420
A4 horizontal (landscape)	210	297
A4 vertical (portrait)	297	210

Use caution when sending electronic drawings between U.S. and International colleagues. Drawing paper sizes will vary. Example: An A-size (11in. x 8.5in.) drawing (280mm x 216mm) does not fit a A4 metric drawing (297mm x 210mm). Use a larger paper size or scale the drawing using the printer setup options.

Start a new session of SolidWorks. Create a new drawing with the default Drawing template. Utilize C ANSI Size paper with no Sheet format displayed.

The sheet border defines the C-size drawing: 22in. x 17in, (558.80mm x 431.80mm). A new Graphics window displays the C ANSI Landscape Drawing, named Draw1.

Landscape indicates that the larger dimension is along the horizontal. A-Portrait and A4-Portrait indicate that the larger dimension is along the vertical.

Landscape	Portrait

Activity: Default Drawing Template

Start a SolidWorks session.

9) Click **Start**, **All Programs** from the Windows Main menu.

10) Click the **SolidWorks 2010** folder.

11) Click the **SolidWorks 2010** application. The SolidWorks Graphics window is displayed.

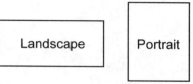

Pin the Menu bar toolbar and the Menu bar menu.

Select the default Drawing template.

12) Click **New** ⬜ from the Menu bar toolbar.

13) Double-click **Drawing** from the Templates tab.

Create a C-Landscape sheet.
14) Select **C (ANSI) Landscape** from the Standard sheet size drop-down menu.

15) **Uncheck** the Display sheet format box.

16) Click **OK** from the Sheet Format/Size dialog box.

Exit the Model View PropertyManager.

17) Click **Cancel** ✖ from the Model View PropertyManager. The FeatureManager is displayed with Draw1 as the default drawing name.

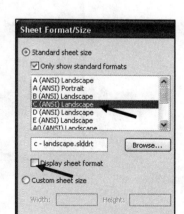

A goal of this book is to expose various SolidWorks design tools and features. The most direct way, may not be always shown.

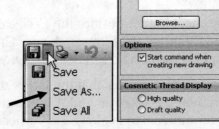

The Model View PropertyManager is displayed if the Start command when creating new drawing box is checked.

Save Draw1.

18) Click **Save As** from the Consolidated Menu bar toolbar.

19) Select the **DRAWING-W-SOLIDWORKS-2010** folder.

20) Click **Save**. The Draw1 FeatureManager is displayed.

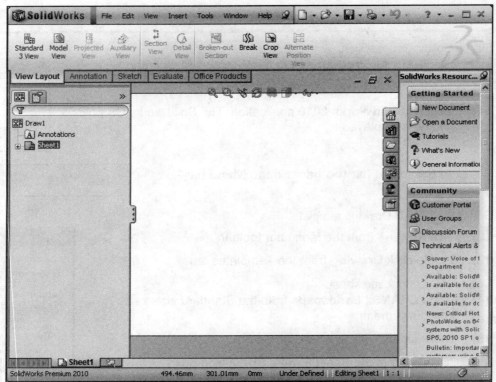

If you do not see the above illustration, right-click inside the Sheet boundary, click Edit Sheet Format. Click Edit Sheet. SolidWorks is presently working on this reported bug.

Activity: Display the Line Format Toolbar

Review the CommandManager options and display the Line Format toolbar.

21) Right-click in the **grey area** of the CommandManager as illustrated.

22) Click **Customize**. The Customize dialog box is displayed. The Toolbars tab is displayed by default.

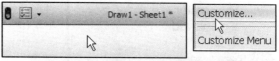

23) Check the **Line Format** box. The Line Format toolbar is displayed. Explore the tabs and your options to customize your options.

24) Click and drag the **Line Format toolbar** off the Graphics window.

Close the Customize dialog box.

25) Click **OK**.

☀ By default, the Show tooltips option is selected. Apply the Customize dialog box to set short cut keys from the keyboard.

Line Format Toolbar

The Line Format toolbar controls the following options: *Layer Properties* 🗔 , *Line Color* 🖉 , *Line Thickness* ≣ , *Line Style* ▦ , *Hide Show edges* ⇄ and *Color Display Mode* ⊾ .

Utilize the Line Format toolbar when creating a Drawing template. Select the tools and menu options that are displayed in bold icons and black text.

The tools and menu options that are displayed in gray are called grayed-out. The gray icon or text cannot be selected. Additional information is required for these options.

☀ You can also display the Line Format toolbar by clicking **View**, **Toolbars**, **Line Format** from the Menu bar menu.

Activity: Create a Keyboard Shortcut

Customize the Keyboard.

26) Click **Tools**, **Customize** from the Menu bar menu. The Customize dialog box is displayed.

Note: There are numerous ways to access commands and menus in SolidWorks.

27) Click the **Keyboard** tab.

28) Select **View** for Categories.

29) Select **Planes** for Commands.

30) Click a **position** inside the Shortcut(s) box.

31) Enter **P** for new shortcut key. Note: Shift+P is displayed in the Shortcut(s) box.

32) Click **OK** from the Customize dialog box.

33) **Save** the drawing. Draw1 is the default name.

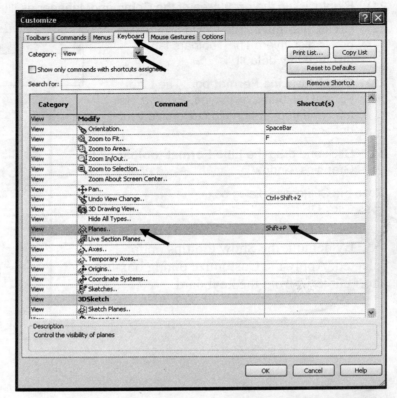

The short cut key P is displayed next to the Planes option in the View menu. Create additional short cut keys as an exercise.

Cursor Feedback

SolidWorks provides system feedback by attaching a symbol to the mouse pointer cursor. The system feedback symbol indicates what you are selecting or what the system is expecting you to select. As you move the mouse pointer across your model, system feedback is provided to you in the form of symbols, riding next to the cursor. The cursor has an important role in the SolidWorks User Interface.

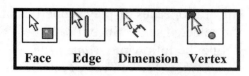

The mouse pointer provides feedback in both the Drawing Sheet and Drawing View modes.

The mouse pointer displays the Drawing Sheet icon when the Sheet properties and commands are executed.

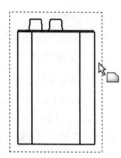

The mouse pointer displays the Drawing View icon when the View properties and commands are executed.

☀ View the mouse pointer for feedback to select Sheet, View, Component and Edge properties in the Drawing.

Sheet Properties display properties of the selected sheet. Right-click in the sheet boundary .

View Properties display properties of the selected view. Right-click on the view boundary .

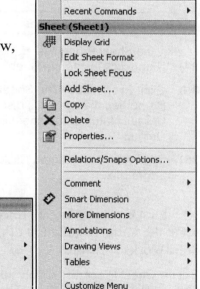

☀ Use the Lock View Position command to prevent a view from being moved by dragging.

☀ Use the Lock View Focus command when you need a view to remain active as you work within it. This allows you to add sketch entities to a view, even when the mouse pointer is close to another view. You can be sure that the items you are adding belong to the view you want.

Sheet Properties

Sheet Properties display properties of the selected sheet. Sheet Properties define the following: *Name of the Sheet*, *Sheet Scale*, *Type of Projection (First angle or Third angle)*, *Sheet Format*, *Sheet Size*, *View label* and *Datum label*.

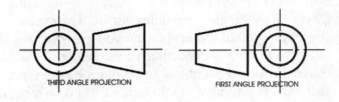

THIRD ANGLE PROJECTION   FIRST ANGLE PROJECTION

The Sheet format and Sheet size are set in the default Drawing template. Review the Sheet Properties. The Standard sheet size option is grayed out.

The Sheet format file extension is *.slddrt. The Sheet format option is grayed out. The C-size paper, width, and height dimensions are listed under the Custom sheet size option.

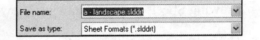

By default, sheet formats are save in the <SolidWorks install directory>\data folder. However formats can be save in any location. The data folder is overwritten when a new version of SolidWorks is loaded. The files will be lost if they are stored here.

Activity: Sheet Properties

Display the Sheet Properties.

34) Right-click inside the **Sheet boundary**.

35) Click **Properties**. The Sheet Properties dialog box is displayed. Default Name of the sheet is Sheet1. Default Scale is 1:1.

36) Set Type of projection. Click the **Third angle** box.

First or Third Angle projection was set at the initial installation of the SolidWorks software.

Exit the Sheet Properties dialog box.

37) Click **OK** from the Sheet Properties dialog box.

The Sheet name is Sheet1. The FeatureManager and Sheet tab display the Sheet name. The Sheet Scale is 1:1. The Preview box contains no Sheet format. Custom sheet size is 22in x 17in (558.80mm x 431.80mm).

Glass Box and Six Principal Views

The Glass box method is a traditional method of placing an object in an *imaginary glass box* to view the six principle views.

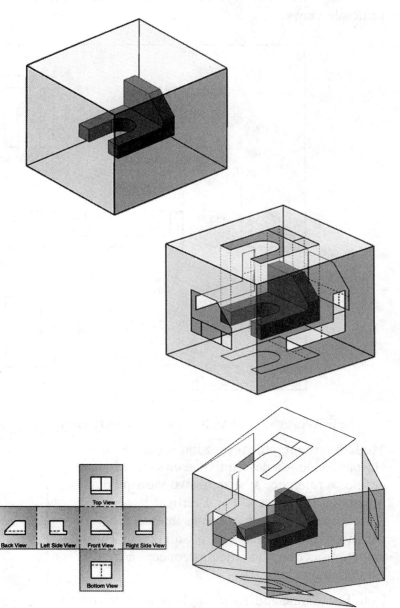

Imagine that the object you are going to draw is placed inside a glass box, so that the large flat surfaces of the object are parallel to the walls of the box.

From each point on the object, imagine a ray, or projector perpendicular to the wall of the box forming the view of the object on that wall or projection plane.

Then *unfold the sides* of the imaginary glass box to create the orthographic projection of the object.

Three are two different types of Angle Projection: First and Third Angle Projection. First Angle Projection is used in Europe and Asia. Third Angle Projection is used in the United States.

Third Angle Projection is used in the book. Imagine that the walls of the box are hinged and unfold the views outward around the Front view. This will provide you with the six principle views.

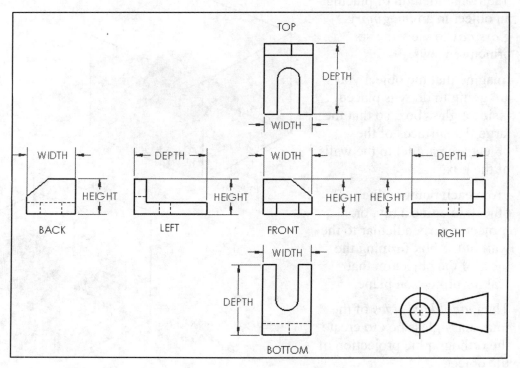

SolidWorks uses BACK view vs. REAR view.

Modern orthographic projection is derived from Gaspard Monge's descriptive geometry. Monge defined a reference system of two viewing planes, horizontal H ("ground") and vertical V ("backdrop"). These two planes intersect to partition 3D space into four quadrants. In Third-Angle projection, the object is conceptually located in quadrant III.

Both First-angle and Third-angle projections result in the same six views; the difference between them is the arrangement of these views around the box.

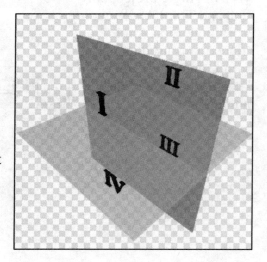

Below is an illustration of First Angle Projection.

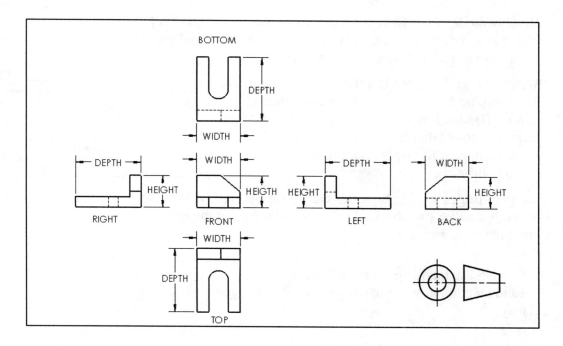

In First Angle projection, the object is conceptually located in quadrant I, i.e. it floats above and before the viewing planes, the planes are opaque, and each view is pushed through the object onto the plane furthest from it.

☀ SolidWorks uses BACK view vs. REAR view.

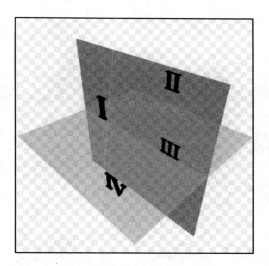

Display Styles / Modes

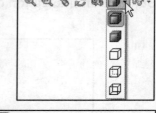

Display modes for a Drawing view are similar to a part except with the addition of the 3D Drawing view tool. This tool provides the ability to rotate the model in an existing view.

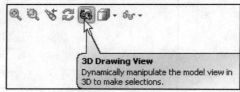

Wireframe and Shaded Display modes provide the best Graphic performance. Mechanical details require Hidden Lines Visible display and Hidden Lines Removed display. Select Shaded/Hidden Lines Removed to display Auxiliary Views to avoid confusion.

Tangent Edges Visible provides clarity for the start of a Fillet edge. Tangent Edges Removed provides the best graphic performance.

 ANSI standards prefers no Tangent Edges display, however individual company standards may display Tangents Edges for clarity.

Tangent Edges are displayed for educational purposes.

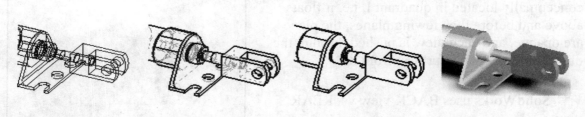

Wireframe   Hidden Lines Visible   Hidden Lines Removed   Shaded

Tangent Edges Visible   Tangent Edges With Font   Tangent Edges Removed

System Options

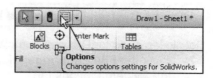

System Options are stored in the registry of the computer. System Options are not part of the document. Changes to the System Options affect all current and future documents. There are hundreds of Systems Options. Review a few of the options in this section.

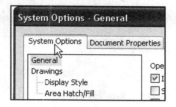

Click the Options ⊟ icon from the Menu bar toolbar to activate the System Options dialog box.

Activity: System Options - Display Style

Set the default display style.

38) Click **Options** ⊟ from the Menu bar toolbar. The System Options - General dialog box is displayed.

39) Click the **Display Style** folder from the System Options tab.

40) Check the **Hidden lines removed** box for the Display style for new views.

41) Check the **Visible** box for the default Tangent edges in the new views. Note: High quality is the default option for display quality.

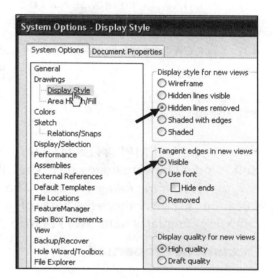

☼ There are two new system properties for drawing documents in SolidWorks 2010: SW-View Name and SW-View Scale. These properties are similar to the system properties SW-Sheet Name and SW-Sheet Scale.

File Locations

System Options, File Locations, Document Templates option determines the path to locate a Custom Drawing template. Add the MY-TEMPLATES folder to the File Locations. The folder listed in the Document Templates option determines the tabs displayed in the New SolidWorks Document dialog box.

Activity: System Options-File Locations

Set file locations for Drawing Templates.

42) Click the **File Locations** folder from the System Options tab.

43) Select **Document Templates** from the Show folders for drop-down menu.

44) Click the **Add** button.

45) Click **Browse**.

46) Select the **DRAWING-W-SOLIDWORKS-2010\MY-TEMPLATES** folder.

47) Click **OK** from the Browse For Folder box.

48) Click **Yes.**

49) Click **OK** from the System Options dialog box.

50) Click **Yes**.

Save Draw1.

51) **Save** Draw1.

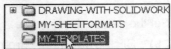

The MY-TEMPLATES tab is displayed in the New SolidWorks Drawing dialog box. The MY-TEMPLATES tab is *not displayed if the folder is empty*. The System Option, File Locations list determines the order of the tabs. Save the Drawing Templates to the MY-TEMPLATES folder.

Document Properties

Document Properties apply to the current document. Set the following: *Drafting Standard*, *Grid/Snap*, *Units*, *Line Fonts*, and *Image Quality* in Document Properties.

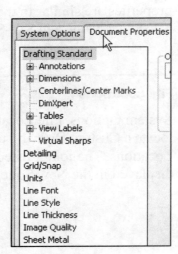

When the current document is saved as a template, the current parameters are stored with the template. New documents that utilize the same template contain the stored parameters.

Conserve drawing time. Set the Document Properties in the Drawing template. Document Properties options contain hundreds of parameters. Examples are addressed in this section. Explore other parameters through SolidWorks Help Topics.

There are numerous text styles and sizes available in SolidWorks. Companies develop drawing format standards and use specific text height for Metric and English drawings.

The ASME Y14.2M-1992(R1998) standard lists the following: *lettering*, *arrowhead*, *line conventions* and *lettering conventions* for engineering drawings and related documentation practices.

Font

Century Gothic is the default SolidWorks font.

Create an assessment page to test that your Printer/Plotter drivers support the default SolidWorks font.

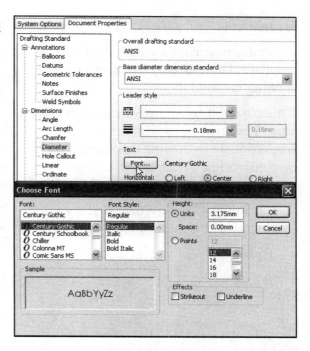

Minimum Drawing Letter Height based on ASME Y14.2.				
Annotation	Inch drawing sizes: A, B, C Metric drawing sizes: A2, A3, A4		Inch drawing sizes: D, E Metric drawing sizes: A0, A1	
	Inch	Millimeter	Inch	Millimeter
Drawing Title, Drawing Size, Cage Code, Drawing Number and Revision letter positioned inside the Title block.	.12in	3mm	.24in	6mm
Section views, Zone letter and numerals.	.24in	6mm	.24in	6mm
Drawing block headings in Title block.	.10in	2.5mm	.10mm	2.5mm
All other characters inside the Sheet boundary. Corresponds to the SW Dimension and Note font.	.12in.	3mm	.12in	3mm.

Arrowheads

Control arrowheads through the Drafting Standard, Dimensions option in an active drawing document.

Utilize a solid filled arrowhead with a 3:1 ratio. The arrowhead width is proportionate to the line thickness. The Dimension line thickness is 0.3mm.

The Dimension arrow is based on the Dimension line. SolidWorks defines arrow size with three options:

- *Height*
- *Width*
- *Length*

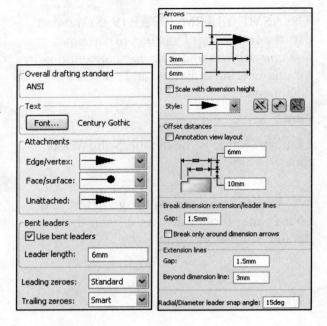

Height corresponds to the arrow width. Width corresponds to the arrow tail length. Length corresponds to the distance from the tip of the arrow to the end of the tail.

The Section line thickness, (Drafting Standard, View Labels, Section) is 0.6mm. The Section arrow is based on the Section line. The Section arrow length is 6mm. The Section arrow width is 2mm.

The illustration displays the default mm values.

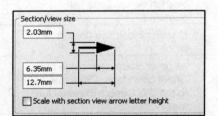

The illustrations are based on SolidWorks SP1.0. The illustrations may vary slightly per your SolidWorks release.

Line Widths

The ASME Y14.2M-1992 (R1998) standard recommends two line widths with a 2:1 ratio. The minimum width of a thin line is 0.3mm. The minimum width of a thick, "normal" line is 0.6mm.

A single width line is acceptable on CAD drawings. Two line widths are used in this Chapter: Thin: 0.3mm and Normal: 0.6mm.

Apply Line Styles in the Line Font Document Properties. Line Font determines the appearance of a line in the Graphics window. SolidWorks styles utilized in this chapter are as follows:

SolidWorks Line Style	Thin: (0.3mm)	Normal: (0.6mm)
Solid		
Dashed		
Phantom		
Chain		
Center		
Stitch		
Thin/Thick Chain		

Various printers/plotters provide variable Line Weight settings. Example: Thin (0.3mm), Normal (0.6mm), and Thick (0.6mm).

Refer to the printer/plotter owner's manual for Line weight setting. Utilize the Document Property, Line Style option to create, save, load, and delete line styles.

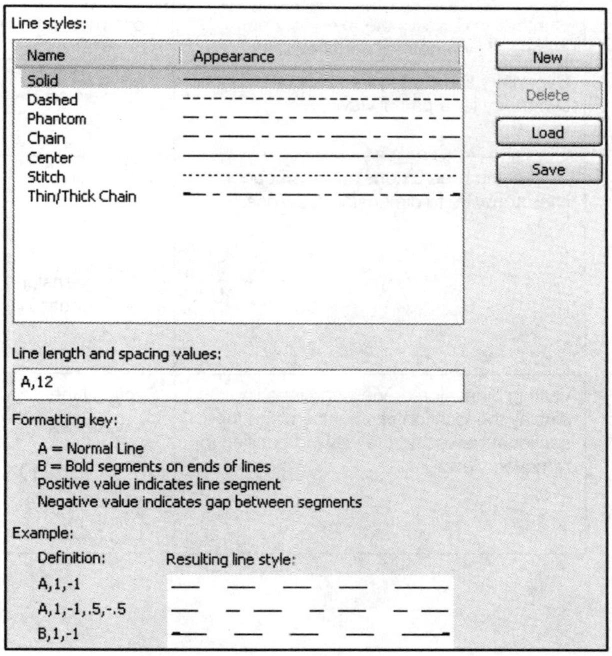

Line styles:

Name	Appearance
Solid	
Dashed	
Phantom	
Chain	
Center	
Stitch	
Thin/Thick Chain	

New
Delete
Load
Save

Line length and spacing values:

A,12

Formatting key:

A = Normal Line
B = Bold segments on ends of lines
Positive value indicates line segment
Negative value indicates gap between segments

Example:

Definition:	Resulting line style:
A,1,-1	
A,1,-1,.5,-.5	
B,1,-1	

Scale large drawing sheets with the Resolution and Scale option located in the File, Page Setup Menu bar menu. Use the Scale to fit option to resize the drawing sheet to the physical paper size.

Use Scale to resize the drawing sheet by a percentage to the physical paper size.

Line Font

The ASME Y14.2M-1992(R1998) standard addresses the type and style of lines used in engineering drawings. Combine different Line Styles and use drawing layers to achieve the following types of ASME lines:

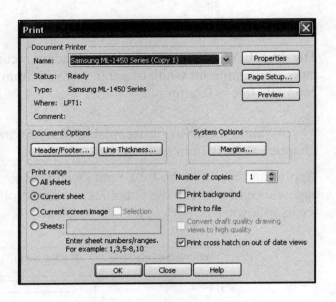

ASME Y14.2-1992(R1998) TYPE of LINE & example:	SolidWorks Line Font Type of Edge:	Style:	Thickness:
Visible line displays the visible edges or contours of a part.	Visible Edge	Solid	Thick "Normal"
Hidden line displays the hidden edges or contours of a part.	Hidden Edge	Dashed	Thin
Section lining displays the cut surface of a part assembly in a section view.	Crosshatch	Solid	Thin Different Hatch patterns relate to different materials
Center line displays the axes of center planes of symmetrical parts/features.	Construction Curves	Center	Thin
Symmetry line displays an axis of symmetry for a partial view.			Sketch Thin Center Line and Thick Visible lines on drawing layer.
Dimension lines/Extension lines/Leader lines combine to dimension drawings.	Dimensions Extension Line Leader Line	Solid	Thin
Cutting plane line or Viewing plane line display the location of a cutting plane for sectional views and the viewing position for removed views.	Section Line View Arrows D D	Phantom Solid	Thick Thick, "Normal"

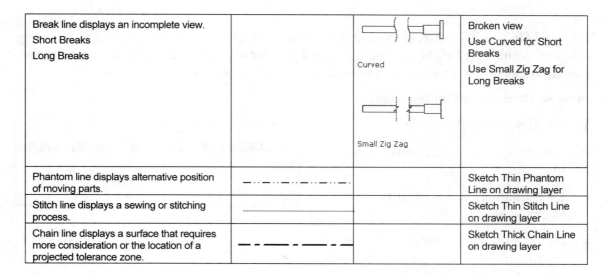

Break line displays an incomplete view. Short Breaks Long Breaks		Curved Small Zig Zag	Broken view Use Curved for Short Breaks Use Small Zig Zag for Long Breaks
Phantom line displays alternative position of moving parts.	— · — · · — · — · — ·		Sketch Thin Phantom Line on drawing layer
Stitch line displays a sewing or stitching process.	··············		Sketch Thin Stitch Line on drawing layer
Chain line displays a surface that requires more consideration or the location of a projected tolerance zone.	— · — · — · —		Sketch Thick Chain Line on drawing layer

The following default lines are defined in SolidWorks: *Solid, Dashed, Phantom, Chain, Center, Stitch, Thin/Thick Chain.*

Define these line types on a separate drawing layer.

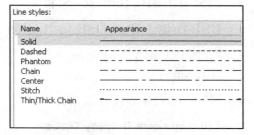

Document Properties-Dimensions

Control the Dimensions options through Document Properties. The Drafting Standard, Dimensions determines the display on the drawing. Millimeter dimensioning and decimal inch dimensioning are the two key types of units specified on engineering drawings.

There are other dimension types specified for commercial commodities such as pipe sizes and lumber sizes. Develop separate Drawing templates for decimal inch units.

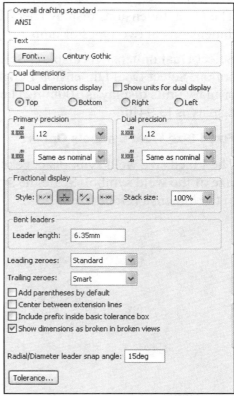

ASME Y14.2-1992(R1998) and the ASME Y14.2M Line Conventions and Lettering standard define text height, arrows and line styles for inch and metric values. Review the Detailing Document Properties options function before entering their values.

Drafting (Dimensioning) Standard

The Drafting standard options are:

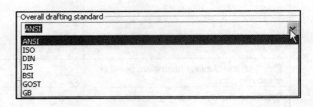

- **ANSI**: American National Standards Institute

- **ISO**: International Standards Organization

- **DIN**: Deutsche Institute für Normumg (German)

- **JIS**: Japanese Industry Standard

- **BSI**: British Standards Institution

- **GOST**: Gosndarstuennye State Standard (Russian)

- **GB**: Guo Biao (Chinese)

Dual dimensions Display Option

The Dual dimensions display check box shows dimensions in two types of units on the drawing.

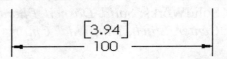

Select Dual dimensions display. Select the On top option. Select Dual Dimension Length units. The primary units display is 100mm. The secondary units display is [3.94]in.

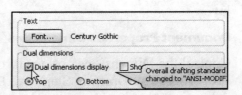

Fixed Size Weld Symbols Option

The Fixed size weld symbols checkbox displays the size of the weld symbol. Scale the symbols according to the dimension font size.

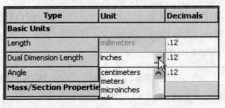

Display Datums per 1982 Option

The Display datums per 1982 checkbox displays the ANSI Y14.5M-1982 datums. Use the ASME Y14.5M-1994(R1999) datums in this text.

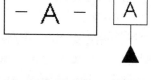

Leading Zeroes and Trailing Zeroes Option

The Leading zeroes list box contains three options:

- **Standard**: Active by default. Zeros are displayed based on the dimensioning standard.

- **Show**: Zeros before decimal points are displayed.

- **Remove**: Zeros are not displayed.

The Trailing zeroes list box contains four options:

- **Smart**: Active by default. Trailing zeros are trimmed for whole metric values. (Conforms to ANSI and ISO standards.)

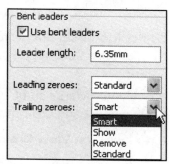

- **Show**: Dimensions have trailing zeros up to the number of decimal places specified in Tools, Options, Document Properties, Units section.

- **Remove**: All trailing zeros are removed.

- **Standard**: Trims trailing zeroes to the ASME Y14.5M-1994 standard.

Alternative Section Display Option

The ASME Y14.2M-1992(R1998) standard supports two display styles. The default section line displays a continuous Phantom line type (D-D).

💡 Check the Alternate section display checkbox to allow for a gap in the section line (B-B).

Centerline Extension and Center Marks Option

The Centerline extension value controls the extension length beyond the section geometry.

Centerlines are created as font lines and arcs in the drawing views.

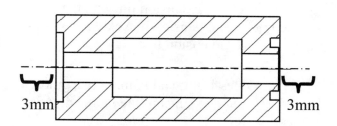

Centerlines should be added to the drawing prior to the addition of dimensions and annotations. You can resize them or modify their appearance. Resize their appearance by dragging the control points on each side of the centerline.

Center marks specify the default center mark size used with arcs and circles. Center marks are displayed with or without Center mark lines.

The Center mark lines extend pass the circumference of the selected circle. Select the Center mark size based on the drawing size and scale.

The Center mark command creates a center mark, or a center point on selected circular edges. Selecting a circle creates a center mark. Selecting an arc creates a center point.

Center Marks should be added to the drawing prior to the addition of dimensions and annotations. You can resize them or modify their appearance.

💡 Center Marks and Centerlines are annotations used to mark circle centers and describe the geometry size on the drawing.

Auto Insert on View Creation Option

Auto insert on view creation locates Center marks on the appropriate entities when a new view is inserted into a drawing. By default Center marks-holes, Center marks-fillets, Center marks-slots, Centerlines, Balloons, and Dimensions marked for drawing options are not checked.

💡 Save detailing time. Uncheck the Center marks option when parts contain multiple size holes and holes positioned at angles. Insert all dimensions and then insert the Center marks tool from the Annotation toolbar.

Extension Lines Option

The ASME Y14.2M-1992(R1998) and ASME Y14.5M-1994(R1999) standard defines extension line length and gap. A visible gap exists between the extension line and the visible line. The extension line extends 3mm - 4mm past the dimension line.

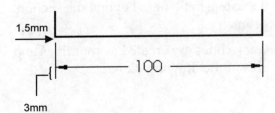

💡 The values 1.5mm and 3mm are a guide. Base the gap and extension line on the drawing size and scale.

Datum Feature Option

The Next label specifies the subsequent upper case letter used for the Datum feature symbol. The default value is A. Successive labels are in alphabetical order. The Datum Display type Per Standard option displays a filled triangular symbol on the Datum feature.

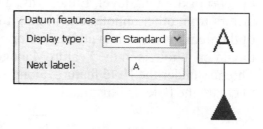

Surface Finish Symbols

For the ISO standard, Surface finish symbols display per the 2002 standard.

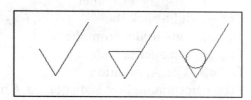

Break Line Option

The Break line gap specifies the size of the gap between the Broken view break lines.

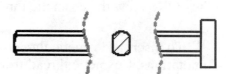

Automatic Update on BOM Option

The Automatic Update on BOM option updates the Bill of Material in a drawing if related model custom properties change.

ITEM NO.	QTY.	PART NO.	MATERIAL
1	1	10-0408	ALUMINUM
2	1	10-0409	STEEL

Set the values in SolidWorks to meet the ASME standard.

☀ Set units before entering values for Detailing options. Units for the Default Templates are determined from initial SolidWorks installation options.

Visible   Hidden

Cosmetic Thread Display Option

The High quality option displays Cosmetic threads visible or hidden in a selected drawing view. A blind hole Cosmetic thread is visible in the Front view and hidden in the Back view.

The Cosmetic thread feature is used to describe the attributes of a specific hole without having to add real threads to the model. It represents the minor diameter of a tread on a boss or the major diameter of a thread on a hole and can include a hole callout.

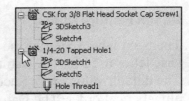

In SolidWorks 2010, the Cosmetic thread can be applied at the part or drawing level. Either way, a cosmetic thread differs from other annotations in that it is an absorbed feature of the item to which it is attached. For example, the cosmetic thread on a hole is in the FeatureManager design tree as Thread1 under the Hole feature, along with the sketches used to create the hole as illustrated.

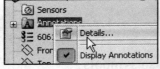

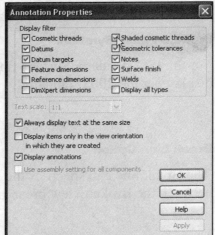

To display a Cosmetic thread, right-click the Annotations folder from the FeatureManager and click Details. The Annotation Properties dialog box is displayed. Check the Cosmetic threads box and the Shaded cosmetic threads box. Click OK. View the cosmetic thread.

To insert a Cosmetic thread, click Insert, Annotations, Cosmetic thread from the Menu bar menu.

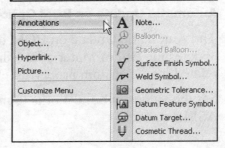

Review the Document Properties before inserting views, dimensions and annotations into your drawing. Modify the Document Properties that correspond to the part. For example, check/uncheck Dual dimension display if required for manufacturing. Uncheck the Auto insert on view creation, Center mark option when a part contains multiple size hole, rotated at different angles.

Activity: Document Properties-Detailing

Set Detailing options.

52) Click **Options** 📋, **Document Properties** tab from the Menu bar toolbar.

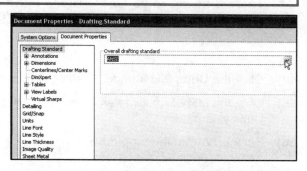

53) Select **ANSI** from the Overall drafting standard drop-down menu. Various options are available depending on the selected standard.

54) Click the **Dimensions** folder.

55) Check the **Dual dimension display** box.

Modify the Dimension Extension line value.

56) Enter **1.5mm** for Extension lines Gap.

57) Enter **3mm** for Extension lines Beyond dimension line.

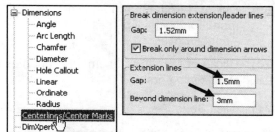

Modify the Centerline / Center Marks.

58) Click the **Centerlines/Center Marks** folder under Dimensions.

59) Enter **3mm** for the Centerline extension.

60) Enter **0.5mm** for the Center marks Size.

Modify the Break line gap.

61) Click the **Detailing** folder under Drafting Standard.

62) Enter **10mm** for the View Break lines Gap.

63) Enter **3mm** for the View break lines Extension.

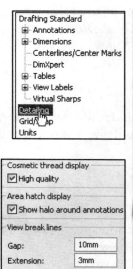

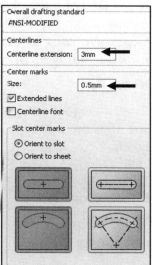

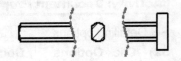

There is no set value for the Break line gap. Increase the value to accommodate a revolved section.

Set units.

64) Click the **Units** folder under Drafting Standard.

65) Click the **MMGS** (millimeter, gram, second) box for Unit system.

66) Select **.12** from the drop-down menu for decimal places for Length units millimeters.

67) Select **inches** from the drop-down menu for Dual Dimension Length.

68) Select **.123** from the drop-down menu for inch Decimal places.

69) Select **.1** from the drop-down menu for Decimal places for Angular units.

70) Click **OK** from the Document Properties - Units dialog box.

71) Click **Save** 🖫.

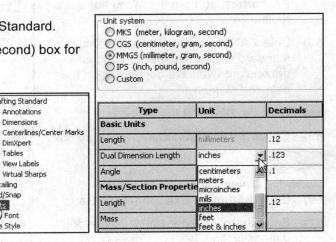

Document Properties, Annotations Font

The Annotations font controls the text height in the Drawing template for the following Annotation types: *Balloons, Datums, Geometric Tolerances, Notes, Surface Finishes* and *Weld Symbols*.

Notes Font

The Notes font option under the Annotations Font specifies the font type and size for notes and view labels.

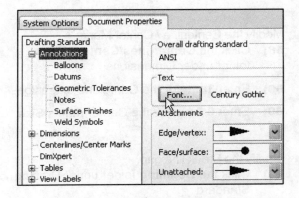

Dimensions Font

The Dimensions font option specifies the font type and size for the dimension text.

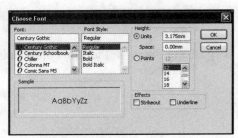

Auxiliary View / Auxiliary View Label Font

The Auxiliary View and the Auxiliary View Label fonts specify the font type and size used for the letter labels on the auxiliary arrow and the auxiliary view label text.

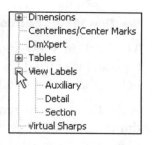

An Auxiliary View in general is similar to a Projected view, but it is unfolded normal to a reference edge in an existing view. The reference edge can be an edge of a part, a silhouette edge, an axis, or a sketched line. If you sketch a line, activate the drawing view first.

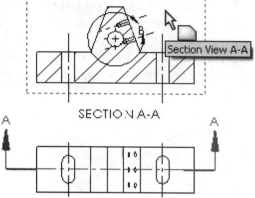

Detail View / Detail View Label Font

The Detail View and the Detail View Label fonts specify the font type and size used for the letter labels on the detail circle and the text below the detail view.

A Detail View in general is used to create a new drawing view which is an enlarged portion of an existing view. The enlarged portion is enclosed using sketch geometry, usually a circle or other closed contour like a spline.

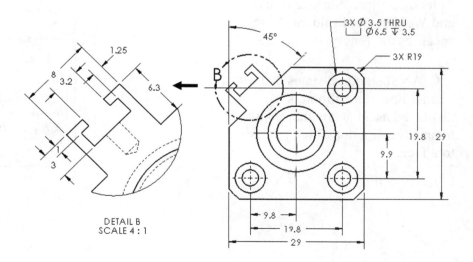

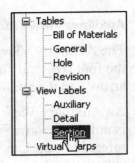

Section View / Section View Label Font

The Section View and the Section View Label fonts specify the font type and size used for the letter labels on the section lines and the text below the Section view.

A Section view in general is used to create a new drawing view that is defined by cutting an existing view with a section line (Sketch).

Some drawing views require or allow sketching within the view, rather than just over the view. These views, most notably sections and details require that the view be active before sketching so that the sketch geometry will be associated with the view.

Annotations Arrow Font

The Annotations font specifies the font type and size used for general annotations.

Balloons, Datums, Geometric Tolerances, Notes, Surface Finished and Weld symbols Font

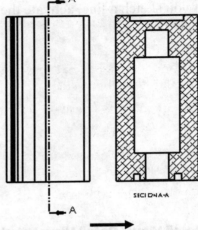

The Balloon, Datum, Geometric Tolerance, Note, Surface Finish and Weld symbol folders specifies the font type and size.

ANSI standard states that a Leader line of a balloon is displayed as an arrow that points to an edge or a dot which points to a face.

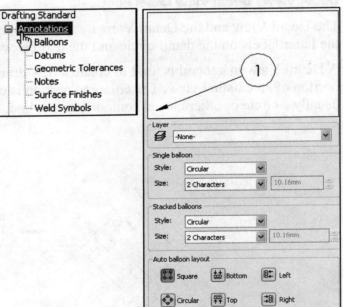

Tables Font

The Tables font varies from company to company. Tables font controls the *Bill of Materials*, *General*, *Hole* and *Revision*.

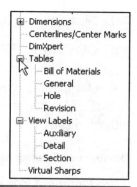

Activity: Document Properties-Annotations Font

Set the Font.

72) Click **Options** ☐, **Document Properties** tab from the Menu bar toolbar.

73) Expand the **Annotations** folder.

74) Click the **Notes** folder.

75) Click the **Font** button. The Choose Font dialog box is displayed.

76) Enter **3mm** for text height.

77) Click **OK** from the Choose Font dialog box.

78) Repeat the above procedure to set Font text height for **Dimensions**, **(View Labels Detail, View Label text)**, **Surface Finishes**, **Weld Symbols**, **Tables**, and **Balloons** font.

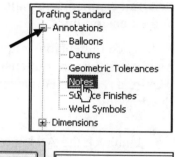

Set the Section and View Arrow font.

79) Click the **Detail** folder under the View Labels folder.

80) Click the **Font** button for View label text.

81) Enter **6mm** for text height.

82) Click **OK** from the Choose Font dialog box.

83) Repeat for the above procedure for the **Section/Section View label text**, and the **Section/Section arrow text**.

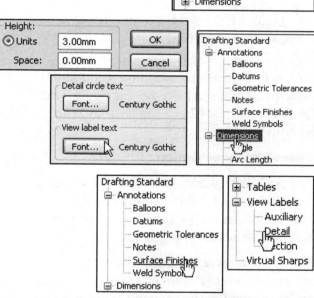

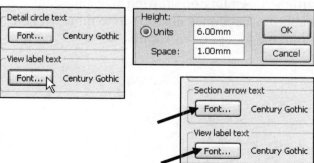

84) Click **OK** from the Document Properties dialog box.

85) Click **Save** 🔲 .

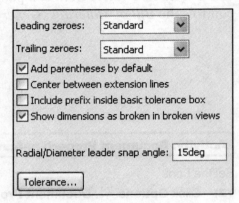

💡 Companies vary the size of their default font. ASME Y14.2 lists the annotation values as minimum letter heights.

Document Properties, Dimensions Options

The Document Properties, Drafting Standard, Dimensions options determine the display of dimensions. The Dimensions option determines the display and position of the text and extension lines.

Reference dimensions require parentheses. Symmetric feature dimensions in the part require a redefined dimensioning scheme in the drawing.

💡 Uncheck the Add parentheses by default to conserve design time.

💡 Add Parenthesis to a dimension in the drawing. Right-click on the dimension text. Click Properties. Check the Display with parentheses box.

Offset Distances Option

The ASME Y14.5M-1994(R1999) standard sets guidelines for dimension spacing. The space between the first dimension line and the part profile is 10mm or greater.

The space between subsequent parallel dimension lines is 6mm or greater. Spacing differs depending on drawing size and scale. Set the From last dimension option to 6mm. Set the From model option to 10mm.

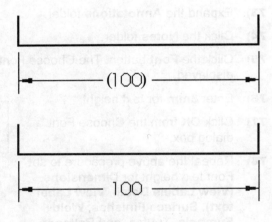

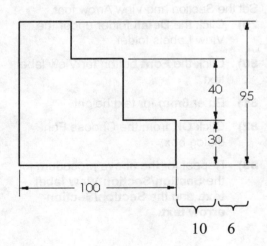

Arrows Option

The Arrows option controls the display of the
Arrowheads. The ASME Y14.2M-1992(R1998)
standard recommends a solid filled arrow head.

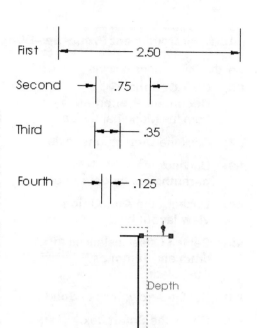

Arrowheads are drawn between extension
lines if space is available. If space is limited, see
the preferred arrowhead and dimension location
order as illustrated.

Double-click the dimension, to access the
control points for the arrowheads in SolidWorks.

Break Dimension/Extension Option

The ASME Y14.5M-1994(R1999) standard states
do not cross dimension lines. Break the extension
line when the dimension line crosses close to
an arrowhead.

Drag the extension line above the arrowhead.
Sketch a new line collinear with the extension
line below the arrowhead.

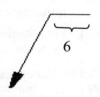

Uncheck the Break around dimension arrows
only option. Control individual breaks in the
drawing for this chapter.

Bent Leader Length Option

Create ASME leader lines with a small
horizontal segment. This is called the Bent
Leader length.

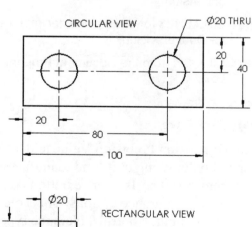

Activity: Document Properties-Dimensions

Set the Dimensions options.

86) Click **Options** 📋, **Document Properties** tab from the Menu bar toolbar.

87) Click the **Dimensions** folder.

88) Uncheck the **Add parentheses by default** box.

89) Uncheck the **Annotation view layout** box.

90) Set the Offset distances to **6mm** and **10mm** as illustrated.

91) Set the Arrow Style to **Solid**.

92) Check the **Smart** box.

93) Enter **1.5mm** for the Gap in the Break dimension extension lines box.

94) Uncheck the **Break around dimension arrows only** box.

95) Enter **6mm** for the Bent leader length (ASME only).

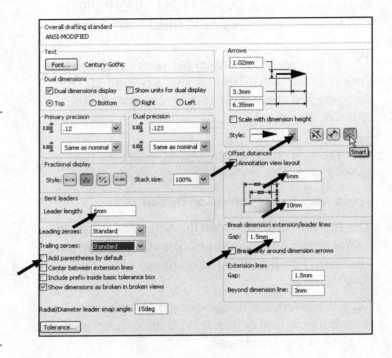

Set the Dimension Precision.

96) The primary units are millimeters. Select **.12** for two place decimal precision for Primary dimension.

97) Select **.123** for three place decimal precision for Dual precision.

98) Click **OK** from the Document Properties dialog box.

Save the drawing.

99) Click **Save** 💾.

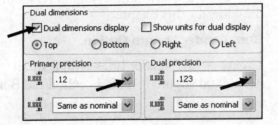

The Dimension Precision Value and Tolerance entries depend on drawing units and manufacturing requirements. The Tolerance button displays the Dimension Tolerance options. The Tolerance type is None by default. Control Tolerance type on individual dimensions.

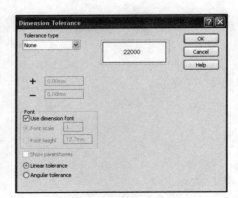

Document Properties-Notes and Balloons Option

Note text positioned on the drawing, outside the Title block use the same font type and height size as the Dimension font. The exceptions to the rule are:

h = text height

2h

- ASME Y14.100M-1998 Engineering Drawing Practices extended symbols.

- Use Upper case letters for all Notes unless lower case is required. Example: HCl – Hardness Critical Item requires a lower case "l".

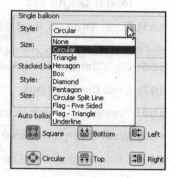

Modify Notes Border Style to create boxes, circles, triangles and other shapes around the text. The Default Border style is set to None. Modify the border height. Use the Size option.

Balloon callouts label components in an assembly and relate them to the item numbers in the Bill of Materials. The default Balloon style is Circular.

Activity: Document Properties - Notes and Balloons

Set the Notes options.

100) Click **Options** ☐ , **Document Properties** tab from the Menu bar toolbar.

101) Expand the **Annotations** folder.

102) Click the **Notes** folder.

103) Check **Bent** for Leader display.

104) Uncheck the **Use document leader length** box.

105) Enter **6mm** for the Leader length.

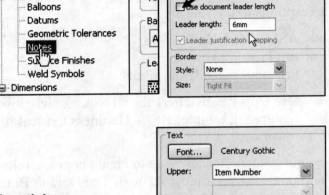

Set the drawing Balloon Properties.
106) Click the **Balloons** folder.

107) Click the **Bent** box.

108) Uncheck the **Use document leader length box**.

109) Enter **6mm** for Leader length.

110) Click **OK** from the Document Properties dialog box.

111) **Save** the drawing.

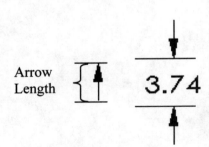

Document Properties - Arrows

Set Arrows Properties according to the ASME Y14.2M-1992(R1998) standard with a 3:1 ratio: Width to Height.

The Length value is the overall length of the arrow from the tip of the arrowhead to the end of the arrow tail. The Length is displayed when the dimension text is flipped to the inside. A Solid filled arrowhead is the preferred arrow type for dimension lines.

Arrow Length ⎰ ↕ 3.74

Activity: Document Properties - Arrows

Set the Dimension Arrow Properties.

112) Click **Options** ▣,
Document Properties tab
from the Menu bar toolbar.

113) Click the **Dimensions**
folder.

114) Enter **1** for the arrow Height
in the Size text box.

115) Enter **3** for the arrow Width.

116) Enter **6** for the arrow Length.

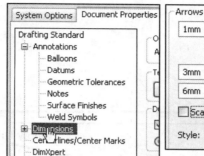
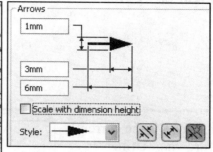

Set the Section View Arrow Properties.
117) Expand the **View Labels** folder.

118) Click the **Section** folder.

Set the arrow style.
119) Under the Section/View size, enter **2** for
Height.

120) Enter **6** for Width.

121) Enter **12** for Length.

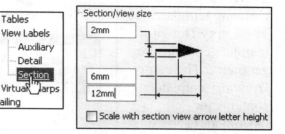

Document Properties - Line Font

The Line Font determines the style and thickness for a particular type of edge in a drawing. Modify the type of edge, style and thickness to reflect the ASME Y14.2M-1992(R1998) standard. The ASME Y14.2M-1992(R1998) standard defines two line weights: 0.3mm and 0.6mm.

Thin Thickness is 0.3mm. Thick (Normal) Thickness is 0.6mm. Review line weights as defined in the File, Page Setup or in File, Print, System Options for your particular printer/plotter. Control the line weight display in the Graphics window.

Activity: Document Properties - Line Font

Set the Line Font Properties.
122) Click the **Line Font** folder.

123) Click **Break Lines** for the Type of edge.

124) Select **Solid** for Style.

Create a Custom Line Thickness.
125) Select **Custom Size** for
Thickness.

126) Enter **0.33**mm for Custom
thickness.

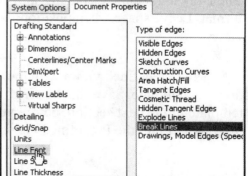

127) Click **OK** from the Document Properties - Line Font dialog box.

Save the drawing.
128) Click **Save**.

Draw1 is the current drawing. Utilize Draw1 to create a Drawing template. The empty Drawing template contains no geometry. The empty Drawing template contains the Document Properties and the Sheet Properties.

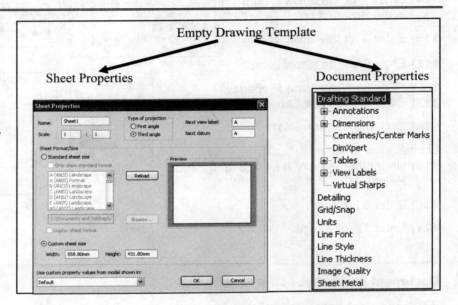

Predefined and Projected Views

In Orthographic Projection - the six principle views are *Top, Front, Right, Back, Bottom* and *Left*. Drawings commonly display the Top, Front, Right, and an Isometric view. You can define a view in a drawing sheet and then populate the view. You can save a drawing document with Predefined views as a document template.

Insert the Top, Front, Right, and Isometric views into the drawing template. Utilize the Predefined command to create the Front and Isometric view. Utilize the Projected view command to create the Right and Top view.

The Drawing template contains a Sheet format. Leave space when positioning views.

☼ Save Predefined views with the drawing template. Save the drawing template in the next section, before you insert a part into the Predefined views.

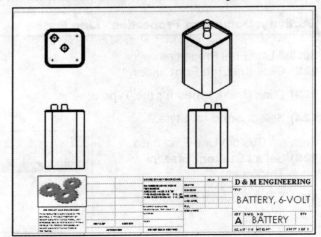

Activity: Insert Predefined and Projected Views

Insert a Front Predefined view.

129) Click **Insert**, **Drawing View**, **Predefined**  from the Menu bar menu.

130) Click the **lower left corner** of the drawing. The Drawing View1 PropertyManager is displayed.

💡 *Front view is the default view in the Orientation dialog box.

131) Click **Hidden Lines Removed** from the Display Style box.

132) Click **OK** ✔ from the Drawing View1 PropertyManager.

Insert a Top Projected view.
133) Click the **View Layout** tab from the CommandManager.

134) Click **Projected view** ⊞ from the View Layout toolbar. The Projected View PropertyManager is displayed.

135) Check the **Use parent style** box to display Hidden Lines Removed.

136) Click a **position** directly above the Front view.

Insert the Right Projected view.

137) Click **Projected View** ⊞ from the View Layout toolbar.

138) Click inside the **Front** view.

139) Click a **position** directly to the right of the Front view.

Insert an Isometric Predefined view.
140) Click inside the **Front** view.

141) Click **Insert**, **Drawing View**, **Predefined** from the Menu bar menu. The Drawing View PropertyManager is displayed.

142) Click a **position** in the upper right corner of the sheet as illustrated.

143) Click *Isometric from the Orientation box.

144) Click **OK** ✔ from the Drawing View4 PropertyManager.

145) Click **Save** 💾. View the drawing FeatureManager. Note the View icons for the Predefined and Projected views.

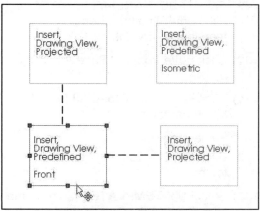

Save As

The Save As option provides the ability to save documents with various file types. The current document is a drawing named Draw1.slddrw. Save the document as a Drawing template (*.drwdot).

🔅 Select the Drawing Templates (*.drwdot) option for Save as type before you browse to the MY-TEMPLATES folder. SolidWorks selects the SolidWorks\data\templates folder by default when you select Drawing Templates (*.drwdot).

Test the Drawing template located in the MY-TEMPLATES folder. Create a new drawing document.

Activity: Save As and Test Drawing Template

Save the empty Drawing Template.

146) Click **Save As** from the Menu bar menu.

147) Select **Drawing Templates (*.drwdot)** from the Save as type.

148) **Browse** and select the **DRAWING-W-SOLIDWORKS-2010\ MY-TEMPLATES** for the Save in file folder.

149) Enter **C-SIZE-ANSI-MM-EMPTY** for the File name. The file extension for the template is .drwdot.

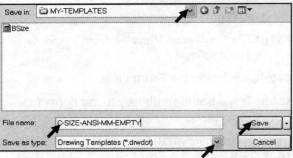

150) Click **Save** from the Save As dialog box.

151) Click **Windows**, **Close All** from the Menu bar toolbar.

Create a new drawing.

152) Click **New** ⬜ from the Menu bar toolbar

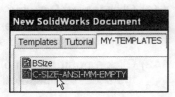

153) Select **MY-TEMPLATES** tab from the New SolidWorks Document dialog box.

154) Double-click **C-SIZE-ANSI-MM-EMPTY**.

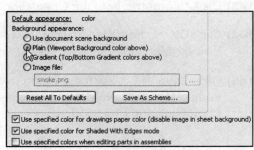

🔅 For improved drawing visibility, the default Drawing Sheet background color is modified to white.

The Sheet Format/Size box displays C (ANSI) Landscape.

155) If required, click **C (ANSI) Landscape**. Click **OK**.

156) Click **Cancel** ✖ from the Model View PropertyManager. Draw2 is the current drawing document. Note the drawing view icons in the FeatureManager.

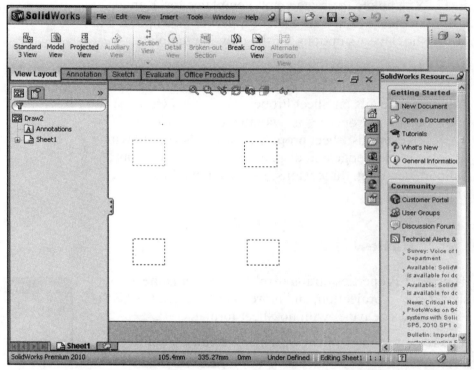

Close all documents.

157) Click **Windows**, **Close All** from the Menu bar menu.

You created a C (ANSI) size drawing with no Sheet format when you selected the C-SIZE-ANSI-MM-EMPTY template from the New SolidWorks Document box. The Drawing template controls sheet size and Document Properties. The Sheet format controls the Title block, company logo, and Custom Properties.

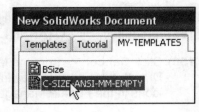

 Conserve design time. Utilize the C-SIZE-ANSI-MM-EMPTY template to create empty templates for A and B size drawings. Modify the Sheet Properties size option and utilize the Save As options for the drawing template.

More Information

Additional details on Sheet Properties, System Options, and Document Properties is available in SolidWorks Help Topics. Keywords: sheet properties, paper (size), drawings (display modes, edge and display), options (annotations, balloon, detailing, dimensions, file locations, font, note, and units).

Review

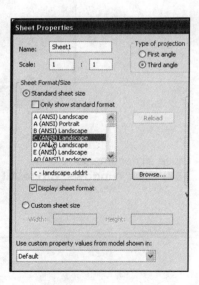

The Sheet Properties option displayed: Sheet name, scale, size, Type of projection, and more. You selected C (ANSI) Landscape size paper with no Sheet format.

You reviewed the System Options Drawings and File Locations. The Drawings Display Style option controlled the display mode and tangent edges of the view.

The File Locations option created the MY-TEMPLATES folder tab in the New SolidWorks Document dialog box.

Document Properties are stored in the current document. You utilized the Detailing (Dimensions, Notes, Balloons, Arrows, and Annotations Font), Line Font, and Units options in the Drawing template. There are hundreds of System Options and Document Properties.

Sheet Format

Customize drawing Sheet formats to create and match your company drawing standards.

A customer requests a new product. The engineer designs the product in one location, the company produces the product in a second location and the field engineer supports the customer in a third location.

The ASME Y14.24M standard describes various types of drawings. Example: The Engineering department produces detail and assembly drawings. The drawings for machined, plastic and sheet metal parts contain specific tolerances and notes used in fabrication.

Manufacturing adds vendor item drawings with tables and notes. Field Service requires installation drawings that are provided to the customer.

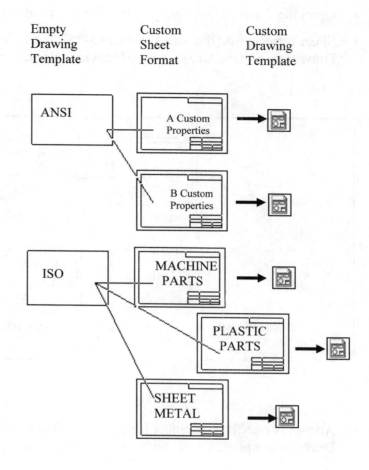

Create Sheet formats to support various standards and drawing types. There are numerous ways to create a custom Sheet format:

- Open a ".dwg" file created with another CAD application. Save the ".dwg" file as a Sheet format.

- Right-click in the Graphics window. Select Edit Sheet Format. Create drawing borders, Title block, notes, and zone locations for each drawing size. Save each drawing format.

- Right-click Properties in the Graphics window. Select Properties. Check the Display Sheet Format option from the Sheet format drop-down menu. Browse to select an existing Sheet format.

- Add an OLE supported Sheet format such as a bitmap file of the Title block and notes. Use the Insert, Object command or Insert, Picture command.

- Utilize an existing AutoCAD drawing to create a SolidWorks Sheet format.

- Open the AutoCAD drawing as the Sheet format. Save the C-FORMAT.slddrt

- Sheet format. Add the Sheet format C-FORMAT.slddrt to the empty C (ANSI) size Drawing template. Create a new Drawing template named C-ANSI-MM.drwdot.

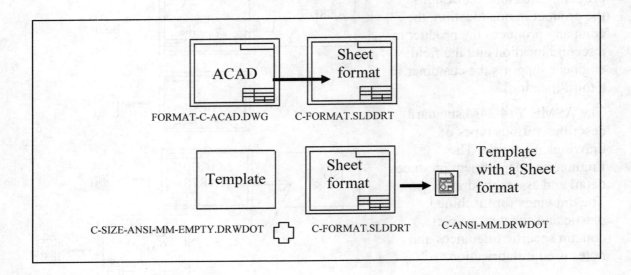

- Add an A (ANSI) size Sheet format, A-FORMAT.slddrt to an empty A (ANSI) size Drawing template. Create an A-ANSI-MM.drwdot Drawing template.

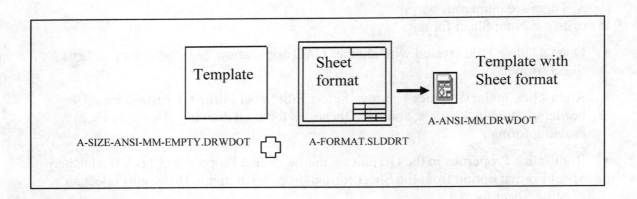

Insert views from the part or assembly into the SolidWorks drawing.

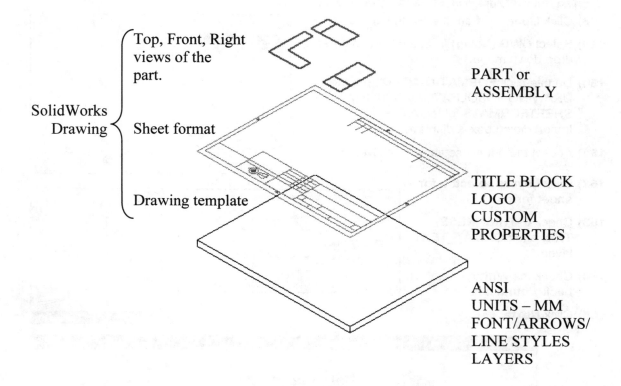

Data imported from other CAD systems for a Sheet format may require editing in SolidWorks. Delete extraneous lines in the imported Sheet format. The drawing sheet contains two modes:

- *Edit Sheet Format*

- *Edit Sheet*

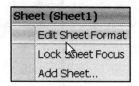

Utilize the *Edit Sheet Format* command to add or modify notes and Title block information. Edit in the *Edit Sheet Format* mode for lines and text created in the AutoCAD Title block.

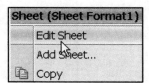

Utilize the *Edit Sheet* command to insert views and dimensions. The sheet boundary and major title block headings are displayed with a THICK line style. Modify the drawing layer THICKNESS.

Activity: Sheet Format, Import From AutoCAD

Open an AutoCAD drawing: FORMAT-C-ACAD.dwg.

158) Click **Open** 📂 from the Menu bar toolbar.

159) Select **DWG (*.dwg)** from the Files of type drop-down menu.

160) Double-click **FORMAT-C-ACAD** from the DRAWING-W-SOLIDWORKS-2010\MY-SHEETFORMATS folder. A DXF / DWG Import dialog box is displayed.

161) Accept the default settings. Click **Next>**.

162) Click **Layers selected for sheet format**.

163) Check **0, THICKNESS, THIN** and **FORMAT_TEXT** layers.

164) Check the **White background** box.

165) Click **Next>**.

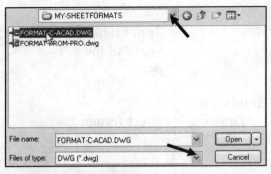

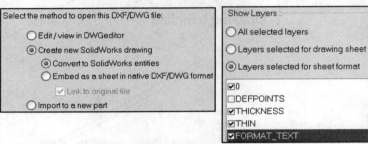

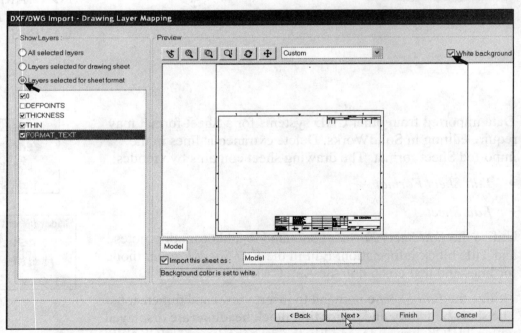

166) Select **Millimeters** for Data units.

167) Select **C-Landscape** for Paper size.

168) Click the **Browse** button.

169) Select the **MY-TEMPLATES** folder.

170) Double-click **C-SIZE-ANSI-MM-EMPTY** for Drawing Template.

171) Enter **0** for the X position.

172) Enter **0** for the Y position.

173) Click **Finish**.

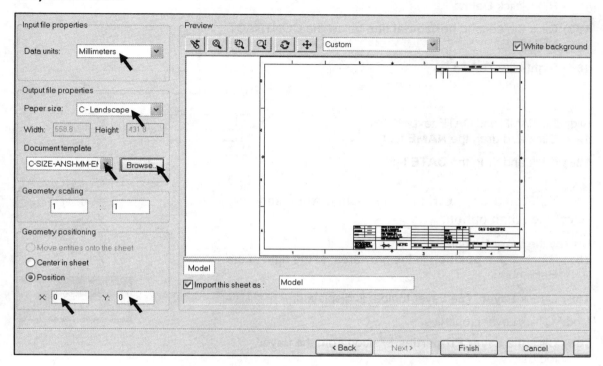

Save the Drawing.

174) Click **Save As** from the Menu bar toolbar.

175) Select the **DRAWING-W-SOLIDWORKS-2010** folder.

176) Enter **Draw3** for File name.

177) Click **Save**.

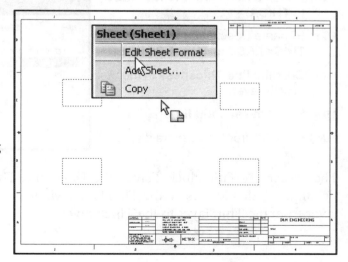

Draw# is the temporary drawing document utilized to create the Sheet format.

Edit the Title block.

178) Right-click in the **Graphics window**.

179) Click **Edit Sheet Format**.

Delete the Title block lines.

180) Zoom in on the Title block.

181) Click the first **horizontal line** below the CONTRACT NUMBER.

182) Right-click **Delete**.

183) Click the second **horizontal line** below the CONTRACT NUMBER.

184) Right-click **Delete**.

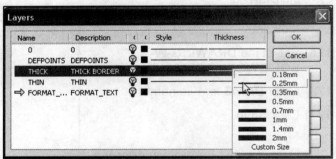

Align the NAME and DATE text.

185) Click and drag the **NAME** text.

186) Click and drag the **DATE** text.

You can use the Ctrl key, right-click Align and select the Align option.

Display the Layer toolbar.

187) Right-click a **position** in the gray area, to the right of the Help menu.

188) Check **Layer**. The Layer toolbar is displayed.

Modify Thick Layer properties.

189) Click the **Layer Properties** icon from the Layer toolbar.

Rename the AutoCAD layer

190) Rename Name from **THICKNESS** to **THICK**.

191) Rename Description from **THICKNESS** to **THICK BORDER**.

192) Click the **line Thickness** in the THICK layer.

193) Select the **second line**.

194) Click **OK** from the Layers dialog box.

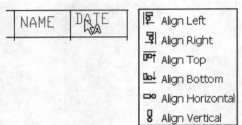

The border and Title block display the Thick line. The left line in the Title block is on the Thin layer. Modify the line layer from the Thin layer to the Thick layer.

Modify a Line layer.

195) Click on the **left line** as illustrated.

196) Click **THICK** layer from the Options box.

197) Click **OK** ✅ from the Line Properties PropertyManager.

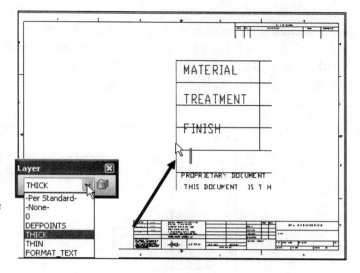

💡 Align the MATERIAL, TREATMENT and FINISH text as an exercise. You will need to retype the MATERIAL, TREATMENT and FINISH text before you align them.

Save the Sheet.

198) Click **Save**.

The C-FORMAT requires additional information and editing in the Title block. The Title block created from AutoCAD only contains text headings such as: Drawing Number, Revision, and Drawn by. Each heading is located in a different box in the Title block.

Insert additional Notes into the Title block in the Edit Sheet Format Mode. The Notes in the Sheet Format are linked to Properties. Properties are variables shared between parts, assemblies, and drawing documents.

💡 View Line segments clearly. The System Options, Drawings, Display sketch entity points option displays the endpoints of the line segments. Check this option before editing the lines in the Title block.

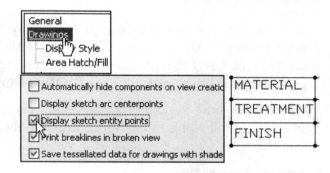

💡 Utilize the Sketch tools to create and edit Title block lines. Utilize dimensions and geometric relations to create Title block lines for A, B, C, D, and E sheet formats according to the ASME Y14.1 Decimal Inch Drawing Sheet Size and Format and ASME Y14.1M Metric Drawing Size and Format.

Utilize the Document Property, Grid/Snap for quick sketching. The ASME Y14.1 Title block is based on 0.125 increments. Set the Document Properties, Grid/Snap to 0.125 (English). The following dimensions below are recommended for A, B, C, and G sizes.

| Detailing |
| Grid/Snap |
| Units |
| Line Font |
| Line Style |

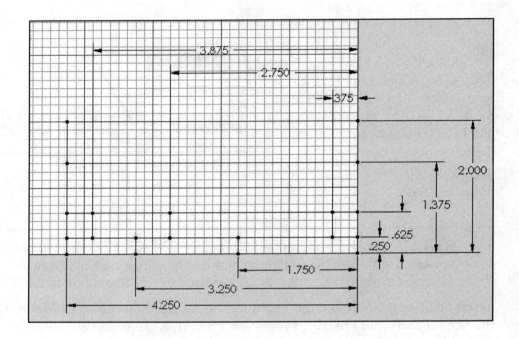

Title Block Notes and Properties

The Title block contains vital part and assembly information. Each company creates a unique version of a Title block. The imported AutoCAD sheet format contains heading names in each area of the Title block such as: TITLE, DWG NO., and SCALE.

Utilize SolidWorks System Properties and User defined Custom Properties to link Notes in the Sheet format to the drawing, part, and assembly.

System Properties

System Properties extract values from the current drawing. System Properties are determined from the SolidWorks documents. Insert System Properties as linked Notes in the Sheet Format.

System Properties begin with the prefix SW. There are two categories of Properties: System Properties and Drawing Specific System Properties.

Set System Properties in the File, Properties, Summary Information dialog box as follows:

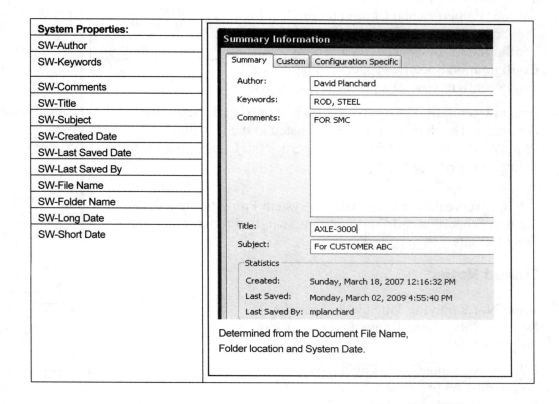

Set Drawing Specific System Properties: SW-Sheet Name, SW-Sheet Scale SW-Sheet Format Size and SW-Template Size in the Sheet Properties dialog box.

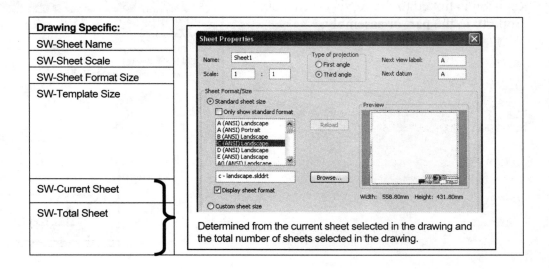

User Defined Properties

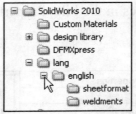

There are two types of User defined Properties: Custom Properties and Configuration Specific Properties. Custom Properties link all of the configurations of a part or an assembly. Configuration Specific Properties link only a single configuration of a part or an assembly.

Assign User defined Property values to named variables in the document. The default variables are listed in the text file \SolidWorks 2010\lang\english, properties.txt. Create your own User defined Property named variables.

Conserve design time. Utilize System Properties and define Custom Properties and Configuration Specific Properties in your sheet formats.

Linked Notes

Insert Notes into the Title block. Link the Notes to SolidWorks Properties and Custom Properties.

Review your company's Engineering documentation practices to determine the Notes displayed in the Title block.

In the next activity, DWG NO. is linked to the SW-File Name System Property. Revision is linked to the Revision Custom Property in the part or assembly.

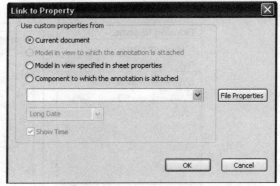

Linked Notes begin with the four different prefixes listed below:

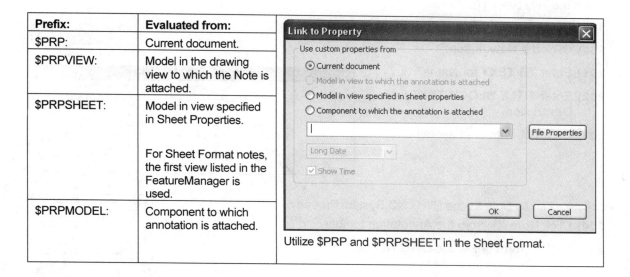

Prefix:	Evaluated from:
$PRP:	Current document.
$PRPVIEW:	Model in the drawing view to which the Note is attached.
$PRPSHEET:	Model in view specified in Sheet Properties. For Sheet Format notes, the first view listed in the FeatureManager is used.
$PRPMODEL:	Component to which annotation is attached.

Utilize $PRP and $PRPSHEET in the Sheet Format.

Linked Notes that reference Custom Properties in the drawing utilize the prefix: $PRP: Enter double quotes to define the property name: Example: $PRP:"CompanyName".

Linked Sheet Format Notes that reference Custom Properties in the part utilize the prefix: $PRPSHEET. Linked Sheet Format Notes are displayed blank in the Edit Sheet mode. Linked Sheet Format Notes are displayed with their property Name in the Edit Sheet Format mode. Example: $PRPSHEET{Material}.

Insert the following Linked Notes:

System Properties Linked to fields in the default Sheet Format. Prefix: $PRP	Custom Properties of drawings linked to fields in the default Sheet Formats. Prefix: $PRP	Custom Properties copied from the default SW Sheet Format to a Custom Sheet Format. Prefix: $PRP		Custom Properties of parts and assemblies linked to the fields in default Sheet Formats. Prefix:$PRPSHEET
SW-File Name (in DWG. NO. field)	CompanyName	DrawnBy	DrawnDate	Description (in TITLE field):
SW-Sheet Scale	CONTRACT NUMBER	CheckedBy	CheckedDate	Weight
SW-Current Sheet		EngineeringApproval	EngAppDate	Material, Finish and TREATMENT
SW-Total Sheets		ManufacturingApproval	MfgAppDate	Revision

User-defined Custom Property Names CONTRACT NUMBER and TREATMENT are displayed in capital letters for clarity. Utilize Large and small letters for Custom Property Names. Create a new layer for the Title block notes. The large yellow arrow in the Name column indicates the current layer.

Activity: Title Block and SW-File Name

Insert the Title block TEXT layer.

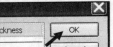

199) Click the **Layer Properties** 🗐 icon.

200) Click the **New** button.

201) Enter **TB TEXT** for Name.

202) Enter **TITLE BLOCK TEXT** for Description.

203) Click **OK** from the Layers box.

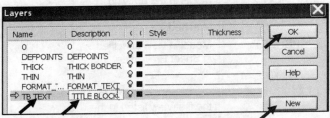

Create a Linked Note for the DWG NO System Property.

204) Click **Note** A from the Annotation toolbar.

205) Click a **point** below the DWG NO. text.

206) Click **Link to Property** 🔗 from the Text Format box.

207) Select **SW-File Name** from the drop-down menu.

208) Click **OK** from the Link to Property dialog box.

209) Click **OK** ✔ from the Note PropertyManager.

210) Position the mouse pointer on the **Draw3** text. The variable name $PRP:"SW-File Name" is displayed.

Save the Drawing.

211) **Rebuild** the drawing.

212) Click **Save**.

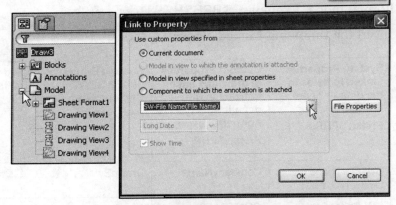

Draw3 is the current file name. The default Draw number varies depending on the number of drawings opened in a SolidWorks session.

The $PRP:"SW-File Name(File Name)" property updates to contain the part or assembly filename. Example: Insert the part 10-0408 into a Drawing template. The filename 10-0408 is linked to the SW-FileName property and is displayed in the DWG NO. box.

What action do you take to control the DWG NO. by a separate property not linked to the part filename? Answer: Create a Note linked to the Custom Property $PRP: "Number" in the Sheet format. Enter the value 45-10032 for the Number Custom Property in the drawing document.

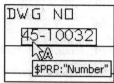

Size, Sheet and Scale Properties

Additional Linked Notes are required in the Title block. Create the SIZE, SHEET and SCALE text with Linked Properties. Position the text below the headings.

The Sheet Scale value changes to reflect the sheet scale properties in the drawing. The Sheet box combines two System Properties: SW-Current Sheet and SW-Total Sheets. The Current Sheet value and Total Sheets value change as additional sheets are added to the drawing.

Activity: Size, Sheet and Scale Properties

Create a Linked Property to the SIZE text.

213) Click **Note** A from the Annotation toolbar.

214) Click a **point** below the SIZE text.

215) Click **Link to Property** from the Text Format box.

216) Select **SW-Sheet Format Size** from the drop-down menu.

217) Click **OK** from the Link to Property dialog box.

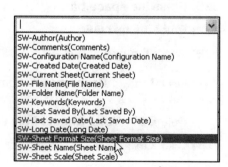

Modify the font size and style of the
SIZE text.
218) Double-click **C** in the SIZE box

219) Enter **3** for font height.

220) Click **Bold** for style.

221) Click **OK** ✓ from the Note PropertyManager.

Create a Linked Property to SCALE.

222) Click **Note** A from the Annotation toolbar.

223) Click a **point** to the right of the SCALE text.

224) Click **Link to Property** 🔗 from the Text Format box.

225) Select **SW-Sheet Scale** from the drop-down menu.

226) Click **OK**. 1:1 is displayed.

227) Click **OK** ✓ from the Note PropertyManager.

Delete text in the Title box.
228) Click the **OF** text in the lower right corner of the title box.

229) Press the **Delete** key.

Combine Link Properties for the SHEET text.
230) Double-click the **SHEET** text.

231) Position the **cursor** at the end of the text.

232) Press the **space bar**.

233) Click **Link to Property** 🔗 from the Text Format box.

234) Select **SW-Current Sheet** from the drop-down menu.

235) Click **OK**.

236) Press the **space bar**.

237) Enter the text **OF**.

238) Press the **space bar**.

239) Click **Link to Property** 🔗 from the Text Format
box.

240) Select **SW-Total Sheets** from the drop-down menu.

241) Click **OK**.

242) Click **OK**.

243) Click **OK** ✓ from the Note PropertyManager.

Save the Drawing.
244) Click **Save**.

Custom Property and Logo Picture

Utilize D&M ENGINEERING or your own value for CompanyName in the next step. The CompanyName Property is controlled through a Custom Property in the Sheet format.

Activity: Custom Property and Logo Picture

Delete the current Company Name Note text.

245) Right-click on the **D&M ENGINEERING** text in the drawing.

246) Click **Edit Text in Window**.

247) Delete **D&M ENGINEERING**.

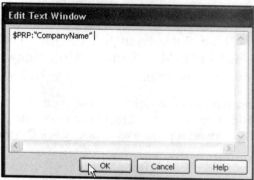

Insert the CompanyName Property.

248) Enter **$PRP:"CompanyName"** in the Note text box.

249) Click **OK**.

250) Click **Link to Property** from the Text Format dialog box.

251) Click the **File Properties** button from the Link to Property box.

252) Click the **Custom** tab from the Summary Information box.

253) Click inside the **Property Name** box.

254) Select **CompanyName**.

255) Click inside the **Value / Text Expression** box.

256) Enter **D&M ENGINEERING** for CompanyName.

257) Click inside the **Evaluated Value** box.

258) Click **OK** from the Summary Information box.

259) Click **OK** from the dialog box.

260) Click **OK** from the Note PropertyManager. View the results.

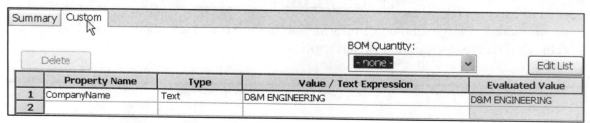

	Property Name	Type	Value / Text Expression	Evaluated Value
1	CompanyName	Text	D&M ENGINEERING	D&M ENGINEERING
2				

The Title block displays the CompanyName Linked Note. The current document stores the CompanyName Property. Select Custom Properties through the Link to Property drop-down menu.

Modify the font of D&M ENGINEERING.
261) Double-click the **D&M ENGINEERING** text.

262) Click **Bold**.

263) Click **OK** ✔ from the Note Property Manager.

Position the mouse pointer over the Linked Note to display the Custom Property value. Utilize Ctrl-A to select all the text in the Note text box.

A company logo is normally located in the Title block. Create a company logo by inserting a picture file or a file as an OLE object into the Title block. Example: The file COMPASS.doc is located in the MY-SHEETFORMATS folder. Utilize any picture file, scanned image, or bitmap.

Insert a picture file for the Sheet Logo.
264) Click **Insert**, **Object** from the Menu bar menu. Note: You can insert a picture as a logo. Click **Create from File**.

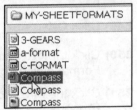

265) Click **Browse**.

266) Double-click **MY-SHEETFORMATS\Compas.doc**.

267) Right-click **OK**. The picture file is displayed on the Sheet.

268) Size the **picture** by dragging the picture handles in Sheet1 as illustrated.

Save the Drawing.
269) Click **Save** 🖫 .

If needed, you can add relations in the sheet format so that any modifications can be easily applied. For instance if you wanted to modify the format for different sheet sizes, or needed to extend a text area

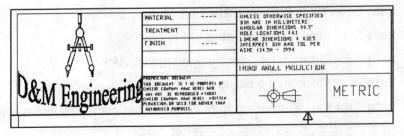

to accommodate a large amount of information in the Title block, then it would be easier to achieve if there were defined sketch entities.

User Defined Custom Property

Your company has a policy that a contract number must be contained in the Title block for all associated drawings in the chapter. The contract number is not a predefined SolidWorks Custom Property. Create a user defined Custom Property named CONTRACT NUMBER. Add it to the drawing Title block. The Custom Property is contained in the sheet format.

Activity: User Defined Custom Property

Create a User defined Custom Property.

270) Click **Note** A from the Annotation toolbar.

271) Click a **point** in the upper left hand corner below the CONTRACT NUMBER text.

272) Click **Link to Property** from the Text Format box.

273) Click the **File Properties** button.

274) Click the **Custom** tab.

275) Click inside the **Property Name** spin box.

276) Enter **CONTRACT NUMBER** for Name.

277) Click inside the **Value / Text Expression** box.

278) Enter **101045-PAP** for Value. Click inside the **Evaluated Value** box.

279) Click **OK** from the Summary Information box.

	Property Name	Type	Value / Text Expression	Evaluated Value
1	CompanyName	Text	D&M ENGINEERING	D&M ENGINEERING
2	CONTRACT NUMBER	Text	101045-PAP	101045-PAP

280) Select **CONTRACT NUMBER** in the Property Name text box. Click **OK** from the Link to Property box. View the results

281) Click **OK** from the Note PropertyManager.

Fit the drawing to the Graphics window.
282) Press the **f** key.

283) Click **Save**.

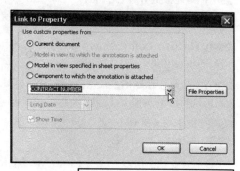
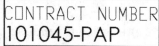

Copy/Paste Custom Properties

Conserve design time. Share information from Templates and Sheet Formats. Copy DrawnBy, DrawnDate, CheckedBy, CheckedDate, EngineeringApproval, EngAppDate, ManufacturingApproval and MfgAppDate from a default SolidWorks C-Sheet format to the Custom C-Format.

Activity: Copy/Paste Custom Properties

Open the default SolidWorks C-size Drawing template.

284) Click **New** ⬜ from the Menu bar toolbar.

285) Select the **Templates** tab.

286) Double-click **Drawing**.

287) Select **C (ANSI) Landscape** for the Sheet format.

288) Check **Display sheet format**. Click **OK**.

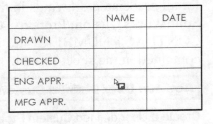

289) If needed, click **Cancel** ✖ from the Model View PropertyManager.

290) **Zoom in** on the NAME and DATE area in the Title block.

Display the Linked text.

291) Click **View**, **Annotation Link Errors** from the Menu bar menu. An Error indicates the value for the Custom Property is empty.

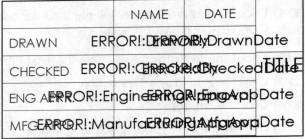

Edit the Sheet format.

292) Right-click in the **sheet boundary**.

293) Click **Edit Sheet Format**.

Copy the drawing Custom Properties.

294) Hold the **Ctrl** key down.

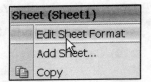

295) Select the **text** in the columns under Name and Date. Do not select the QA text row.

296) Release the **Ctrl** key.

297) Press **Ctrl + C**.

298) **Return** to the active custom C-Sheet format drawing.

299) Click a **position** between the NAME and DATE column and the CHECKED and ENG APPR. row.

Paste the information.

300) Press **Ctrl + V**.

301) Drag the **text** to center in the NAME column and DATE column.

302) Position the **mouse pointer** on the DrawnBy text. The Custom Property $PRP:"DrawnBy" is displayed.

Hide the Linked text.

303) Click **View**; uncheck **Annotation Link Errors** from the Menu bar menu.

Insert Custom Property DrawnBy.

304) Click **File**, **Properties** from the Menu bar menu.

305) Click the **Custom** tab.

306) Select **DrawnBy** for Property Name.

307) Enter your name, example **DCP,** in the Value / Text Expression box.

308) Click inside the **Evaluated Value** box.

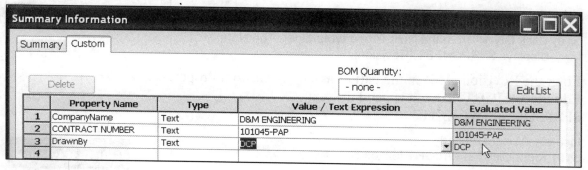

Summary Information

	Property Name	Type	Value / Text Expression	Evaluated Value
1	CompanyName	Text	D&M ENGINEERING	D&M ENGINEERING
2	CONTRACT NUMBER	Text	101045-PAP	101045-PAP
3	DrawnBy	Text	DCP	DCP
4				

BOM Quantity: - none -

309) Click **OK**.

310) Click **Save**.

🔅 In this example, you saved the DrawnBy Custom Property with the Sheet format. The DrawnBy Custom Property may also be left blank in the Sheet format and entered by the designer in the drawing.

	NAME	DATE
DRAWN	DCP	
CHECKED		

Custom Properties in Parts and Assemblies

Define Custom Properties in parts and assemblies through the ConfigurationManager, Properties option. Insert Custom Properties from a part or assembly into the drawing. Create Description, Weight, Material, and Revision Custom Properties as Linked Notes in the sheet format. Enter values for these Custom Properties in the part or assembly.

Activity: Custom Properties in Parts and Assemblies

Insert the Description Property.

311) Click **Note** A from the Annotation toolbar.

312) Click a **position** to the right of the TITLE.

313) Enter **$PRPSHEET:"Description"**.

314) Click **OK** ✔ from the Note PropertyManager.

The Note displays $PRPSHEET:{Description}. Enter the
Description value in the part or assembly Custom Properties.
The value is linked to the TITLE box Note.

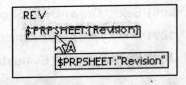

Insert the Revision Property.

315) Click **Note A** from the Annotation toolbar.

316) Click a **position** below the REV text.

317) Enter **$PRPSHEET:"Revision"**.

318) Click **OK** ✔ from the Note PropertyManager. The Note
displays $PRPSHEET:{Revision}.

Enter the Revision value in the part or assembly Custom Properties.
Edit the WEIGHT text and append the text
$PRPSHEET:"WEIGHT".

Insert the Weight Property.

319) Right-click the **WEIGHT** text on Sheet1.

320) Click **Edit Text in Window**.

321) Delete the **WEIGHT** text.

322) Enter **$PRPSHEET:"Weight"**.

323) Click **OK** from the Edit Text Window dialog box.

324) Click **OK** ✔ from the Note PropertyManager.

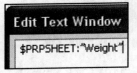

SCALE 1:1	$PRPSHEET:{Weight}	SHEET 1 OF 1

Insert the Material Property.

325) Delete the ------ to the right of the MATERIAL
box.

326) Click **Note A** from the Annotation toolbar.

327) Enter **$PRPSHEET:"Material"** to the right of
the MATERIAL box.

328) Click **OK** ✔ from the Note PropertyManager.

329) **Repeat** for TREATMENT.

330) Enter **$PRPSHEET:"Treatment"** to the right
of the TREATMENT box.

331) **Repeat** for FINISH.

332) Enter **$PRPSHEET:"Finish"** to the right of the
FINISH box.

333) Click **Save** 💾.

Description, Revision, Weight, Material, and Finish are predefined Custom Properties. Assign values in the part and assembly. The TREATMENT Custom Property is not defined. Create the TREATMENT Custom Property Name and value in the part through the ConfigurationManager, Custom Properties, or a Design Table.

General Notes

General notes are annotations that describe additional information on a drawing. Conserve drawing time. Place common general notes in the Sheet format. The Engineering department stores general notes in a Notepad file, GENERALNOTES.TXT. General notes are usually located in a corner of a drawing.

Activity: General Notes

334) Minimize the **SolidWorks window**. Do not close.

Create general notes from a text file.
335) Double-click on the Notepad file, **MY-SHEETFORMATS\GENERALNOTES.TXT**.

336) Click **Ctrl + A** to select the text in the Notepad file.

337) Click **Ctrl + C** to copy the text into the windows clipboard.

338) Return to the open document in SolidWorks. Click the **Alt + tab**.

339) Click **Note A** from the Annotation toolbar.

340) Click a **point** in the lower left hand corner of the Sheet.

341) Click **inside** the Note text box.

Paste the three lines of text.
342) Click **Ctrl + V**.

343) Click **OK** ✔ from the Note PropertyManager.

344) Click **Save**.

GERERALNOTES
Text Document
1 KB

GERERALNOTES - Notepad

File Edit Format View Help

```
1. DIMENSION PER ANSI 14.5 STANDARD.
2. REMOVE ALL BURRS.
3. ENGINEERING MUST REVIEW PROTOTYPE BEFORE MFG.
```

1. DIMENSION PER ANSI 14.5 STANDARD.
2. REMOVE ALL BURRS.
3. ENGINEERING MUST REVIEW PROTOTYPE BEFORE MFG.

Tables

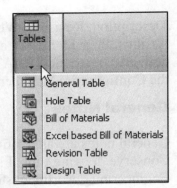

Various general SolidWorks tables are available: *General Table, Hole Table, Bill of Materials, Excel based Bill of Materials, Weldment Cut list, Revision Table and Design Table*. Each table contains an Anchor point. An Anchor point locates the Table position in the Sheet format. Access to the Anchor point is through the Table entry in the FeatureManager.

The Revision Table documents the history of a drawing. Locate the Revision Table Anchor point in the upper right corner of the sheet format. Address other tables in future projects.

Activity: Revision Table-Anchor Point

Delete the current Revision Table created in the AutoCad format.
345) **Zoom in** on the upper right corner of the Sheet Format.

346) Window-select the
Revision Table.

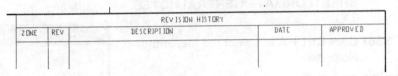

347) Right-click **Delete** to
remove all imported
table lines and text.

Return to the drawing sheet.
348) Right-click in the **Graphics window**.

349) Right-click **Edit Sheet**.

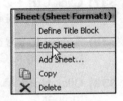

Fit the drawing to the Graphics window.
350) Press the **f** key.

Set the default layer.
351) Click **None** from the Layer text box.

Set the Revision Table anchor point.
352) **Expand** Sheet Format1 in the Drawing FeatureManager.

353) Right-click **Revision Table Anchor1**.

354) Click **Set Anchor**.

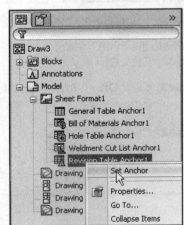

355) Click a **position** in the upper right corner of the Title block. You are in the Edit Sheet Format mode.

356) Click **Save** 🖫 .

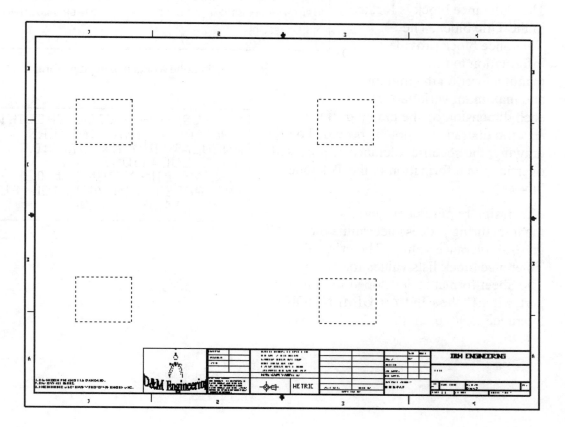

Two additional areas of the Title block require editing. Address this action as an exercise. The AutoCAD format utilized blocks in the original Proprietary Document statement.

The paragraph was imported. Letters are missing. Each line is a separate block.

PROPRIETARY DOCUMENT

THIS DOCUMENT IS T HE PROPERTY OF
<INSERT COMPANY NAME HERE> AND
 MAY NOT BE REPRODCUED WTHOUT
<INSERT COMPANY NAME HERE> WRITTEN
PERMISSION, OR USED FOR AOTHER THAN
 AUTHORIZED PURPOSES.

Imported from Autocad, in block format.

Delete the old note. Retype the note in SolidWorks. Modify the text font to Century Gothic.

```
PROPRIETARY DOCUMENT

THIS DOCUMENT IS THE PROPERTY OF D&M ENGINEERING AND
MAY NOT BE REPRODUCED WITHOUT D&M ENGINEERING
WRITTEN PERMISSION, OR USED FOR ANY OTHER UN-AUTHORIZED
PURPOSES.
```

Recreated in SolidWorks in paragraph format.

The Tolerance block is located in the Title block. The Tolerance block provides information to the manufacturer on the minimum and maximum variation for each dimension on the drawing. If a specific tolerance or note is provided on the drawing, the specific tolerance or note will override the information in the Tolerance block.

```
UNLESS OTHERWISE SPECIFIED
DIM ARE IN MILLIMETERS
ANGULAR DIMENSIONS ±0.3°
HOLE LOCATIONS ±0.1
LINEAR DIMENSIONS ± 0.2|
INTERPRET DIM AND TOL PER
ASME Y14.5M - 1994
```

The design requirements and the manufacturing process determine the general tolerance values. The original Tolerance block lists values for inch parts. The Sheet format is developed for a metric part. Modify the LINEAR DIMENSIONS tolerance to +/- 0.2mm.

 **Review**

The Sheet format contains System Properties, Custom Properties and General Notes. SW-File Name, SW-Sheet Scale, SW-Current Sheet and SW-Total Sheets were Notes in the Sheet format linked to System Properties.

CompanyName, CONTRACT NUMBER, DrawnBy, and DrawnDate were Notes in the sheet format linked to the Drawing Custom Properties. DrawnBy and DrawingDate were copied from an existing default Sheet format.

Description, Revision, Material, Weight, Finish and TREATMENT were Notes in the sheet format linked to Custom Properties in the part and assembly.

You inserted a file for a company logo and General Notes from a text file. You utilized a table anchor point to position future Revision Tables in the Title block.

Create Sheet formats for different parts types. Example: sheet metal parts, plastic parts and high precision machined parts. Create Sheet formats for each category of the parts that are manufactured with unique sets of Notes and Custom Properties.

The illustrations are based on SolidWorks SP1.0. The illustrations may vary slightly per your SolidWorks release.

Review the Engineering Drawing Practices in your company as they relate to Custom Properties and Sheet formats. Create a table. List the following:

- Identify the required Sheet formats.

- Identify the required SolidWorks Properties to control the design process.

- Identify the required Custom Properties to control the design process.

- Determine the required values for each Property.

- Determine the correct location to define the Property: part, assembly, or drawing.

Save Sheet Format and Drawing Template

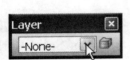

The Sheet format (*.slddrt) and Drawing template (*.drwdot) utilize two different commands to save the current drawing document (.drw). Utilize the File, Save Sheet Format option to create the Sheet format. Store Sheet formats in your MY-SHEETFORMATS folder.

Utilize the Save As command and select the Drawing template option to create the Drawing template. Combine the C-FORMAT Sheet format with the empty Drawing template. The C-FORMAT Sheet format is contained in every sheet of the drawing in the C-ANSI-MM Drawing template.

Save the Sheet format and Drawing templates in the Edit Sheet mode. Insert Views into the drawing in Edit Sheet mode. Views can't be displayed in the Edit Sheet Format mode. Set the layer option to None. The current layer is saved in the Drawing template.

Create a new drawing to test the Sheet format and the Drawing template. The Add Sheet option inserts a second sheet into the current drawing.

Activity: Save Sheet Format and Save Drawing Template

Set the Layer.
357) If needed, click **None** from the Layers toolbar.

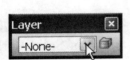

Save the Sheet format.
358) Click **File, Save Sheet Format** from the Menu bar menu.

359) Enter **C-FORMAT** in the MY-SHEETFORMATS folder.

360) Click **Save**.

Close all documents.
361) Click **Windows, Close All** from the Menu bar menu.

Combine the C-SIZE-ANSI-MM-EMPTY template with the C-FORMAT Sheet format.

362) Click **New** ☐ from the Menu bar menu.

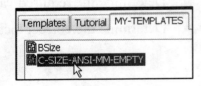

363) Double-click **C-SIZE-ANSI-MM-EMPTY** from the MY-TEMPLETES folder.

364) Right-click in the **Graphics window**.

365) Click **Properties**.

366) Click the **Standard Sheet size** box.

367) Click **Browse**.

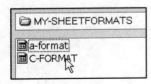

368) Double-click **C-FORMAT** from the MY-SHEETFORMATS folder.

369) Check **Display sheet format**.

370) Click **OK** from the Sheet Properties dialog box.

Save the Drawing Template.
371) Click **Save As** from the Menu bar toolbar.

372) Select **Drawing Template (*drwdot)** for Save as type.

373) Select **MY-TEMPLATES** for Save in folder.

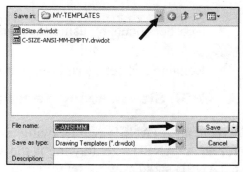

374) Enter **C-ANSI-MM** for File name.

375) Click **Save**.

Close all documents.
376) Click **Windows**, **Close All** from the Menu bar menu.

Verify the template.
377) Click **New** ⬚ from the Menu bar toolbar.

378) Click the **MY-TEMPLATES** tab.

379) Double-click the **C-ANSI-MM** template. The C-ANSI-MM Drawing template is displayed with the Sheet format.

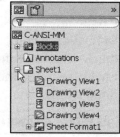

Add Sheet2
380) Right-click in **Sheet1**.

381) Click **Add Sheet**.

382) Click **No**. Sheet2 is displayed.

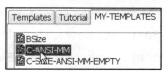

Save the drawing.
383) Click **Save As** from the Menu bar toolbar.

384) Select the **DRAWING-W-SOLIDWORKS-2010** folder.

385) Enter **Draw6** for Filename.

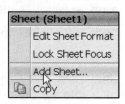

Close all files.
386) Click **Windows**, **Close All** from the Menu bar menu.

🔆 Drawing sheets are ordered as they are created. The names are displayed in the FeatureManager design tree and as Excel-style tabs at the bottom of the Graphics window. Activate a sheet by right-clicking in FeatureManager design tree and clicking Activate or click the tab name.

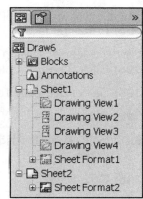

🔆 *When adding a sheet, if the system can't locate the Sheet format, add the Sheet format in File Location under System Options or Browse to the correct Sheet format location.*

Reorder sheets by using the standard drag and drop technique with the tabs.

 Rename a sheet by right-clicking the drawing tab, click Rename.

A (ANSI) Size Drawing Template

Create an A (ANSI) size Drawing template and an A (ANSI) size Sheet format. Text size for an A (ANSI) size drawing is the same as a C (ANSI) size drawing. Utilize the empty C (ANSI) size Drawing template to copy the Document Properties.

Create an A-ANSI-MM Drawing template. Add an A (ANSI) size Sheet format. SolidWorks copies the Document Properties in the C (ANSI) size Drawing template to the A-size Drawing template. The MY-SHEETFORMATS folder contains a predefined Sheet format named, A-FORMAT. The A-FORMAT contains geometry, text, and dimensions. The current layer is set to None. The Drawing template controls the units.

Activity: A (ANSI) Drawing Template

Create a new A (ANSI) Drawing template.

387) Click **New** ⬚ from the Menu bar toolbar.

388) Double-click **C-SIZE-ANSI-MM-EMPTY**.

389) Select **A (ANSI) Landscape** for Standard sheet size.

390) Uncheck **Display Sheet Format**.

391) Click **OK**.

392) Click and drag the **pre-determined views** into the Sheet boundary.

Fit the template to the Graphics window.
393) Press the **f** key.

Save the A-size Drawing Template.
394) Click **Save As** from the Menu bar toolbar.

395) Select **Drawing Templates** for Save as type.

396) **Browse** to the MY-TEMPLATES file folder.

397) Enter **A-SIZE-ANSI-MM-EMPTY** for File name.

398) Click **Save**.

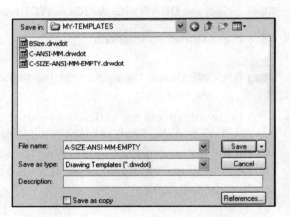

Load the Custom A-size Sheet format.
399) Right-click in the **Graphics window**.

400) Click **Properties**.

401) Click **Standard sheet size** for the Sheet format.

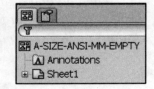

402) Click **Browse**.

403) Double-click **a-format** in the MY-SHEETFORMATS folder.

404) Check **Display sheet format**.

405) Click **OK**. Note: The current layer is set to None.

Save the new Drawing Template.
406) Click **Save As** from the Menu bar toolbar.

407) Select **Drawing Templates(*.drwdot)** for Save as type.

408) Select the **MY-TEMPLATES** file folder.

409) Enter **A-ANSI-MM**.

410) Click **Save**.

Close all documents.
411) Click **Windows**, **Close All** from the Menu bar toolbar.

Verify the template.
412) Click **New** from the Menu bar toolbar.

413) Click the **MY-TEMPLATES** tab.

414) Double-click the **A-ANSI-MM** template. The new drawing is displayed in the Graphics window.

Close all documents.
415) Click **Windows**, **Close All** from the Menu bar menu.

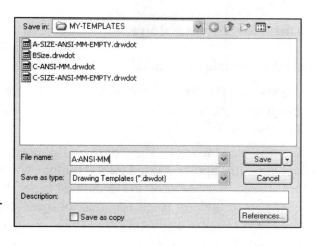

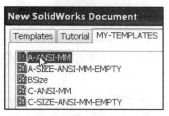

Chapter Summary

In this chapter, you created a Custom C-size and A-size Drawing template and Sheet format. The Drawing template and Sheet format contained global drawing and detailing standards.

You obtained and applied drawing properties that reflect the ASME Y14 Engineering Drawing and Related Drawing Practices. You performed the task of importing an AutoCAD drawing to create and modify a Custom Sheet format.

The Sheet format utilized System Properties and User defined Custom Properties through Linked Notes. The A-ANSI-MM and C-ANSI-MM Drawing templates and A-FORMAT and C-FORMAT Sheet formats are use in the next Chapter.

Review additional topics in the chapter exercise. Example: Create drawing templates for inch Document Properties. Import a Pro\ENGINEER Sheet format into SolidWorks.

Chapter Terminology

ANSI: American National Standards Institute.

ASME: American Society of Mechanical Engineers. ASME is the publisher of the Y14 Engineering Drawing and Related Documentation Practices. ASME Y14.5M-1994 is a revision of ANSI Y14.5-1982.

CommandManager: The CommandManager is a Context-sensitive toolbar that dynamically updates based on the toolbar you want to access. By default, it has toolbars embedded in it based on the document type. When you click a tab below the Command Manager, it updates to display that toolbar. For example, if you click the **Sketches** tab, the Sketch toolbar is displayed.

Coordinate System: SolidWorks uses a coordinate system with origins. A part document contains an original Origin. Whenever you select a plane or face and open a sketch, an Origin is created in alignment with the plane or face. An Origin can be used as an anchor for the sketch entities, and it helps orient perspective of the axes. A three-dimensional reference triad orients you to the X, Y, and Z directions in part and assembly documents.

Cursor Feedback: The system feedback symbol indicates what you are selecting or what the system is expecting you to select. As you move the mouse pointer across your model, system feedback is provided.

DimXpertManager: The DimXpertManager lists the tolerance features defined by DimXpert for a part. It also displays DimXpert tools that you use to insert dimensions and tolerances into a part. You can import these dimensions and tolerances into drawings. DimXpert is not associative.

Drawing: A 2D representation of a 3D part or assembly. The extension for a SolidWorks drawing file name is .SLDDRW. Drawing refers to the SolidWorks module used to insert, add, and modify views in an engineering drawing.

Drawing Template: A document that is the foundation of a new drawing. The drawing template contains document properties and user-defined parameters such as sheet format. The extension for the drawing template filename is .DRWDOT.

Drawing Sheet: A page in a drawing document.

FeatureManager: The FeatureManager design tree located on the left side of the SolidWorks window provides an outline view of the active part, assembly, or drawing. This makes it easy to see how the model or assembly was constructed or to examine the various sheets and views in a drawing. The FeatureManager and the Graphics window are dynamically linked. You can select features, sketches, drawing views, and construction geometry in either pane.

Heads-up View toolbar: A transparent toolbar located at the top of the Graphic window.

Hidden Lines Removed (HLR): A view mode. All edges of the model that are not visible from the current view angle are removed from the display.

Hidden Lines Visible (HLV): A view mode. All edges of the model that are not visible from the current view angle are shown gray or dashed.

Import: The ability to open files from other software applications into a SolidWorks document. The A-size sheet format was created as an AutoCAD file and imported into SolidWorks.

Layers: Simplifies a drawing by combining dimensions, annotations, geometry and components. Properties such as: display, line style, and thickness are assigned to a named layer.

Menus: Menus provide access to the commands that the SolidWorks software offers. Menus are Context-sensitive and can be customized through a dialog box.

Model: 3D solid geometry in a part or assembly document. If a part or assembly document contains multiple configurations, each configuration is a separate model.

Mouse Buttons: The left, middle, and right mouse buttons have distinct meanings in SolidWorks. Use the middle mouse button to rotate and Zoom in/out on the part or assembly document.

OLE (Object Linking and Embedding): A Windows file format. A company logo or EXCEL spreadsheet placed inside a SolidWorks document are examples of OLE files.

Origin: The model origin is displayed in blue and represents the (0,0,0) coordinate of the model. When a sketch is active, a sketch origin is displayed in red and represents the (0,0,0) coordinate of the sketch. Dimensions and relations can be added to the model origin, but not to a sketch origin.

Part: A 3D object that consist of one or more features. A part inserted into an assembly is called a component. Insert part views, feature dimensions and annotations into 2D drawing. The extension for a SolidWorks part filename is .SLDPRT.

Plane: To create a sketch, choose a plane. Planes are flat and infinite. Planes are represented on the screen with visible edges.

Properties: Variables shared between documents through linked notes.

Sheet: A page in a drawing document.

Sheet Format: A document that contains the following: page size and orientation, standard text, borders, logos, and Title block information. Customize the Sheet format to save time. The extension for the Sheet format filename is .SLDDRT.

Sheet Properties: Sheet Properties display properties of the selected sheet. Sheet Properties define the following: Name of the Sheet, Sheet Scale, Type of Projection (First angle or Third angle), Sheet Format, Sheet Size, View label, and Datum label.

System Feedback: Feedback is provided by a symbol attached to the cursor arrow indicating your selection. As the cursor floats across the model, feedback is provided in the form of symbols riding next to the cursor.

System Options: System Options are stored in the registry of the computer. System Options are not part of the document. Changes to the System Options affect all current and future documents. There are hundreds of Systems Options.

Templates: Templates are part, drawing, and assembly documents that include user-defined parameters and are the basis for new documents.

Toolbars: The toolbar menus provide shortcuts enabling you to access the most frequently used commands. Toolbars are Context-sensitive and can be customized through a dialog box.

Questions

1. Name the drawing options defined in the Drawing template.

2. Name five drawing items that are contained in the Sheet format.

3. Identify the paper dimensions required for an A (ANSI) Landscape size horizontal drawing.

4. Identify the paper dimensions required for an A4 horizontal drawing.

5. Name the Size option you select in order to define a custom paper width and height.

6. Identify the primary type of projection utilized in a drawing in the United States.

7. Describe the steps to display and modify the Properties in a drawing sheet.

8. Identify the location of the stored System Options.

9. Name five Display Modes for drawing views.

10. True or False. SolidWorks Line Font Types define all ASME Y14.2 type and style of lines.

11. Identify all Dimensioning Standards Options supported by SolidWorks.

12. Identify 10 drawing items that are contained in a Title block.

13. SolidWorks Properties are saved with the _____ format.

14. The Drawing template ends with the SolidWorks file extension _____.

15. A Sheet format ends with the SolidWorks file extension _____.

16. An AutoCAD drawing ends with the file extension _____.

17. Describe the procedure to insert a picture into the Sheet format.

18. True or False. Custom Properties are defined only in the Drawing template.

Exercises

Notes for Exercise 2.1 through Exercise 2.3:

Create Drawing templates for both inch and metric units. ASME Y14.5M has different rules for English and Metric unit decimal display.

English decimal display: If a dimension value is less than 1in, no leading zero is displayed before the decimal point. See Table 1 for details.

Metric decimal display: If a dimension value is less than 1mm, a leading zero is displayed before the decimal point. See Table 1 for details.

Specify General Tolerances in the Title block. Specific tolerances are applied to an individual dimension.

Select ANSI for the SolidWorks Dimensioning Standard. Select inch or metric for Drawing units.

Table 1 Tolerance Display for INCH and METRIC DIMENSIONS (ASME Y14.5M)		
Display	Inch	Metric
Dimensions less than 1	.5	0.5
Unilateral Tolerance	$1.417^{+.005}_{-.000}$	$36^{\ 0}_{-0.5}$
Bilateral Tolerance	$1.417^{+.010}_{-.020}$	$36^{+0.25}_{-0.50}$
Limit Tolerance	.571 .463	14.50 11.50

Exercise 2.1:

Create an A-size ANSI Drawing template using inch units. Use an A-FORMAT Sheet format. Create a C-size ANSI Drawing template using inch units. Use a C-FORMAT Sheet format.

The minimum ASME Y14.2M letter height for the Title block is displayed in Table 2. Create three new Layers named:

- DETAILS

- HIDE DIMS

- CNST DIMS (Construction Dimensions)

Create new Layers to display the CHAIN, PHANTOM, and STITCH lines.

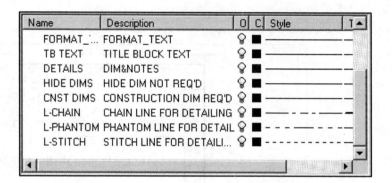

TABLE 2	
Minimum Letter Height for TITLE BLOCK	
(ASME Y14.2M)	
Title Block Text	Letter Height (inches) for A, B, C Drawing Size
Drawing Title, Drawing Size, Cage Code, Drawing Number, Revision Letter	.12
Section and view letters	.24
Drawing block letters	.10
All other characters	.10

Exercise 2.2:

Create an A4(horizontal) ISO Drawing template. Use Document Properties to set the ISO dimension standard and millimeter units.

Exercise 2.3:

Modify the SolidWorks drawing template A4-ISO. Edit Sheet Format to include a new Sheet Metal & Weldment Tolerances box on the left hand side of the Sheet format, Figure EX2.3.

Display sketched end points to create new lines for the Tolerance box. Click Options, System Options, Sketch from the Menu bar toolbar. Check Display entity points. The endpoints are displayed for the Sketched lines.

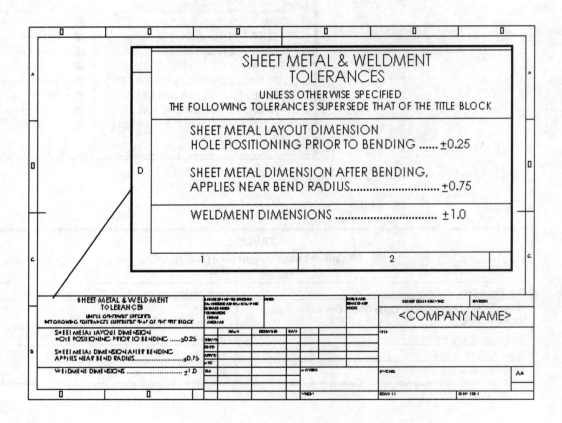

Figure EX2.3

SHEET METAL & WELDMENT TOLERANCES box

Courtesy of Ismeca, USA Inc. Vista, CA.

Exercise 2.4:

You are not required to have Pro/E to perform the following exercise. Your company uses SolidWorks and Pro/ENGINEER to manufacture sheet metal parts, Figure EX1.4. Import the empty A-size drawing format, FORMAT-A-PRO-E.DWG located in the DRAWING-W-SOLIDWORKS-2010 file folder. The document was exported from Pro/E as a DWG file. Save the Pro/E drawing format as a SolidWorks Sheet format.

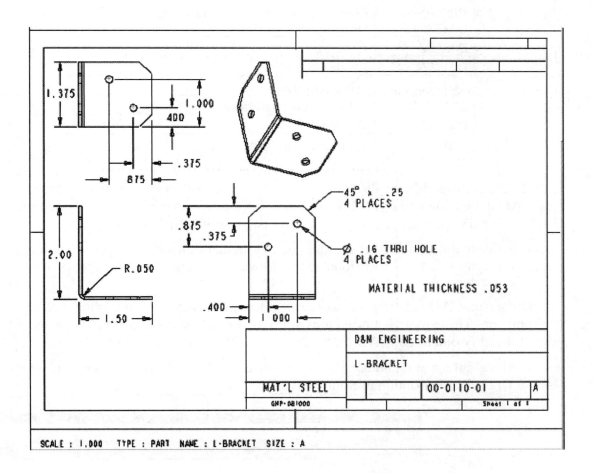

Figure EX2.4
Sheet Metal Strong Tie Reinforcing Bracket,
Courtesy of Simpson Strong Tie Corporation, CA, USA.

Exercise 2.5:

You are required to have AutoCAD to perform the following exercise. Your company uses SolidWorks and AutoCAD. Open an A-size Drawing template from AutoCAD. Review the Dimension Variables (DIMVARS) in AutoCAD. Record the DIMSTATUS for the following variables:

AutoCAD:	Function:
DIMTXSTY	Dimensioning Text Style
DIMASZ	Arrow size
DIMCEN	Center Mark size
DIMDEC	Decimal Places
DIMTDEC	Tolerance Decimal Places
DIMTXT	Text Height
DIMDLI	Space between dimension lines for Baseline dimensioning

Identify the corresponding values in SolidWorks Document Properties to contain the AutoCAD dimension variables. Utilize Help, Moving from AutoCAD to SolidWorks. Use CommandMap, Draw Toolbar, and Dimension Toolbar in this exercise.

Define Favorite dimension style settings for a particular dimension. Apply Favorite dimension styles to other dimensions on the drawing, part and assembly documents.

Early AutoCAD drawing formats contain fonts not supported in a Windows environment. These fonts imported into SolidWorks will be misaligned in the Sheet Format. Modify older AutoCAD formats to a True Type Font in SolidWorks.

For additional information on the transition between 2D AutoCAD and 3D SolidWorks, Use the Draw Toolbar option in SolidWorks help.

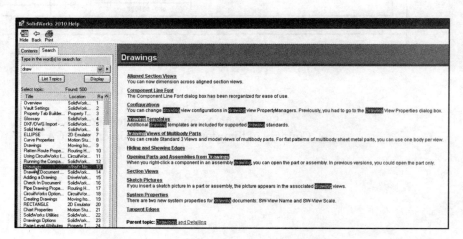

Chapter 3

Drawings and Various Drawing Views

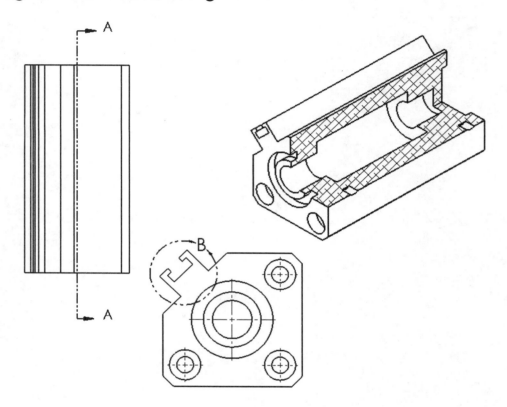

Below are the desired outcomes and usage competencies based on the completion of this Chapter.

Desired Outcomes:	Usage Competencies:
Three Drawings: • TUBE • ROD • COVERPLATE	• Ability to create the following drawing views: Standard, Isometric, Auxiliary, Section, Broken Section, Detail, Half Section (Cut-away), Crop, Projected Back, and more.
	• Ability to create multi-sheet drawings from various part configurations.

Notes:

Chapter 3 - Drawings and Various Drawing Views

Chapter Objective

Create three drawings: TUBE, ROD and COVERPLATE. Insert the following drawing views: *Front Top, Right, Isometric, Auxiliary, Detail, Section, Crop, Broken Section, Half Section, Revolved Section, Offset Section, Removed, Projected, Aligned Section and more.* Insert, modify, suppress, un-suppress and delete drawing views.

Work between multiple parts, configurations, and sheets to create the required drawing views. Insert annotations and dimensions. Apply a Design Table.

On the completion of this chapter, you will be able to:

- Create a single Sheet drawing.

- Add multiple sheets to a drawing.

- Work between part configurations in a Design Table.

- Insert Predefined views and Named views.

- Insert an Auxiliary, Detail, and Section views.

- Insert Broken Section, Half Section, Offset Section and Aligned Section views.

- Add a configuration to a part.

- Insert an Area Hatch.

- Comprehend Orthographic projection: First angle and Third angle.

- Insert dimensions and Annotations.

- Utilize the following SolidWorks tools and commands: *Model View, Projected View, Auxiliary View, Section View, Aligned Section View, Standard 3 View, Broken-out Section View, Horizontal Break View, Vertical Break View, Crop View and Alternate Position View.*

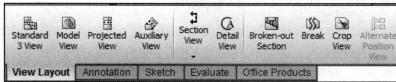

Chapter Overview

A customer approaches the Engineering
department to address the current Air
Cylinder for a new product application. In
the new application, there is an interference
concern with the positions of the current Air
Cylinder switches.

The engineering team proposes a new design
that would re-positions the switches in a 45°
grooved track.

The design incorporates three individual
parts: *TUBE*, *ROD* and *COVERPLATE*. The
parts are mated to create the CYLINDER in
the Air Cylinder assembly.

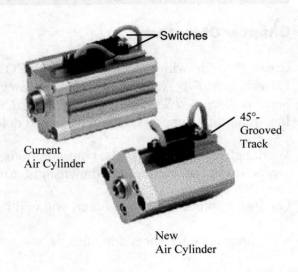

🔅 Mates create Geometric relationships
between assembly components. As you
add mates, you define the allowable
directions of linear or rotational motion of
the components. You can move a
component within its degrees of freedom,
visualizing the assembly's behavior.

The Marketing manager for the Air
Cylinder product line reviews the new
proposed assembly in SolidWorks.

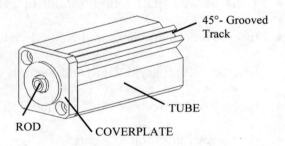

Courtesy of SMC Corporation of America
The feature dimensions for components utilized in this
assembly have been modified for educational purposes.

The design team decides to incorporate the
new design in its standard product line.
The original designer that developed the
current Air Cylinder was transferred to a
different company division.

You are part of the CYLINDER project development team. All design drawings must
meet the company's drawing standards.

What is the next step? Create drawings for various internal departments, namely:
production, purchasing, engineering, inspection and manufacturing.

First, review and discuss the features used to create the three parts. The three parts are:

*   ROD

*   TUBE

*   COVERPLATE

Second, create three drawings:

*   ROD

*   TUBE

*   COVERPLATE

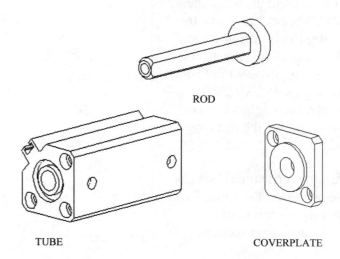

ROD

TUBE   COVERPLATE

A SolidWorks drawing document consists of a single sheet or multiple sheets. The ROD drawing consists of three sheets.

Use three separate drawing sheets to display the required information for the ROD drawing.

The first drawing sheet utilizes the Short Rod configuration. ROD-Sheet1 contains three Standard views, (Principle views) and an Isometric view.

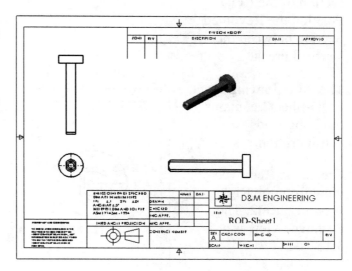

The three Standard views are:

*   Top view

*   Front view

*   Right view

Utilize the Predefined views in the Drawing template to create the first drawing sheet.

The second drawing sheet, ROD-Sheet2 contains the Long Rod configuration. Use a drawing sheet scale of 2:1 to display the Front detail view. Using a 2:1 scale, the Right view is too long for the drawing sheet.

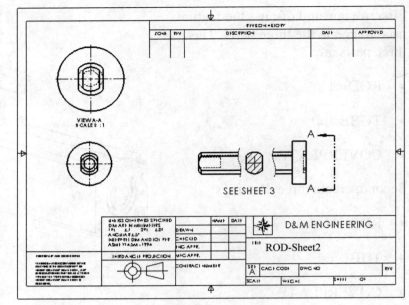

Use a Vertical Break view to represent the Long Rod configuration with a constant cross section.

Add a Revolved Section view to represent the cross section of the ROD. Position the Revolved Section between the Vertical break.

The third drawing sheet, ROD-Sheet3 contains the Long Rod configuration.

Create the Removed view from the Right view in Sheet2. The Removed view is at a 3:1 scale.

Combine two Detail views to construct the Isometric view.

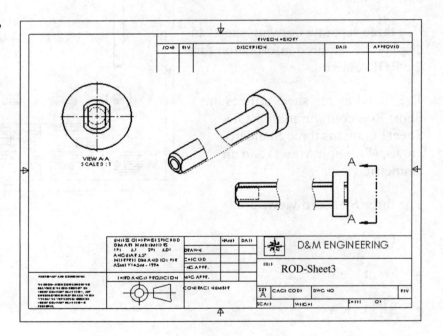

When adding a sheet, if the system can't locate the Sheet format, add the Sheet format in File Location under System Options or Browse to the correct Sheet format location.

The TUBE drawing consists of one sheet with eight views. The TUBE drawing contains:

Three Standard views and:

1.) Projected Back view

2.) Section view

3.) Detail view

4.) Auxiliary view

5.) Half Section Isometric view

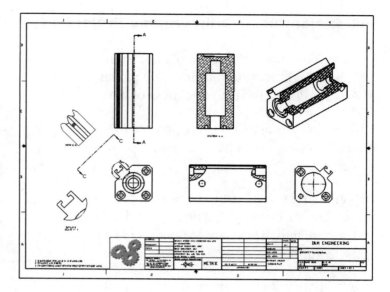

The COVERPLATE drawing consists of two drawing sheets. There are two part configurations:

- Without Nose Holes

- With Nose Holes

The first drawing sheet utilizes the Without Nose Holes configuration.

COVERPLATE-Sheet1 contains the following views: Front view, Right view, and an Offset Section view.

The second drawing sheet utilizes the With Nose Holes configuration.

COVERPLATE-Sheet2 contains the Front view and the Aligned Section view.

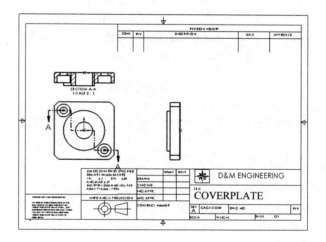

☀ Use the DrawCompare tool to highlight the differences between two selected drawings. Click **Tools**, **Compare**, **DrawCompare**.

First, let's review the fundamentals of Orthographic projection before you create any drawings.

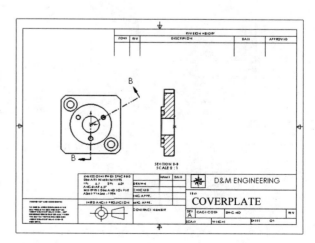

Fundamentals of Orthographic Projection

The three default ⊥ reference planes: Front, Top, and Right represent infinite 2D planes in 3D space. Planes have no thickness or mass.

Orthographic projection is the process of projecting views onto parallel planes with ⊥ projectors.

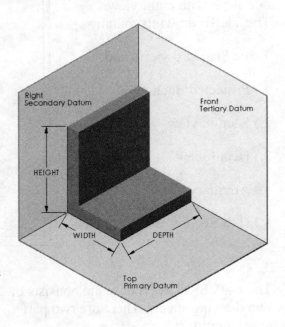

In Geometric tolerancing, the default reference planes are the Primary, Secondary, and Tertiary ⊥ datum planes. These are the planes used in manufacturing.

The Primary datum plane contacts the part at a minimum of three points. The Secondary datum plane contacts the part at a minimum of two points. The Tertiary datum plane contacts the part at a minimum of one point.

The part view orientation depends on the Sketch plane of the Base feature. Compare the Front Plane, Top Plane and Right Plane. Each Extruded Base (Boss-Extrude1) feature utilizes an L-shaped 2D profile.

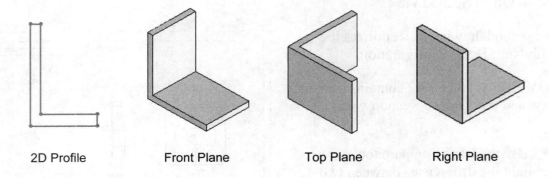

2D Profile   Front Plane   Top Plane   Right Plane

The six principle views of Orthographic projection listed in the ASME Y14.3M standard are: *Top, Front, Right side, Bottom, Rear, & Left side.* SolidWorks Standard view names correspond to these Orthographic projection view names.

ASME Y14.3M Principle View Name:	SolidWorks Standard View:
Front	Front
Top	Top
Right side	Right
Bottom	Bottom
Rear	Back
Left side	Left

In the Third Angle Orthographic projection example below, the standard drawing views are: Front, Top, Right, and Isometric.

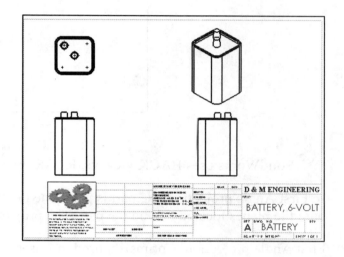

There are two Orthographic projection drawing systems.

- First Angle projection

- Third Angle projection

The systems are derived from positioning a 3D object in the first or third quadrant.

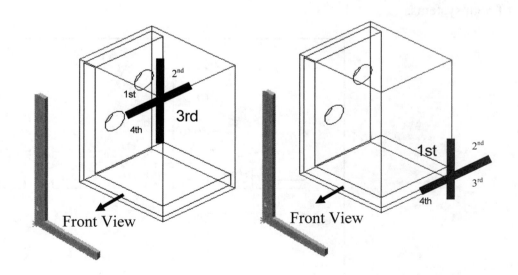

In Third Angle projection, the part is positioned in the third quadrant. The 2D projection planes are located between the viewer and the part.

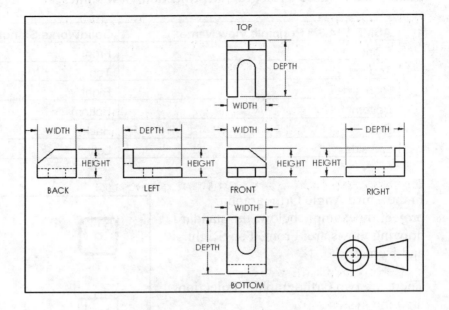

☀ SolidWorks uses BACK view vs. REAR view.

In First Angle projection, the part is positioned in the first quadrant. Views are projected onto the planes located behind the part. The projected views are placed on a drawing.

First Angle projection is primarily used in Europe and Asia. Third angle projection is primarily used in the U.S. & Canada and is based on the ASME Y14.3M Multi and Sectional View Drawings standard. Designers should have knowledge and understanding of both systems.

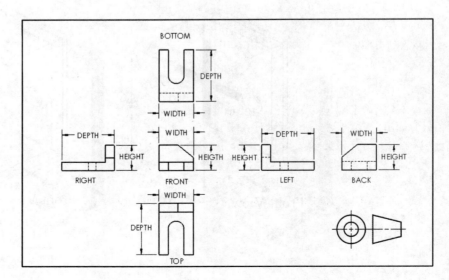

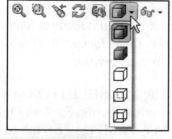

SolidWorks provides the user with numerous view options from the Standard Views, View, and the Heads-up View toolbar. The Heads-up View toolbar provides the following tools: **Zoom to Fit** , **Zoom to Area** , **Previous View** , **Rotate View** , **3D Drawing View** , Display Style drop-down menu , and **Hide/Show Items** .

3D Drawing View provides the ability to manipulate the model view in 3D to help select a point, edge or face.

Review the ROD Part and Configurations

Configurations are variations of a part. The ROD part consists of two configurations:

- Short Rod configuration

- Long Rod configuration

The first ROD drawing sheet contains the Short Rod configuration. The second and third ROD drawing sheets contain the Long Rod configuration.

A drawing utilizes views, dimensioning, tolerances, notes, and other related design information from the part. When you modify a feature dimension in a part, the drawing automatically updates. The part and the drawing share the same file structure. Do not delete or move the part document.

If you did not create the A-ANSI-MM and C-ANSI MM Drawing templates in Chapter 2, utilize the Drawing templates and Sheet formats located in the folder DRAWING-W-SOLIDWORKS-2010\CHAPTER2-TEMPLATES-SHEETFORMATS on the CD. Add the folder to the File Locations section under System Options if needed.

DRAWING-W-SOLIDWORKS-2010
- CHAPTER2-TEMPLATES-SHEETFORMATS
- Chapter 3 Homework
- Chapter 5
- CSWA Chapter 7 models
- Exercises
- MY-SHEETFORMATS
- MY-TEMPLATES

🔆 *When adding a Sheet to a drawing, if the system can't locate the Sheet format, add the Sheet format in File Location under System Options or Browse to the correct Sheet format location.*

The MY-SHEETFORMATS folder contains the Sheet formats. Note: In some network environments, System Options are valid for the current session of SolidWorks. Add the MY-TEMPLATES tab to the New SolidWorks Document dialog box. If the MY-TEMPLATES tab is not displayed, utilize the System Options, File Locations, Drawing Templates option described in Chapter 2.

Perform the following recommended tasks before starting the ROD drawing:

1. Open the part.

2. View the dimensions in each feature.

3. Move the feature dimensions off the profile.

4. View the configurations of the part.

There are two dimension types displayed in a drawing:
- Projected - 2D dimensions.

- True - Accurate model dimensions.

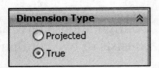

🔆 SolidWorks specifies Projected type dimensions for Standard and Custom Orthogonal views and True type dimensions for Isometric, Dimetric, and Trimetric views.

🔆 Locate the parts required for this chapter in the DRAWING-W-SOLIDWORKS-2010 file folder on the CD in the book.

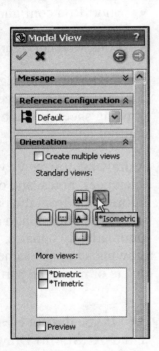

🔆 Feature dimensions in the part by default contain the Mark dimension to be imported into a drawing option. The Insert Model Items option places the Marked feature dimensions in the drawing.

💡 Clarify model items in the part. Position the feature dimensions and annotations off the part before you insert the model items into the drawing.

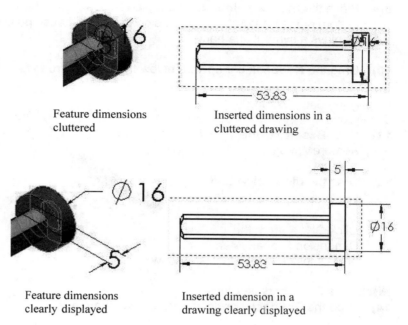

Feature dimensions cluttered

Inserted dimensions in a cluttered drawing

💡 Gaps need to be address between the model and the extension lines.

💡 Clutter feature dimensions create clutter drawing views.

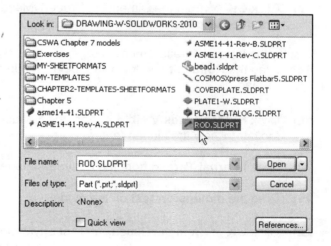

Feature dimensions clearly displayed

Inserted dimension in a drawing clearly displayed

Activity: Review the ROD Part and Configurations

Start a SolidWorks session.

1) Click **Start**, **All Programs** from the Windows Main menu.

2) Click the **SolidWorks 2010** folder.

3) Click the **SolidWorks 2010** application.

Open the ROD part.

4) Click **Open** 📂 from the Menu bar toolbar.

5) Select the **DRAWING-W-SOLIDWORKS-2010** folder.

💡 Copy all files and folders from the CD in the book to your hard drive. Work from your hard drive.

6) Select **Part** for Files of type.

7) Double-click **ROD**. The Rod is displayed in the Graphics window.

8) Display the **Default** configuration.

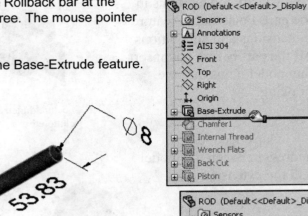

Review the ROD part features.

9) Place the **mouse pointer** over the blue Rollback bar at the bottom of the FeatureManager design tree. The mouse pointer displays a symbol of a hand.

10) Drag the **Rollback** bar upward below the Base-Extrude feature.

Display the Base-Extrude dimensions.

11) Click **Base-Extrude** from the FeatureManager.

12) Drag the **dimension text** off the model.

13) Click **OK** ✔ from the Dimension PropertyManager or click inside the Graphics window.

Display the Chamfer dimensions.
14) Drag the **Rollback** bar downward below Chamfer1.

15) Click **Chamfer1** from the FeatureManager.

16) Drag the **dimension text** off the model.

17) Click **OK** ✔ from the Dimension PropertyManager or click in the Graphics window.

Display the Internal Thread dimensions.
18) Drag the **Rollback** bar downward below the Internal Thread.

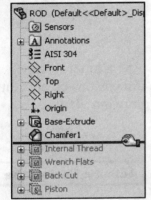

19) Click **Hidden Lines Visible** ⬚ from the Heads-up View toolbar to view the hidden feature.

20) Click **Internal Thread** from the FeatureManager.

21) Drag the **dimension text** off the model.

22) Click **OK** ✔ from the Dimension PropertyManager.

Display the Back Cut dimensions.
23) Drag the **Rollback** bar downward below Back Cut.

24) Click **Back Cut** from the FeatureManager.

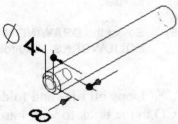

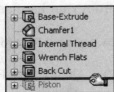

25) Click **Wireframe** from the Heads-up View toolbar.

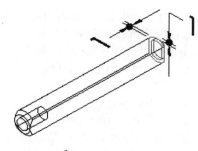

26) Drag the **dimension text** off the model.

27) Click **OK** ✔ from the Dimension PropertyManager.

Display the Piston dimensions.
28) Drag the **Rollback** bar downward below Piston.

29) Click **Piston** from the FeatureManager.

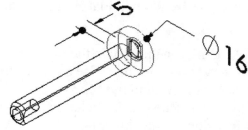

30) Drag the **dimension text** off the model.

31) Click **OK** ✔ from the Dimension PropertyManager.

Display the ROD part configurations.
32) Click the **ConfigurationManager** tab at the top of the FeatureManager.

33) Double-click the **Long Rod** configuration. View the Long Rod configuration.

Fit the ROD to the Graphics window.
34) Press the **f** key.

35) Double-click the **Short Rod** configuration. View the Short Rod configuration.

☀ Press the z key to Zoom out or the middle mouse button. Press the f key to fit the model to the Graphics window.

Return to the ROD FeatureManager.
36) Click the **FeatureManager** tab. The Short Rod is the current configuration.

Fit the ROD to the Graphics window.
37) Press the **f** key.

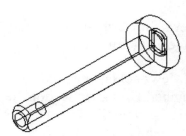

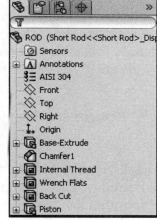

The Internal Thread utilizes an Extruded Cut feature sketched on the Front Plane. Internal Threads require specific notes. Use a Hole Callout in the Drawing to annotate the Internal Thread in Chapter 4.

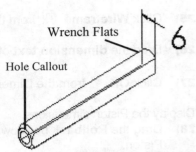

Wrench Flats

Hole Callout

Locate the profile for the Wrench Flats on the Back Plane. The design engineer uses a Symmetric relation with the Right Plane. Add a centerline in the drawing to represent the Wrench Flat symmetry in Chapter 4.

Utilize symmetry in the part whenever possible. This conserves rebuild time. Use Symmetric relations in the sketch. Use Mirror All and the Mirror Feature in the part. Symmetric dimension schemes and relations defined in the part require added dimensions in the drawing.

Create fully defined sketches. A minus sign (-) displayed in the FeatureManager indicates an under defined Sketch. Sketch1 through Sketch5 are fully defined. Fully defined sketches provide marked dimensions, address faster rebuild times, and create fewer configuration problems.

ROD Drawing: Sheet1-Short Rod Configuration

The ROD drawing contains three drawing sheets. Sheet1 contains the Short Rod configuration, three Standard views, (Principle views) and an Isometric view. Insert Standard views and the Isometric view as Predefined views created in the A-ANSI-MM drawing template. The FeatureManager displays the Drawing view names. Predefined views, Named Model views, and Projected views are given a sequential numbered drawing view name.

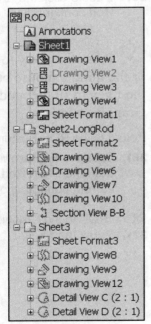

Rename drawing views for clarity. Click inside the view entry in the FeatureManager. Enter the new name.

Detail views and Section views are label with their view name followed by a letter or number. Example: Section view A-A. Reposition the drawing views. Drag the drawing view by its green view boundary or a drawing entity inside the view.

Provide approximately 1in. - 2in., (25mm - 50mm) between each view for dimension placement. The Right and Top views align to the Front view position. The Isometric view is free to move and contains no alignment. The Sheet, View, Edge, and Component contain specific properties. Select the right mouse button on an entity to review the Properties.

To nudge a view, select the view boundary. Press an arrow key to move a view by a set increment. Utilize the System Option, Drawings, Keyboard movement increment, to set the nudge value.

Activity: ROD Drawing-Sheet1

Note: If you did not create the A-ANSI-MM and C-ANSI MM drawing templates in Chapter 2, utilize the Drawing templates and Sheet formats located in the folder DRAWING-W-SOLIDWORKS-2010\CHAPTER2-TEMPLATES-SHEETFORMATS on the CD. If needed, add the folder to the File Locations section under System Options.

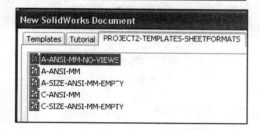

Select the A-ANSI-MM Drawing Template.

38) Click **New** ☐ from the Menu bar toolbar.

39) Click the **MY-TEMPLATES** tab.

40) Double-click **A-ANSI-MM**.

Save the empty drawing.
41) Click **Save As** from the Consolidated Menu bar toolbar.

42) Select **DRAWING-W-SOLIDWORKS-2010** for Save in.

43) Enter **ROD** for File name.

44) Enter **ROD DRAWING** for Description.

45) Click **Save**. The ROD drawing FeatureManager is displayed.

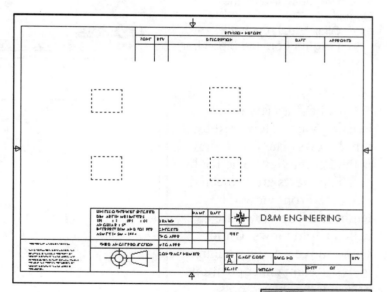

Display the Layer toolbar.
46) Click **View**, **Toolbars**, **Layer** from the Menu bar menu.

47) Select **None** for Layer Properties.

Insert the Predefined Views.
48) Click **Window**, **Tile Horizontal**
 Tile Horizontally from the Menu bar menu. The ROD-Sheet1 drawing and ROD part are displayed.

49) Click and drag the **ROD** ROD (Short Rod) icon from the Part FeatureManager into the drawing Graphics window.

50) **Maximize** ☐ the ROD drawing.

If needed, de-activated the Origins.
51) Click **View**; uncheck **Origins** from the Menu bar menu.

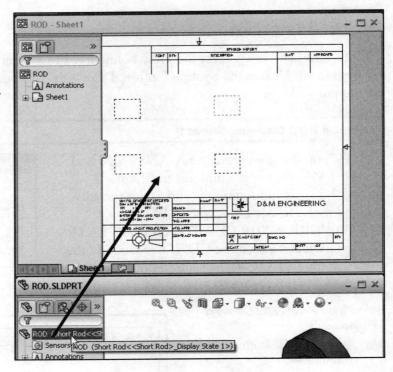

A Parent view is an existing view referenced by other views. The Front view is the Parent view. The Right and Top views are Projected from the Front view. The Right and Top views are called Child views. Child views move relative to Parent views. Retain exact positions between the views, press Shift while dragging the views.

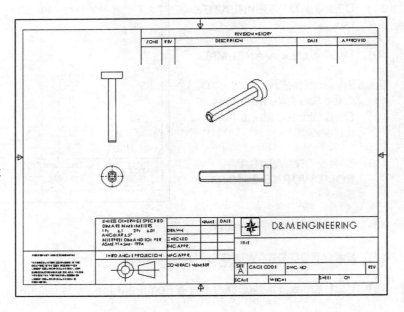

Move the drawing views.

52) Click inside the view boundary of **Drawing View4**, (Isometric view). The mouse pointer displays the Drawing View  icon. The view boundary is displayed.

53) Position the **mouse pointer** on the edge of the view until the Drawing Move View icon is displayed.

54) Click and drag the **Isometric** view in an upward direction.

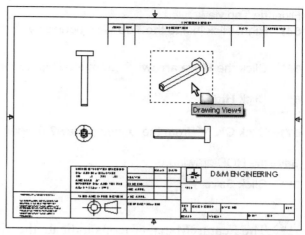

Display the Sheet properties.

55) Position the **mouse pointer** in the middle of the Sheet. The mouse pointer displays the Sheet icon.

56) Right-click in the **sheet area**, (large white space).

57) Click **Properties**. Review the Properties of the Sheet.

58) Click **OK** from the Sheet Properties dialog box.

Display the view properties.

59) Position the **mouse pointer** inside the Top view area. The mouse pointer displays the Drawing View icon.

60) Click inside the **view area**. The view boundary turns blue.

Display the edge and component properties.

61) Locate the mouse pointer on the **vertical line** in the Top view as illustrated. The vertical line turns blue. The mouse pointer displays an Edge icon, the Edge properties and the Component properties.

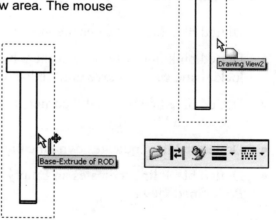

Display the Isometric view shaded.

62) Click inside the **Isometric view** boundary.

63) Click **Shaded With Edges** from the Drawing View4 PropertyManager.

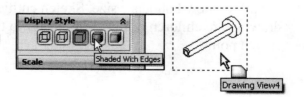

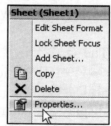

Hide the Top view.
64) Right-click inside the **Top** view boundary.

65) Click the **More arrow** ⟱ from the Pop-up menu.

66) Click **Hide**.

67) Click **OK** ✔ from the Drawing View2 PropertyManager.

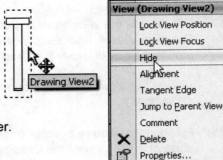

Save the ROD drawing.
68) Click **Save** 🖫 .

💡 The FeatureManager icons indicate the visible and hidden views. Modify the view state quickly with the FeatureManager.

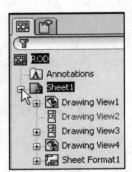

The 🖽 Drawing View2 icon displays hidden views. The 🖻 Drawing View1 icon displays visible Model views. The 🖽 Drawing View3 icon displays visible Projected views. Utilize Show to display a hidden view. Right-click the view name in the FeatureManager. Select the Show option.

View Boundary Properties and Lock View Options

The view boundary displays different colors to indicate various states as follows:

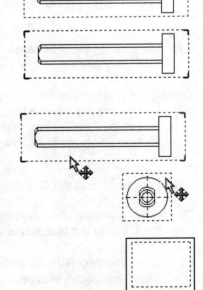

- Dotted blue line indicates the view is selected.

- Dotted pink line with solid corners indicates the view is locked and cannot move until unlocked.

- Dotted blue line with solid corners indicates the view is selected and locked.

- Dotted red line indicates dynamic highlighting.

- Dotted black line indicates an Empty view or Predefined view.

💡 Model geometry and sketch geometry determine the size of the view boundary. Annotations and dimensions do not affect view boundary size. Sketch entities in the drawing are children of the view closest to the initial sketch point.

As a drawing becomes populated with views, utilize the Lock options to control annotation and sketch geometry into the view or the sheet. The Lock View Position, Lock View Focus, and the Lock Sheet Focus options provide the following:

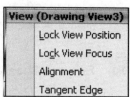

- **Lock View Position**: Secures the view at its current position in the sheet. Right-click in the drawing view to Lock View Position. To unlock a view position, right-click and select Unlock View Position.
- **Lock View Focus**: Adds sketch entities and annotations to the selected locked view. Double-click the view to activate Lock View Focus. To unlock a view, right-click and select Unlock View Focus or double click outside the view boundary.

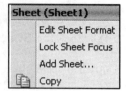

- **Lock Sheet Focus**: Adds sketch entities and annotations to the selected sheet. Double-click the sheet to activate Lock Sheet Focus. To unlock a sheet, right-click and select Unlock Sheet Focus or double click inside the sheet boundary.

ROD Drawing: Sheet2 - Long Rod Configuration

The second sheet of the ROD drawing, ROD-Sheet2 utilizes the Long Rod configuration.

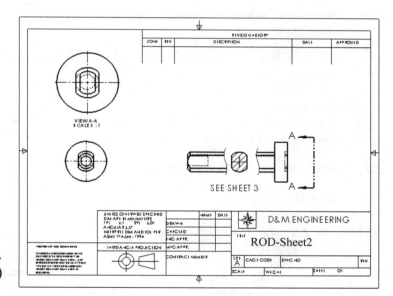

Add ROD-Sheet2. Copy the Front view from Sheet1 to Sheet2. Select the Long Rod configuration.

Insert a Projected Right view. Use a Sheet scale of 2:1 to display the Front details.

The Right view is too long for the sheet using the scale of 2:1. Insert a Broken (or interrupted) view with a vertical break in the Right view. The Broken view represents the Long Rod with a constant cross section. Dimensions associated with the Broken view reflect the actual model values.

The Add Sheet tab is located at the bottom of the Graphics window.

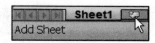

Activity: ROD Drawing-Sheet2 Projected View and Break View

Add Sheet2 to the ROD drawing.

69) Click the **Add Sheet** tab located at the bottom of the Graphics window. Sheet2 is displayed. Note: At this time, there is a bug with SP1.0. If needed, Browse and apply the correct Sheet format from the MY-SHEETFORMATS folder.

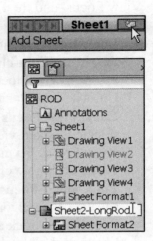

70) Rename **Sheet2** to **Sheet2-LongRod**.

The Custom a-format is the default Sheet format. Sheet2-LongRod is displayed.

Copy the Front view from Sheet1 to Sheet2.

71) Click the **Sheet1** tab. Click inside **Drawing View1**, (Front) view.

Copy the view.

72) Click **Edit**, **Copy** from the Menu bar menu

73) Click the **Sheet2-LongRod** tab.

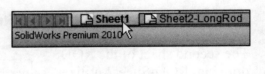

74) Click a view **position** in the lower left corner.

Paste the view.

75) Click **Edit**, **Paste** from the Menu bar menu. Drawing View5 is displayed.

Modify the view Scale.

76) Click inside the **Drawing View5** view boundary. The Drawing View5 PropertyManager is displayed.

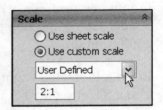

77) Check the **Use custom scale** box.

78) Select **User Defined**.

79) Enter **2:1**. Click **OK** ✔ from the Drawing View5 PropertyManager.

Modify the ROD configuration.

80) Right-click **Properties** in the Drawing View5 view boundary.

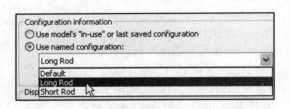

81) Select **Long Rod** from the Use Named Configuration drop-down menu. Click **OK**.

Insert a Projected view.

82) Click **Projected View** ⊟ from the View Layout toolbar.

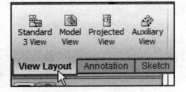

83) Click a **position** to the right of the Front view. DrawingView6 is displayed.

Modify the Scale to fit the drawing.

84) Click inside the **Drawing View6** boundary.

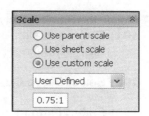

85) Check the **Use custom scale** box.

86) Select **User Defined**.

87) Enter **.75:1**.

88) Click **OK** ✔ from Drawing View6 PropertyManager.

89) Drag **Drawing View6** in Sheet2.

Insert a Vertical Zig Zag Break in the Right view.

90) Click inside the **Drawing View6** boundary.

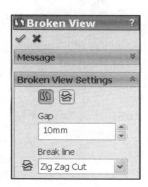

91) Click **Break** ⧖ from the View Layout toolbar. The Broken View PropertyManager is displayed. Vertical is the default setting. Gap equals 10mms.

92) Click a **position** as illustrated to create the left vertical break line towards the Internal Thread.

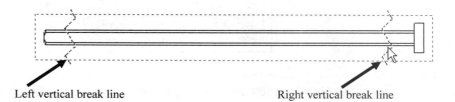

Left vertical break line   Right vertical break line

93) Click a **position** as illustrated to create the right vertical break line towards the Piston.

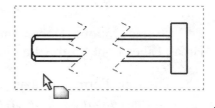

94) Click **OK** ✔ from the Broken View PropertyManager.

95) Right-click inside the **Drawing View6** boundary.

96) Click **Un-Break View**. View the results.

97) Right-click inside the **Drawing View6** boundary.

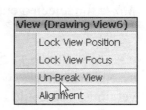

98) Click **Break View**.

99) Click inside the **Drawing View6** boundary.

100) Check the **Use parent scale** box.

Modify the Break line style.

101) Click on the left **Break line**. The Broken View PropertyManager is displayed.

102) Select **Curve Cut** to display the curved break line.

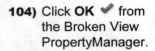

103) Enter **20mm** for Gap.

104) Click **OK** from the Broken View PropertyManager.

Save the ROD drawing.
105) **Rebuild** the drawing.

106) Click **Save**.

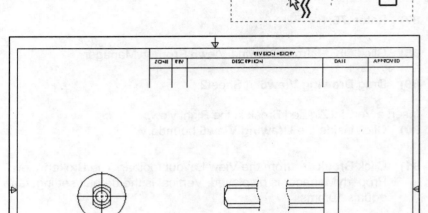

Modify the Break Lines display. Right-click on the Break line. Select: *Straight Cut, Curve Cut, Zig Zag Cut,* or *Small Zig Zag Cut.*

Utilize Options, Document Properties, Line Font to modify the Break Lines Font for the drawing document.

The Line Format toolbar controls: *Layer Properties, Line Color, Line Thickness, Line Style, Hide / Show Edges, Color Display Mode* for selected entities.

In SolidWorks 2010, when you right-click a component in an assembly drawing, you can open the part or assembly. In previous versions, you could only open the part.

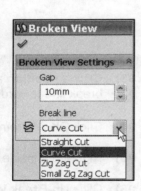

ROD Drawing: Sheet3 - Long Rod Configuration

Add ROD-Sheet3. Sheet3
utilizes a Removed view.
Utilize a Removed view
when additional space is
required to display the view.

There is no Removed view
tool. Use an Auxiliary view
off the right edge of the
Broken view to create a
Removed view.

Copy the Removed view
from ROD-Sheet2 to ROD-
Sheet3.

Utilize the Auxiliary view
A-A arrows to indicate that
the view is not projected
from the Broken view.

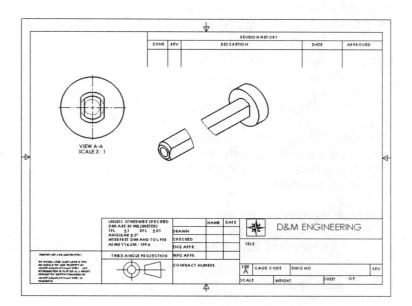

Use upper case letters, Example: View A-A to
associate the viewing plane to the Removed view.
Indicate the sheet name below the view name when a
Removed view does not fit on the same sheet.

Combine Drawings tools and work outside the
sheet boundary to produce the Removed view,
Revolved Section view, and Broken Isometric view.

Click the View Palette icon in the Task Pane.
Click the drop-down arrow from the View Palette
menu to view an active saved model or click the
Browse button to locate a model. Click and drag the
desired view/views into the active drawing Sheet.

*When adding a Sheet to a drawing, if the system
can't locate the Sheet format, add the Sheet format in
File Location under System Options or Browse to the
correct Sheet format location.*

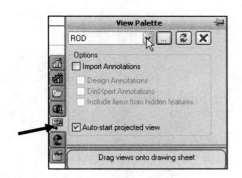

Activity: ROD Drawing - Sheet3 Removed View

Insert a Removed view.
107) Click inside the **Right view** boundary.

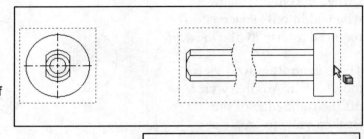

108) Click **Auxiliary view** from the View Layout toolbar. The Auxiliary View PropertyManager is displayed.

109) Click the **right vertical edge** of the Right view as illustrated. The Auxiliary view and arrows are displayed.

110) Hold the **Ctrl** key down.

111) Click a **position** above the Front view.

112) Release the **Ctrl** key.

Modify the Scale of the Top view.
113) Click **Use custom scale**.

114) Select **User Defined**.

115) Enter **3:1**. Click **OK** from the Drawing View 7 PropertyManager.

116) Drag the **VIEW A-A, SCALE 3:1** text below the Top view.

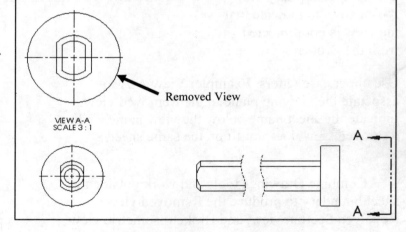

Removed View

VIEW A-A
SCALE 3 : 1

117) Rebuild the drawing.

The Ctrl key prevents the Removed view from creating an aligned relationship to the Vertical Break. The Broken Right view is the parent view of the Removed view. Select both views to copy the Removed view to Sheet3.

Add Sheet3 to the ROD drawing.
118) Click the **Add Sheet** tab. The third Sheet is displayed. Note: At this time, there is a bug with SP1.0. If needed, Browse and apply the correct Sheet format from the MY-SHEETFORMATS folder.

119) Save the drawing.

Copy the Removed view from Sheet2 to Sheet3.

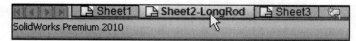

120) Click the **Sheet2-LongRod** tab.

121) Hold the **Ctrl** key down.

122) Click the **Broken Right** view.

123) Click the **Removed View A-A**. The Multiple Views PropertyManager is displayed.

124) Release the **Ctrl** key. Press **Ctrl + C**. Click **Yes**.

Paste the views.
125) Click the **Sheet3** tab. Click a **position** on the left top side of Sheet3.

126) Press **Ctrl + V**. The two views are pasted on Sheet3.

127) Move the views in Sheet3 as illustrated. Zoom out. Press the **z** key approximately 2 times.

128) Drag the **Break Right view** off Sheet3 to the right of the Title block as illustrated.

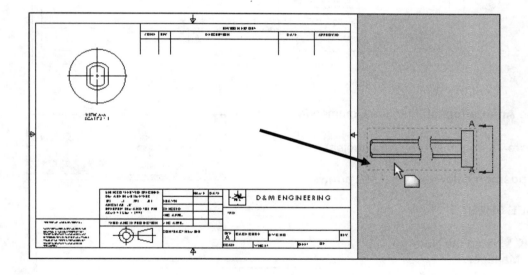

Modify Annotations.
129) Click the **VIEW A-A** text.

130) Right-click **Edit Text in Window**.

131) Enter **SEE SHEET2** on the third line.

132) Click **OK**.

133) Click **inside** Sheet3 to deselect.

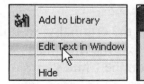
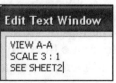

Move the Removed view on Sheet2.
134) Click the **Sheet2-LongRod** tab.

135) Click and drag the **Removed view** boundary to the left of Sheet2 as illustrated.

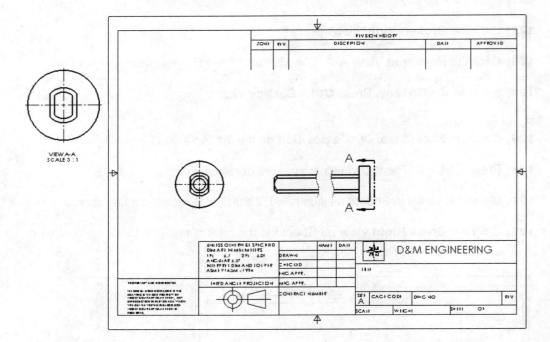

Add a Note.
136) Click the **Annotation** tab from the CommandManager.

137) Click **Note** A from the Annotation toolbar.

138) Click a **position** below the View A-A arrows.

139) Enter **SEE SHEET 3**.

140) Click **OK** ✔ from the Note
PropertyManager.

141) Drag the **View A-A** arrows to the right of
the view.

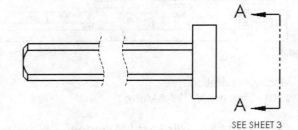

SEE SHEET 3

The Parent view is the original view utilized
to create the Child views: *Auxiliary*, *Section*
and *Detail*. Position the Child views on the
same drawing sheet as the Parent view. If
no space exists on the current sheet, move the Child view to a new Sheet. Label the Child
view with the Parent view Sheet number. Utilize the Note tool from the Annotate toolbar,
"See Sheet X" where X is the number of the Parent sheet.

Sheets larger than B size contain Zone letters and numbers inside their margins. Place the Zone location below the "SEE SHEET #" text for drawing sizes larger than B. Letters and numbers in the sheet boundary create a grid indicating the exact zone location.

Example:

```
┌─────────────────┐
│   SEE SHEET 2   │
│    ZONE A2      │
└─────────────────┘
```

ROD Drawing - Revolved Section

A Revolved Section represents the cross section of the Rod. There is no Revolved Section tool. Copy the Broken Right view. Utilize a Section view to create the Revolved Section between the two Break lines. Align the Revolved Section horizontally to the Right view.

Activity: ROD Drawing-Revolved Section

Increase the default break line gap from 10mm to 25mm.

142) Click **Options** 📧 , **Document Properties** tab from the Menu bar toolbar.

143) Click the **Detailing** folder under Document Properties.

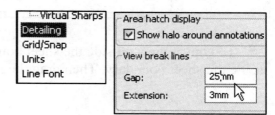

144) Enter **25** in the View break lines Gap box.

145) Click **OK** from the Document Properties - Detailing dialog box.

146) **Rebuild** the drawing.

147) Click **Save**.

Zoom in on the Graphics window.

148) Press the **z** key until Sheet2 is approximately ½ its original size.

Copy and Paste the Vertical Break Right view.

149) Click inside the **Vertical Break** view boundary; Drawing View6.

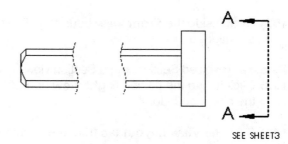

SEE SHEET3

150) Click **Ctrl + C**.

151) Click a **position** above the Right view.

152) Click **Ctrl + V**.

153) Drag the copied **view** off the sheet boundary to the right of the Vertical Break Right view.

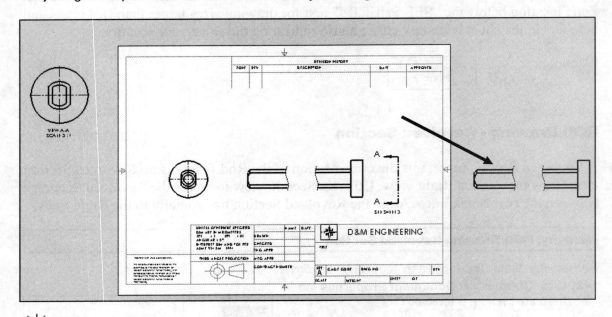

💡 To copy a view outside the sheet boundary, select a view to copy. Click a position inside the sheet boundary. Then drag the new view off the sheet boundary.

Align the views.
154) Right-click inside the **copied Right view**.

155) Click **Alignment**.

156) Click **Align Horizontal by Origin**. The mouse pointer displays the Alignment icon

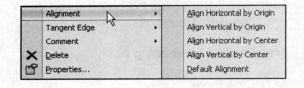

157) Click inside the **Front view** boundary, Drawing View5. The two views are aligned.

Create a Revolved Section with a Section view.
158) Click inside the copied **Right view** boundary to the right of the sheet boundary.

159) Click the **View Layout** tab from the CommandManager.

160) Click **Section View** ⫴ from the View Layout toolbar. The Section View PropertyManager is displayed. The Line Sketch tool is displayed

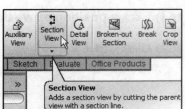

161) Sketch a **vertical line** to the left of the copied Vertical Break and to the right of the Internal Thread feature. **Flip** the arrows to the left if required.

162) Place the **cross section** between the Vertical Break Lines.

Set the Scale.
163) Check the **Use custom scale** box.

164) Select **User Defined** from the drop-down menu.

165) Enter **.75:1**.

166) Click **OK** ✔ from the Section View PropertyManager. Note: If you clicked a position inside of the view boundary of Drawing View6 on the previous page, the text: SEE SHEET3 would be displayed.

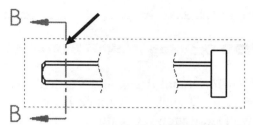

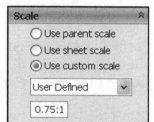

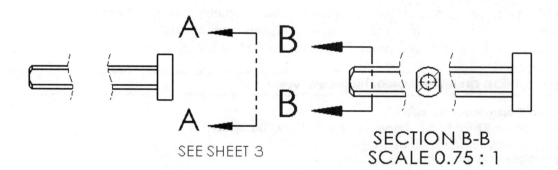

SEE SHEET 3

SECTION B-B
SCALE 0.75 : 1

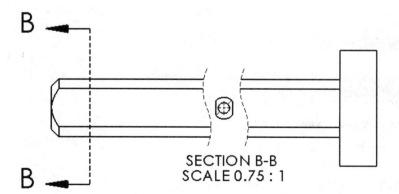

SECTION B-B
SCALE 0.75 : 1

SEE SHEET3

Save the ROD drawing.

167) Click **Save** 🖫 .

ROD Drawing-Broken Isometric View

The Horizontal Break and Vertical Break options work
only in 2D views. A Broken Isometric view utilizes
two Detail views. Create a front Detail view and then a
back Detail view.

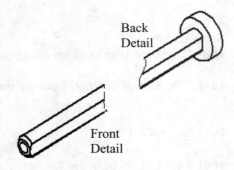

Position the two Detail views. Utilize a Sketch Line to
align the Front Detail and the Back Detail. Create the
Sketch Line on the Construction Drawing layer.

Select the Detail views and utilize the Default
Alignment option to move both views together. Create
layers in a drawing document for construction
geometry and dimensions.

Sketched geometry in the drawing links to the current view. Select the view and the view
boundary turns blue. Sketch the geometry and the geometry moves with the view.
Specify line color, thickness and line style. Add New entities to the active layer. Turn
layers on/off to simplify drawings. Shut layers off when not in use.

Activity: ROD Drawing-Broken Isometric View

Create a Broken Isometric view.
168) Click the **SHEET3** tab. **Zoom out** on the Sheet boundary.

Insert an Isometric view.

169) Click **Model View** 🖾 from the View Layout toolbar. ROD is an active
part document.

170) Click **Next** ⊙ . *Isometric is selected by default.

171) Click a **position** above the Right view, off the ROD-Sheet3 boundary.
The Drawing View12 PropertyManager is displayed.

172) Right-click inside the **Drawing View12** view boundary.

173) Click **Properties**.

174) Select the **Long Rod** configuration.

175) Click **OK**. Click **OK** ✓ from the Drawing View12 PropertyManager.

176) Click and drag the **views** as illustrated.

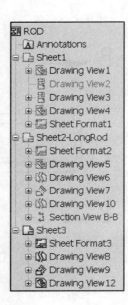

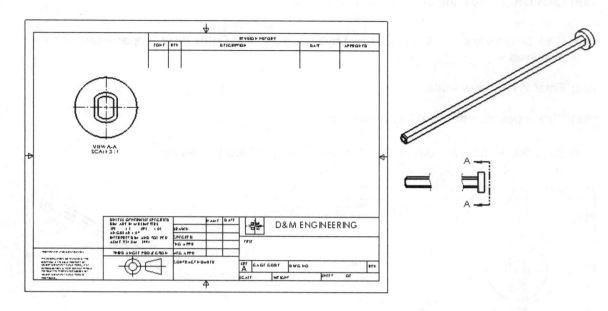

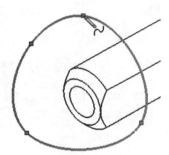

Create a Detail C view.
177) Zoom in on the Internal Thread.

178) Click the **Sketch** tab from the CommandManager.

179) Click **Spline** from the Sketch toolbar.

180) Sketch a **closed Spline** around the Internal Thread.

181) Click **OK** from the Spline PropertyManager.

182) Click **Detail View** from the View Layout toolbar. The Detail View PropertyManager is displayed.

183) Enter **2:1** for view scale.

184) Click a **position** to the right of the Removed view in the Sheet boundary as illustrated.

185) Click **OK** from the Detail View C PropertyManager.

DETAIL C
SCALE 2 : 1

Create Detail D.
186) Click the **Sketch** tab from the CommandManager.

187) Click **Spline** from the Sketch toolbar.

188) Sketch a **closed Spline** around the Piston end as illustrated.

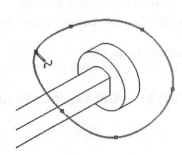

189) Click **OK** ✔ from the Spline PropertyManager.

190) Click **Detail View** Ⓐ from the View Layout toolbar. The Detail View PropertyManager is displayed.

191) Enter **2:1** for view scale.

192) Click a **position** in Sheet3 as illustrated.

193) Click **OK** ✔ from the Detail View PropertyManager. View the results.

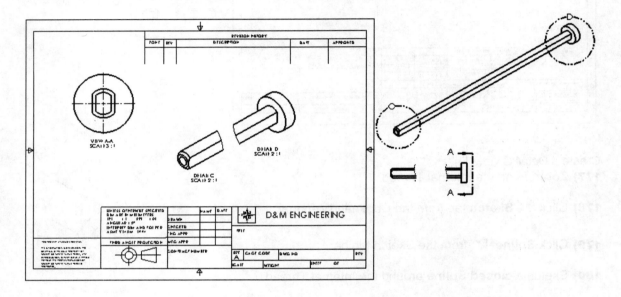

💡 Do not delete the Parent views outside the Sheet boundary. The Detail C and Detail D text is dependent on the Isometric view. Sketching Splines for Broken Isometric views requires practice. Sketch the Spline back portion in Detail C similar to the Spline front portion in Detail D. Right-click on the Detail Circle. Select Edit Sketch to return to the original Spline.

Display the Layer toolbar.
194) Click **View**, **Toolbars**, **Layer** from the Menu bar menu.

Display the Layers dialog box.
195) Click the **Layer Properties** 🖪 icon.

Create a new layer.
196) Click the **New** button.

197) Enter **Construction** for Name.

198) Enter **Construction View Lines** for Description. Note: The layer is on when the Light Bulb 💡 is yellow.

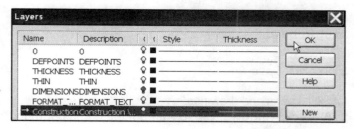

199) Select **Red** for Color.

200) Select **Dashed** for Style.

201) Click **OK** from the Layers dialog box.

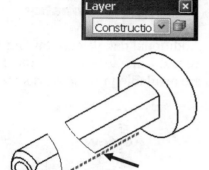

Sketch a line.
202) Click inside the **Detail C** view boundary.

203) Click **Line** ╲ from the Sketch toolbar.

204) Sketch a **line parallel** to the lower profile line on Detail C as illustrated.

Move the Detail D view.
205) Drag **Detail D** until the bottom edge is approximately aligned with the red Line.

Lock View position.
206) Click inside the **Detail C** view boundary.

207) Hold the **Ctrl** key down.

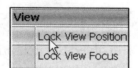

208) Click inside the **Detail D** view boundary.

209) Release the **Ctrl** key.

210) Right-click **Lock View Position**.

Hide the red line.
211) Click the **Layer Properties** 🗗 icon.

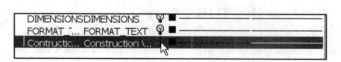

212) Click the **Light Bulb** 💡 to turn off the Construction layer.

213) Click **OK** from the Layers dialog box.

Return to the default layer.
214) Select **None** from the Layer toolbar.

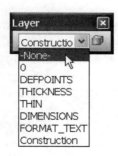

Fit the drawing to the Graphics window.
215) Press the **f** key.

Save the ROD drawing.
216) Rebuild the drawing.

217) Click **Save** .

Close all parts and drawings.
218) Click **Windows**, **Close All** from the Menu bar menu.

 More Information

Additional details on Drawing Views, Hide, Add Sheet, Horizontal Break, Vertical Break, Line Font, Dimension Type, Align, Spline, Note, and Layers are available in SolidWorks Help Topics.

Review

The ROD drawing consisted of three sheets. Sheet1 contained the Front, Top, Right, and Isometric view for the Short Rod configuration. The Drawing template in Project 2 stored the Predefined views.

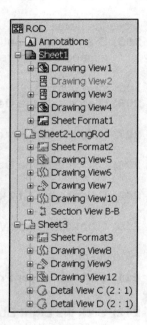

Sheet2 contained a copied Front view and a Vertical Break Right view. The views utilized the Long Rod configuration. The Revolved Section utilized the Section view positioned outside the sheet boundary.

Sheet3 contained a Removed view and a Broken Isometric view. The Removed view utilized an Auxiliary view on Sheet2. The Broken Isometric view was created with two Detail views.

Review the TUBE Part

Perform the following recommended tasks before starting the TUBE drawing:

* Verify the TUBE part

* View and move feature dimensions

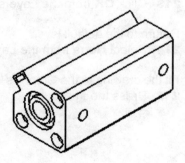

Position feature dimensions off the part before creating the drawing. Dimension schemes defined in the part require changes in the drawing. Design engineers use different dimensioning schemes than those required by manufacturing engineers.

Example 1: The design engineer references the depth dimensions 27.75mm and 32.75mm to the Front Plane for the Tube Extrusion feature. The engineer's analysis calculations also reference the Front Plane.

The manufacturing engineer requires an overall depth of 60.50mm (27.75mm + 32.75mm) referenced from the front face. Create the overall depth dimension of 60.50mm for the drawing in Chapter 3.

Example 2: The design engineer references the depth dimensions to the Front Plane for the Stoke Chamber (Depth1 = 17.50mm and Depth2 = 17.50mm).

The manufacturing engineering requires an overall depth of 35.00mm.

Example 3: An Extruded Cut feature creates the Stroke Chamber as an internal feature. Display the Stroke Chamber dimensions in the Section view of the drawing. Reference added dimensions from the front face in the Section view.

Activity: Review the TUBE Part

Review the TUBE part.

219) Click **Open** from the Menu bar toolbar.

220) Double-click **TUBE** from the DRAWING-W-SOLIDWORKS-2010 folder. The TUBE FeatureManager is displayed.

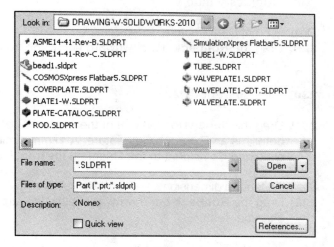

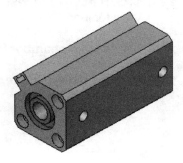

Execute various display modes.

221) Click **Hidden Line Visible** ⬚ from the Heads-up View toolbar. Internal features are displayed.

222) Click **Hidden Lines Removed** ⬚ from the Heads-up View toolbar. Internal features are hidden.

Review the TUBE part features.

223) Place the **mouse pointer** over the blue Rollback bar at the bottom of the FeatureManager design tree.

224) Drag the **Rollback** bar upward to below the tube extrusion feature.

225) Click **tube extrusion** from the FeatureManager.

226) Drag the **dimension text** off the model.

227) If needed, flip the **dimension arrows** to view the text.

228) Click **OK** ✔ from the Dimension PropertyManager.

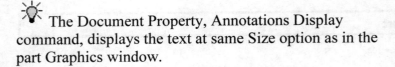

🔆 The Document Property, Annotations Display command, displays the text at same Size option as in the part Graphics window.

Display Front Detail feature dimensions.

229) Drag the **Rollback** bar downward below the front detail1 feature.

230) Click on **front detail1**.

231) Drag the **dimension text** off of the model. The front detail1 is an Extruded Cut feature. A 17mm circle is sketched Coincident to the Origin on the front face.

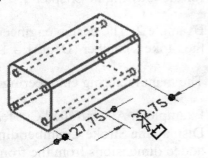

View the feature dimensions.

232) Drag the **Rollback** bar downward below the stroke chamber feature.

233) Click **Hidden Line Visible** ⬚ from the Heads-up View toolbar.

234) Click **stroke chamber** from the FeatureManager.

235) Drag the **dimension text** off the model.

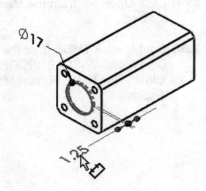

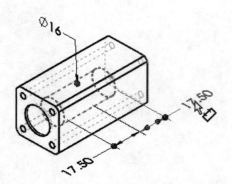

Display the Nose feature dimensions.
236) Drag the **Rollback** bar downward below the nose feature.

237) Click the **nose** feature from the FeatureManager. The Nose feature requires a Detail view.

Display the Bore feature dimensions.
238) Drag the **Rollback** bar downward below the bore feature.

239) Click the **bore** feature from the FeatureManager. The Cut requires a Section view. The circular sketch profile is extruded on both sides of the front plane with two different Depth options.

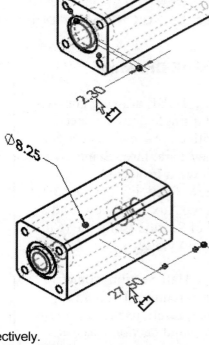

240) Drag the **dimension text** off the model.

Display the Port feature dimensions.
241) Drag the **Rollback** bar downward below the ports feature.

242) Click the **ports** feature from the FeatureManager.

243) Drag the **dimension text** off the model.

Display the 45 AngleCut, switchgroove, and the M2.0 hole respectively.
244) Drag the **Rollback bar** downward under switchgroove. The switchgroove requires a Detail view. The M2.0 hole requires an Auxiliary view.

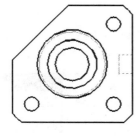

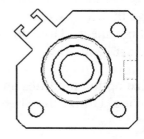
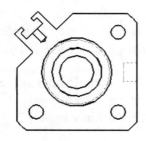

45 AngleCut   SwitchGroove   M2.0 hole

Display the Cbore Front and Cbore Rear
245) Right-click on the **switchgroove** feature.

246) Click **Roll to End**. The Rollback bar is positioned at the end of the FeatureManager.

247) Click the **Cbore Front** feature from the FeatureManager. The feature is displayed in blue in the Graphics window.

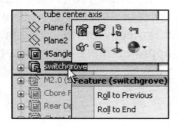

248) Rotate the part to view the Rear Detail and Cbore Rear features. The Rear Detail and Cbore Rear requires a Back Projected view in the drawing.

249) Click **Isometric** 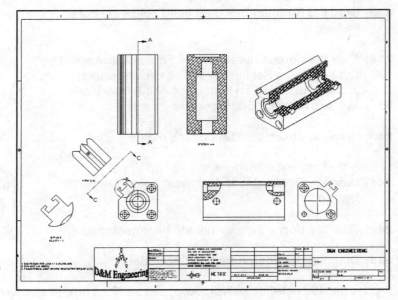 view from the Heads-up View toolbar.

250) Click **OK** ✔ from the Dimension PropertyManager.

TUBE Drawing

The TUBE drawing consists of a single drawing sheet with eight views. The eight views are: three Standard views, a Projected Back view, Section view, Detail view, Auxiliary view, and a Half Section Isometric (Cut away) view.

The Half Section Isometric view requires two part configurations named: *Entire Part* and *Section Cutaway*.

Utilize an A-ANSI-MM Drawing template. Insert the four Predefined views: Front, Top, Right, and Isometric. There is not enough space on an A-size drawing. You have two options: enlarge the sheet size or move additional views to multiple sheets. How do you increase the sheet size? Utilize Sheet Properties.

The Sheet Properties, Size option modifies an A-size drawing to a C-size drawing. Utilize the Sheet format you created in Chapter 2.

Projected views display the part or assembly by projecting an Orthographic view using the First angle or Third angle projection. Recall that Third angle projection is set in Sheet Properties in the Drawing template. Insert a Project view to create the Back view. Provide approximately 1in. - 2in., (25mm - 50mm) between views.

Activity: TUBE Drawing

Create the TUBE drawing.

251) Click **New** ☐ from the Menu bar toolbar.

252) Click the **MY-TEMPLATES** tab.

253) Double-click **A-ANSI-MM** from the SolidWorks Document dialog box.

Save the drawing.

254) Click **Save As** from the Consolidated Menu bar toolbar.

255) Select **DRAWING-W-SOLIDWORKS-2010** for Save in folder.

256) Enter **TUBE** for File name.

257) Enter **TUBE DRAWING** for Description.

258) Click **Save**.

Insert the Predefined views.

259) Click **Window**, **Tile Horizontally** from the Menu bar menu. Drag the **TUBE** 🗂 TUBE icon from the Part FeatureManager into the drawing Graphics window. The Front, Top, Right, and Isometric views are displayed in the drawing.

260) **Maximize** the TUBE drawing.

If needed, deactivate the Origins.

261) Click **View**; uncheck **Origins** from the Menu bar menu.

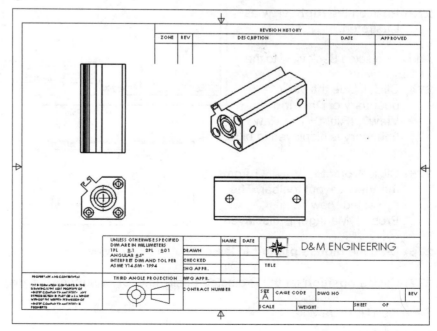

Modify Sheet Properties.

262) Right-click in the **Graphics window**.

263) Click **Properties**.

264) Enter **2:1** for sheet Scale.

265) Select **C (ANSI) Landscape** for Sheet Format/Size.

266) Click the **Browse** button.

267) Double-click **C-FORMAT** from the MY-SHEETFORMATS folder.

268) Click **OK** from the Sheet Properties dialog box.

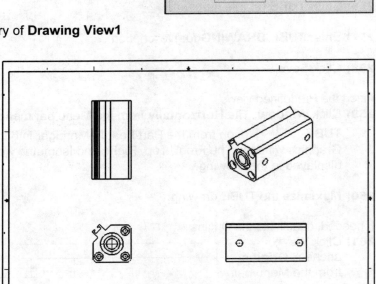

Move the TUBE drawing views.

269) Click inside the view boundary of **Drawing View1** (Front). The view boundary is displayed in blue.

270) Position the **Front** view as illustrated.

271) Position the **Top** view as illustrated.

272) Drag the **Isometric** view as illustrated.

273) Position the **Right** view as illustrated.

Add a Projected Back view to the TUBE drawing.

274) Click inside the view boundary of **Drawing View3**, (Right). The view boundary is displayed in blue.

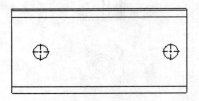 

275) Click **Projected View** 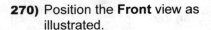 from the View Layout toolbar. The Projected View PropertyManager is displayed.

276) Drag the **mouse pointer** to the right of the Right view.

277) Click a **position** for the Projected Back view. Drawing View5 is displayed.

Save the TUBE drawing.

278) Click **Save** .

TUBE Drawing-Section View and Detail View

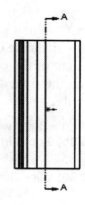

How many views are utilized in a drawing? The number of views in a drawing depends on how many views are required to define the true shape and size of the part.

The TUBE part requires additional drawing views to display interior features and to enlarge features. Display the interior TUBE part features with a Section view.

A Section view defines a cutting plane with a sketched line in a view perpendicular to the view. Create a Full Section view by sketching a section line in the Top view.

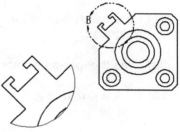

A Detail views enlarge an area of an existing view. Specify location, shape and scale. Create a Detail view from a Section view at a 4:1 scale.

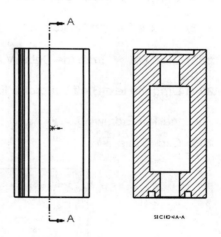

Activity: TUBE Drawing-Section View and Detail View

Add a Section view to the TUBE drawing.
279) Display the Origins. Click **View**; check **Origins** from the Menu bar menu.

280) Click inside the view boundary of **Drawing View2**, (Top). The view boundary is displayed in blue.

281) Click **Section View** ⇥ from the View Layout toolbar. The Section View PropertyManager is displayed.

282) Sketch a **vertical section line** Coincident with the Right Plane, through the Origin. The line must extend pass the profile lines.

☼ If needed, right-click Edit Sketch on the Section line, to locate the sketched Section line at the part Origin. Select the line. Select the origin. Add a Coincident relation. Save and exit the sketch.

283) Click a **position** to the right Drawing View2 (Top) view. The section arrows point to the right. If required, click **Flip direction**.

284) Click **OK** ✔ from the Section View A-A PropertyManager.

When you create a Section view, you can specific
the distance of the cut, so the Section view does not create
a cut of the entire drawing view. Do not display origins
on the final drawing. This is for illustration purposes
only.

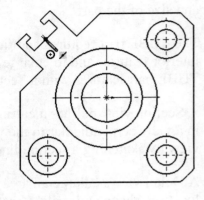

Add a Detail view to the TUBE drawing.
285) **Zoom in** on the upper left corner of Drawing View1.

286) Click **Detail View** Ⓐ from the View Layout toolbar. The
Circle Sketch tool is activated.

287) Click the **middle** of the switchgroove in the Front view as
illustrated.

288) Drag the **mouse pointer** downwards as illustrated.

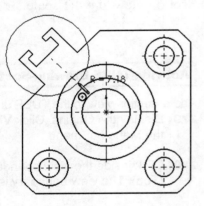

289) Click a **position** just below the large circle to create a
sketched circle.

290) Click the **position** to the bottom left of DrawingView1,
(Front). The Detail View name is B.

Set the scale.
291) Check the **Use custom scale** box.

292) Enter **4:1** in the Custom Scale text box.

293) Click **OK** ✔ from the Detail View B PropertyManager.

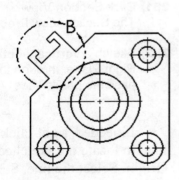

294) Drag the text **B** off the profile lines.

Save the TUBE drawing.
295) Click **Save** 💾 .

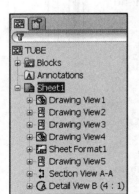

DETAIL B
SCALE 4 : 1

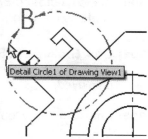

To modify the size of the Detail view, position the mouse pointer on the Detail circle. The mouse pointer displays the

Detail icon. Right-click and select Edit Sketch. Drag the circumference of the sketch circle. Click OK from the Circle PropertyManager. Click Rebuild to update the Detail view.

The Detail view profile is a circle. When a non-circular view is required, sketch the closed profile first. Then select the Detail view.

Verify view names. The A, B, & C view names increment sequentially for Section views, Detail views and Auxiliary views. If you delete the view, the view name still increments by a letter. Modify the view name in the PropertyManager for a specific view.

TUBE Drawing-Broken-out Section View, Auxiliary View and Crop View

A Broken-out Section view removes material to a specified depth to expose the inner details of an existing view. A closed profile defines a Broken-out Section view.

An Auxiliary view displays a plane parallel to an angled plane with true dimensions. A primary Auxiliary view is hinged to one of the six principle views. Create a primary Full Auxiliary view that references the Front view.

Display the M2.0 Hole information. Create a Partial Auxiliary view from the Full Auxiliary view. Sketch a closed profile in an active Auxiliary view. Use the Crop view tool to create a Partial Auxiliary view.

Activity: TUBE Drawing-Broken-out Section View, Auxiliary View, and Crop View

---

Add the first Broken-out Section view to the TUBE drawing.
296) Click inside the view boundary of **Drawing View3**, (Right).

297) Click **Hidden Line Visible** . The hidden lines do not clearly define the internal front features of the part.

Create a Broken-out Section view.
298) Click the **Sketch** tab from the CommandManager. The Sketch toolbar is displayed.

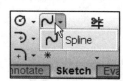

299) Click **Spline** from the Sketch toolbar.

300) Sketch a **closed Spline** in the top left corner. The Spline contains the Cbore Front feature.

301) Click **Broken-out Section**  from the Layout View toolbar. The Broken-out Section PropertyManager is displayed.

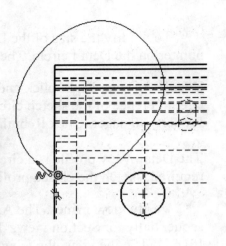

302) Enter **5**mm for Depth.

303) Check the **Preview** box to insure that the Cbore Front is displayed.

304) Click **OK** from the Broken-out Section PropertyManager.

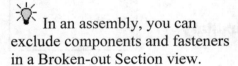 In an assembly, you can exclude components and fasteners in a Broken-out Section view.

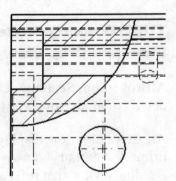

Add a second Broken-out Section view to the TUBE drawing.
305) Click the **Sketch** tab from the CommandManager.

306) Click **Spline** ⌒ from the Sketch toolbar.

307) Sketch a **closed Spline** in the top right corner of Drawing View3. The Spline contains the Cbore Rear feature.

308) Click **Broken-out Section**  from the View Layout toolbar.

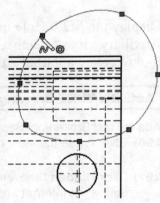

309) Enter **5**mm for Depth.

310) Check the **Preview** box.

311) Click **OK** from the Broken-out Section PropertyManager.

312) Click **inside** Drawing View3.

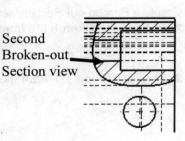

Second Broken-out Section view

Display no hidden lines.

313) Click **Hidden Lines Removed** .

314) Click **OK** ✓ from the Drawing
View3 PropertyManager.

Fit the drawing to the Sheet.
315) Press the **f** key.

Deactivate the Origins.
316) Click **View**; uncheck **Origins** from
the Menu bar menu.

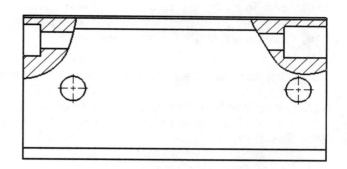

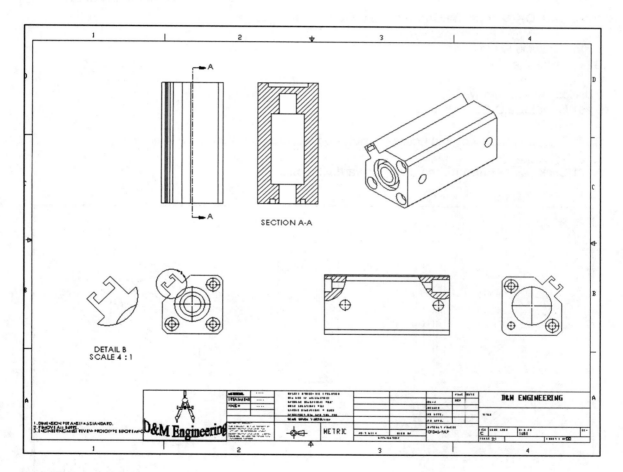

Save the TUBE drawing.
317) Click **Save** .

Add an Auxiliary view to the TUBE drawing.
318) Zoom in on the left top side of Drawing View1.

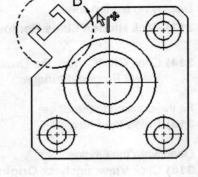

319) Click the **left angled edge** as illustrated.

320) Click **Auxiliary View** from the View Layout toolbar.

321) Click a **position** to the upper left of Drawing View1 (Front). The location selected is the center of the Full Auxiliary view.

322) Enter **C** for the View Name.

323) Click **OK** from the Drawing View PropertyManager.

Fit the Drawing to the Sheet.
324) Press the **f** key.

Position the view arrows.
325) Click **Line C-C**.

326) Drag the **midpoint** and position it between the Auxiliary view and Front view.

327) Click each **endpoint** and drag it towards the midpoint.

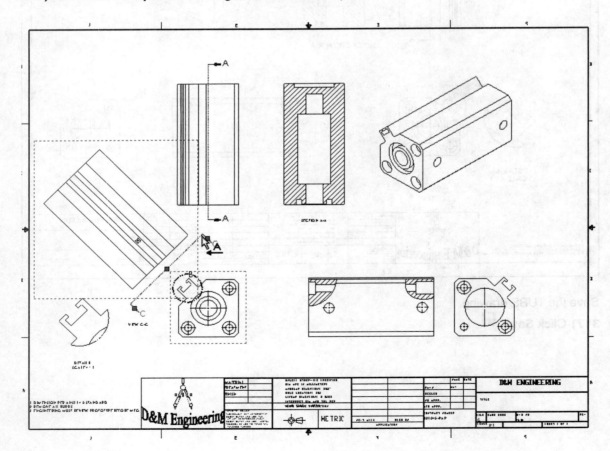

Sketch a closed profile in the active Auxiliary view.

328) Click the **Sketch** tab from the CommandManager.

329) Click **Spline** ∿ from the Sketch toolbar. The first point is Coincident with the left line of the switchgroove.

330) Sketch **7 Points** to create the closed Spline. The last point is Coincident with the right line of the switchgroove.

Sketch three lines.

331) Click **Line** \ from the Sketch toolbar.

332) Sketch the **first line**, the mouse pointer displays Endpoint inference.

333) Sketch the **second line** Collinear with the bottom edge of the Auxiliary view. The first point and second point display Endpoint inference.

334) Sketch the **third line**. The last point must display Endpoint interference with the first point of the Spline.

335) Right-click **Select**.

336) Window-Select the **three lines** and the **Spline**. The Properties PropertyManager is displayed. The selected entities are displayed in the Selected Entities box.

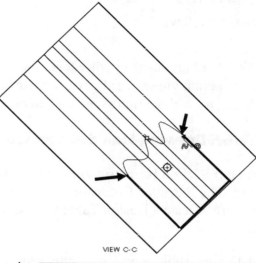

VIEW C-C

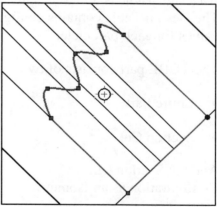

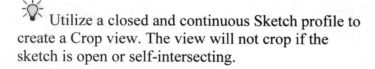 Utilize a closed and continuous Sketch profile to create a Crop view. The view will not crop if the sketch is open or self-intersecting.

Crop the view.

337) Click **Crop View** 🖾 from the View Layout toolbar to display the partial Auxiliary view.

338) Click **OK** ✔ from the Properties PropertyManager.

Fit the drawing to the Sheet.

339) Press the **f** key.

Position the view.

340) Drag the **C-C view arrow** between the Auxiliary view and the Front view.

341) Drag the **VIEW C-C** text below the Auxiliary view.

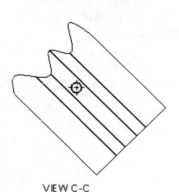

VIEW C-C

342) Click **OK** ✔ from the Note PropertyManager.

Save the TUBE drawing.

343) Click **Save** 🖫 .

🔆 Position views in other locations on the sheet when space is limited. The Auxiliary and Section views are aligned to their Parent view. Press the Ctrl key before selecting the Auxiliary and Section view tools in order to position the views anywhere on the sheet.

TUBE Drawing-Half Section Isometric (Cut-Away) View

A Half Section Isometric view in the TUBE drawing requires a Cut feature created in the part. The Extruded Cut feature removes ¼ of the TUBE part. Create an Extruded Cut feature. Create a Design Table to control the Suppressed State of the Extruded Cut feature.

A Design Table is an Excel spreadsheet that represents multiple configurations of a part. The Design Table contains configuration names, parameters to control and assigned values for each parameter.

The TUBE part consists of two configurations:

- Entire Part

- Section Cut

Add the Section Cut Configuration as an Isometric view.

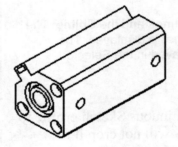 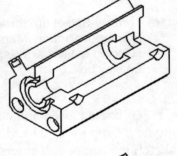

Insert an Area Hatch pattern in the Isometric view. A Hatch Pattern, (section lining or cross sectioning) represents an exposed cut surface based on the material.

Entire Part

The Hatch type, ANSI38(Aluminum) represents the TUBE material.

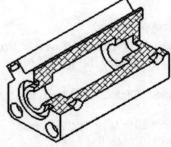

Hatch Cut

| **Activity: TUBE Drawing-Half Section Isometric-Cut Away View** |

Open the TUBE part.

344) Right-click inside the **Front view** boundary.

345) Click **Open Part**. The TUBE FeatureManager is displayed

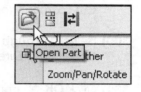

Insert a cut.

346) Click **Front view** ⬦ from the
Heads-up View toolbar.

347) Right-click the **front face** of the
TUBE in the Graphics window.

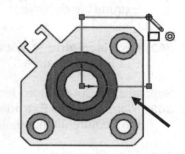

348) Click **Sketch** ✏ from the
Context toolbar.

349) Click **Corner Rectangle** ▢ from
the Consolidated Sketch toolbar.

350) Sketch a **rectangle** through the
Origin as illustrated.

351) Right-click **Select** to deselect the
sketch tool.

Add a Collinear relation between the top horizontal line and the top
edge.

352) Click the **top horizontal** line.

353) Hold the **Ctrl** key down.

354) Click the **top edge**.

355) Release the **Ctrl** key.

356) Click **Collinear** ⟋ from the Add Relations box.

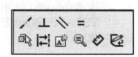

☼ Right-click and use the Pop-up Context toolbar to insert
Geometric relations.

357) Add a **Collinear** relation between the right vertical line and the
right edge.

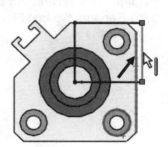

Add an Extruded Cut Feature.

358) Click the **Features** tab from the CommandManager.

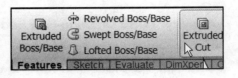

359) Click **Extruded Cut** from the Feature toolbar. The Cut-Extrude PropertyManager is displayed.

360) Select **Through All** for End Condition in Direction 1.

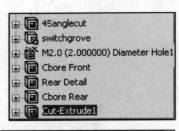

361) Click **OK** ✔ from the Cut-Extrude PropertyManager. Cut-Extrude1 is displayed.

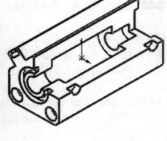

362) Click **Isometric** ⬦. View the Cut-Extrude feature.

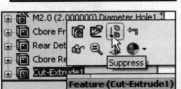

Suppress the Cut-Extrude1 feature.

363) Right-click **Cut-Extrude1** from the FeatureManager.

364) Click **Suppress**.

Insert a Design Table.

365) Click **Insert**, **Tables**, **Design Table** from the Menu bar menu.

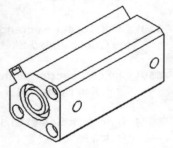

366) Check the **Blank** box for Source.

367) Click **OK** ✔ from the Design Table PropertyManager.

368) Click **$STATE@Cut-Extrude1** from the Parameters box.

369) Click **OK** from the Add Rows and Columns dialog box. The Design Table for the TUBE is displayed in the upper left corner. $STATE@Cut-Extrude1 is displayed in Cell B2.

Rename the first configuration.

370) Rename the text **First Instance** to **Entire Part**.

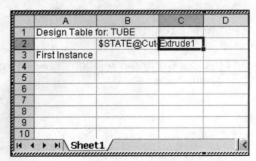

Create the second configuration.
371) Enter **Section Cut** in Cell A4.

372) Enter **S** in Cell B3.

373) Enter **U** in Cell B4.

Close the Design Table.
374) Click inside the **Graphics window**.

375) Click **OK**. Both TUBE configurations are created.

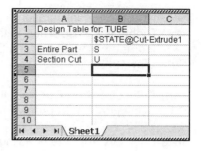

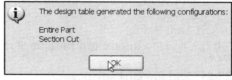

Click Edit, Design Table, Edit Table from the Menu bar menu to access an existing Design Table or Right-click the Design Table icon in the ConfigurationManager and select Edit Table.

The Design Table abbreviation for Suppressed is S. The abbreviation for Unsuppressed is U.

Display the TUBE part configurations.
376) Click the **ConfigurationManager** tab.

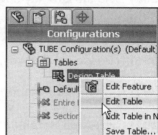

377) Double-click **Entire Part** from the ConfigurationManager.

378) Double-click **Section Cut** from the ConfigurationManager. View the results.

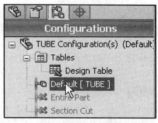

Display the TUBE part default configuration.
379) Double-click **Default** from the ConfigurationManager.

Return to the TUBE part FeatureManager.
380) Click the **Part FeatureManager** tab.

Save the TUBE part.
381) Click **Save** .

Open the TUBE drawing.
382) Right-click **Tube (Default)** from the FeatureManager.

383) Click **Open Drawing**. The TUBE drawing is displayed.

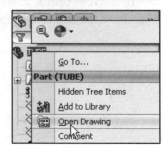

Select the TUBE configuration.

384) Right-click **Properties** in the Isometric view boundary, Drawing View4.

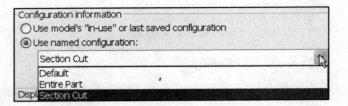

385) Select **Section Cut** from the Named Configuration drop-down menu.

386) Click **OK** from the Drawing View Properties dialog box. The Section Cut configuration is displayed.

Insert Area Hatch.

387) Click the **inside top face** as illustrated.

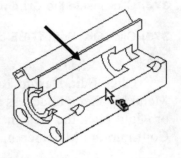

388) Hold the **Ctrl** key down.

389) Click the **inside bottom face** as illustrated.

390) Release the **Ctrl** key.

391) Click the **Annotation** tab from the CommandManager.

392) Click **Area Hatch/Fill** ▨ from the Annotation toolbar.

Change the Area Hatch type.

393) Select **ANSI38 (Aluminum)** from the Pattern drop-down menu.

394) Select **2** from the Scale drop-down menu.

395) Click **OK** ✔ from the Area Hatch/Fill PropertyManager.

Fit the drawing to the Sheet.

396) Press the **f** key.

Save the TUBE drawing.

397) Click **Save** 💾 .

The Section view and Broken-out Section view requires the Aluminum Property for the Area Hatch.

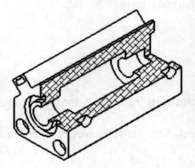

Activity: TUBE Part-Edit Material

Open the TUBE part.
398) Right-click inside the **Isometric view** boundary.

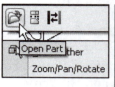

399) Click **Open Part**. The TUBE FeatureManager is displayed.

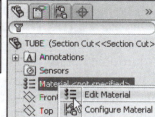

Set Material type.
400) Right-click **Material** in the FeatureManager.

401) Click **Edit Material**. The Material dialog box is displayed.

402) **Expand** Aluminum Alloys. Select **6061 Alloy**. Click **Apply**.

403) Click **Close** from the Material dialog box.

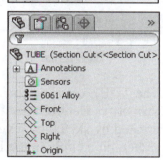

Return to the TUBE drawing.
404) Click **Window**, **Tube-Sheet1** from the Menu bar menu. **Rebuild** the drawing to display the Aluminum hatch pattern in the remaining views.

405) Click **Save** .

Close all files.
406) Click **Windows**, **Close All** from the Menu bar menu.

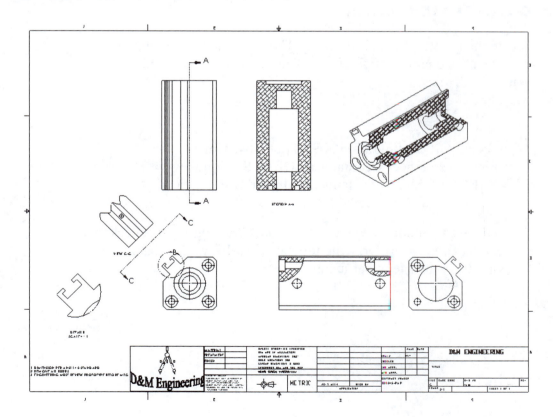

The views required for the TUBE drawing are complete. Insert dimensions and notes for the TUBE drawing in Chapter 4. Note: Utilize Detail View option to create a detail of a preexisting Detail View of a Crop View.

 More Information

Additional details on Drawing Views, Section, Detail, Auxiliary, Area Hatch, Design Tables, Sheet Properties and Broken-out Section are available in Online help. Keywords: Drawing Views (auxiliary, configuration, detail), Model View, Section views, Auxiliary views, Detail views, Design Tables(Suppress), Broken-out Section and Spline.

 Review

The TUBE drawing consisted of a single sheet with eight different views. Sheet Properties were utilized to modify the Sheet size from A to C. The Section view was created by sketching a vertical line in the Top view. The Detail view was created by sketching a circle in the Front view. A Partial Auxiliary view utilized the Crop view tool. The Right view was modified with the Broken-out Section tool.

The Design Table controlled the suppression state of an Extruded Cut feature in the TUBE part. The Isometric view utilized the Section Cut configuration. The Area Hatch utilized the Aluminum material in the Isometric view.

COVERPLATE Drawing

Create the COVERPLATE drawing. The COVERPLATE drawing consists of two part configurations. The first part configuration is With Nose Holes.

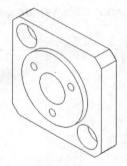

The second part configuration is Without Nose Holes. COVERPLATE-Sheet 1 contains an Offset Section view. COVERPLATE-Sheet2 contains an Aligned Section view.

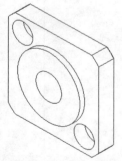

The Start command when creating new drawing box is checked by default. To view the Drawing toolbar, click View, Toolbars, Drawing from the Menu bar menu.

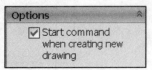

Insert a new Front view with the Model View tool. Delete the Predefined views created with the drawing template. Create a new layer to locate and hide all Center marks on a single layer. Insert an Offset Section view and a Right view.

Copy the Front view from Sheet1 to Sheet2. Modify the configuration. Insert an Aligned Section view.

Activity: COVERPLATE Drawing

Open the COVERPLATE part.
407) Click **Open** from the Menu bar toolbar.

408) Double-click the **COVERPLATE** part.

Display the dimensions.
409) Click on each **feature name**. View the dimensions.

Display the COVERPLATE part configurations.
410) Drag the **Split Bar** downward to split the FeatureManager.

411) Click the **ConfigurationManager** tab.

412) Double-click **With Nose Holes** configuration.

413) Double-click **Without Nose Holes** configuration.

414) Double-click **Default [COVERPLATE]** configuration.

Create the COVERPLATE drawing.
415) Click **New** from the Menu bar toolbar.

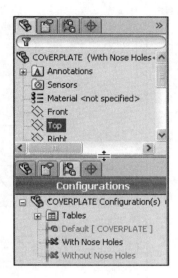

416) Double-click the **A-ANSI-MM** drawing template. COVERPLATE is the open document displayed in the Model View PropertyManager.

417) Click **Next** from the Model View PropertyManager.

418) Click *****Front** from the Orientation box.

419) Click a **position** in the lower left corner of the drawing.

Set the View Scale.
420) Click **Use custom scale**.

421) Select **User Defined**.

422) Enter **1.5:1**.

423) Click **OK** from the Projected View PropertyManager. Drawing View5 is displayed in the FeatureManager.

Delete the Predefined empty views.
424) Hold the **Ctrl** key down.

425) Click **Drawing View1**, **Drawing View2**, **Drawing View3** and **Drawing View4**.

426) Release the **Ctrl** key. Press the **Delete** key.

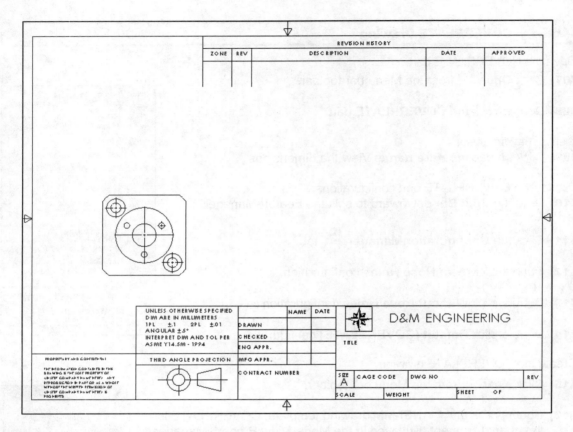

427) Click **Yes to all** to delete the four predefined views. Drawing View5 is displayed.

Modify the configuration.
428) Right-click **Properties** inside the Front view boundary, (Drawing View5).

429) Select **Without Nose Holes** for view configuration. Click **OK**.

Display the Layers dialog box.
430) Click **Layer Properties** 📇 icon.

Create a new layer.
431) Click the **New** button. Enter **Centermarks**
for Name.

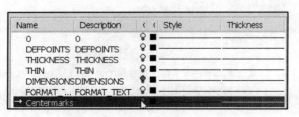

432) Click the **Light Bulb** 💡 icon to turn off
layer display. Click **OK**.

Place the Center marks on the new layer.
433) Hold the **Ctrl** key down.

434) Click the **Center marks** in the Front view.

435) Release the **Ctrl** key.

436) Select **Centermarks** for layer.

437) Click **OK** ✔ from the Center Mark PropertyManager.

438) Click **Save** 🖫.

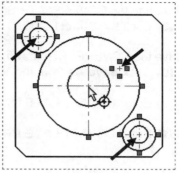

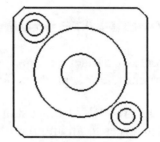

🔆 Control Center mark display before you insert dimensions.

Control Center marks with two options:
- **Option 1**: When the Document Property, Auto insert on view creation option is checked, place Center marks on a separate layer. Turn off the layer to add dimensions and construction geometry in the drawing.
- **Option 2**: Uncheck the Auto insert on view creation option to control individual Center marks. Save the setting in the Drawing template. Position dimensions, then apply the Center Mark tool from the Annotation toolbar.

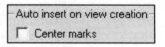

Display the None layer.
439) Click **Layer** drop-down menu.

440) Click **None** for current layer.

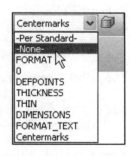

Copy the Front view.
441) Click inside the **Front view** boundary. Press **Ctrl + C**.

Add COVERPLATE-Sheet2.
442) Right-click the **Sheet1** tab.

443) Click **Add Sheet**.

Copy the Front view from Sheet1 to Sheet2.
444) Click a **position** on the left side of Sheet2.

445) Press **Ctrl + V**. Right-click **Properties** in the view boundary.

446) Select **With Nose Holes** from the Configuration text box.

447) Click **OK**. A pattern of 3 holes is displayed.

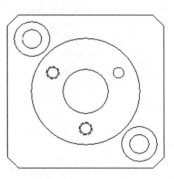

Return to the COVERPLATE-Sheet1.
448) Click the **Sheet1** tab.

Save the COVERPLATE drawing.
449) Click **Save As** from the Menu bar toolbar.

450) Enter **COVERPLATE** for Drawing Name.

451) Enter **COVERPLATE DRAWING** for Description.

452) Click **Save** 🖫 .

COVERPLATE Drawing-Offset Section View and Aligned Section View

Create an Offset Section view by drawing a sketched line. Draw sketch lines in perpendicular segments. Section A-A displays the offsets in a single plane.

In the ASME Y14.3M standard, an Aligned Section occurs when features lend themselves to an angular change in the direction of the cutting plane. The bent cutting plane and features rotate into a plane perpendicular to the line of sight of the sectional view. Create an Aligned Section with a sketched line.

Activity: COVERPLATE Drawing-Offset Section View and Aligned Section View

Display the Origin and Temporary Axes on Sheet1.
453) Click **View**; check **Origins** from the Menu bar menu.

454) Click **View**; check **Temporary Axes** from the Menu bar menu.

Select the view.
455) Click inside the **Front view** boundary.

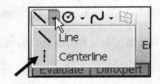

Sketch an open contour with 5 connecting center line segments.
456) Click **Centerline** ¦ from the Sketch toolbar.

457) Position the **mouse pointer** on the circumference of the upper left Cbore. The center point is displayed.

458) Drag the **mouse pointer** directly to the left. A blue dashed line, aligned with the center point is displayed.

459) Click the **start point** to the left of the vertical profile line.

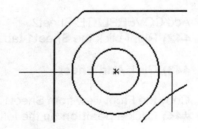

460) Drag the mouse pointer over the **circumference** of the Bore to display the center point.

461) Sketch a **vertical centerline** to the left of the Bore circle.

462) Sketch a **horizontal centerline** through the center of the Bore.

463) Drag the mouse **pointer** over the circumference of the lower right Cbore to display the center point.

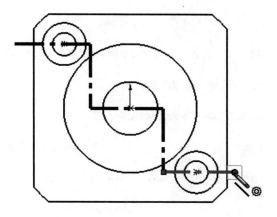

464) Sketch a **vertical centerline**. Sketch a horizontal centerline.

465) Place the **end point** of the last line segment to the right of the vertical profile line.

Add Relations to the Center points.
466) Click **Point** ✳ from the Sketch toolbar. The

Point ✳ icon is displayed.

467) Click the center point of the **top left circle** and the **bottom right circle**.

468) Right-click **Select** to deselect the Point Sketch toolbar.

469) Click the **center point** of the left circle.

470) Hold the **Ctrl** key down.

471) Click the **first horizontal line**.

472) Release the **Ctrl** key.

473) Click **Coincident**.

474) Click the **center point** of the right circle.

475) Hold the **Ctrl** key down.

476) Click the **third horizontal** line.

477) Release the **Ctrl** key.

478) Click **Coincident**.

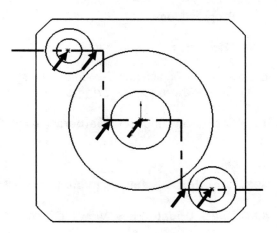

479) Click the **Origin**.

480) Hold the **Ctrl** key down.

481) Click the **second horizontal** line.

482) Release the **Ctrl** key.

483) Click **Coincident**.

484) Click **OK** ✔ from the Properties PropertyManager.

485) Select the five **Center line segments**.

Create the Offset Section view.
486) Click **Insert**, **Drawing View**, **Section** from the Menu bar menu or click Section View from the View Layout toolbar.

487) Click a **position** above the Front view as illustrated.

488) The section arrows point downward. If required, click **Flip direction**.

489) Click **OK** ✔ from the Section View A-A PropertyManager.

490) Click **Save**.

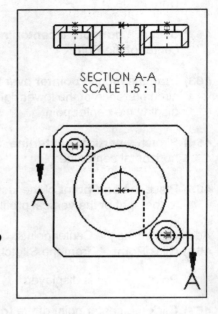

SECTION A-A
SCALE 1.5 : 1

Deactivate the Origins and Temporary Axes.
491) Click **View**; uncheck **Origins** from the Menu bar menu.

492) Click **View**; uncheck **Temporary Axes** from the Menu bar menu.

Modify the Edit Pull-down menu.
493) Click **Edit**, **Customize menu** from the Menu bar menu.

494) Check **Update View**. View the default settings.

🔅 Update the view if light hatching appears across the view boundary. Utilize Update View to update a single view. Utilize Update All Views or Rebuild to update all drawing views.

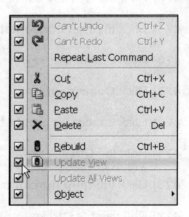

Add a Projected Right view.
495) Click inside the **Front view** boundary.

496) Click **Projected View** from the View Layout toolbar.

497) Click a **position** to the right of the Front view.

498) Click **Hidden Lines Removed**.

499) Click **OK** from the Projected View PropertyManager

Save the COVERPLATE drawing.

500) Click **Save**.

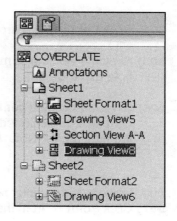

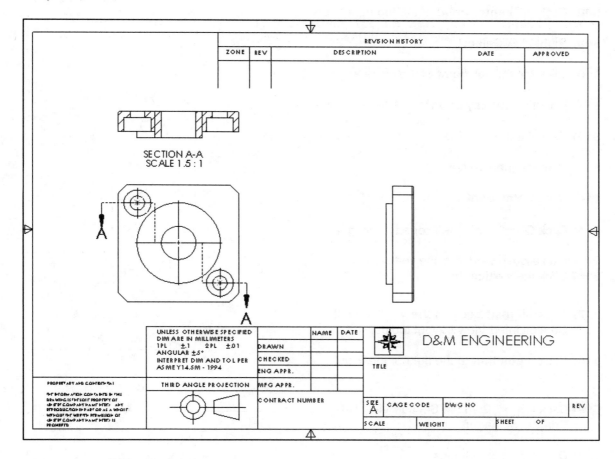

Return to COVERPLATE-Sheet2.
501) Click the **Sheet2** tab. Display the **Origins**.

Create an Aligned Section view.
502) Click inside the **Drawing View6** view boundary. The PropertyManager is displayed.

503) Click the **Sketch** tab from the CommandManager.

504) Click **Centerline** from the Sketch toolbar.

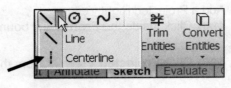

505) Sketch a **vertical centerline** through the bottom hole to the Origin.

506) Sketch an angled **centerline** from the Origin though the right hole as illustrated. The endpoint must extend beyond the right profile. Note: Delete the Center mark if required.

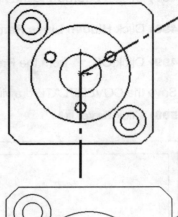

Add Relations to the center points.
507) Click **Point** ✳ from the Sketch toolbar.

508) Click the **center point** of the top right circle.

509) Right-click **Select**.

510) Click the **center point** of the circle.

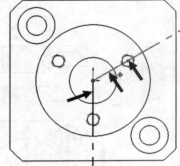

511) Hold the **Ctrl** key down.

512) Click the **angled line**.

513) Release the **Ctrl** key.

514) Click **Coincident**.

515) Click **OK** ✅ from the PropertyManager.

Project an aligned view from the vertical line.
516) Click the **vertical line**.

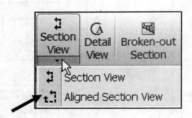

517) Click **Aligned Section View** ⌐ from the Consolidated View Layout toolbar.

518) Click a **position** to the right of the Front view.

519) Click **OK** ✅ from the Section View B-B PropertyManager.

520) Deactivate the Origins.

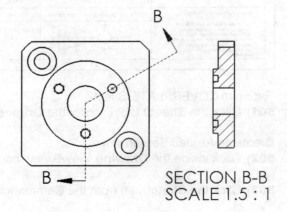

SECTION B-B
SCALE 1.5 : 1

Save the COVERPLATE drawing.
521) Click **Save** 💾.

Additional View Options and View Properties

There are additional options for Section views and Aligned Section views. When do you use a Section view versus an Aligned Section view? Answer: Utilize two sketch line segments for the Aligned Section view. Utilize one, three or more sketch line segments and arc segments for the Section view.

💡 Select a vertical or horizontal sketched line before you create the Aligned view. Otherwise, the bent sketched line creates the aligned view at an angle.

Create a Half Section view by sketching two perpendicular lines segments for the section line. The available Section view options are: *Partial section*, *Display only cut faces(s)*, *Auto hatching*, and *Display surface bodies*.

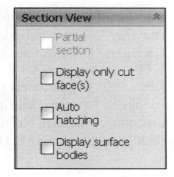

The Partial section option creates a portion of the Section view when the section line is smaller than the view geometry. The Display only cut faces(s) option shows only the surfaces cut by the section line in the Section view. The Auto hatching option displays the hatch pattern for the model material. The Display surface bodies option only displays the surface of the model.

The Right Projected view on Sheet 1 utilized the View tools to set the entire view to Hidden Lines Visible or Hidden Lines Removed.

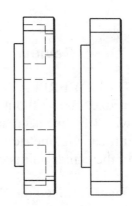

View Properties list the view type, model file and configuration name. The Show Hidden Edges option controls the display of a feature's hidden lines in a specific view.

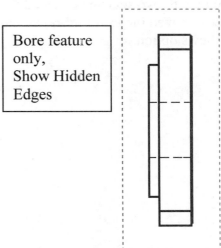

Bore feature only, Show Hidden Edges

As models become complex, hidden lines are difficult to distinguish. One technique is to create multiple views and display only specific features with hidden lines.

Example: Right-click Properties in the Right view, select Show Hidden Edges. Expand the Drawing FeatureManager. Expand Sheet1. Expand the Right view, Drawing View8. Click the Bore feature.

To display the Bore feature hidden edges, set the display mode option in the drawing view to Hidden Lines Removed.

More Information

Additional details on Offset Section, Aligned Section, Update Drawing Views, Configurations, Customizing menus, Show and Geometric Relations are available in SolidWorks help.

Keywords: Section view (Drawings, Aligned), Section lines (stepped), Update (Drawing views), Drawing (configurations), Customize (menus), Relations (geometric, add) and Show (hidden edges in drawing).

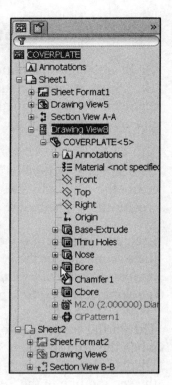

 **Review**

The COVERPLATE drawing consisted of two Sheets. Sheet1 utilized the Without Nose Holes Configuration. A sketched line with five line segments created the Offset Section view. You utilized Geometric relations to define the sketched line relative to the center points of the Cbore.

Sheet2 utilized the With Nose Holes Configuration. A sketched line with two segments created the Aligned Section view. You customized the Edit Pull-down menu by adding the Update Views option.

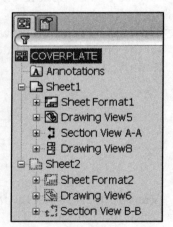

Multi-view Drawings - View Layout toolbar

The information in this section is provided in order to create additional Multi-view drawings and to understand the tools which are available in the View Layout toolbar. There are no step-by-step instructions in this section.

Multiple views represent the true shape of the part. The Model View tool selects a Named view from the part Orientation list. The default orientation is the Current Model view. The View Layout toolbar contains numerous tools to create Multiple view drawings. They are:

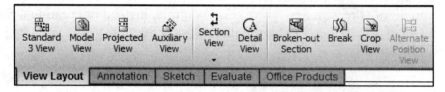

Standard 3 View: Provides the ability to create three related default Orthographic views of a part or assembly displayed at the same time.

Model View: Provides the ability to create a new drawing. Note: SolidWorks part and assembly documents support 3D annotations according to the ASME Y14.41-2003 standard. Annotation views are indicated by an A on the view icon.

Projection View: Provides the ability to create a Projected view from a previously defined Orthogonal view.

Auxiliary View: Provides the ability to create an Auxiliary view by selecting an angled edge from a previously defined view. An Auxiliary View is similar to a Projected view, but it is unfolded normal to a reference edge in an existing view.

Section View: Provides the ability to create a Section View cutting the Parent view with a section line. The Section view can be a straight cut section or an offset section defined by a stepped section line. The section line can also include Concentric arcs.

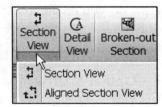

Aligned Section View: Provides the ability to create an Aligned Section view in a drawing through a model, or portion of a model, that is aligned with a selected section line segment. The aligned section view is similar to a Section view, but the section line for an aligned section comprises two or more lines connected at an angle.

Detail View: Provides the ability to create a Detail view in a drawing to display how a portion of a view, usually at an enlarged scale. This detail may be of an Orthographic view, a Non-planar (Isometric) view, a Section view, a Crop view, an Exploded assembly view, or another Detail view.

Broken-out Section View: A Broken-out Section is part of an existing drawing view, not a separate view. A closed profile, usually a Spline, defines the Broken-out section. Material is removed to a specified depth to expose inner details. Specify the depth by setting a number or by selecting geometry in a drawing view.

Break: Provides the ability to apply a broken (or interrupted) view in a drawing. Broken views make it possible to display the drawing view in a larger scale on a smaller size drawing sheet. Note: Reference dimensions and model dimensions associated with the broken area reflect the actual model values.

Crop view: You can crop any drawing view except a Detail View, a view from which a Detail View has been created, or an Exploded view. A Crop view can save steps because you do not create a new view. For example, instead of creating a Section View and then a Detail View, then hiding the unnecessary Section View, you can just crop the Section View directly.

Alternative Position view: Provides the ability to superimpose one drawing view precisely on another. The Alternate Position is displayed by default with phantom lines. Alternate Position Views are often used to show the range of motion of an assembly.

How do you create a single view drawing? Answer: Create the drawing by using a Named view with the Model view tool or apply the View Palette. Use a Parametric note to represent material thickness from the Annotation toolbar.

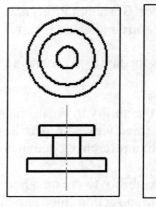 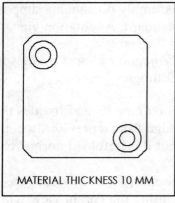

MATERIAL THICKNESS 10 MM

2 View Drawing   1 View Drawing

How do you create a two view drawing? Answer: There are three options:

- **Option 1**: Create the Standard views: Front, Top, and Right. Hide one of the views.

- **Option 2**: Create a Named view with the Model view tool. Insert a Projected view.

- **Option 3**: Apply the View Palette tool from the Task Pane and click and drag the required views.

Develop the part based on the assembly and symmetry. Orient the part based on its position in the assembly. Orient the part to build symmetry between features and sketch geometry. Create a new drawing for the assembly and part before these documents are complete. Utilize the drawing to understand assembly layout, interference and part fabrication.

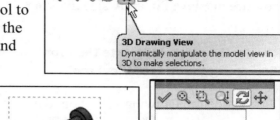

Use the Model view tool, Rotate view tool, 3D Drawing View tool and the Projection view tool to orient the part in a fabrication drawing. Select the view orientation that minimizes hidden lines and outlines the profile of the feature. The ASME Y14.3M standard defines other view types not required in this chapter. These views are applied to different types of drawings.

Auxiliary View

A Primary Auxiliary view: VIEW A is aligned and adjacent to the angled edge of the principle Front view.

A Secondary Auxiliary view: VIEW B is aligned and adjacent to a Primary Auxiliary view, VIEW A. Select an edge in the Primary Auxiliary.

In SolidWorks, Secondary Auxiliary views are created from a Primary Auxiliary view. Use the Auxiliary View to create the Secondary Auxiliary view.

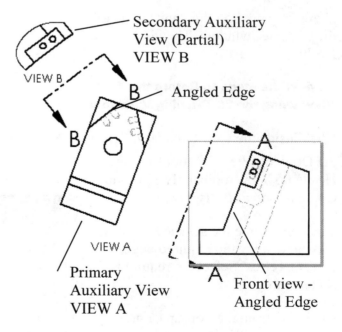

Rotate Drawing View

Views can be rotated to fit within the sheet boundary. The angle and direction of rotation is placed below the view title.

Example: A Front view and Projected Left view are displayed in an A-size drawing.

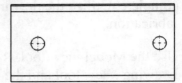

Review the steps to Rotate the Front View using the Rotate View tool

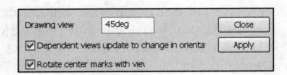

Click inside the Drawing view boundary.

Click Rotate View ↻ from the Heads-up View toolbar.

Enter the Drawing view angle from the Rotate Drawing View dialog box. Example: 45°.

The Left view depends on the Front view and rotates by 45°. Note: Select Rotate

View ↻ and drag the view boundary in the Graphics window. The view rotates freely.

Review the steps to Rotate the Front View using the 3D Drawing View tool

Click inside the view boundary. Select the 3D Drawing View ⊞ tool from the Heads-up View toolbar. The Pop-up Context toolbar is displayed.

Click and rotate the selected drawing view to display the required edge, face, or vertex. Select the required sketch entity.

Click OK from the Pop-up Context toolbar to exit 3D Drawing View.

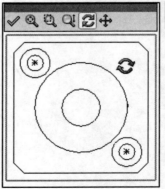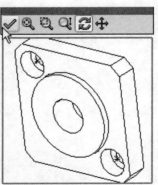

Steps to create a new Rotated View

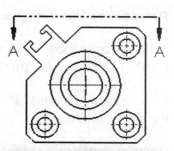

Select the Section View ⤵ tool. Sketch a straight section line above the Front view. Click the view boundary to rotate.

Click Rotate ⟳ from the Heads-up View toolbar. Enter the Drawing view angle from the Rotate Drawing View dialog box.

Break alignment of the rotated view to position the view in a new location. Right-click Alignment, click Break Alignment. Realign the view if required.

Add a note with view name, rotated angle and direction.
Example: VIEW A-A, ROTATED 90 CCW.

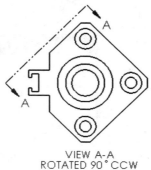

VIEW A-A
ROTATED 90° CCW

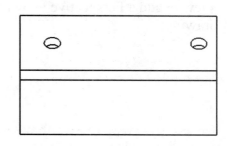

Perspective View in a part

A Perspective view is the view normally seen by the human eye. Parallel lines recede into the distance to a vanishing point.

Utilize **View**, **Display**, **Perspective** to create a perspective view of the active model.

Create a Perspective view short cut key. Press the space bar on your keyboard. The Orientation dialog box is displayed.

Click the New View ✤ tool. The Name View dialog box is displayed.

Enter Perspective for View name. Click OK. The Perspective view is added to the Orientation dialog box.

Utilize the Perspective view from the Heads-up View toolbar. Utilize Model View to add a Perspective view into a drawing.

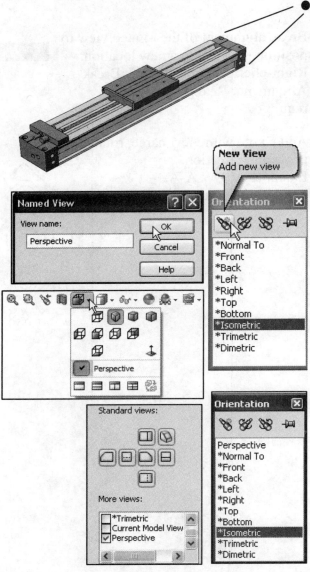

Alternative Position View

The Alternative Position 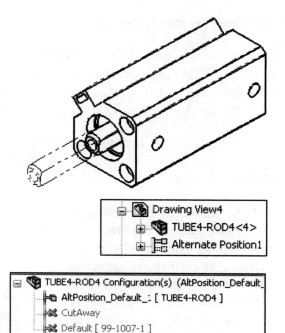 tool displays two configurations of an assembly in a drawing.

Click the Alternative Position tool from the View Layout toolbar. There are two options:

Define the Alternate Position in the drawing.

Create a configuration in the assembly and

reference the Alternate Position in the drawing.

Suppress mates in the assembly to create the Alternate Position. The Alternate Position displays the first configuration in dark visible lines and the second configuration in light gray line style. The FeatureManager displays the Alternate Position configuration in the drawing and in the assembly.

Empty View

The Empty view tool creates a blank view not tied to the part or assembly. Utilize Insert, Empty from the Menu bar menu to create the view.

Insert multiple sketched entities, dimensions, relations and annotations into an Empty view. Move, Hide, and Layer Properties apply to an Empty view.

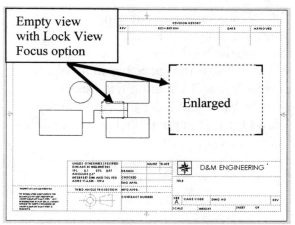

Utilize the Lock View Focus option from the Pop-up menu to link all inserted entities to the Empty view. Geometry inserted outside the view boundary maintains its relationship with the Empty view.

Relative To Model View

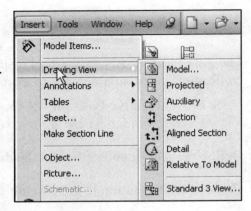

The Relative To Model tool defines an Orthographic view based on two orthogonal faces or places in the model. Utilize Tile Horizontal to display the drawing and the model.

Select the drawing for the active window. Select Insert, Drawing View, Relative To Model from the Menu bar menu.

The Graphics window displays the model. Select the First orientation from the model. This is the primary reference in the drawing. Select the Second orientation from the model. This is the secondary reference in the drawing.

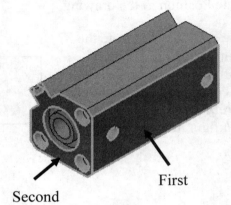

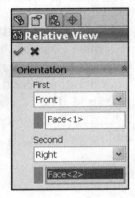

First

Second

Click OK from the Relative View PropertyManager to return to the drawing. Position the view on the drawing.

Name additional drawing views required in the part. Position the model in the graphics window. Press the space bar to invoke the current View Orientation list. Select Named View and enter the view name. Views created in the model are accessible in the drawing.

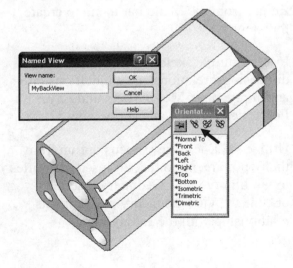

Chapter Summary

In this chapter, you displayed and created Standard, Isometric, Auxiliary, Section, Broken-out Section, Detail, and Half Section (Cut-away) views.

Feature dimensions in the part were positioned off the profile. Part configurations were reviewed. You obtained the ability create a new drawing, use SolidWorks Drawing tools and other related view commands.

You reviewed the Fundamentals of Orthographic projection for first angle and third angle projection systems. You created multi-sheet drawings from various part configurations. The three drawings that you created were:

1. TUBE drawing

2. ROD drawing

3. COVERPLATE drawing

The ROD drawing consisted of three Sheets. The TUBE drawing consisted of a single Sheet. The COVERPLATE drawing consisted of two Sheets. Practice creating drawings, views and more options in the project exercises. Insert dimensions from the part and create new annotations in Chapter 4.

Chapter Terminology

Alternate Position View: A drawing view superimposed in phantom lines on the original view. Utilized to show range of motion of an assembly.

Area hatch: Apply a crosshatch pattern or solid fill to a model face, to a closed sketch profile, or to a region bounded by a combination of model edges and sketch entities. Area hatch can be applied only in drawings.

Auxiliary view: An Auxiliary View is similar to a Projected View, but it is unfolded normal to a reference edge in an existing view.

Balloon: Labels parts in an assembly, typically including item numbers and quantity. In drawings, the item numbers are related to rows in a bill of materials (BOM). Create balloons in a drawing document or in a note.

Bill of Materials: A table inserted into a drawing to keep a record of the parts used in an assembly.

Broken out Section: A drawing view that exposes inner details of a drawing view by removing material from a closed profile, usually a spline.

CommandManager: The CommandManager is a Context-sensitive toolbar that dynamically updates based on the toolbar you want to access. By default, it has toolbars embedded in it based on the document type. When you click a tab below the Command Manager, it updates to display that toolbar. For example, if you click the **Sketches** tab, the Sketch toolbar is displayed.

ConfigurationManager: The ConfigurationManager is located on the left side of the SolidWorks window and provides the means to create, select, and view multiple configurations of parts and assemblies in an active document. You can split the ConfigurationManager and either display two ConfigurationManager instances, or combine the ConfigurationManager with the FeatureManager design tree, PropertyManager, or third party applications that use the panel.

Copy and Paste: Utilize copy/paste to copy views from one sheet to another sheet in a drawing or between different drawings.

Detail view: A portion of a larger view, usually at a larger scale than the original view. Create a detail view in a drawing to display a portion of a view, usually at an enlarged scale. This detail may be of an orthographic view, a non-planar (isometric) view, a section view, a crop view, an exploded assembly view, or another detail view.

Drawing: A 2D representation of a 3D part or assembly. The extension for a SolidWorks drawing file name is .SLDDRW. Drawing refers to the SolidWorks module used to insert, add, and modify views in an engineering drawing.

Edit Sheet: The drawing sheet contains two modes. Utilize the Edit Sheet command to insert views and dimensions.

Edit Sheet Format: The drawing sheet contains two modes. Utilize the Edit Sheet Format command to add or modify notes and Title block information. Edit in the Edit Sheet Format mode.

Empty View: An Empty View creates a blank view not tied to a part or assembly document.

Extruded Cut feature: Projects a sketch perpendicular to a Sketch plane to remove material from a part.

FeatureManager: The FeatureManager design tree located on the left side of the SolidWorks window provides an outline view of the active part, assembly, or drawing. This makes it easy to see how the model or assembly was constructed or to examine the various sheets and views in a drawing. The FeatureManager and the Graphics window are dynamically linked. You can select features, sketches, drawing views, and construction geometry in either pane.

First Angle Projection: Standard 3 Views are in either third angle or first angle projection. In first angle projection, the front view is displayed at the upper left and the other two views are the top and left views.

Handle: An arrow, square, or circle that you drag to adjust the size or position of an entity such as a view or dimension.

Heads-up View toolbar: A transparent toolbar located at the top of the Graphic window.

Layers: Simplifies a drawing by combining dimensions, annotations, geometry and components. Properties such as: display, line style, and thickness are assigned to a named layer.

Lock View Focus: Adds sketch entities and annotations to the selected locked view. Double-click the view to activate Lock View Focus. To unlock a view, right-click and select Unlock View Focus or double click outside the view boundary.

Lock View Position: Secures the view at its current position in the sheet. Right-click in the drawing view to Lock View Position. To unlock a view position, right-click and select Unlock View Position.

Lock Sheet Focus: Adds sketch entities and annotations to the selected sheet. Double-click the sheet to activate Lock Sheet Focus. To unlock a sheet, right-click and select Unlock Sheet Focus or double click inside the sheet boundary.

Menus: Menus provide access to the commands that the SolidWorks software offers. Menus are Context-sensitive and can be customized through a dialog box.

Model: 3D solid geometry in a part or assembly document. If a part or assembly document contains multiple configurations, each configuration is a separate model.

Mouse Buttons: The left, middle, and right mouse buttons have distinct meanings in SolidWorks. Use the middle mouse button to rotate and Zoom in/out on the part or assembly document.

Model View: A specific view of a part or assembly. Standard named views are listed in the view orientation dialog box such as isometric or front. Named views can be user-defined name for a specific view.

Origin: The model origin is displayed in blue and represents the (0,0,0) coordinate of the model. When a sketch is active, a sketch origin is displayed in red and represents the (0,0,0) coordinate of the sketch. Dimensions and relations can be added to the model origin, but not to a sketch origin.

Parent View: A Parent view is an existing view in which other views are dependent on.

Projected View: Projected views are created for Orthogonal views using one of the following tools: Standard 3 View, Model View, or the Projected View tool from the View Layout toolbar.

Relative view: The Relative View defines an Orthographic view based on two orthogonal faces or places in the model.

Section line: A line or centerline sketched in a drawing view to create a section view.

Section view: Create a Section View in a drawing by cutting the Parent view with a section line. The section view can be a straight cut section or an offset section defined by a stepped section line. The section line can also include concentric arcs.

Sheet Format: A document that contains the following: page size and orientation, standard text, borders, logos, and Title block information. Customize the sheet format to save time. The extension for the sheet format filename is .SLDDRT.
Sheet: A page in a drawing document.

Spline: A sketched 2D or 3D curve defined by a set of control points.

Standard views: The three orthographic projection views, Front, Top and Right positioned on the drawing according to First angle or Third angle projection.

Suppress: Removes an entity from the display and from any calculations in which it is involved. You can suppress features, assembly components, and so on. Suppressing an entity does not delete the entity; you can unsuppress the entity to restore it.

System Feedback: Feedback is provided by a symbol attached to the cursor arrow indicating your selection. As the cursor floats across the model, feedback is provided in the form of symbols riding next to the cursor.

Third Angle Projection: Standard 3 Views are in either third angle or first angle projection. In third angle projection, the default front view from the part or assembly is displayed at the lower left, and the other two views are the top and right views.

Toolbars: The toolbar menus provide shortcuts enabling you to access the most frequently used commands. Toolbars are Context-sensitive and can be customized through a dialog box.

View Palette: Use the View Palette, located in the Task Pane, to insert drawing views. It contains images of standard views, annotation views, section views, and flat patterns (sheet metal parts) of the selected model. You can drag views onto the drawing sheet to create a drawing view.

Questions:

1. Name the three default Reference Planes: _____, _____ and
    _____.

2. Identify the six principle drawing views in Orthographic Projection:

    _____, _____, _____, _____,

    _____, _____.

3. Name the two Orthographic projection systems: _____,
    _____ .

4. A drawing contains multiple _____ of a part.

5. True or False. Delete the part when a drawing is complete.

6. True of False. All drawings contain a single part configuration.

7. A Design Table is inserted into two document types. Identify the two documents.

8. Describe the difference between View properties and Sheet properties.

9. Identify the tool from the View Layout toolbar that is used to browse and create a view in a drawing.

10. Describe the procedure to copy a view from one sheet to another sheet in the same drawing.

11. True or False. Drawing Layers exist in a SolidWorks drawing.

12. Identify the command used to change the Scale of a Detailed view.

13. Describe the procedure to display internal features, "view" of a part in a drawing.

14. You created a multi-sheet drawing. On the first sheet, the correct Sheet format is displayed. On the second sheet, an incorrect Sheet format is displayed. Identify the procedure to modify the Sheet Properties to display the correct Sheet format.

15. The Alternative Position view tool is located in the View Layout toolbar. Identify the menu location to find additional information on the Alternative Position view tool.

16. Identify the following View Layout tools:

A　　B　　C　　D　　E　　F　　G　　H　　I

Exercises:

Exercise 3.1: FLATBAR - 3 HOLE Drawing

Note: Dimensions are enlarged for clarity. Utilize inch, millimeter, or dual dimensioning.

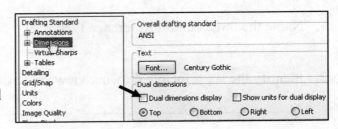

- Create the ANSI-IPS Third Angle Projection FLATBAR - 3HOLE drawing. First create the part from the drawing - then create the drawing. Use the default A (ANSI)-Landscape Sheet Format/Size.

- Insert a Shaded Isometric view. No Tangent Edges displayed.

- Insert a Front and Top view. Insert dimensions. Insert 3X - EQ. SP. Insert the Company and Third Angle Projection icon. Add a Parametric Linked Note for MATERIAL THICKNESS. Note: All needed icons are located in the Chapter 3 Homework folder on the CD. Copy the folder to your hard drive.

- Hide the Thickness dimension in the Top view. Insert needed Centerlines.

- Insert Custom Properties for Material (2014 Alloy), DRAWNBY, DRAWNDATE, COMPANYNAME, etc.

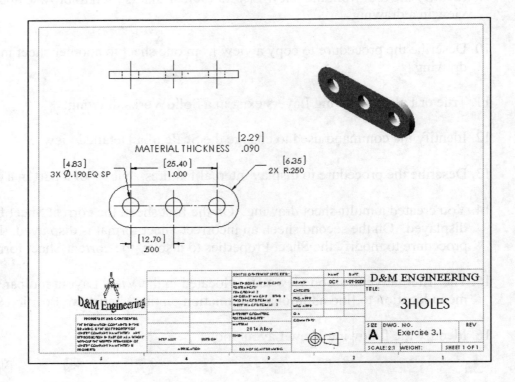

Exercise 3.2: CYLINDER Drawing

Create the ANSI - IPS - Third Angle CYLINDER drawing.

- First create the part from the drawing - then create the drawing. Use the default A (ANSI)-Landscape Sheet Format/Size.

- Insert the Front and Right view as illustrated. Insert dimensions. Think about the proper view for your dimensions!

- Insert Company and Third Angle projection icons. The icons are available in the homework folder. Note: All needed icons are located in the Chapter 3 Homework folder on the CD. Copy the folder to your hard drive.

- Insert needed Centerlines and Center Marks. Insert Custom Properties: Material, Description, DrawnBy, DrawnDate, CompanyName, etc. Note: Material is AISI 1020.

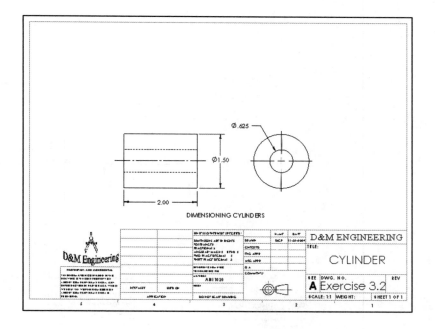

- Utilize the Mass Properties tool from the Evaluate toolbar to calculate the volume and mass of the CYLINDER part. Set decimal places to 4.

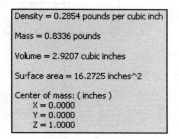

Density = 0.2854 pounds per cubic inch

Mass = 0.8336 pounds

Volume = 2.9207 cubic inches

Surface area = 16.2725 inches^2

Center of mass: (inches)
   X = 0.0000
   Y = 0.0000
   Z = 1.0000

Exercise 3.3: PRESSURE PLATE Drawing

Create the ANSI - IPS - Third Angle PRESSURE PLATE drawing.

- First create the part from the drawing - then create the drawing. Use the default A-Landscape Sheet Format/Size.

- Insert the Front and Right view as illustrated. Insert dimensions. Think about the proper view for your dimensions!

- Insert Company and Third Angle projection icons. The icons are available in the homework folder. Note: All needed icons are located in the Chapter 3 Homework folder on the CD. Copy the folder to your hard drive.

- Insert needed Centerlines and Center Marks.

- Insert Custom Properties: Material, Description, DrawnBy, DrawnDate, CompanyName, etc. Note: Material is 1060 Alloy.

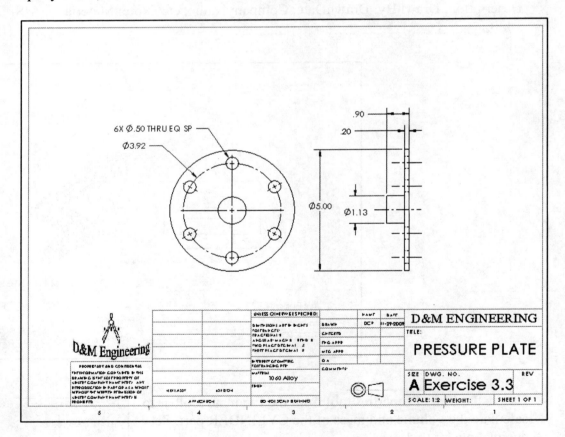

Exercise 3.4: **LINKS Assembly Drawing**

- Create the LINK assembly. Utilize three different FLATBAR configurations and a SHAFT-COLLAR. You are the designer. Create the four needed parts.

- Create the LINK assembly drawing as illustrated. Use the default A-Landscape Sheet Format/Size.

- Insert Company and Third Angle projection icons. The icons are available in the homework folder. Remove all Tangent Edges. Note: All needed icons are located in the Chapter 3 Homework folder on the CD. Copy the folder to your hard drive.

- Insert Custom Properties: Description, DrawnBy, DrawnDate, CompanyName, etc.

- Insert a Bill of Materials as illustrated with Balloons.

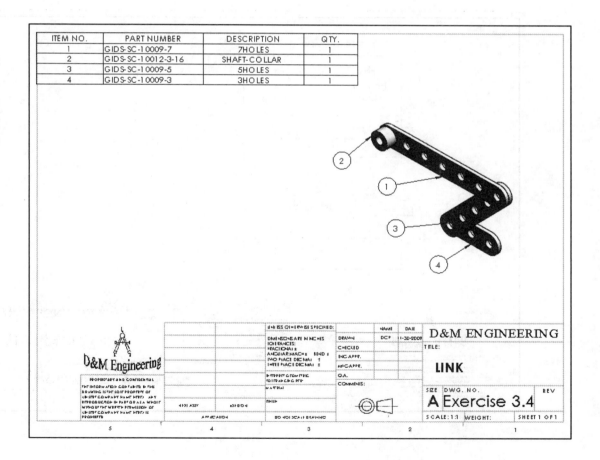

ITEM NO.	PART NUMBER	DESCRIPTION	QTY.
1	GIDS-SC-10009-7	7HOLES	1
2	GIDS-SC-10012-3-16	SHAFT-COLLAR	1
3	GIDS-SC-10009-5	5HOLES	1
4	GIDS-SC-10009-3	3HOLES	1

Exercise 3.5: PLATE-1 Drawing

Create the ANSI - MMGS - Third Angle PLATE-1 drawing.

- First create the part from the drawing - then create the drawing. Use the default A-Landscape Sheet Format/Size.

- Insert the Front and Right view as illustrated. Insert dimensions. Think about the proper view for your dimensions!

- Insert Company and Third Angle projection icons. The icons are available in the homework folder.

- Insert needed Centerlines and Center Marks.

- Insert Custom Properties: Material, Description, DrawnBy, DrawnDate, CompanyName, etc. Note: Material is 1060 Alloy.

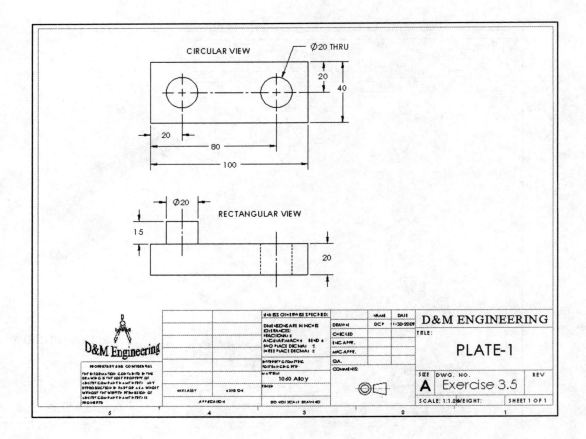

Exercise 3.6: FLATE-PLATE Drawing

Create the ANSI - IPS - Third Angle PLATE-1 drawing.

- First create the part from the drawing - then create the drawing. Use the default A-Landscape Sheet Format/Size. Remove all Tangent Edges.

- Insert the Front, Top, Right and Isometric view as illustrated. Insert dimensions. Think about the proper view for your dimensions!

- Insert Company and Third Angle projection icons. The icons are available in the homework folder. Note: All needed icons are located in the Chapter 3 Homework folder on the CD. Copy the folder to your hard drive.

- Insert needed Centerlines and Center Marks.

- Insert Custom Properties: Material, Description, DrawnBy, DrawnDate, CompanyName, Hole Annotation, etc. Note: Material is 1060 Alloy

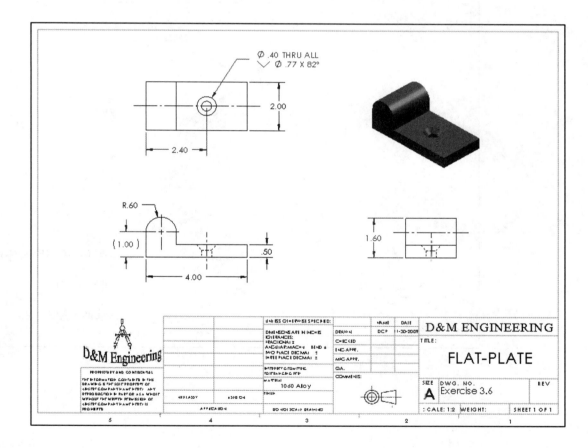

Exercise 3.7: LINKAGE-2 Drawing

- Create a new drawing named, LINKAGE-2.

- Insert an Isometric view, shaded view of the LINKAGE-2 Assembly. The LINKAGE-2 Assembly is located in the Chapter 3 Homework folder on the CD.

- Define the PART NO. Property and the DESCRIPTION Property for the AXLE, FLATBAR- 9HOLE, FLATBAR - 3HOLE and SHAFT COLLAR.

- Save the LINKAGE-2 assembly to update the properties. Return to the LINKAGE-2 Drawing. Insert a Bill of Materials with Auto Balloons as illustrated.

- Insert the Company and Third Angle Projection icon. Insert Custom Properties for DRAWNBY, DRAWNDATE and COMPANYNAME

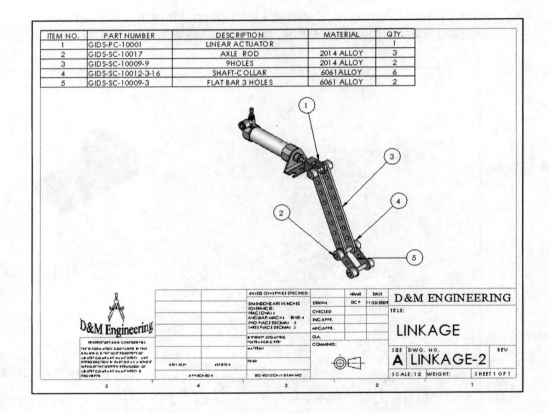

ITEM NO.	PART NUMBER	DESCRIPTION	MATERIAL	QTY.
1	GIDS-PC-10001	LINEAR ACTUATOR		1
2	GIDS-SC-10017	AXLE ROD	2014 ALLOY	3
3	GIDS-SC-10009-9	9HOLES	2014 ALLOY	2
4	GIDS-SC-10012-3-16	SHAFT-COLLAR	6061 ALLOY	6
5	GIDS-SC-10009-3	FLAT BAR 3 HOLES	6061 ALLOY	2

Exercise 3.8: eDrawing

Create an eDrawing of the LINKAGE-2 drawing. A SolidWorks eDrawing is a compressed document that does not require the corresponding part or assembly. SolidWorks eDrawing is animated to display multiple views and dimensions. Review the eDrawing On-line Help for additional functionality.

- Click Publish eDrawing File from the Menu bar menu.

- Click the Play button.

- Click the Stop button.

- Save the LINKAGE-2 eDrawing.

- Return to the LINKAGE2 drawing.

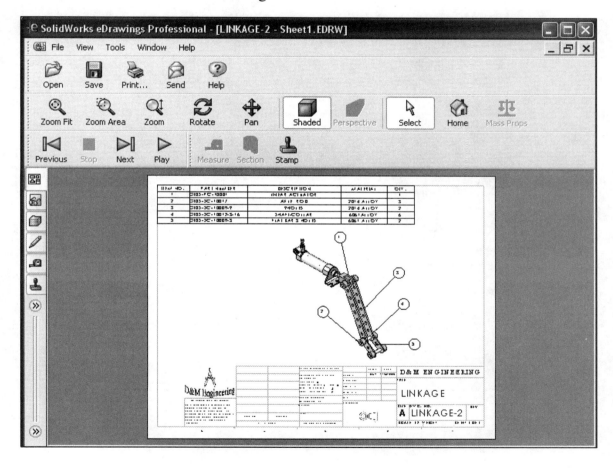

Notes:

Chapter 4

Fundamentals of Detailing

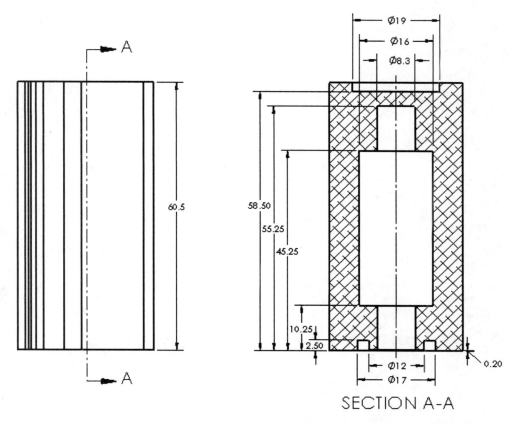

SECTION A-A

Below are the desired outcomes and usage competencies based on the completion of this Chapter. Note: Drawing refers to the SolidWorks module used to insert, add, and modify views in an engineering drawing. Detailing refers to the SolidWorks module used to insert, add, and modify dimensions and notes in an engineering drawing.

Desired Outcomes:	Usage Competencies:
Two Detail drawings: • TUBE drawing with detailing • COVERPLATE drawing with detailing	• Ability to insert, add and modify dimensions.
	• An understanding of inserting and adding Annotations.
	• Knowledge of dimensioning standards.

Notes:

Chapter 4 - Fundamentals of Detailing

Chapter Objective

Details are the drawing dimensions and notes required to document part features. Create two detailed drawings:

- TUBE

- COVERPLATE

On the completion of this chapter, you will be able to:

- Insert and modify drawing view dimensions.

- Add and address Annotations.

- Insert Hole Callouts, Center Marks, and Centerlines.

- Use various methods to move, hide, show, suppress, and un-suppress drawing views.

- Apply the ASME Y14.5 standard for Types of Decimal Dimensions.

- Add Modifying Symbols and Hole Symbols.

- Utilize the following SolidWorks tools and commands: *Smart Dimension, Model Items, Autodimension, Note, Balloon, AutoBalloon, Surface Finish, Weld Symbol, Geometric Tolerance, Datum Feature, Datum Target, Hole Callout, Area Hatch/Fill, Block, Center Mark* and *Centerline*.

Chapter Overview

You inserted and added views for the TUBE, ROD and COVERPLATE drawings in Chapter 3. In this Chapter, you will insert, add, and modify dimensions and obtain an understanding of inserting and adding various annotations in a drawing.

Details are the drawing dimensions and annotations required to document part features. There are two types of dimensions: Inserted dimensions and Added dimensions. Inserted dimensions are feature dimensions.

Feature dimensions are created in the part and inserted into the drawing. Inserted dimensions are associative. Modify a dimension in the drawing and the feature dimension is modified in the part.

Added drawing dimensions are called Reference dimensions. Reference dimensions are driven by part features. Driven dimensions are called Reference dimensions. You cannot edit a Driven or Reference dimension.

Add annotations such as: Notes, Hole Callouts, and Center Marks to the drawing document from the View Layout toolbar.

The design intent of this project is to work with dimensions inserted from parts and to incorporate them into the drawings. Explore methods to move, hide, and add dimensions to adhere to a drawing standard.

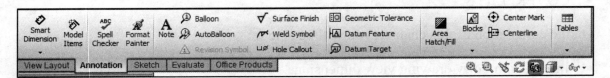

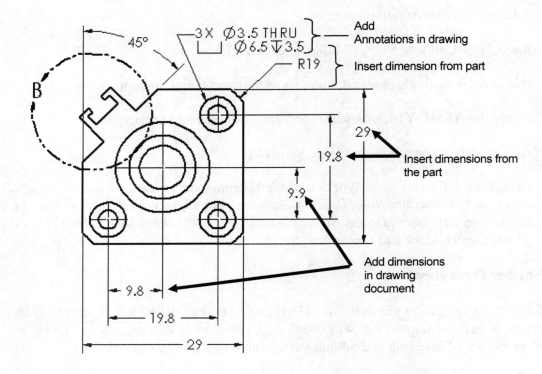

Work between multiple parts, drawings, and sheets. Add annotations to the drawing that reference part dimensions.

A goal of this book is to expose various SolidWorks design tools and features. The most direct way may not be always shown.

💡 There are other solutions to the dimensioning schemes illustrated in this chapter. The TUBE, COVERPLATE, and exercise drawings are sample drawings; they are not complete. A drawing requires tolerances, materials, Revision Tables, Engineering Change Orders, and other notes prior to production and release.

Review a hypothetical "worse case" drawing situation. You just inserted dimensions from a part into a drawing. The dimensions, extensions lines and arrows are not in the correct locations. How can you improve the position of these details? Answer: Apply an engineering drawing standard.

No:	Situation:
1	Extension line crosses dimension line. Dimensions not evenly spaced.
2	Largest dimension placed closest to profile.
3	Leader lines overlapping
4	Extension line crossing arrowhead.
5	Arrow gap too large.
6	Dimension pointing to feature in another view. Missing dimension – inserted into Detail view (not shown).
7	Dimension text over centerline, too close to profile.
8	Dimension from other view – leader line too long.
9	Dimension inside section lines.
10	No visible gap.
11	Arrows overlapping text.
12	Incorrect decimal display with whole number (millimeter), no specified tolerance.

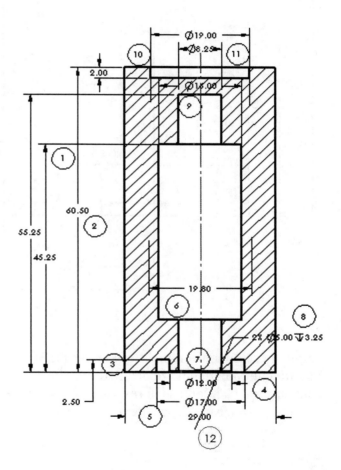

💡 Dimensions are displayed in millimeters in this chapter.

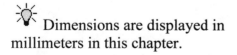

The ASME Y14.5M standard defines an engineering drawing standard. Review the twelve changes made to the drawing to meet the standard.

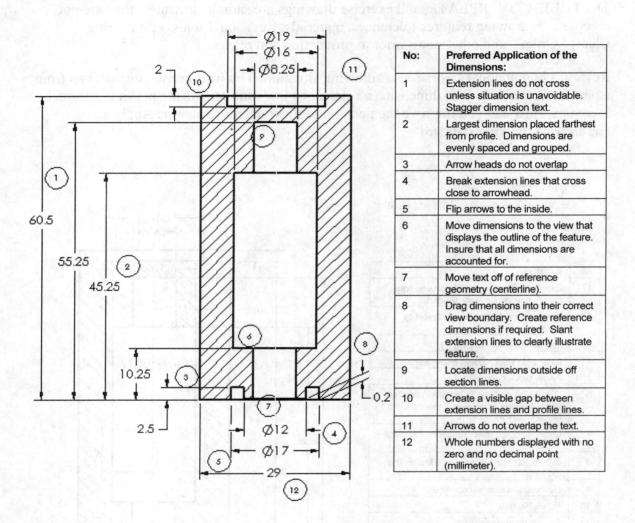

No:	Preferred Application of the Dimensions:
1	Extension lines do not cross unless situation is unavoidable. Stagger dimension text.
2	Largest dimension placed farthest from profile. Dimensions are evenly spaced and grouped.
3	Arrow heads do not overlap
4	Break extension lines that cross close to arrowhead.
5	Flip arrows to the inside.
6	Move dimensions to the view that displays the outline of the feature. Insure that all dimensions are accounted for.
7	Move text off of reference geometry (centerline).
8	Drag dimensions into their correct view boundary. Create reference dimensions if required. Slant extension lines to clearly illustrate feature.
9	Locate dimensions outside off section lines.
10	Create a visible gap between extension lines and profile lines.
11	Arrows do not overlap the text.
12	Whole numbers displayed with no zero and no decimal point (millimeter).

Apply these dimension practices to the TUBE, COVERPLATE, and exercise drawings. Manufactured parts utilize detailed drawings. A mistake on a drawing can cost your company substantial loss in revenue. The mistake could result in a customer liability lawsuit. In other words, as the designer, dimension and annotate your parts clearly to avoid common problems.

Leading zeros, trailing zeros, and number of zeros to the right of the decimal point are important in dimension and tolerance display.

There are different rules for the display of decimal dimensions and tolerances based on millimeter and inch units. Review the below table.

TYPES of DECIMAL DIMENSIONS (ASME Y14.5M)			
Description:	**UNITS: MM**	**Description:**	**UNITS: INCH**
Dimension is less than 1mm. Zero precedes the decimal point.	0.9 0.95	Dimension is less than 1 inch. Zero is not used before the decimal point.	.5 .56
Dimension is a whole number. Display no decimal point. Display no zero after decimal point.	19	Express dimension to the same number of decimal places as its tolerance. Add zeros to the right of the decimal point. If the tolerance is expressed to 3 places, then the dimension contains 3 places to the right of the decimal point.	1.750
Dimension exceeds a whole number by a decimal fraction of a millimeter. Display no zero to the right of the decimal.	11.5 11.51		

TOLERANCE DISPLAY FOR METRIC AND INCH DIMENSIONS (ASME Y14.5M)		
Description:	**UNITS: MM**	**UNITS: INCH**
Dimensions less than 1	0.5	.5
Unilateral Tolerance	$36^{\,0}_{-0.5}$	$1.417^{+.005}_{-.000}$
Bilateral Tolerance	$36^{+0.25}_{-0.50}$	$1.417^{+.010}_{-.020}$
Limit Tolerance	14.50 11.50	.571 .463

The SolidWorks dimensioning standard is set to ANSI. Trailing zeroes is set to Smart. The primary unit is millimeters in this chapter.

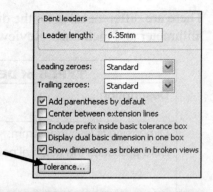

SolidWorks displays a leading zero for millimeter dimensions less than one. SolidWorks displays no decimal point and no zero after the decimal point for whole number dimensions.

Click **Options**, **Document Properties** tab, **Dimensions** folder, **Tolerance** [Tolerance...] button to control tolerance type.

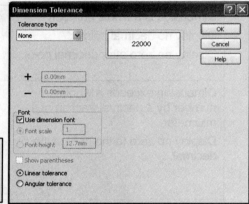

Click **Options**, **Document Properties** tab, **Dimensions** folder to address precision.

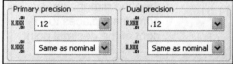

Access the Tolerance/Precision option for an active drawing from the Dimension PropertyManager.

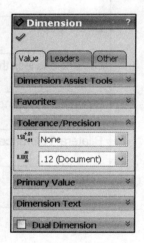

Modify individual millimeter dimensions from the Dimension PropertyManager if the decimal fraction ends in a zero.

- Example 1: Set Precision Primary Units to .12 places. The drawing dimension displays 0.55. The number of decimal places is two. No change is required.

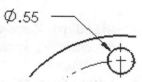

- Example 2: The drawing dimension displays 0.50. Control individual dimension precision through the Dimension Properties Tolerance/Precision text box.

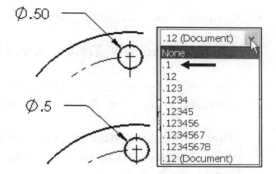

Modify the dimension Primary Units display to .X, (one decimal place). The drawing dimension displays 0.5.

General tolerance values apply to all dimensions on a drawing except reference dimensions and material stock sizes. Tolerance values are displayed with 1, 2 and or 3 decimal places.

Values differ for machined parts, plastic parts, sheet metal parts, castings and other manufacturing processes.

```
UNLESS OTHERWISE SPECIFIED
DIM ARE IN MILLIMETERS
1PL      ±0.2      2PL      ±0.05
ANGULAR ±.5°
INTERPRET DIM AND TOL PER
ASME Y14.5M - 1994
```

- Example: 1PL is ±0.2. The dimension 0.9 has a tolerance value of ±0.2. The feature dimension range is 0.7mm - 1.1mm. The tolerance equals 1.1mm - 0.7mm = 0.4mm.

- Example: 2PL is ±0.05. The dimension 0.95 has a tolerance value of ±0.05. The feature dimension range is 0.90mm - 1.00mm. The tolerance equals 1.00mm - 0.90mm = 0.10mm.

The Document Property, Leading zeroes has three options:

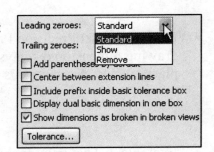

- **Standard**: Zeros are displayed based on the dimensioning standard.

- **Show**: Zeros before decimal points are displayed.

- **Remove**: Zeros do not displayed.

The Document Property, Trailing zeroes has four options:

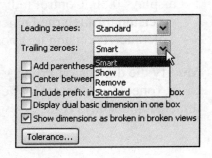

- **Smart**: Trailing zeros are trimmed for whole metric values. (Conforms to ANSI and ISO standards.)

- **Show**: Dimensions have trailing zeros up to the number of decimal places specified in Options, Document Properties tab, Units.

- **Remove**: All trailing zeros are removed.

- **Standard**: Trims trailing zeroes to the ASME Y14.5M-1994 standard.

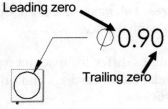

Trailing zeroes, Smart option removes all zeros to the right of the decimal point for whole numbers. The Show option displays the number of zeros equal to the number of places specified in the Units option. The Remove option displays no trailing zeros to the right of the dimension value. The Standard option trims trailing zeroes to the ASME Y14.5M-1994 standard.

Set the Trailing zeroes option to Smart. Control individual dimensions with the Primary Units Precision option. The Trailing zeroes option does not affect tolerance display. The Tolerance/Precision display for a drawing is located in the Dimension PropertyManager. In the drawing, the Tolerance/Precision box determines specific display for individual dimensions.

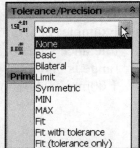

Tolerance Type

A Tolerance type is selected from the available drop down list in the Dimension PropertyManager. The list is dynamic. A few examples of Tolerance type display are listed below:

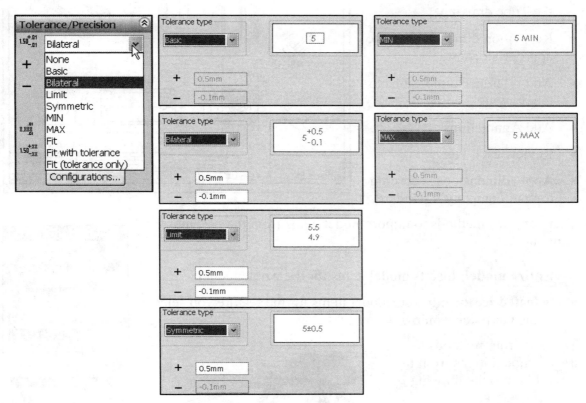

- Example: View the illustrated model. Review the Tolerance, Precision, and Dimension Text in the model.

- 2X Ø.190 - Two holes with a diameter of .190. Precision is set to three decimal places.

- 2X R.250 - Two corners with a radius of .250. Precision is set to three decimal places.

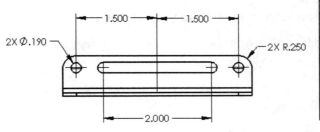

TUBE Drawing-Detailing

Detailing the TUBE drawing
requires numerous steps.
Example:

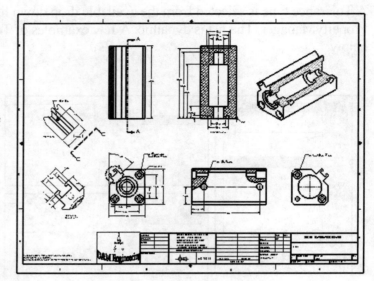

- Insert part dimensions into
  the Tube drawing.

- Reposition dimensions to the
  appropriate view.

- Add reference dimensions to
  the drawing.

- Add Annotations.

- Review each view.

- Apply dimensions according
  to your company's standard.

There are two methods to import model items from the part into the
drawing:

- **Entire model**: Inserts model items for the whole model.

- **Selected feature**: Inserts model items for the feature you select
  in the Graphics window.

There are four methods to
import model items from the
assembly into the drawing.

- **Entire model**: Inserts
  model items for the
  whole model.

- **Selected feature**: Inserts
  model items for the
  feature you select in the
  Graphics window.

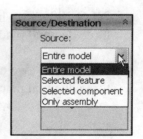

- **Selected component**:
  Inserts model items for
  the component you select in the Graphics window.

- **Only assembly**: Inserts model items for assembly features only.

How do you reposition numerous dimensions and annotations? Answer: One view at a time. Use the following tips:

- Hide views temporarily when not in use.

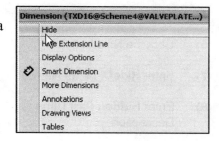

- Hide dimensions that are not longer required. Utilize a layer to turn on\off dimensions. Utilize Hide\Show to control dimension display. Do not delete them. It takes less time to show a hidden dimension that to create one.

- Temporarily move views to see dimensions on top of other views.

- Deactivate the dimension parenthesis when creating baseline dimensions.

- Review each feature to determine if all feature dimensions and Geometric relations are accounted for in the appropriate view.

- Review each view for center marks, center lines, hole callouts and other annotations.

Work with layers to control the display of dimensions. Create the two new layers named; Details and HideDims. Insert dimensions from the part on the Details layer. Add dimensions and annotations on the Details layer. Move dimensions inserted from the part and not required to detail the drawing to the HideDims layer. The HideDims layer is turned off.

SolidWorks truncates layer names to 26 characters, converts lower case letters to upper case letters and replaces typed spaces in layer names with underscores. Review the view names in the FeatureManager before you Insert Dimensions. Dimensions are displayed in a specific order. First, SolidWorks imports dimensions into all section views and detail views. Next, the dimensions are positioned in the standard views.

Activity: TUBE Drawing-Detailing

Open the TUBE drawing.

1) Click **Open** 📂 from the Menu bar toolbar.

2) Select **Drawing** for file type.

3) Double-click **TUBE**. Uncheck the **Dual dimensions display** box in the Document Properties box.

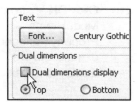

Display the Layer toolbar.

4)   Check **View**, **Toolbars**, **Layer** from the Menu bar menu.

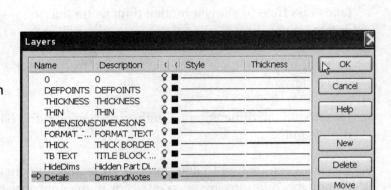

Create a new layer

5)   Click the **Layer Properties** 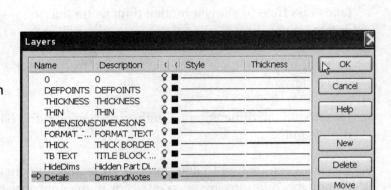 icon.

6)   Click the **New** button.

7)   Enter **HideDims** for Name.

8)   Enter **Hidden Part Dims** for Description.

9)   Click the **Light Bulb** to turn the HideDims layer off. Select **Red** for Color. Click **OK**.

10)   Click the **New** button. Enter **Details** for Name.

11)   Enter **DimsandNotes** for Description. The Layer is On when the Light Bulb is yellow.

12)   Enter **Blue** for Color. Accept the default Style and Thickness. Click **OK**. Details layer is the current layer.

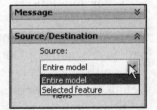

Insert dimensions for the entire model.

13)   Click a **position** inside the sheet boundary and outside any view boundary. Note: No Drawing view boundaries are selected.

14)   Click **Model Items** from the Annotation toolbar.

15)   Select **Entire model**. Accept the defaults.

16)   Click **OK** from the Model Items PropertyManager. The dimensions are displayed in blue.

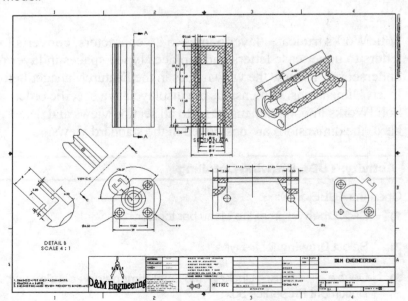

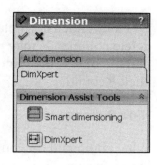

⛉ The illustrated dimensions may vary from your drawing. Import dimensions into the most appropriate view.

⛉ The Dimension PropertyManager provides the ability to dimension a drawing with Smart dimensioning or DimXpert.

Temporarily hide views when not in use.

17) Right-click inside the **Right view** boundary; Drawing View3.

18) Click **Hide**.

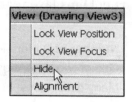

Hide dimensions from the Half Section Isometric view.

19) Click inside the **Half Section Isometric view** boundary.

20) Drag the **view** to the right, away from the Section view dimensions.

21) Click and drag the **dimension text** until you view each dimension.

22) Hold the **Ctrl** key down.

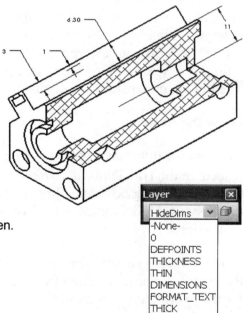

23) Click the **11**, **3**, **1** and **6.30** dimension text.

24) Release the **Ctrl** key.

25) Select the **HideDims** layer from the Dimension PropertyManager.

26) Click **OK** ✅ from the Dimension PropertyManager. The selected dimensions are hidden.

27) Select the **Details** layer from the Layer toolbar.

Save the TUBE drawing.

28) Click **Save** 💾 .

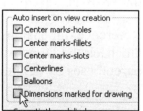

⛉ Marked dimensions can be inserted automatically as the views are created using the option **Tools, Options, Document Properties, Detailing, Auto insert on view creation**.

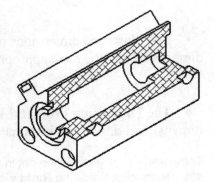

For dimensions placed on a hidden layer, hide and delete commands may not completely remove all of the graphic bits. If the dimensions are not erased completely, click Rebuild.

Hide Dimensions

What command do you select when dimensions are no longer required? Answer: There are two options: HideDims layer or the Hide command.

Number of Dimensions:	Command Sequence:
One or two dimensions	Select the dimensions. Right-click, Hide.
Many dimensions	Place the dimensions on the HideDims layer. Turn off the HideDims layer.

Hide dimensions versus delete dimensions. Use caution when deleting a dimension. You may require the dimension in the future. How do you restore the hidden dimensions? Answer: Utilize View, Hide/Show Annotations from the Menu bar menu. The hidden dimensions are displayed in a small box.

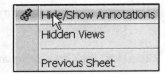

Show Dimensions

Click on the dimension text to display the Dimension PropertyManager. Dimensions placed on the HideDims layer remain turned off. To display the layer, click On from the Layers dialog box. The dimensions added to a drawing are called Reference dimensions. Model dimensions drive Reference dimensions.

Model dimensions are created in a part or an assembly. A Reference dimension cannot be changed. The dimension for the overall length and Stroke Chamber are defined from the Front reference plane. The part dimension scheme was the engineer's intent. As the detailer, define the dimensions to a base line. Hide the dimensions to avoid superfluous dimensions.

Reference dimensions may be displayed with parentheses. Uncheck the Dimensions Document Property, Add parentheses by default option to conserve design time.

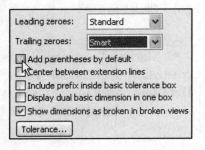

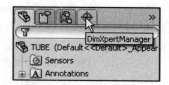

DimXpert applies dimensions in drawings so that manufacturing features, patterns, slots, pockets, etc. are fully-defined. Click the DimXpertManager tab or the DimXpert tab from the CommandManager to access the available DimXpert tools. DimXpert is part of the SWIFT family of features. DimXpert is explored later in the book.

The ASME Y14.5M-1994 standard uses parenthesis to represent an Overall and an Intermediate Reference dimension. Control the dimensions that contain a parenthesis to adhere to your company's drawing standard. Select Properties on the dimension text.

Uncheck the Display with parenthesis option to control the individual Reference dimensions.

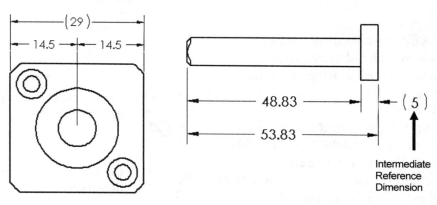

TUBE Detailing-Section View, Top View and Detail View

There are numerous techniques utilized to detail a view. Start with the Section view. The Model Items tool from the Annotate toolbar inserted the majority of the required dimensions into the Section view.

Move the Section view away from the Top view to view the dimensions. The Top view requires an overall vertical dimension. Modify the Precision of the dimension to one decimal place.

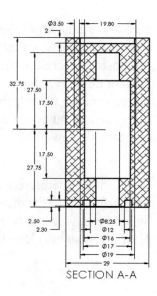

Place inserted part dimensions not required on
the HideDims layer. Insert a Baseline
Dimension for the vertical dimensions, modify
extension lines and center dimension text.
Move dimensions from the Section view to
the Front view.

There is a horizontal dimension
required to describe Front-
Detail1 in the Section view. The
Ø17 dimension was created in
the TUBE part.

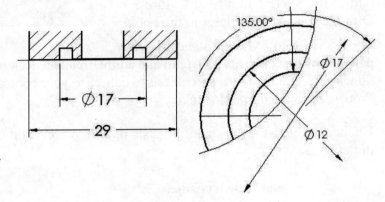

☀ Where is the dimension?
Answer: Look for the
dimension in the Detail view if
the Ø17 is not displayed in the
Section view.

SolidWorks inserts dimensions into the
Section view and Detail view. Then
SolidWorks inserts dimensions into the
remaining views.

The Ø17 text is located in the Detail view if
the Detail view contains the Front-Detail1
feature. A small part of the circle is
displayed in the Detail view. The leader line
is long and extends into the boundary of the
Front view.

Move the Ø17 text from the Detail view to
the Section view. Create a vertical
dimension referencing the bottom
horizontal edge. Use the Hole Callout to
dimension the Counterbore. Move
dimensions and add dimensions to the Front
and Detail view.

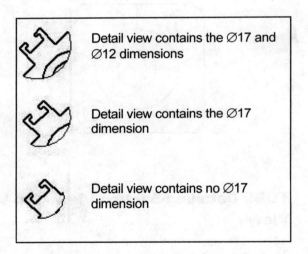

☀ Driven or Reference Dimensions can be
added directly to the drawing at any time to supplement or replace the model dimensions.
Several methods can be used including Standard dimensions, Baseline, Chamfer or Ordinate.
They can also be added using the Autodimension tool.

Activity: TUBE Drawing Detailing-Section View, Top View, and Detail View

Temporarily move the Section view.
29) Drag the **Section view** boundary to the right until the dimension text is off the Top view.

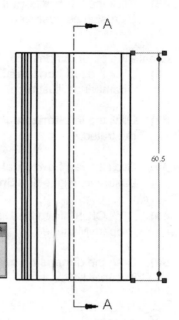

Create the overall depth dimension.
30) Click inside the **Top view** boundary. If needed, **hide** all dimensions in the Top view.

31) Click **Smart Dimension** ✎ from the Sketch toolbar.

32) Click the **right vertical line** in the Top view.

33) Position the **60.50** dimension text to the right of the Top view. A visible gap exists between the extension lines and the right vertical profile lines.

34) Select **.1** from the Primary Unit Precision text box. The 60.5 dimension text is displayed.

35) Click **OK** ✔ from the Dimension PropertyManager. View the results.

Hide the vertical dimensions in the Section view A-A as illustrated.
36) Click the **vertical dimensions**.

37) Select the **HideDims** layer.

38) Click **OK** ✔ from the Dimension PropertyManager.

Insert Baseline dimensions.
39) Select the **Details** layer from the Layer toolbar.

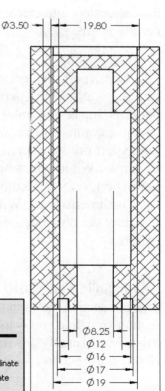

Create the first dimensions for the Stroke Chamber.
40) Click inside the **Section view A-A** view boundary.

41) Click **Smart Dimension** ✎ from the Sketch toolbar.

42) Right-click **More Dimensions**.

43) Click **Baseline**. The

Baseline ⊞ icon is displayed.

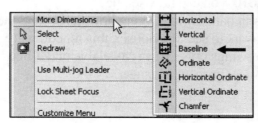

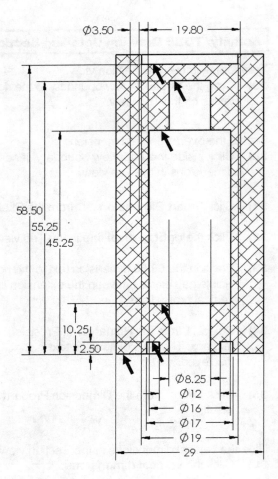

44) Click the **lower left horizontal line** of the Stroke Chamber as illustrated. Click the **left horizontal line** of the Nose as illustrated.

45) Click the **left horizontal line** of the Tube Extrusion as illustrated.

Create the other dimensions.
46) Click the **left horizontal line** of the Stroke Chamber as illustrated.

47) Click the **left horizontal line** of the Bore as illustrated.

48) Click the **left horizontal line** of the Cbore as illustrated. Right-click **Smart Dimension**.

49) Click **OK** ✅ from the Dimension PropertyManager.

50) Drag the **dimension text** to the left as illustrated.

🔅 All drawing views with dimensions require internal gaps between the visible feature line and extension lines. Zoom in on the dimension, click the dimension, and create the gap with the blue control points.

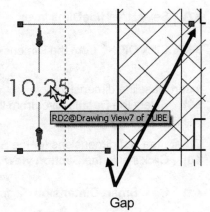

Gap

🔅 DimXpert differs from Autodimension in two key ways: DimXpert Recognizes patterns, linear and polar dimensions with instance counts and countersink holes, and DimXpert produces predictable results. Example: When you select an edge in DimXpert, only the feature represented by the edge is dimensioned. With autodimensioning, you may get unwanted dimensions to several features.

🔅 In SolidWorks 2010, you can now set the depth of section views in parts by specifying how far beyond the section view line you want to see. Previously, this functionality existed in assembly drawings only. This is available under Section Depth in the Section View PropertyManager.

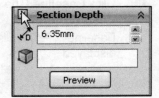

🔆 Select a line segment not a point to create a linear dimension. Fillet and Chamfer features remove points.

Center the dimension text between the extension lines.
51) Right-click on the **10.25** dimension text.

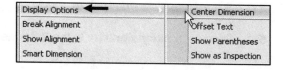

52) Click **Display Options**.

53) Click **Center Dimension**.

54) Click **OK** ✔ from the Dimension PropertyManager.

🔆 Baseline dimensions are aligned. Right-click Properties, Break Alignment to remove aligned dimensions. Click Show Alignment to display dimensions that are aligned. Uncheck the Center Dimension to position text along the extension lines.

55) Review the dimensions and view positions. If required, click and drag the **Section view**, **dimensions** and the **extension lines** of the vertical dimensions to create needed gaps.

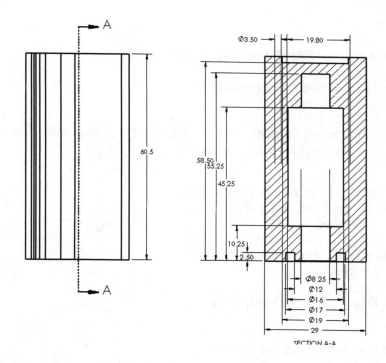

The vertical dimensions are equally spaced and positioned off the profiles. The Top and Section views are adequately spaced. The text and arrows are visible. There is a gap between the profile and vertical extension lines.

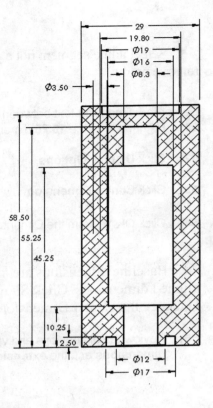

Move the bottom horizontal dimensions to the top in the Section view.

56) Click and drag the Ø**8.25** bottom horizontal dimension text to the top of the Section view A-A approximately 10mm above the top horizontal profile.

57) Set Primary Unit Precision to **.1**.

58) Drag each **extension line** to the top vertex of the Bore to create a gap.

59) Click and drag the Ø**16** text upward above the Ø8.3 text.

60) Drag the extension lines to the **top vertex** of the Bore.

61) Repeat for the other **illustrated dimension** text.

Align the top horizontal dimensions.

62) Hold the **Ctrl** key down.

63) Click the Ø**8.3**, Ø**16**, and Ø**19** dimension text.

64) Release the **Ctrl** key.

65) Click **Tools**, **Dimensions**, **Align Parallel/Concentric** from the Menu bar menu.

66) Click **OK** ✔ from the Dimension PropertyManager.

💡 The Dimension Document Property, Offset distances, From last dimension option controls the spacing between parallel dimensions.

Move dimensions from the Section view A-A to the Front view.

67) Press the **z** key until the Front view and the Section view are displayed.

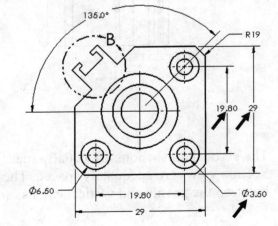

68) Click the **29** dimension text in the Section view. Hold the **Shift** key down.

69) Drag the **29** dimension text to the inside of the Front view.

70) Release the **Mouse button**. Release the **Shift** key.

71) Perform the same procedure for **19.8** and Ø**3.50** in the Section view. Note Position the text in the Front view in the next section.

72) Hide the **11** dimension with the Hide option.

💡 The Leaders tab in the Dimension PropertyManager Provides the ability to access the Witness/Leader Display box. The Witness/Leader Display box provides the ability to select arrow style, direction, and type.

💡 Selecting multiple entities becomes a challenge on a large drawing. To move, copy, or modify multiple entities, select the first entity. Hold the Ctrl key down and select the remaining entities. The first selection clears all previously selected entities.

Move the horizontal dimension text.
73) Click the Ø**12** dimension text at the bottom of the Section view.

74) Drag the Ø**12** dimension text upward to a position 10mm below the bottom horizontal profile line.

75) Drag each **extension line** off the profile. Do not use the Nose vertex. The Nose feature is too close to the bottom horizontal line of the Tube to utilize the vertex.

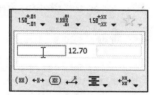

💡 New for 2010 is the dimension Pop-up dialog box in the Graphics window. This saves mouse travel to the Dimension PropertyManager to modify dimension, tolerance, leader and more.

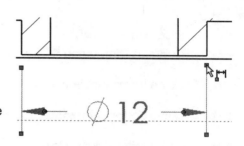

Align the horizontal dimensions.
76) Click the Ø**12** dimension text.

77) Hold the **Ctrl** key down.

78) Click the Ø**17** dimension.

79) Release the **Ctrl** key.

80) Click **Tools**, **Dimensions**, **Align Parallel/Concentric** from the Menu bar menu.

81) Click **OK** ✔ from the Dimension PropertyManager.

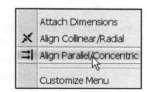

Position the Section A-A text below the bottom horizontal dimensions.
82) Center the **Section A-A** text.

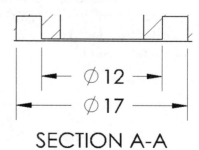

SECTION A-A

Insert a Centerline.

83)   Click inside the **Section view A-A** boundary.

84)   Click **Centerline** 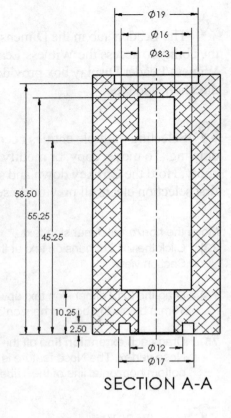 from the Annotation toolbar.

85)   Click **OK** ✔ from the Centerline PropertyManager.

Insert Centerlines quickly. Utilize the view boundary, two edges, two sketched entities (expect Splines), face or feature to manually insert a Centerline annotation. Utilize the Offset text option to position the text angled, outside the dimension arrows.

Add a vertical dimension with Offset.

86)   Click **Smart Dimension** ✎ from the Sketch toolbar.

87)   Click the **horizontal line** of the Nose.

88)   Click the **bottom horizontal line** of the Tube Extrusion.

89)   Click a **position** directly to the right.

90)   Drag the **dimension** to the right, off the Section view.

91)   Click **OK** ✔ from the Dimension PropertyManager.

Display offset text.

92)   Click the **0.20** dimension text.

93)   Click the **Value** tab in the Dimension PropertyManager

94)   Click the **Offset Text** button.

To slant the dimension, position the mouse pointer at the end of the extension line. Drag the extension line to create the angled dimension.

SECTION A-A

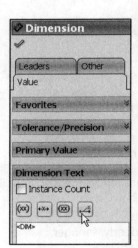

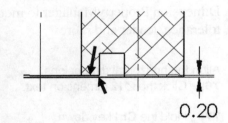

0.20

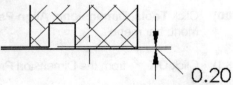

0.20

95) Select **.1** from the Tolerance/Precision text box. The 0.2 dimension is displayed.

96) Click **OK** ✓ from the Dimension PropertyManager.

Save the TUBE drawing.

97) Click **Save** 🖫 .

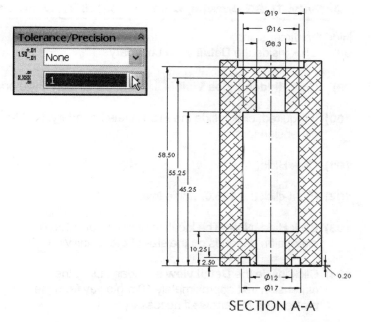

SECTION A-A

TUBE Drawing-Detailing Detail View, and Front View

Review the status of the Front view and Detail view. Dimensions are not clear or Dimensions are on top of each other. Dimensions are too far or too close to the profile.

Hide the 11 and 135° dimensions in the Detail view or Front view with the Hide option. Replace the 135° obtuse angle with an acute angle. Create an acute angle dimension from a construction line Collinear with the left vertical edge in the Front view.

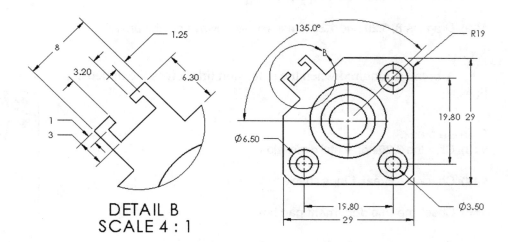

DETAIL B
SCALE 4 : 1

Activity: TUBE Drawing-Detailing Detail View and Front View

Hide the dimensions.

98) Click inside the **Detail view** boundary.

99) Click **Hidden Lines Visible**  from the Display Style box.

100) If required, click inside the **Front view** boundary. Right-click the **11** dimension text.

101) Click **Hide**.

102) Right-click the **135.0°** angle text.

103) Click **Hide**. Note: The location of the 11 and 135.0° dimension depends on the size of the Detail view.

104) Click inside the **Detail view** boundary. Drag the **1** dimension text approximately 10mm away from the profile. **Flip** the arrows if necessary.

105) Drag the **3** text to the left of the 1 text.

106) Select the **1** dimension text.

107) Hold the **Ctrl** key down.

108) Select the **3** dimension text.

109) Release the **Ctrl** key.

110) Click **Tools**, **Dimensions**, **Align Parallel/ Concentric** from the Menu bar menu.

111) Click **OK** ✔ from the PropertyManager.

112) Drag the **8**, **3.20** and **1.25** dimension text away from the profile.

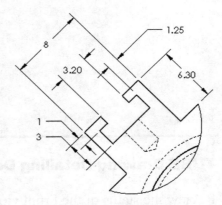

DETAIL B
SCALE 4 : 1

🔅 A break is required when the extension lines cross the dimension lines.

Create a break.

113) Click the **3.20** horizontal dimension.

114) Check the **Break Lines** check box.

115) Check the **Use document gap** box.

116) Click **OK** ✔ from the Dimension PropertyManager.

Set the Precision
117) Click the **3.20** dimension. Hold the **Ctrl** key down.

118) Click the **6.30** dimension. Release the **Ctrl** key.

119) Select **.1** from the Primary Unit Precision text box. The dimensions 3.2 and 6.3 are displayed.

120) Click **OK** ✓ from the Dimension PropertyManager.

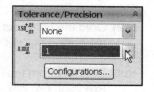

Align the dimensions.
121) Click the **8** dimension. Hold the **Ctrl** key down.

122) Click the **3.2** and **1.25** dimension.

123) Release the **Ctrl** key.

124) Click **Tools**, **Dimensions**, **Align Parallel/Concentric** from the Menu bar menu.

125) Position the **DETAIL B** text below the profile.

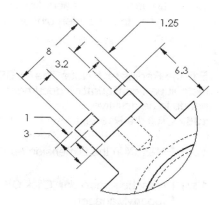

DETAIL B
SCALE 4 : 1

Save the TUBE drawing.
126) Click **Save** 🖫 .

🔆 The default Break dimension extension/leader lines Gap value is set in Tools, Options, Document Properties, Dimensions, Break dimension extension/leader lines for an active drawing document.

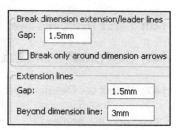

🔆 If the Hide option is utilized to hide an annotation, and you want to display the annotation on the sheet, select View, Hide/Show Annotations from the Menu bar menu. The hidden annotations are displayed in gray. Click the needed annotation to be displayed.

Move and Hide dimensions in the Front view.
127) Click inside the **Drawing View1** view boundary.

128) Drag the vertical **29** dimension text off the profile to the right.

129) Drag the vertical **19.80** dimension to the right.

130) Select **.1** from the Primary Unit Precision text box.

131) Drag the horizontal **29** dimension text below the profile.

132) Drag the horizontal **19.80** dimension below the profile.

133) Select **.1** from the Primary Unit Precision text box.

134) Drag the **R19** dimension upward. The arrow of the leader line is aligned to the centerpoint of the arc.

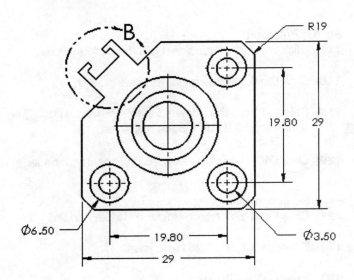

Edit the Radius text. Note: The TUBE Default part configuration document needs to be activtive.
135) Click the **R19** text.

136) Enter **3X** in the Dimension text box.

137) Press the **space bar**. Click **OK** ✔ from the Dimension PropertyManager.

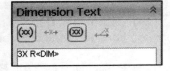

Hide dimensions.
138) Click the Ø**3.50** dimension text. Hold the **Ctrl** key down.

139) Click the Ø**6.50** dimension text. Release the **Ctrl** key.

140) Select **HideDims** layer from the Dimension PropertyManager.

141) Click **OK** ✔ from the Dimension PropertyManager.

142) Select the **Details** layer from the Layer toolbar.

Dimension the angle cut.

143) Click **Smart Dimension** ✎ from the Sketch toolbar.

144) Click the **left vertical profile line** and the **top angled edge**.

145) Position the **dimension** inside the acute angle.

146) Select **None** from the Primary Units Precision box.

147) Click **OK** ✔ from the Dimension PropertyManager.

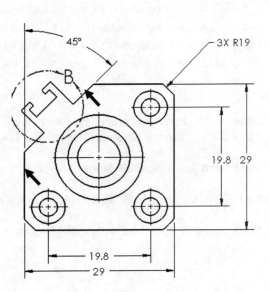

Save the TUBE drawing.

148) Click **Save** 💾 .

🔆 Edge selection is important. Select the top angled edge, not the bottom angle edge. The bottom angle edge extension line overlaps the profile line and does not produce a gap.

TUBE Drawing-Detailing Right View, Back View, and Holes

The Right view contains a series of holes that require annotations. Display the Right view. Reposition dimensions and add annotations. The Back view requires additional annotations to detail a Counterbore.

Simple Holes and other circular geometry utilize various display options: *Display As Radius, Display As Linear, Define by Hole Wizard, Show Parentheses and Show as Inspection.*

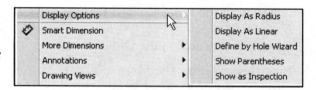

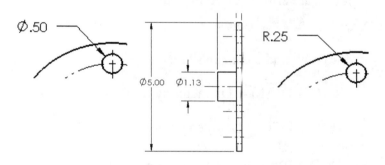

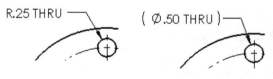 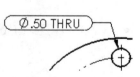

🔆 You can also utilize the Dimension PropertyManager - Leaders tab to affect the display option: *Outside, Inside, Smart, Arrow type, Radius, Diameter, Linear, Perpendicular to Axis, and Use document bend length.*

Flip arrows by selecting the blue control point on the arrowhead. Arrows alternate between the outside position and the inside position.

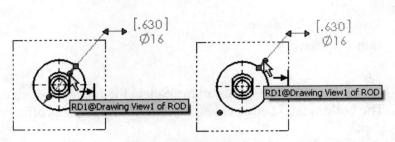

Counterbore holes in the Right view require a note. Use the Hole Callout to dimension the holes. The Hole Callout function creates additional notes required to

dimension the holes. The dimension standard symbols are displayed automatically when you insert holes created with the Hole Wizard feature.

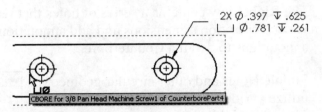

Symbols are located in the Dimension Properties text box. The More button displays additional Symbol libraries. Symbols are also accessed from the Variables button.

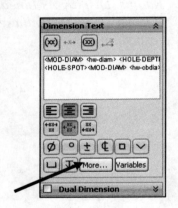

A few command commands are:

- <MOD-DIAM>: Diameter symbol ∅.

- <MOD-DEG>: Degree symbol °.

- <MOD-PM>: Plus / Minus symbol ±.

- <MOD-CL>: CenterLine symbol ℄.

- <MOD-BOX>: Square symbol ☐.

- <HOLE-SINK>: CounterSink symbol ∨.

- <HOLE-SPOT>: Counterbore symbol ⌴.

- <HOLE-DEPTH>: Depth/Deep symbol ⊽.

- <DIM>: Dimension value.

The text in brackets <>, indicates the <library name – symbol name>. Place the number of holes (3) and the multiplication sign (X) before the diameter dimension. Example: 3X<MOD-DIAM><DIM> THRU EQ SP is displayed on the drawing as: 6X ⌀.50 THRU EQ SP.

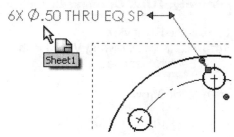

Two Extruded Cut features created the Counterbore in the Front view. The third Extruded Cut feature created the Counterbore in the Back. The Extruded Cut features did not produce the correct Counterbore Hole Callout according to a dimensioning standard. Utilize the Hole Callout tool to create the correct annotation. The mouse pointer displays the Hole Callout ⌴⌀ icon, when the Hole Callout tool is active.

Create two Parametric notes to represent the Counterbore in the Front and Back view. A Parametric note contains dimensions from a part or drawing. Modify the dimension and the Parametric note to reflect the new value. Utilize the Centerline tool and Center Mark tool from the Annotation toolbar. Centerlines are composed of alternating long and short dash lines. The lines identify the center of a circle, axes, or cylindrical geometry.

Center Marks represent two perpendicular intersecting centerlines. Adjust adjacent extension lines after applying Center Marks.

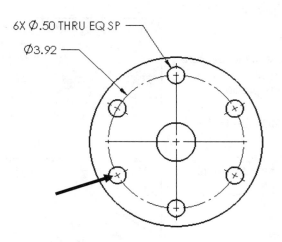

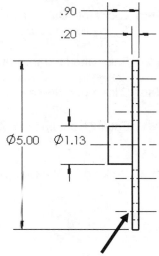

Activity: TUBE Drawing-Detailing Right View, Back View and Holes

Display the Right view.

149) Right-click **Drawing View3** in the FeatureManager.

150) Click **Show**.

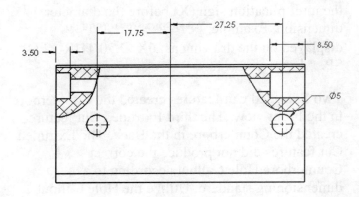

Hide dimensions.

151) Click the Ø5 dimension text.

152) Press the **Ctrl** key.

153) Click the **3.50**, **8.50**, **17.75**, and **27.25** dimension text.

154) Release the **Ctrl** key.

155) Select the **HideDims** layer from the Dimension PropertyManager.

156) Click **OK** ✔ from the Dimension PropertyManager.

157) Select the **Details** layer from the Layer toolbar.

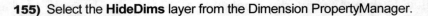

Dimension the Ports.

158) Click **Hole CallOut** ⊔∅ from the Annotation toolbar.

159) Select the **circumference** of the left Port.

160) Click a **position** above the profile.

161) Enter **2X** before the <MOD-DIAM> text.

162) Click **Yes** to the Break Link with Model dialog box.

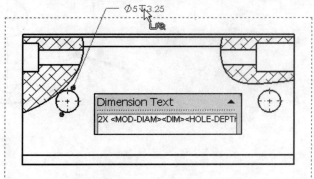

163) Press the **space** key.

164) Click **OK** ✔ from the Dimension PropertyManager.

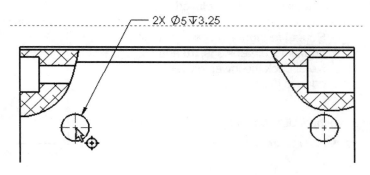
2X ⌀5▼3.25

💡 Inserting text into a Hole Callout annotation in the drawing produces the Break Link with the Model dialog box. Modify the part dimension from ∅5 to ∅6 and the drawing annotation updates. Manually edit the dimension text from ∅5 to ∅6 in the Hole Callout and the part dimension remains unchanged.

Add the vertical and horizontal dimensions.

165) **Hide** the Center Marks on the Port holes.

166) Click **Smart Dimension** 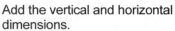 from the Annotation toolbar.

167) Click the **bottom horizontal edge**.

168) Click the left side of the **circumference** of the first circle.

169) Click a **position** to the left of the vertical profile line. The 14.50 dimension text is displayed.

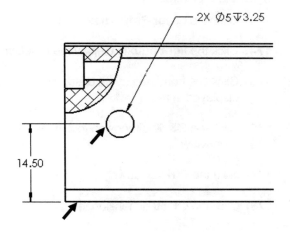
2X ⌀5▼3.25
14.50

170) Select **.1** from the Primary Unit Precision text box. The 14.5 dimension text is displayed.

171) Repeat for above procedure for the horizontal dimensions; **10** and **55**. Note: Click the lower left vertical edge to the gap.

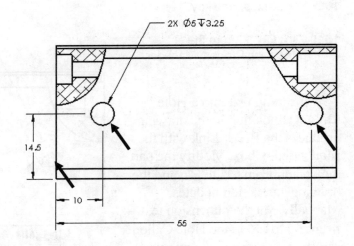

Save the TUBE drawing.

172) Click **Save** 💾 .

💡 Select edges, not vertices when creating linear dimensions. Select the circumference of the circle not the Center Mark annotation when referencing the center point of circular geometry.

Show the HideDims layer.

173) Click the **Layer Properties** 📄 icon.

174) Click the **light bulb** to display the HideDims layer.

175) Click **OK** from the Layers dialog box. The dimensions are displayed in red.

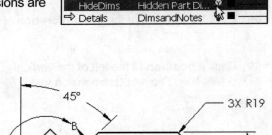

176) Click the ∅**3.50** dimension text in the Front view.

177) Hold the **Ctrl** key down.

178) Click the ∅**6.50** dimension text.

179) Release the **Ctrl** key.

180) Select the **Details** layer from the Dimension PropertyManager.

181) Click **OK** ✔ from the PropertyManager. The dimensions are on the Details layer, and are displayed in blue.

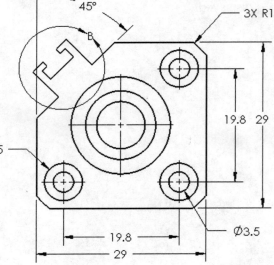

Modify the Precision.

182) Select **.1** Primary Unit Precision for the ∅3.5 and ∅6.5 dimension text.

Insert a Note.

183) Click **Note** $\mathbf{A}$ from the Annotation toolbar.

184) Click the **circumference** of the top right Counterbore in the Front view

185) Click a **position** to the top right of the view. Note: The Details layer is the active layer in the drawing.

186) Enter **3X**.

187) Click the ⌀**3.5** dimension text in the Front view.

188) Enter **THRU**.

189) Press the **Enter** key.

190) Click the **Add Symbol** button.

191) Select **Hole Symbols** for Symbol library.

192) Click **Counterbore (Spotface)**.

193) Click **OK**.

194) Click the ⌀**6.5** dimension text.

195) Enter<**HOLE-DEPTH**>.

196) Press the **space** bar.

197) Enter **3.5**.

198) Click **OK** from the Note PropertyManager.

Hide the diameter dimensions.

199) Click the ⌀**3.5** dimension in the Front view.

200) Hold the **Ctrl** key down.

201) Click the ⌀**6.5** dimension.

202) Release the **Ctrl** key.

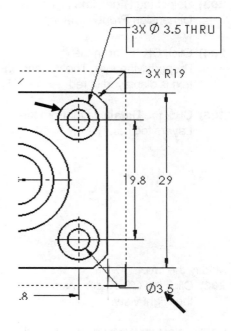

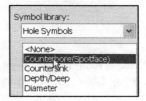

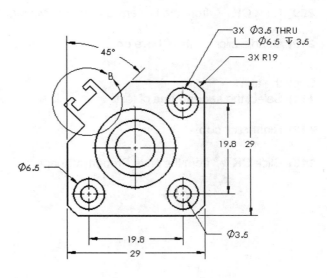

203) Select the **HideDims** layer from the Dimension PropertyManager.

204) Click **OK** ✔ from the PropertyManager. The dimension text is displayed in red.

205) Click the **Details** layer from the Layers toolbar.

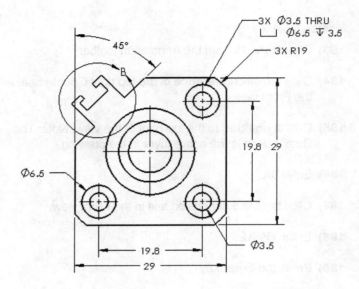

Modify the layer.
206) Click the ⌀**8.50** dimension text in the Right view.

207) Select the **Details** layer from the PropertyManager.

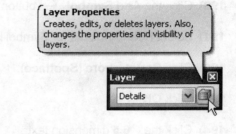

Add a Note to the Counterbore Rear.
208) Click **.1** for Primary Unit Precision. The 8.5 dimension is displayed.

209) Click **OK** ✔ from the Dimension PropertyManager.

210) Double-click on the **Cbore note** in the Front view.

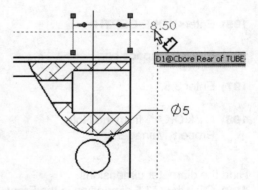

Copy the text.
211) Select the **second line** of text.

212) Right-click **copy**.

213) Click **OK** ✔ from the Note PropertyManager.

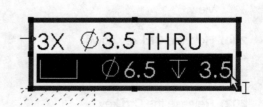

214) Click **Note** A from the Annotation toolbar.

215) Click the **circumference** of the top left Counterbore in the Back view.

216) Click a **position** for the Note.

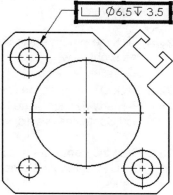

Paste the Note.
217) Click-right **Paste**.

Edit the Note.
218) Enter **2X** at the start of the line.

219) Press the **space** bar.

220) Delete the **3.5** Note text.

221) Click the **8.5** dimension text in the Right view.

222) Click **OK** ✔ from the Note PropertyManager.

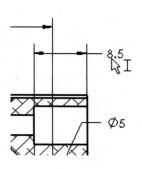

Hide the 8.5 dimension.
223) Click the **8.5** dimension text in the Right view.

224) Select the **HideDims** layer from the Dimension PropertyManager.

225) Click **OK** ✔ from the Dimension PropertyManager.

226) Turn the **HideDims layer off**.

227) Click the **Details** layer from the Layers toolbar.

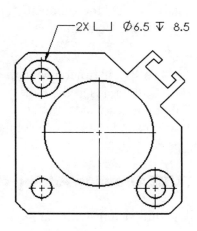

Delete automatically inserted Center Marks in the Right view before you investigate the next step.

Add Center Marks and a Centerline to the Right view.
228) Click **Center Mark** ⊕ from the Annotation toolbar.

229) Click the **Linear Center Mark** button.

230) Check the **Connection lines** box.

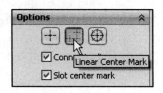

231) Click the circumference of the **left Port** in the Right view.

232) Click the circumference of the **right Port** in the Right view.

233) Click **OK** ✔ from the Center Mark PropertyManager. The two Center Marks and Centerline are displayed.

234) Drag the **centerlines** and **extension** lines off the Center Marks. Do not overlap the Center Marks.

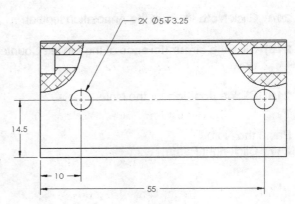

The desired Centerline did not work if you select the top/bottom edges. The top edge is the Switch feature, not the extruded Tube feature. To display the Centerline for this feature, select Hidden Lines Visible. Select the silhouette top and bottom edges of the Bore feature to create the Centerline.

To specify tolerance in the Hole Callout, insert the Hole Callout. Click inside the Dimension Text box and select the Tolerance type.

$$2X \; \varnothing \, 5 \, {}^{+0.5}_{0} \, \overline{\underline{V}} \, 3.3$$

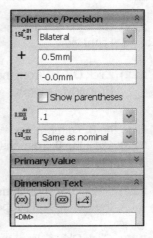

TUBE Drawing-Adding Dimensions

Add dimensions with the Smart Dimension tool in the drawing. The TUBE holes utilized symmetry in the initial Base sketch.

The profile contains horizontal and vertical construction lines sketched from the Origin to a midpoint. A Symmetric relationship with vertical and horizontal construction lines create a fully defined sketch. No additional dimension is required from the Origin to the center point of the hole.

Create new dimensions to locate the holes in relationship to the center of the Bore. Adjust all vertical and horizontal dimensions. Stagger and space dimension text for clarity. Create a gap between the extension lines and the Center Mark. The Auxiliary view is the last view to move and to add dimensions. Use a Hole Callout to specify size and depth. Add a dimension to locate the center of the hole. Move extension lines off the profile.

Activity: TUBE Drawing-Adding Dimensions

Create a vertical dimension in Drawing View1.

235) Click **Smart Dimension** ✎ from the Sketch toolbar.

236) Click the **circumference** of the small right bottom hole.

237) Click the **circumference** of the center circle.

238) Drag the **9.90** dimension to the right of the vertical profile line. Note: If required, delete the small **Center Mark** at the center of the Front view.

239) Click **.1** for Primary Unit Precision. The 9.9 dimension is displayed.

240) Drag the other vertical **dimensions** to the right. **Flip** the dimension arrows if required.

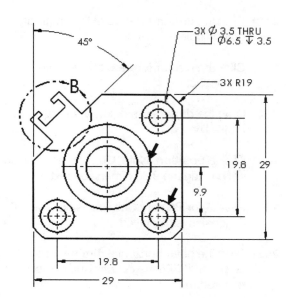

💡 The Arc Condition option in the Dimension PropertyManager provides the ability to set the dimension between arcs or circles. The First arc condition specifies where or the arc or circle the distance is measured. The Second arc condition specifies where on the second selected item the distance is measured, when both items are arcs or circles.

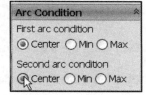

Align dimensions.
241) Click the **9.9** dimension text.

242) Hold the **Ctrl** key down.

243) Click the **19.8** and **29** dimension text.

244) Release the **Ctrl** key.

245) Click **Tools, Dimensions, Align Parallel/Concentric** from the Menu bar menu.

246) Click **OK** ✔ from the Dimension PropertyManager.

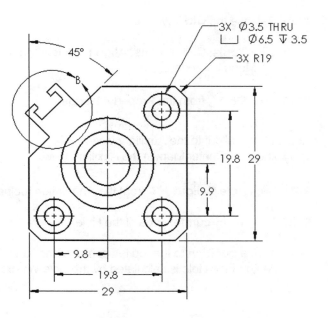

Create a horizontal dimension.

247) Click **Smart Dimension** ◇ from the Sketch toolbar.

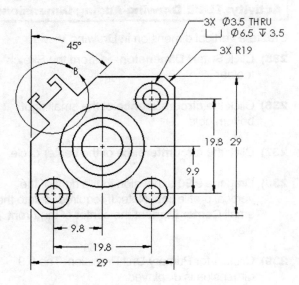

248) Click the **circumference** of the small left bottom hole.

249) Click the **circumference** of the center bottom hole.

250) Drag the **dimension** below the horizontal profile line.

251) Click a **position**. Note: Clicking the position will provide the 9.80 dimension text.

252) Click **.1** for Primary Unit Precision. The 9.8 dimension is displayed.

253) Drag the other horizontal **dimensions** downward. **Flip** the dimension arrows if required.

254) Drag the **29** dimension text to the right of the 19.8 dimension text.

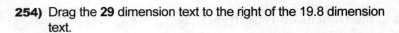

255) Click the **9.8** dimension text.

256) Hold the **Ctrl** key down.

257) Click the **19.8** and **29** dimension text.

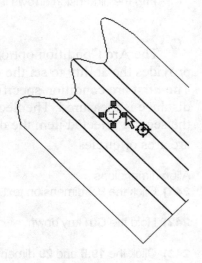

258) Release the **Ctrl** key.

259) Click **Tools**, **Dimensions**, **Align Parallel/Concentric** from the Menu bar menu.

260) Click **OK** ✔ from the PropertyManager.

Add a Hole Callout to the Auxiliary view.
261) **Hide** the Center Mark in the Auxiliary view.

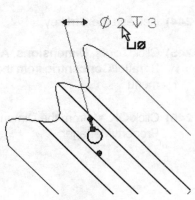

262) Click **Hole Callout** ⊔ø from the Annotation toolbar.

263) Click the **circumference** of the Hole.

264) Click a **position** to the top left corner of the view. The depth of the Hole is calculated by the Hole Wizard.

Add dimensions.

265) Click **Smart Dimension** 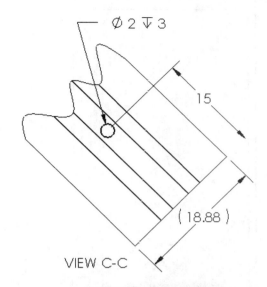 from the Annotation toolbar.

266) Click the **circumference** of the small hole.

267) Click the **bottom edge**.

268) Click a **position** to the right off the profile.

269) Click the **left edge**.

270) Click the **right edge**.

271) Click a **position** below the profile.

Modify the reference dimension.
272) Click the **18.88** dimension text.

273) Click **Add Parentheses** in the Dimension Text box.

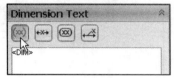

Insert a Center Mark.

274) Click **Center Mark** ⊕ from the Annotation toolbar. The Center Mark PropertyManager is displayed. Single Center Mark is the default option.

275) Click the **center circle** as illustrated.

276) Click the **Single Center Mark** box.

277) Enter **0** for Angle to rotate the Center Mark.

278) Click **OK** ✔ from the Center Mark PropertyManager.

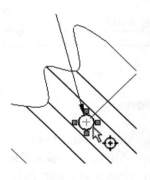

Fit the Model to the Sheet.
279) Press the **f** key.

Save the TUBE drawing.
280) Click **Save** 🖫 .

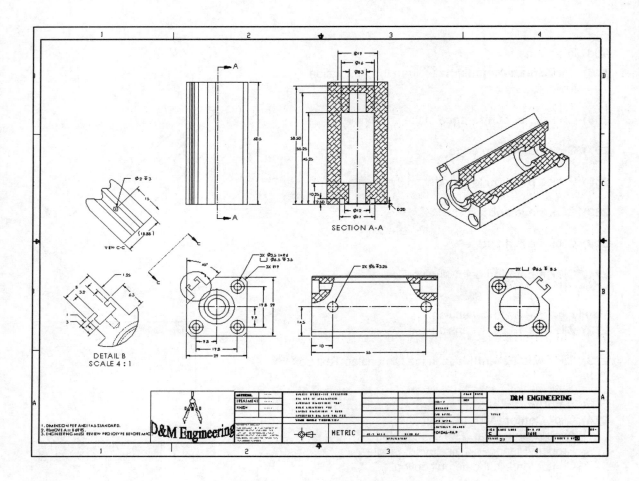

⚲ More Information

Additional details on Dimension, Layer, Insert Model Items, Hide/Show, Document Properties, Display Options, Align, Precision, Break Dimension Lines, Symbols, Hole Callout, Center Mark, Centerline and Parametric Note are available in SolidWorks help.

Keywords: Dimensions (align, copy, display, driven, move and reference), Layers (drawing), Insert (dimensions into drawings), Hide (dimensions, drawing views), Options (drawings) Display (drawing views), Align (dimensions), Precision(display), Break Lines, Symbols (in note text), Hole Callouts, and Parametric note.

In SolidWorks 2010, when you right-click a component in an assembly drawing, you can open the part or assembly. In previous versions, you could open the part only.

Review

The TUBE drawing consisted of a single sheet with eight different views. Each view contained dimensions and annotations. You utilized layers to hide and display dimensions and annotations.

Feature dimensions were inserted from the part into the drawing. Dimensions were relocated in the view and moved to different views. Added dimensions were created in the drawing. Display options and alignment were used to modify the dimensions. Hole Callout annotations utilized symbols and dimension values to create Parametric notes.

Detailing Tips

The Hole Wizard feature created the M2 hole in the part. The M2 hole sketch utilized a Midpoint and Horizontal Geometric relation. No dimensions were required to position the hole.

Where do you create dimensions? Do you return to the part and change your dimension scheme to accommodate the drawing? Answer: No. Build the dimensioning scheme and design intent into the part.

Build parts with symmetric relationships. Use a line of symmetry in a sketch. Add Geometric relationships. Add reference dimensions in the drawing to detail part geometric relations such as Equal and Symmetry.

Modify part sketches and features to accommodate a drawing. Fully defined sketches are displayed in black. Drag sketch dimensions off the profiles. Insert part dimensions into the drawing.

Position dimensions in the best view to document the feature.

Move dimensions with the Shift key. Copy dimensions with the Ctrl key. Select a position inside the new view boundary to place the dimensions.

☀ Utilize drawing layers to hide unwanted part dimensions, annotations, and construction geometry created in the drawing.

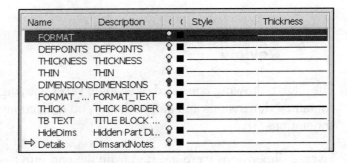

Add additional layers to control notes and various line fonts. Control the Layer display with the On/Off option.

The TUBE drawing contained dimensions from over 10 features. The Insert Model Items, Entire model option, displayed numerous dimensions. How do you display hundreds of feature dimensions for a part? Answer: Utilize the following tips:

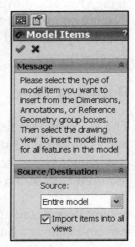

☀ Organize dimension and annotation display with the FeatureManager. Select the feature from the FeatureManager. Select Insert Model Items, Selected Feature option. Repeat for multiple features from the top to the bottom of the FeatureManager.

☀ Utilize a two-view approach. Create a copy of the view and position the new view outside the sheet boundary. The copy of the view is called the "sloppy copy". Select the sloppy copy view boundary. Select Insert Model Items for the selected view. Utilize Ctrl-Select to choose multiple dimensions. Move the required dimensions from the sloppy copy to the original view inside the sheet boundary.

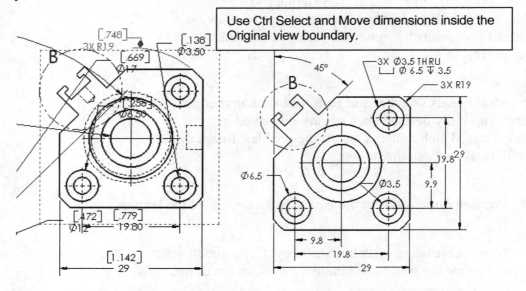

Sloppy Copy (Insert Model Items by View)   Move entities to Final view

Create multiple part configurations with a Design Table. Configurations conserve design time and provide a record of the changes in a single part file.

Example: A Design Table controls the Suppressed/UnSuppressed State of the all around Fillet features. Utilize the Suppress configuration in the drawing. Replace the Fillet features with a note. To modify the note attachment point to the bent leader line, first position the note on the drawing. Select the note and then select the Attachment Leader Style

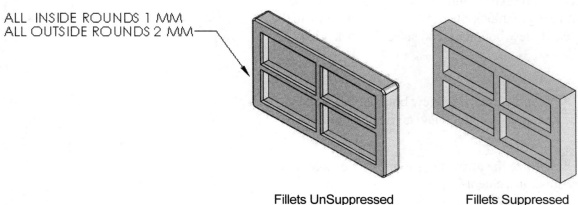

ALL INSIDE ROUNDS 1 MM
ALL OUTSIDE ROUNDS 2 MM

Fillets UnSuppressed   Fillets Suppressed

Drawings contain multiple sheets and views. The Lock Sheet Focus and the Lock View Focus options assist in complex drawings.

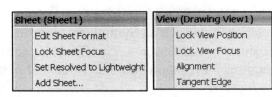

System Options, Drawings, Automatically scale new drawing views activation option scales new drawing views to fit the drawing sheet, regardless of the paper size selected.

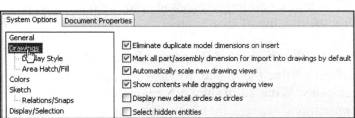

Selecting the preferred view with the mouse is difficult when view boundaries overlap. Sketch entities belong to the view closest to the mouse pointer when you begin sketching.

Lock Sheet Focus and Lock View Focus temporarily halt Dynamic drawing view activation. The Lock Sheet Focus allows you to add entities to the sheet. Entities reference the sheet not a view.

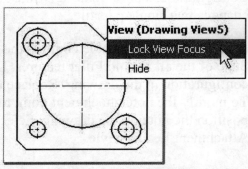

NOTE STAYS WITH VIEW

Lock View Focus allows you to add entities to a view, even when the mouse pointer is close to another view. Entities reference only the Locked View.

To reactivate the Dynamic drawing view activation option, right-click in the sheet boundary and select Unlock Sheet Focus, or right-click in the locked view boundary and select Unlock View Focus.

☀ Double-click any view boundary to activate the Dynamic drawing view activation option.

☀ Utilize the arrow keys to move views or notes by small increments.

COVERPLATE Drawing-Detailing

The COVERPLATE utilizes Geometric relationships such as Symmetric to define the position of the features. The ∅8.25 dimension requires a Precision value of 2 decimal places.

All of the remaining dimensions require a Precision value of 1 or None.

Modify the Document Properties Precision value to 1 decimal place. Review the geometric relations. What additional dimensions and annotations are required in the drawing? Answer: Locate the Counterbore with respect to the Center Hole with a linear dimension in the drawing. Add a Chamfer annotation in the drawing.

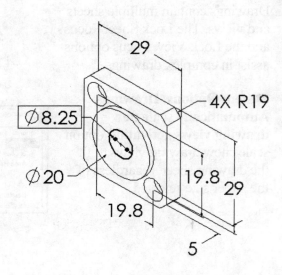

The COVERPLATE-Sheet1 Front view utilizes the Without Nose Holes configuration. Activate the part configuration to modify the dimension in the Front view. You cannot edit a dimension in the sheet unless the configuration is active

A Cosmetic Thread displays the major and minor diameter of a thread. Control a Cosmetic Thread as an annotation in the part or in the drawing. The Hole Wizard tapped hole contains a Cosmetic Thread option. Insert a Cosmetic Thread into COVERPLATE-Sheet2. Activate the With Nose Holes part configuration to modify the annotation.

Activity: COVERPLATE Drawing-Detailing

Set Document Precision to 1 decimal place.
281) **Open** the COVERPLATE drawing.

282) Click the **Sheet1** tab.

283) Click **Options** , **Document Properties** tab, **Dimensions** from the Menu bar toolbar.

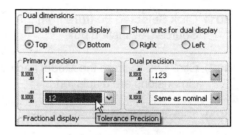

284) Select **1** for Primary precision dimension value.

285) Select **.12** for Tolerance Precision.

286) Click the **Units** folder.

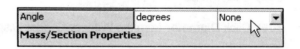

287) Select **None** for Angular dimension value.

288) Click **OK** from the Document Properties – Units dialog box.

Create a Hole Callout.
289) Click **Hole Callout** ⊔∅ from the Annotation toolbar. The Hole Callout PropertyManager is displayed.

290) Click the **Counterbore circumference** in Drawing View5.

291) Click a **position** above the profile.

292) Enter **2X** in the Dimension Text box.

293) Click **Yes** in the Break Link with Model dialog box.

294) Click the **space** bar.

295) Click **OK** from the Dimension PropertyManager.

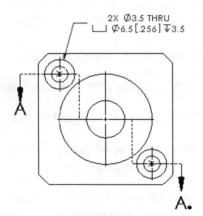

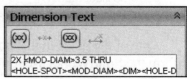

Insert the Model Item for individual features.

296) Click the **circumference** of the small center Bore feature in the Front view.

297) Hold the **Ctrl** key down.

298) Click the **circumference** of the large center Nose feature.

299) Release the **Ctrl** key.

300) Click **Model items** from the Annotation toolbar. The Model Items PropertyManager is displayed.

301) Click **Selected Feature** from the Source/Destination box.

302) Click **OK** from the Model Items PropertyManager. Two dimensions are displayed.

303) Click the Ø**8.25** dimension text.

304) Click the **Leaders** tab.

305) Click **Diameter** from the Witness/Leader Display dialog box.

306) Click the **Value** tab.

307) **Uncheck** the Dual Dimension box.

308) Click **OK** from the Dimension PropertyManager.

309) Click the Ø**8.25** dimension text.

310) Click the Ø**20 dimension** text.

311) **Uncheck** the Dual Dimension box.

312) Click **OK** from the Dimension PropertyManager.

313) **Eliminate** all dual dimensions in the drawing view as illustrated.

One of the goals in this book, is to inform the SolidWorks user on different ways to perform the same function.

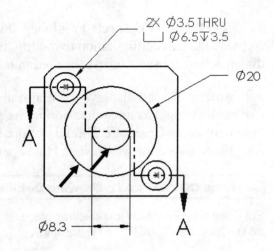

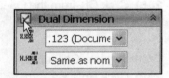

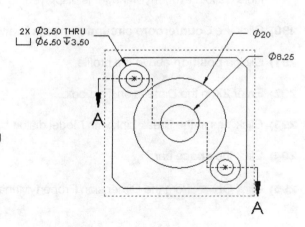

Insert the Model Item for the Section view.
314) Click inside the **Section view** boundary.

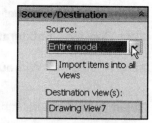

315) Click **Model Items**  from the Annotation toolbar. The Model Items PropertyManager is displayed.

316) Select **Entire model** from the Source/Destination box.

317) Click **OK** ✔ from the Model Items PropertyManager. The dimensions are displayed.

318) **Eliminate** all dual dimensions in the Drawing. Un-check the Dual dimensions display box from Document Properties.

319) **Eliminate** all trailing zeros on the dimensions.

320) Hide the ∅**6.5**, ∅**3.5** and the **3.5** dimension text.

321) Drag the horizontal dimensions **29** and **19.8** 10mm away from the Profile line. A gap exists between the extension lines and profile.

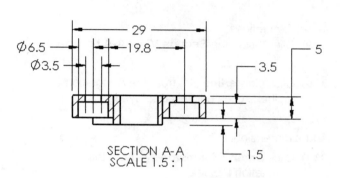

SECTION A-A
SCALE 1.5 : 1

Open the part.
322) Right-click in the **Section view A-A** boundary.

323) Click **Open Part**. The COVERPLATE is displayed in the Graphics window.

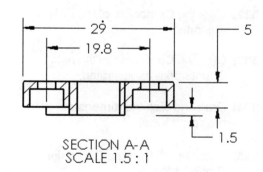

SECTION A-A
SCALE 1.5 : 1

💡 The view utilizes the Without Holes Configuration.

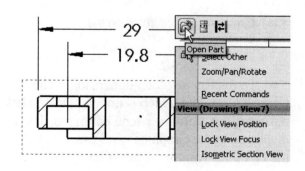

Select the No Holes Configuration.

324) Click the **ConfigurationManager** tab.

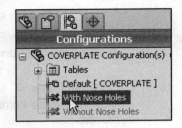

325) Double-click **Without Nose Holes**.

Return to the FeatureManager.

326) Click the **FeatureManager** tab.

Return to the COVERPLATE drawing

327) Right-click on the **COVERPLATE** name in the FeatureManager.

328) Click **Open Drawing**. The COVERPLATE drawing is displayed.

Insert Centerlines.

329) Click inside the **Section View A-A** boundary.

330) Click **Centerline** from the Annotation toolbar. A centerline is displayed.

Add a dimension.

331) Click **Smart Dimension** from the Annotation toolbar.

332) Click the **Centerline** of the Hole as illustrated.

333) Click the **Centerline** of the right Counterbore as illustrated.

334) Drag and click the **dimension** off the profile.

335) Click **OK** from the Dimension PropertyManager.

336) **Eliminate** trailing zeros on the dimension.

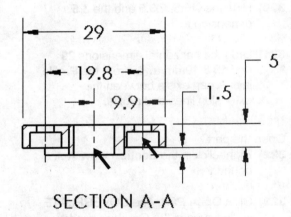

SECTION A-A

To display a hidden dimension in the Graphics window which is not on a layer, click **View, Hide/Show Annotations** from the Menu bar menu. The Hidden dimensions are displayed in the Graphics windows. Click the **dimension** to show in the Graphics window. Click **View, Hide/Show Annotation** from the Menu bar menu to return to the Graphics window.

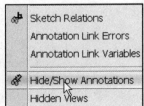

Insert the remaining dimensions.
337) Click a **position** in the sheet boundary.

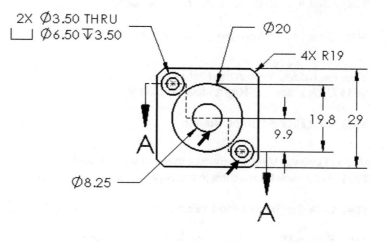

338) Click **Model Items** from the Annotation toolbar. Select **Entire Model**.

339) Click **OK** from the Model Items PropertyManager. Note: If needed, modify the drawing view scale to 1:1 to fit the inserted dimensions.

340) **Eliminate** all trailing zeros.

Create a vertical dimension in the Front view.
341) Click inside the **Front view** boundary. Click **Smart Dimension** .

342) Click the **circumference** of the right Counterbore. Click the **circumference** of the small center circle. Click a **position** to the right of the profile.

343) Click **OK** from the PropertyManager.

Apply the 3D Drawing View tool from the Heads-up View toolbar to select difficult edges or faces in a drawing view.

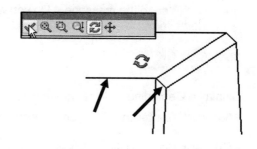

If the extension line references the arc tangent, drag the endpoint of the extension line to the center point to create a center-to-center dimension.

Create a Chamfer dimension in the Right view.
344) Click inside the **Right view** boundary.

345) **Zoom in** on the top right corner.

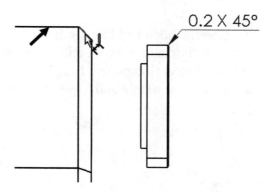

346) Click the **Smart Dimension** tool.

347) Right-click **More Dimensions** from the Pop-up menu. Click **Chamfer**.

348) Click the small **angled edge**. Click the top **horizontal edge**.

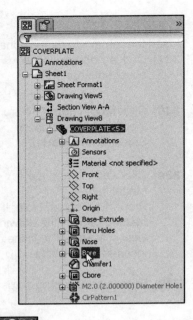

349) Click a **position** to place the dimension.

350) Click **OK** ✔ from the Dimension PropertyManager.

View the hidden lines in the Right view.
351) Click inside the **Right view** boundary.

352) Click **Hidden Lines Visible**.

Modify Drawing View Properties to display the Bore feature.
353) Right-click **Properties** in the Right view.

354) Click the **Show Hidden Edges** tab.

355) **Expand** the FeatureManager for the Drawing View8 (Right).

356) Click the **Bore** feature.

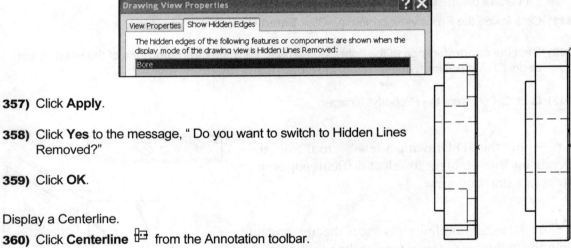

357) Click **Apply**.

358) Click **Yes** to the message, " Do you want to switch to Hidden Lines Removed?"

359) Click **OK**.

Display a Centerline.
360) Click **Centerline** ⊞ from the Annotation toolbar.

361) Click **OK** ✔ from the Centerline PropertyManager.

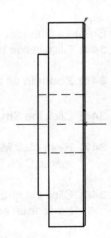

Visible　　　Removed

💡 Control individual line display with the Show/Hide option. Control individual Line font. Right-click a component in the drawing. Select Component Line Font. Select the Type of edge, Line style, Line weight and Layer. Click OK.

Save the COVERPLATE drawing.
362) Click **Save** 💾 .

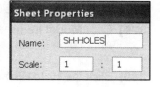

Add a new Sheet.
363) Right-click on the **Sheet1** tab.

364) Click **Add Sheet**. Sheet3 is the default
Sheet Name.

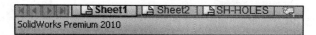

365) Enter **SH-HOLES** for sheet name.

Modify the sheet order.
366) Drag **SH-HOLES** upward in the FeatureManager.

367) Position **SH-HOLES** below Sheet1.

Open the COVERPLATE part.
368) Open **COVERPLATE**. Select the **With
Nose Holes** configuration.

369) Expand the **M2.0 Diameter Hole1** feature
in the FeatureManager.

370) Right-click **Sketch7**. Click **Show**.

Insert a Relative view into the SH-HOLES Sheet.
371) Click **Windows**, **Tile Horizontal** from the Menu bar menu.

372) Click inside **COVERPLATE-SH-HOLES** Sheet.

373) Click **Insert**, **Drawing View**, **Relative to Model** from the Menu bar
menu. The Relative View PropertyManager is displayed.

374) Click the **front face** of the COVERPLATE part for First orientation
as illustrated.

375) Click the **right face** of the part for the Second orientation as
illustrated. Click **OK** ✔ from the Relative View PropertyManager.

Place the view.
376) Click a **position** on the left side of the SH-HOLES sheet.

377) Create a Custom Scale of **2:1** for the Relative view.

378) Click **OK** ✔ from Drawing View10 PropertyManager.

Insert Dimensions for the M2.0 hole.

379) Click **Model Items**  from the Annotation toolbar.

380) Click the **Hole Wizard Locations** box.

381) Click the **Hole Callout** box.

382) Click **Selected feature**.

383) Click the **top right hole** (Seed feature).

384) Click **OK** ✔ from the Model Items PropertyManager.

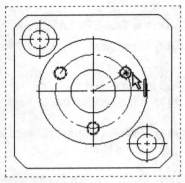

385) Drag the **30°** dimension text off the profile.

386) Right-click the **∅14** dimension text.

387) Click **Display Options**.

388) Click **Display As Diameter**.

389) Drag the **dimensions** off the Profile.

390) Click **OK** ✔ from the PropertyManager.

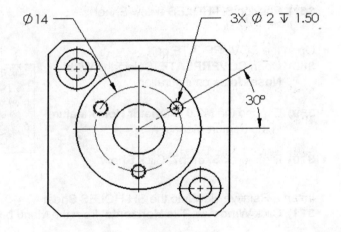

Create an Angular dimension.

391) If needed, hide the **Center Marks** in the top right M2 circle and the center circle.

392) Click **View**, check **Origins** from the Menu bar menu.

393) Sketch a **centerline** from the Origin to the center of the top right M2 circle.

394) Sketch a **centerline** from the Origin to the center of the top left M2 circle.

395) Click the **Smart Dimension** ✏ tool.

396) Click the **first centerline**.

397) Click the **second centerline**.

398) Click a **position** above the profile.

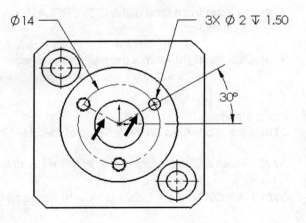

399) Click **OK** from the Make Dimension Driven dialog box.

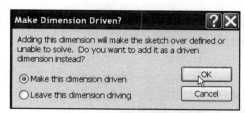

400) Click the **120°** text in the Graphics window.

401) Enter **3X** before the dimension text as illustrated.

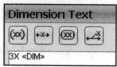

Add a Cosmetic Thread.
402) Click the **right M2 hole** (Edge<1>).

403) Click **Insert**, **Annotations**, **Cosmetic Thread** ⋓ from the Menu bar menu. The Cosmetic Thread PropertyManager is displayed.

404) Select **None**.

405) Select **Blind**.

406) Enter **1.5** for Depth. Accept the defaults.

407) Click **OK** ✔ from the Cosmetic Thread PropertyManager.

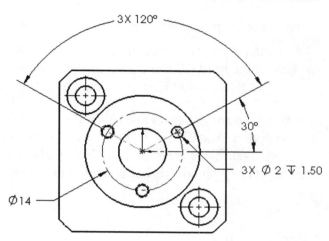

Display the Cosmetic Thread in the FeatureManager.
408) **Expand** the COVERPLATE FeatureManager.

409) **Expand** the Hole Wizard feature. The Cosmetic Thread is added to the M2.0 hole feature.

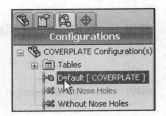

Save the COVERPLATE drawing.
410) Click **Save** 🖫 .

Return to the COVERPLATE part.
411) Click the **Default** configuration.

412) Click **Save** 🖫 .

413) Click **Windows**, **Close All** from the Menu bar menu.

The Cosmetic Thread represents the outside thread diameter of the hole or the inside thread diameter of a boss. Insert the Cosmetic Thread Annotation in the part, assembly or drawing.

The Hole Wizard, Tapped Hole also utilizes the Cosmetic Thread option. Add Cosmetic thread with thread callout option in the part creates the corresponding Hole Callout in the drawing. The Cosmetic Thread is a sub-entry in the CirPattern1 feature.

Insert and add dimensions and annotations as an exercise to
complete the COVERPLATE drawings.

You added annotations in the COVERPLATE drawing.
In Chapter 5 create annotations in a new part and insert annotations
into a drawing. Utilize Model Items to insert the following: Datums,
Datum Targets, Geometric tolerances, Notes, Surface finish, and
Weld annotations.

More Information

Additional details on Dimension Precision, Hole Callout, Aligned
Section View, Section View, Chamfer, Relative View, View
Properties, Grid and Cosmetic Thread are available in SolidWorks
help.

Keywords: Precision (options), section views (aligned, section view PropertyManager),
chamfer (dimensions), relative to model views, grid, properties (drawing views), and cosmetic
threads (display).

 **Review**

The COVERPLATE drawing consisted of three Sheets. Sheet1 utilized an Aligned Section
view. Sheet2 utilized an Offset Section view. Sheet3 was renamed SH-HOLES and utilized a
Relative view.

An Aligned Section required two sketched line segments. The Offset Section required 5
sketched line segments. Additional options for the Section views were discussed.

The Dimension, Chamfer option inserted an annotation for the Chamfer feature. The Chamfer
option required the chamfered edge, reference line and a placement position for the
annotation. You utilized the Drawing View Properties to control the display of the hidden
lines of the Bore feature. Sheet SH-HOLES was positioned in the FeatureManager as the
second sheet in the drawing. The Relative view utilized the part to locate the front and right
faces.

The M2 Hole Wizard dimensions were inserted into the drawing.

Modifying Features

The design process is dynamic. We do not live in a static world. Explore the following changes to the COVERPLATE, With Nose Holes configuration in Exercise 4.1.

Decrease the Boss diameter to Ø17. The drawing dimension decreases. The Dimension text position is unchanged. Feature changes in the part that modify size require simple or no changes in the drawing.

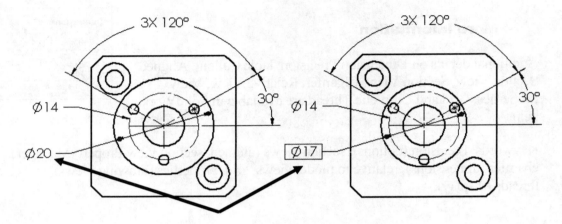

When a part has multiple configurations, dimension changes modify one or more configurations. Modify the 30° to 45° dimensions in the drawing. Check the This Configuration option from the Modify box.

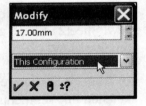

The part configuration COVERPLATE-With Nose Holes controls the 30° dimension. The COVERPLATE-With Nose Holes is the current configuration of the part.

If you receive a warning message, "the part was saved in a different configuration", open the part and set the configuration to With Nose Holes before you change a dimension.

Change the number of holes from 3 to 4 in the Circular Pattern. The change from 3 to 4 instances requires a drawing modification.

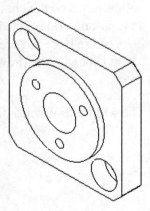

The number of instances, changes from 3 to 4.
Modify the angle from 30° to 45°. Add new
centerline and Center Marks.

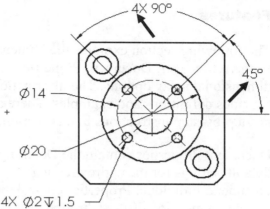

Insert the part Reference geometry into the
drawing. Utilize Insert Model Items to display
Axes, Curves, Planes, Surfaces, Points,
Routing points and Origins.

Control the display of Reference geometry
through the View menu: Planes, Axes,
Temporary Axes, Origins, Coordinate
Systems, Sketches, etc. The options in the
View menu control the display for the entire
sheet.

How do you control the display of a plane in a
single drawing view? Answer: Create
configurations to control the state of a plane in
the part. The State Property controls the
Suppress/Unsuppress reference geometry such
as: *Plane, Axis, Coordinate System, and Point.*

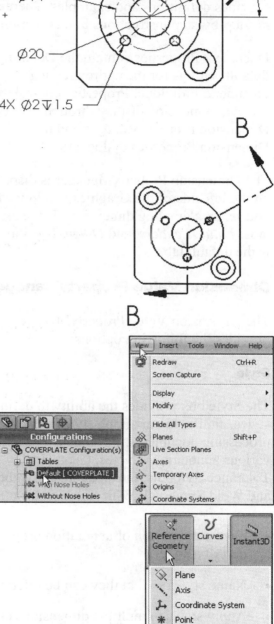

Additional Information-Dimension PropertyManager and Dimensioning Features

The following section explores the Dimension PropertyManager, Document Properties, and dimension display options. The information provides definitions and examples. There are no step-by-step instructions in this section.

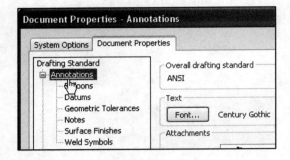

Document Properties contain the Detailing default settings for the entire drawing document. Individual Properties control the selected dimension display through the Dimension PropertyManager and the Dimension Properties dialog box.

The Dimension PropertyManager is displayed on the left side of the Graphics window when you select a drawing dimension. Three are three tabs: *Value*, *Leaders*, and *Other*. The Value tab is the default tab.

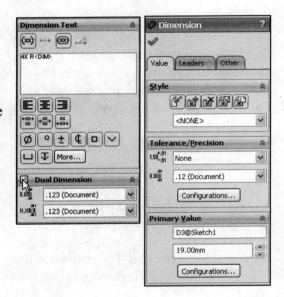

Dimension Value PropertyManager

The Dimension Value PropertyManager provides the following options:

Style

The Style box provides the ability to define styles, similar to paragraph styles in word processing documents, for dimensions and various annotations (Notes, Geometric Tolerance Symbols, Surface Finish Symbols, and Weld Symbols). With styles, you can:

- Save a dimension or annotation property as part of a style.

- Name styles so that they can be referenced.

- Apply styles to multiple dimensions or annotations.

- Add, update, and delete styles.

- Save and load styles. You can also load styles saved from other documents and located in other folders.

Style Type:	File extension:
Dimensions	.sldfvt
Notes	sldnotfvt
Geometric Tolerance Symbols	.sldgtolfbt
Surface Finish Symbols	.sldsffvt
Weld Symbols	.sldweldfvt

💡 Style live in the original model. Modify an inserted dimension in the drawing and the Favorites in the drawings change the Favorites in the part.

Tolerance/Precision

The Tolerance/Precision box defines a Callout value. Select a dimension in an active drawing. The Tolerance/Precision box provides the following options:

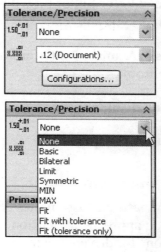
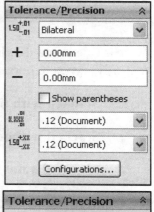

- **Tolerance Type**: Select from the drop-down menu: (None, Basic, Bilateral, Limit, Symmetric, etc). The list is dynamic. Example: Types for chamfer dimensions are limited to None, Bilateral, and Symmetric.

- **Maximum Variation**: Input a value.

- **Minimum Variation**: Input a value.

- **Show parentheses**: Parentheses are available for Bilateral, Symmetric, and Fit with tolerance types. When selected, parentheses bracket the tolerance values. Parenthesis are available for Fit with tolerance if you specify Hole Fit or Shaft Fit, but not both.

- **Primary Unit Precision**: Select the number of digits after the decimal point from the drop-down menu for the dimension precision.

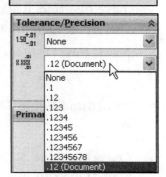

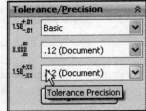

- **Tolerance Precision**: Select the number of digits after the decimal point for tolerance values.

- **Classification**: Available only for Fit, Fit with tolerance, or Fit (tolerance only) types. Classification can be User Defined, Clearance, Transitional, or Press. Select a classification from the list. When you select either Hole Fit or Shaft Fit, the list for the other category (Hole Fit or Shaft Fit) is filtered based on the classification.

- **Hole Fit**: Available only for Fit, or Fit with tolerance, or Fit (tolerance only) types. Select from the lists, or type any text.

- **Shaft Fit**: Available only for Fit, or Fit with tolerance, or Fit (tolerance only) types. Select from the lists, or type any text.

- **Fit tolerance display**: Available only for Fit, Fit with tolerance, or Fit (tolerance only) types. Choose from:

  o **Stacked with line display**

  o **Stacked without line display**

  o **Linear display**

- **Configurations**: For parts and assemblies only. Provides the ability to apply the dimension tolerance to specific configurations for driven dimensions only.

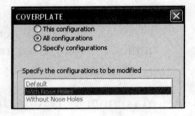

See SolidWorks help for additional information and details.

Primary Value

The Text Dimension box provides the ability to add tolerances to a dimension that you have overridden add, or modify the selected dimension in the drawing.

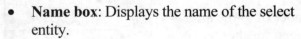

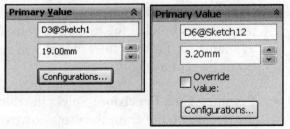

- **Name box**: Displays the name of the select entity.

- **Dimension Value**. Displays the selected dimension in the drawing view.

- **Override value**: Select to override the primary value. If you clear **Override value**, the dimension returns to its original value but retains the tolerance.

- **Configurations**: For parts and assemblies only. Provides the ability to apply the dimension tolerance to specific configurations for driven dimensions only.

Text Dimension

The Text Dimension box provides the ability to add, or modify the selected dimension in the drawing. Select the drawing dimension. The dimension is displayed automatically in the center text box, represented by <DIM>. Place the pointer anywhere in the text box to insert text. If you delete <DIM>, you can reinsert the value by clicking Add Value. The Text Dimension box provides the following options:

- **Add Parenthesis:** Inserts Parenthesis around the dimension.

- **Center Dimension:** Centers the dimension.

- **Inspection Dimension**: Inserts an Inspection dimension.

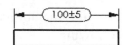

- **Offset Text:** Offset text relative to the dimension.

- **Justify**: You can justify text horizontally and, for some standards such as ANSI, you can justify the leader vertically.

    o **Horizontal - Left Justify, Center Justify, Right Justify**

    o **Vertical - Top Justify, Middle Justify, Bottom Justify**

- **Symbols**: Click to place the pointer where you want a symbol. Click a symbol icon (for Diameter, Degree, etc) or click the More option to access the Symbol Library. The symbol is represented by its name in the text box, and the actual symbol is displayed in the Graphics window.

Dual Dimension

The Dual Dimension box provides the ability to specify that the dimension is displayed in both the document's unit system and the dual dimension units. Both units are specified in **Tools, Options, Document Properties, Units**.

- **Primary Unit Precision:** Select the number of digits after the decimal point from the list for the dimension value.

- **Tolerance Precision:** Select the number of digits after the decimal point for tolerance values.

Type	Unit	Decimals
Basic Units		
Length	inches	.12
Dual Dimension Length	inches	.123
Angle	degrees	.12

Dimension Leaders PropertyManager

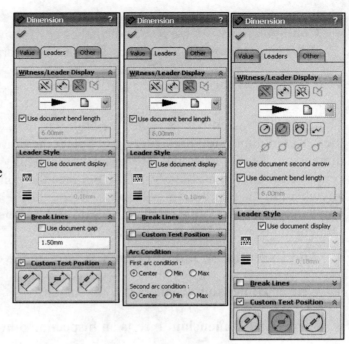

The Dimension Leaders PropertyManager is document and dimension dependent.

If you select multiple dimensions, only the properties that apply to all the selected dimensions are available. The Leaders tab in the Dimension PropertyManager provides the following options:

Witness/Leader Display

The Witness/Leader Display box provides the ability to position the following:

- **Leader display location**: **Outside, Inside, Smart, and Directed Leader**.

- **Arrow style**: Provides the ability to select **13 Arrow Styles**.

- **Leader display**: **Radius, Diameter, Linear, Multi-jog Leader, Two Arrows / Solid Leader, Two Arrows / Open Leader, One Arrow / Solid Leader, One Arrow / Open Leader.**

- **Use document bend length**. Checked by default.

- **Use document second arrow**. Checked by default.

 Smart specifies that arrows automatically appear outside of extension lines if the space is too small to accommodate the dimension text and the arrowheads.

Arrow style and Leader display are document dependent.

Leader Style

You can define Leader styles, similar to paragraph styles in word processing documents, for dimensions and various annotations (Notes, Geometric Tolerance Symbols, Surface Finish Symbols, and Weld Symbols).

Break Line

The Break Lines box provides the ability to select the dimension and extension lines to break when crossing other dimension or extension lines in drawings:

- **Use document gap**: Select to use the document default set in Tools, Options, Document Properties, Dimensions.

- **Gap**: Enter a value if you do not use the document's default.

Custom Text Position

The Custom Text Position box provides the following options: **Solid leader, aligned text**, **Broken leader, horizontal text**, and **Broken leader, aligned text**.

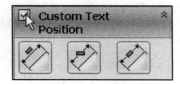

 See SolidWorks help for additional information and details.

Arc Condition

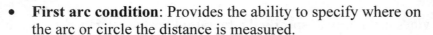
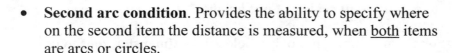

The Arc Condition box provides the ability to set how to dimension between an arc or a circle:

- **First arc condition**: Provides the ability to specify where on the arc or circle the distance is measured.

- **Second arc condition**. Provides the ability to specify where on the second item the distance is measured, when <u>both</u> items are arcs or circles.

Example: The **First arc condition** is **Center**, and the **Second arc condition** is set as illustrated.

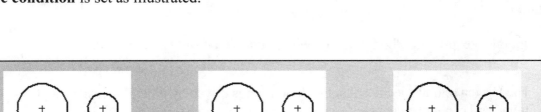

| Center (default) | Min (closest point) | Max (farthest point) |

Dimension Other PropertyManager

The Dimension Other PropertyManager provides the ability to specify the display of dimensions. If you select multiple dimensions, only the properties that apply to all the selected dimensions are available.

Override Units

The Override Units box provides the ability to override the document's units defined in the Units options section. Specify the unit type for the selected dimension. The available options depend on the type of dimensions that you selected. For example, an **Angular Unit** can be **Degrees**, **Deg/Min**, **Deg/Min/Sec**, or **Radians**.

Text Fonts

The Text Fonts box provides the following options:

- **Dimension font: Provides the ability to** specify the font used for the dimension. Either select **Use document's font**, as defined in the Annotations Font section, or clear the check box and click the Font option to select a new font type, style, and size for the selected items.

- **Tolerance font**. Provides the ability to specify the font used for the tolerance dimension. Select **Use dimension font** to use the same font as for dimensions. Clear **Use dimension font** to specify **Font scale** or **Font height**.

- **Fit tolerance font** (For **Fit** tolerance types only). Select **Use dimension font** to use the same font as for dimensions. Clear **Use dimension font** to specify **Font scale** or **Font height**.

Options

The Options box provides the following two options: **Read only** and **Driven**.

The Driven option specifies that the dimension is driven by other dimensions and conditions, and cannot be changed.

Layer

The Layer box provides the ability to select a layer in the drawing.

Dimension Properties Dialog Box

The Dimension Properties dialog box contains additional options to control the selected dimension.

In tight spaces control the arrow, extension line, and dimension line display.

Both arrowheads do not fit in the tight space. Modify the bottom arrowhead to a straight line.

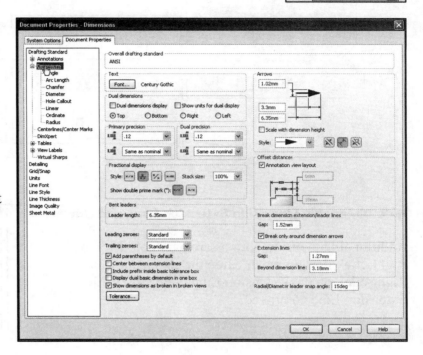

For the document, the Document Properties, Dimensions: *Angle, Arc Length, Chamfer, Diameter, Hole Callout, Linear, and Radius* folders address Leaders to control leader lines and text.

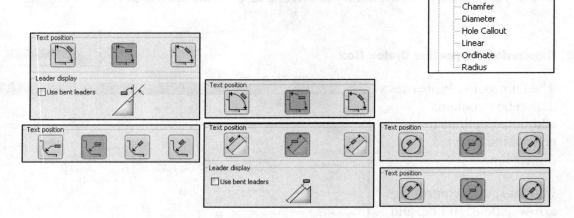

Hide Dimension Line, Hide Extension Line, and Driven

Additional Dimension options are available with the Right-click Pop-up menu. Hide the Extension Line. Right-click on the Extension Line. Select the Hide Extension Line command.

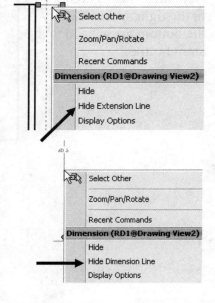

Right-click on the Dimension Line. Select Hide Dimension Line. Select the left and right lines between the dimension to hide both lines.

Modify an inserted model dimension to a Driven dimension in the drawing. Other dimensions and conditions drive a Driven dimension. Check the Driven option in the Pop-up menu or in the Dimension PropertyManager Options box.

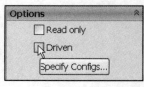

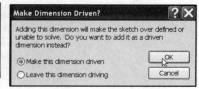

Dimension Schemes

There are various dimension schemes for arcs. The dimensioning scheme of the part utilized symmetry and equal relations between the two arcs.

How do you determine the design intent of a sketch, if you did not create the model? Answer: Review the geometric relations.

Locate Display\Delete Relations Display... Relations in the Sketch toolbar.

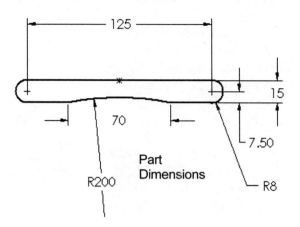

Foreshortened Radii

The Dimension tool draws large radii outside the sheet boundary or overlaps a second view. A Foreshortened radius inserts three line segments on the leader line.

When you dimension to a foreshortened radius or diameter, the dimension also appears as a zigzag.

Check the Foreshortened radius check box in the Dimension Leaders PropertyManager or Right-click Display Options, Foreshortened. Drag the blue endpoints of the foreshortened radius if required to fit within the view.

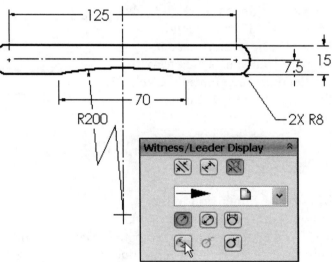

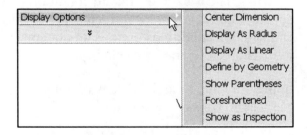

Partially Rounded Ends, Center/Min/Max Arc Condition

The distance between the two
center points of the arc
determines the current overall
dimension, 125. Return to the
part sketch to redefine the
dimension scheme.

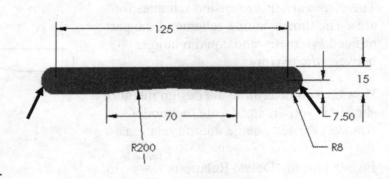

Delete the overall dimension.
Click Smart Dimension. Select
each arc to redefine the overall
length. Do not select the center
point.

Select the dimension, 125. Click
Max for the First arc condition
from the Dimension Leaders
PropertyManager. Click Max for
the Second arc condition. Click OK
from the PropertyManager. The
overall arc dimension is 141.

Save and Exit the sketch. Return to
the drawing.

Modify the dimension in the
drawing. Enter 2X for the radius
text. Add center marks to indicate the center of the
radii. Create a gap. Add centerlines to complete the
drawing. The Max and Min arc condition options
appear when dimensions reference arc edges. The Max
and Min arc conditions options do not appear when
dimensions reference arc center points.

In the drawing, drag the extension line to modify the
Max, Min, Center arc condition.

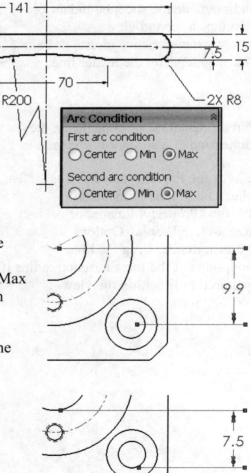

Display Option, Offset Text

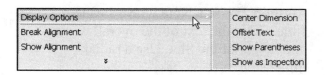

The Pop-up Display Options controls the dimension display. In tight spaces, utilize the Offset Text to position the dimension text off the dimension line.

Slotted Holes

Slotted Holes utilized symmetry in the part. Redefine the dimensions for the Slot Cut according to the ASME 14.5M standard. The ASME 14.5M standard requires that the dimension references the arc edge.

The Radius value is not dimensioned. Select each arc to create a center/min/max arc condition in the part.

Insert the part into the drawing. The end radii are indicated.

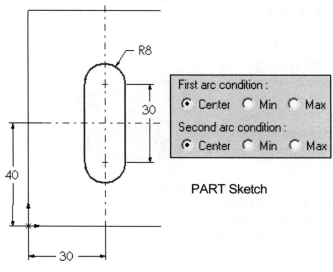

PART Sketch

No dimension is labeled. There are three methods to dimension a slot in the drawing. Modify the dimension properties to create one of the following:

Method 1: Select Center for the First Arc condition. Select Center for the Second Arc condition.

Create a linear dimension between the two vertical lines of the slot. Create a radial dimension. Delete the radius value.

Enter the text 2X R. Add two Center Marks and a Centerline between the two arcs.

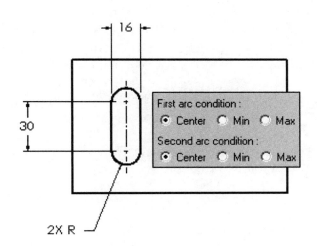

Method 2: Use a Note with a Leader Line. Enter the text of the overall width and height of the Slot. Use a radial dimension.

Enter the 2X R text. Add two intersecting centerlines.

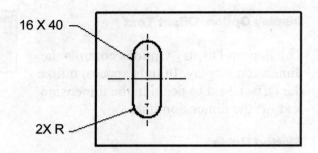

Method 3: Select Max for the First Arc condition. Select Max for the Second Arc condition.

Create a linear dimension between the two vertical lines of the slot.

Create a radial dimension. Delete the radius value. Enter 2X R text.

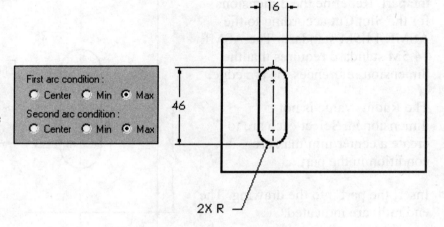

Grid/Snap

The Document Properties, Dimensions, Snap text to grid option positions the dimension text at the grid snap points in a drawing or sketch. The snap points are located at the intersection of two perpendicular grid lines. Control Grid and Snap options through the Document Properties, Grid/Snap option.

Location of Features

The information is provided to you in order to explore other dimensioning methods.

Rectangular coordinate dimensioning locates features with respect to one another, from a datum or an origin.

There are two methods:

- **Base Line Dimensioning**

- **Ordinate Dimensioning**

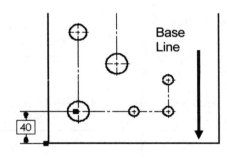

Base Line Dimensioning

Create Base Line Dimensions. Select a Base Line. Select a feature (hole). Select a location for the dimension text.

Select the remaining features in order from smallest to largest.

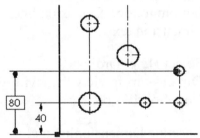

Base Line dimensions are aligned dimensions. To insert a new dimension between existing dimensions, break the alignment with the text closest to the new value.

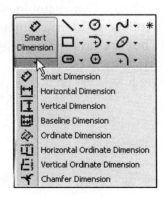

Ordinate Dimension

Create Horizontal Ordinate Dimensions.
Select Tools, Dimension, Horizontal Ordinate
from the Menu bar menu or use
Autodimension PropertyManager.

Select the Origin or vertex for a zero location.
All other dimensions are measured from this
location.

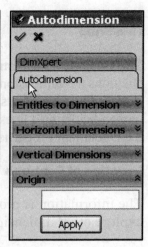

Select a location for the
dimension text below the
profile. Select a feature
(hole). Select the remaining
features in order from left
to right.

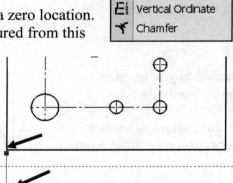

Create Vertical Ordinate
Dimensions. Select
Vertical Ordinate. Select the Origin of vertex for
zero location.

Select a location for the dimension text off the
profile. Select a feature (hole).

Select the remaining features in order from
bottom to top. Extension lines will jog to fit
dimension text.

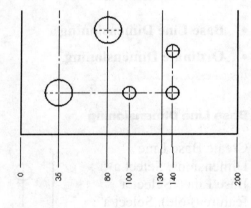

Select Help, Ordinate
Dimensions to view the .avi file
from SolidWorks.

Baseline Dimensioning and
Ordinate Dimensioning
produce reference dimensions.
They are driven dimensions
from the part.

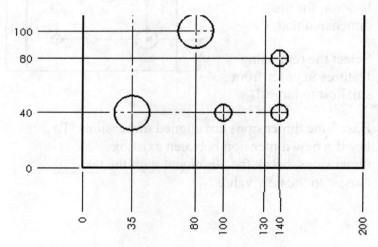

Part features drive Baseline and Ordinate dimensions. To insert a new Ordinate dimension, right-click on an existing dimension. Click Add to Ordinate.

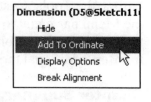

Hole Tables label holes on the drawing. The labels locate each hole based on an X-Y coordinate system. Explore Hole Tables in Chapter 5.

TAG	X LOC	Y LOC	SIZE
A1	35	40	∅25 THRU
A2	80	100	∅25 THRU
A3	80	180	∅25 THRU
A4	130	260	∅25 THRU
B1	35	140	∅20 THRU
B2	130	210	∅20 THRU
C1	100	40	∅12 THRU
C2	140	40	∅12 THRU
C3	140	80	∅12 THRU

Hole Table for TABLE-PLATE-LABELS

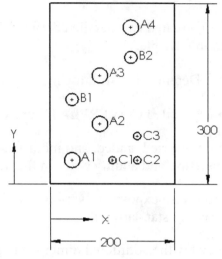

View Layout Toolbar and Annotation Toolbar

The CommandManager displays the Annotation toolbar and the View Layout toolbar. In Chapter 3 and Chapter 4 you utilized the default tools in the View Layout and the Annotation toolbars.

Locate additional tools in the Menu bar menu:

- **Insert, Drawing View**

- **Insert, Annotations**

- **Tools, Dimensions**

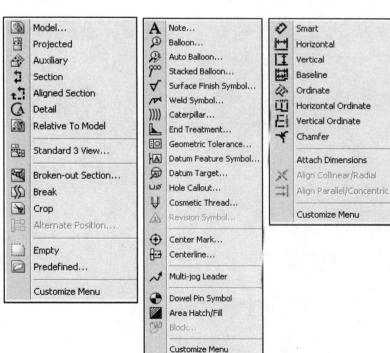

Utilize the Tools, Customize from
the Menu bar menu to modify a
toolbar. Select the Commands tab
to insert additional tools.

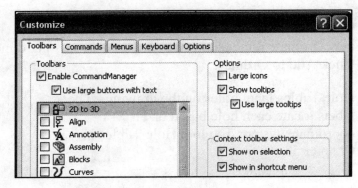

Chapter Summary

You created two detailed drawings
in this chapter:

- Detailed TUBE drawing

- Detailed COVERPLATE drawing

You inserted, added, and modified dimensions along with obtaining an understanding of
inserting and adding notes in the detailed drawings.

You were exposed to various methods to move, hide, and add dimensions that adhere to a
drawing standard.

Review the additional dimensioning options in the Dimension PropertyManager,
Dimension Property dialog box and Pop-up menu. Apply your skills to detail the ROD
drawing and other drawings in the chapter exercises.

Chapter Terminology

Annotation: An annotation is a text note or a symbol that adds specific information and design intent to a part, assembly, or drawing. Annotations in a drawing include: specific note, hole callout, surface finish symbol, datum feature symbol, datum target, geometric tolerance symbol, weld symbol, balloon, and stacked balloon, center mark, centerline marks, area hatch, and block.

AutoDimension: The Autodimension tool provides the ability to insert reference dimensions into drawing views such as baseline, chain, and ordinate dimensions.

Baseline dimensions: Dimensions referenced from the same edge or vertex in a drawing view.

Balloon: Labels parts in an assembly, typically including item numbers and quantity. In drawings, the item numbers are related to rows in a bill of materials (BOM). Create balloons in a drawing document or in a note.

Bill of Materials: A table inserted into a drawing to keep a record of the parts used in an assembly.

Broken out Section: A drawing view that exposes inner details of a drawing view by removing material from a closed profile, usually a spline.

Center Mark: A cross that marks the center of a circle or arc.

Centerline: An axis of symmetry in a sketch or drawing displayed in a phantom font.

ConfigurationManager: The ConfigurationManager is located on the left side of the SolidWorks window and provides the means to create, select, and view multiple configurations of parts and assemblies in an active document. You can split the ConfigurationManager and either display two ConfigurationManager instances, or combine the ConfigurationManager with the FeatureManager design tree, PropertyManager, or third party applications that use the panel.

CommandManager: The CommandManager is a Context-sensitive toolbar that dynamically updates based on the toolbar you want to access. By default, it has toolbars embedded in it based on the document type. When you click a tab below the Command Manager, it updates to display that toolbar. For example, if you click the **Sketches** tab, the Sketch toolbar is displayed.

Copy and Paste: Utilize copy/paste to copy views from one sheet to another sheet in a drawing or between different drawings.

Cosmetic thread: An annotation that represents threads.

Crosshatch: A pattern (or fill) applied to drawing views such as section views and broken-out sections

Detailing: Detailing refers to the SolidWorks module used to insert, add, and modify dimensions and notes in an engineering drawing.

Design Table: An Excel spreadsheet that is used to create multiple configurations in a part or assembly document.

Dimension: A value indicating the size of feature geometry.

Dimension Line: A line that references dimension text to extension lines indicating the feature being measured.

DimXpert for Parts: A set of tools that applies dimensions and tolerances to parts according to the requirements of the ASME Y.14.41-2003 standard.

Document: A file containing a part, assembly, or drawing.

Drawing: A 2D representation of a 3D part or assembly. The extension for a SolidWorks drawing file name is .SLDDRW. Drawing refers to the SolidWorks module used to insert, add, and modify views in an engineering drawing.

Edit Sheet: The drawing sheet contains two modes. Utilize the Edit Sheet command to insert views and dimensions.

Edit Sheet Format: The drawing sheet contains two modes. Utilize the Edit Sheet Format command to add or modify notes and Title block information. Edit in the Edit Sheet Format mode.

Equation: Creates a mathematical relation between sketch dimensions, using dimension names as variables, or between feature parameters, such as the depth of an extruded feature or the instance count in a pattern.

Extension line: The line extending from the profile line indicating the point from which a dimension is measured.

Face: A selectable area (planar or otherwise) of a model or surface with boundaries that help define the shape of the model or surface. For example, a rectangular solid has six faces.

FeatureManager: The FeatureManager design tree located on the left side of the SolidWorks window provides an outline view of the active part, assembly, or drawing. This makes it easy to see how the model or assembly was constructed or to examine the various sheets and views in a drawing. The FeatureManager and the Graphics window are dynamically linked. You can select features, sketches, drawing views, and construction geometry in either pane.

First Angle Projection: Standard 3 Views are in either third angle or first angle projection. In first angle projection, the front view is displayed at the upper left and the other two views are the top and left views.

Foreshortened radius: Helpful when the centerpoint of a radius is outside of the drawing or interferes with another drawing view: Broken Leader.

Fully defined: A sketch where all lines and curves in the sketch, and their positions, are described by dimensions or relations, or both, and cannot be moved. Fully defined sketch entities are displayed in black.

Geometric Tolerance: A set of standard symbols that specify the geometric characteristics and dimensional requirements of a feature.

Graphics window: The area in the SolidWorks window where the part, assembly, or drawing is displayed.

Heads-up View toolbar: A transparent toolbar located at the top of the Graphic window.

Hole Callouts: Hole callouts are available in drawings. If you modify a hole dimension in the model, the callout updates automatically in the drawing if you did not use DimXpert.

Leader: A solid line created from an annotation to the referenced feature.

Model Item: Provides the ability to insert dimensions, annotations, and reference geometry from a model document (part or assembly) into a drawing.

Ordinate dimensions: Chain of dimensions referenced from a zero ordinate in a drawing or sketch.

Origin: The model origin is displayed in blue and represents the (0,0,0) coordinate of the model. When a sketch is active, a sketch origin is displayed in red and represents the (0,0,0) coordinate of the sketch. Dimensions and relations can be added to the model origin, but not to a sketch origin.

Rebuild: A tool that updates (or regenerates) the document with any changes made since the last time the model was rebuilt. Rebuild is typically used after changing a model dimension.

Reference dimension: Dimensions added to a drawing document are called Reference dimensions, and are driven; you cannot edit the value of reference dimensions to modify the model. However, the values of reference dimensions change when the model dimensions change.

Relative view: A relative (or relative to model) drawing view is created relative to planar surfaces in a part or assembly.

Rollback: Suppresses all items below the rollback bar.

Parametric note: A Note that references a SolidWorks dimension or property.

Precision: Controls the number of decimal places displayed in a dimension.

Silhouette edge: A curve representing the extent of a cylindrical or curved face when viewed from the side.

Suppress: Removes an entity from the display and from any calculations in which it is involved. You can suppress features, assembly components, and so on. Suppressing an entity does not delete the entity; you can unsuppress the entity to restore it.

Tangent Edge: The transition edge between rounded or filleted faces in hidden lines visible or hidden lines removed modes in drawings.

Weld Finish: A weld symbol representing the parameters you specify.

Questions:

1. Dimensions in a drawing are _____ from a part or _____ in the drawing.

2. Drawing Notes, Hole Callout, and Center Mark tools are located in the SolidWorks _____ toolbar.

3. Identify the order in which dimensions are inserted into a drawing with the various views: Standard views, Section views and Detail views.

4. True or False. Feature dimensions are inserted into an Empty drawing.

5. Identify the command to select when dimensions are no longer required.

6. Describe a Reference dimension in SolidWorks.

7. Describe the procedure to move a part dimension from one view to a different view.

8. List and describe three methods to dimension simple holes and circular geometry.

9. True or False. Cosmetic Threads added in the drawing are automatically inserted into the referenced part.

10. A drawing references multiple part configurations. A dimension is changed on a drawing. Identify the three Modify options that appear in the Modify dialog box.

11. Name three different types of Reference geometry created in a part that is inserted into a drawing.

12. Describe the procedure to create a Foreshortened radius.

13. Identify the arc conditions that are required when dimensioning the overall length of a slot.

14. Provide a definition for Baseline Dimensioning.

15. Provide a definition for Ordinate Dimensioning.

16. Identity the following symbols:

Exercises

Exercise 4.1:

Open the COVERPLATE part. Decrease the Boss diameter to ∅17.

Open the COVERPLATE drawing. Modify the M2 hole location from 30° to 45°.
Change the number of M2 holes from 3 to 4 in the Circular Pattern.

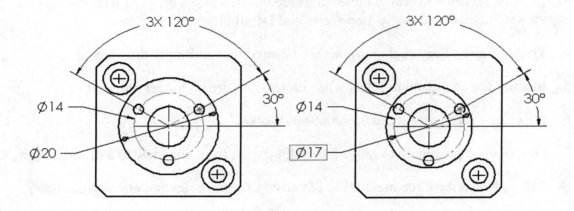

Add a new centerline and redefine the dimension. Reposition the dimensions and edit the
note quantity of M2 holes from 3 to 4. Insert Center Marks to complete the drawing.

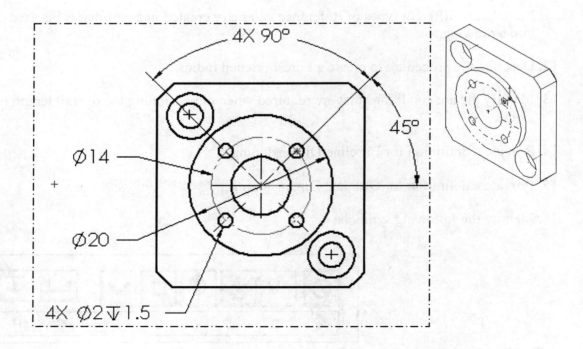

Exercise 4.2:

Create a new drawing for the RADIUS-ROUNDED END part. Locate the part in the DRAWING-W-SOLIDWORKS-2010\Exercises folder. Add a Foreshorten Radius for the R200.

Create an overall dimension for the partially rounded ends. Modify the Radius text according to the ASME standard. Add Centerlines and Center Marks.

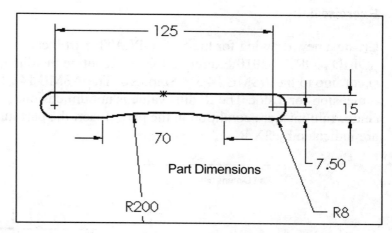

Part Dimensions

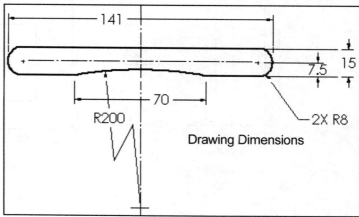

Drawing Dimensions

Exercise 4.3:

Dimension chamfers in the drawing. Create a new part called C-BLOCK. Sketch an L-shaped Extruded Base feature. Add two different size CHAMFER features. The dimensions are not provided.

Create the C-BLOCK drawing. Insert chamfer dimensions into a drawing. Click Smart Dimension from the Sketch toolbar. Right-click in the Graphics window. Select Chamfer. The mouse pointer changes to .

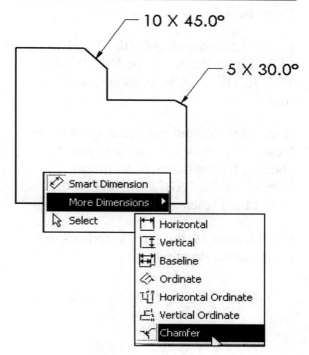

Select the chamfered edge. Select one of the lead-in edges. Click in the Graphics window to place the dimension and to display the CHAMFER.

Exercise 4.4:

Create a new drawing for the SLOT-PLATE part located in the DRAWING-W-SOLIDWORKS-2010\Exercises folder. Redefine the dimensions for the Slot Cut according to the ASME 14.5M Standard. The ASME 14.5M Standard requires an outside dimension for a slot. The Radius value is not dimensioned. Select each arc to create a center/min/max arc condition in the part. Insert the part into the drawing. The end radii are indicated by 2X R.

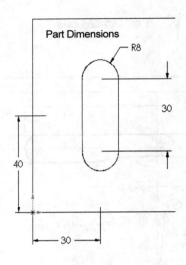

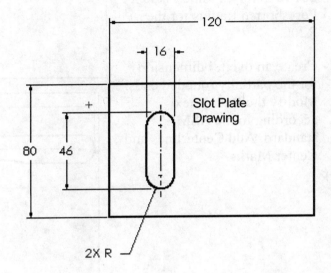

Exercise 4.5:

Create a new drawing for the TABLE-PLATE part located in the DRAWING-W-SOLIDWORKS-2010\exercises folder.

Rectangular coordinate dimensioning locates features with respect to one another, from a datum or an origin. Dimension the TABLE-PLATE with Base Line Dimensioning.

Insert Center Marks and Centerlines to complete the drawing.

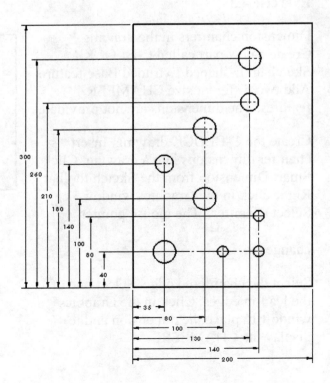

Exercise 4.6:

Create a new drawing for the TABLE-PLATE part located in the DRAWING-W-SOLIDWORKS-2010\Exercise folder. Dimension the TABLE-PLATE with Ordinate Dimensioning.

Insert Center Marks and Centerlines to complete the drawing.

To insert an Ordinate dimension for a new feature, right-click on an existing dimension and select the Add to Ordinate option.

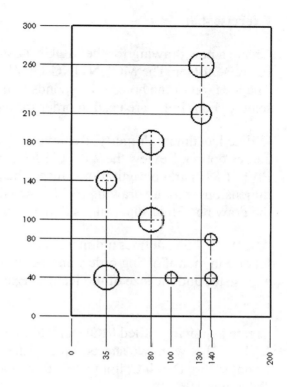

Exercise 4.7:

Detail the ROD Drawing.

The ROD requires dimensions for both the Long and Short part configuration. Dimension the Short configuration on Sheet1. Dimension the Long configuration on Sheet2 and Sheet3 in this section.

Utilize Hole Callout, Center Mark and Centerline from the Annotations toolbar.

Utilize the Display As Radius option for the Front view diameter dimension.

Modify the 2X R4. Utilize the Displays As Linear option.

Modify the 8 dimension. Utilize the Display As Diameter option.

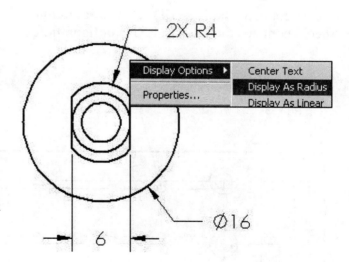

Exercise 4.8:

Create a new drawing for the MOUNTINGPLATE-CYLINDER part located in the Exercise folder. The MOUNTING-CLYLINDER contains a square pattern of 4 holes. The location of the holes corresponds to the initial sketch of the TUBE Base Extrude feature. Four holes are used in order for the TUBE to be mounted in either direction.

Utilize Document Property, Remove Trailing zeroes option. Review the 2 PATTERN and 3 PATTERN part configurations. Insert the part dimensions into the drawing. Add dimensions in the drawing. Hide superfulous dimensions.

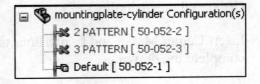

ASME Y14.5M defines a dimension for a repeating feature in the following order: number of features, an X, a space and the size of the feature. Example: 12X Ø3.5.

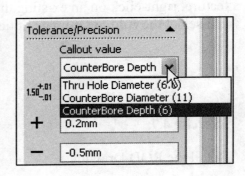

Create a drawing called MOUNTINGPLATE-CYLINDER with two sheets. Modify the CounterBore Depth Callout value to include Tolerance +0.2/-0.5.

Sheet1 contains the 3 PATTERN configuration.
Sheet2 contains the 2 PATTERN configuration.

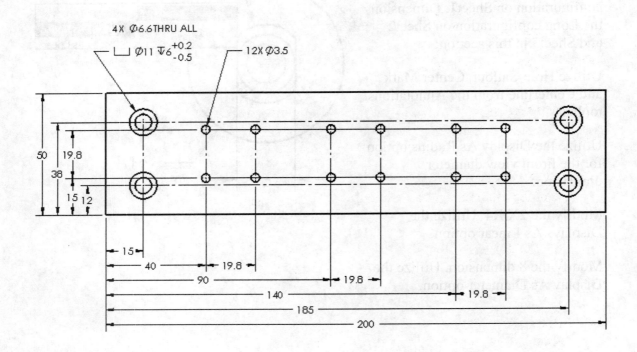

Chapter 5

Assembly Drawings

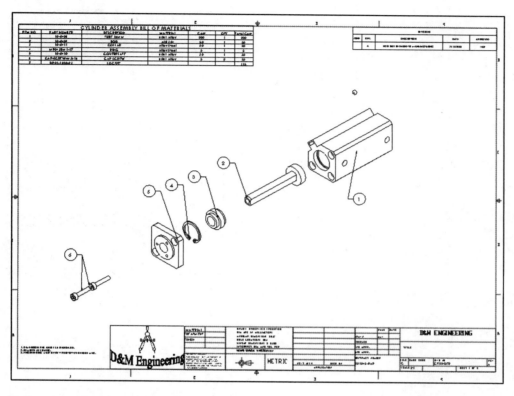

Below are the desired outcomes and usage competencies based on the completion of this Chapter.

Desired Outcomes:	Usage Competencies:
Two Drawings and a Assembly: • CYLINDER assembly with Custom Properties and a Design Table	• Ability to create an assembly with multiple configurations.
	• An understanding of Custom Properties and SolidWorks Properties.
• CYLINDER drawing • COVERPLATE4 drawing	• Ability to create an assembly drawing using multiple part and assembly configurations.
• Bill of Materials and Revision Table.	• Knowledge to develop and incorporate a Bill of Materials and Revision Tables.

Notes:

Chapter 5 - Assembly Drawings

Chapter Objective

You will create the
following in this chapter:

- CYLINDER assembly
  with Custom Properties
  and a Design Table.

- CYLINDER drawing
  with multiple sheets
  and a Bill of Materials.

- COVERPLATE4
  drawing with a
  Revision Table.

Insert an Isometric
Exploded view in the CYLINDER assembly. Add Custom
Properties to each part to describe: Material, Mass, Description,
and Cost parameters. Insert a Design Table in the CYLINDER
assembly to create six different configurations of the assembly.

Insert a Revision Table into the COVERPLATE4 drawing and the
CYLINDER drawing. An Engineering Change Order (ECO)
requires a Revision letter in the Revision Table and the Title
blocks of the part and assembly drawings. Create three sheets for
the CYLINDER drawing:

- Sheet1: Isometric Exploded view, Balloon labels, and a Bill of
  Materials.

- Sheet2: Multiple configurations of the CYLINDER assembly
  with corresponding Bill of Materials.

- Sheet3: Show/Hide options and configurations in drawing views.

Create a single sheet for the COVERPLATE4 drawing:

- Sheet1: Insert a Revision Table and Revisions.

On the completion of this chapter, you will be able to:

- Insert an assembly with multiple configurations into a drawing.

- Display the Exploded view in the drawing.

- Insert Balloons and Bill of Materials.

- Edit and format the Bill of Materials.

- Add Custom Properties to the components of the CYLINDER assembly.

- Link Custom Properties in the drawing

- Modify View Properties in the drawing.

- Insert Revisions and modify the REV linked property in the Title block.

- Utilize the following SolidWorks tools and commands: *Custom Properties, Note, Balloon, Auto Balloon, Stacked Balloon, Bill of Materials, Exploded View, Revision Table, Design Library* and *View Palette*.

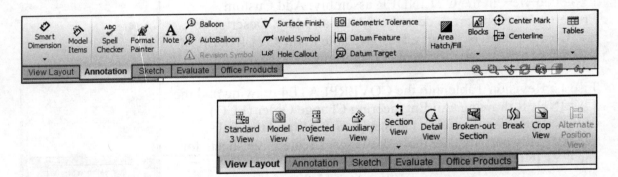

Chapter Overview

The Manufacturing and Marketing department requires a CYLINDER drawing. Marketing needs part and assembly views for their on-line catalog. Manufacturing requires a Bill of Materials for the assembly configuration.

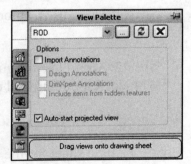

Creating a Bill of Materials is an automatic function that uses a table similar to the Hole Table and the Revision Table. Changes at the assembly level (deletions, reordering, additions and so on) are reflected in the BOM.

The CYLINDER drawing consists of multiple configurations of the CYLINDER assembly and the Bill of Materials.

Sheet1 contains an Exploded Isometric View with a Bill of Materials.

The Revision Table, REV letter is linked to the REV letter in the Title block of the drawing.

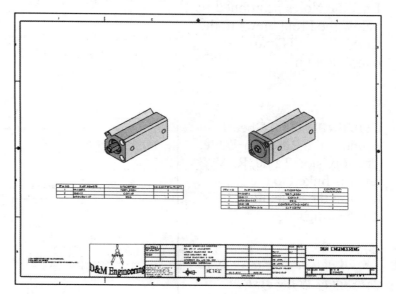

Sheet2 contains two CYLINDER configurations. The COVERPLATE and CAP-SCREWS are suppressed in the top left Isometric view.

The two parts: COVERPLATE and CAP-SCREWS are unsuppressed in the top right Isometric view.

The Bill of Materials reflects the two different configurations.

In SolidWorks 2010, when you right-click a component in an assembly drawing, you can open the part or assembly. In previous versions, you could only open the part.

Insert Custom properties in a part - they propagate to the Design Table. Insert Custom properties in a Design Table - they propagate to the part if the link is active.

A goal of this book is to expose various SolidWorks design tools and features. The most direct way may not be always shown.

Sheet3 contains the CUTAWAY, Default CYLINDER configuration, and the CYLINDER Design Table.

Sheet3 also contains two Front views of the COVERPLATE part. The left Front view displays the WithNoseHoles configuration. The right Front view displays the WithoutNoseHoles configuration.

Link the Notes positioned below the Front views to the COVERPLATE part configuration.

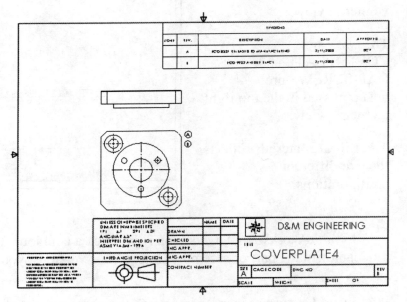

COVERPLATE4-Sheet1 contains the Revision Table. The Revision Table, REV letter is linked to the REV letter in the Title block of the drawing.

When adding a Sheet to a drawing, if the system can't locate the Sheet format, add the Sheet format in File Location under System Options or Browse to the correct Sheet format location.

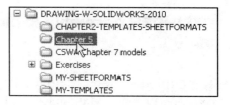

🔆 Utilize the CYLINDER assembly and other components: CAP-SCREW-M3x16, COLLAR, COVERPLATE4, RING, ROD4, TUBE4, and TUBE4-ROD4 located in DRAWING-W-SOLIDWORKS-2010\Chapter 5 folder on the CD in the book. Copy all needed files and folders to your hard drive.

The components contain the parts, Design Tables, and Custom Properties required for the three sheets in the CYLINDER drawing. Work between five different document types in this project: drawing, assembly, part, Design Table and Bill of Materials. The illustrations specify the document type.

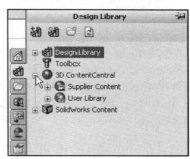

🔆 Utilize Ctrl Tab to toggle between the open drawing, assembly and part.

🔆 SMC Corporation of America manufactures the CYLINDER assembly. The model files were obtained from 3D ContentCentral. The components were modified for educational purposes.

The RING and CAP-SCREW-M3x16 part were obtained from the SolidWorks\toolbox and modified for the chapter.

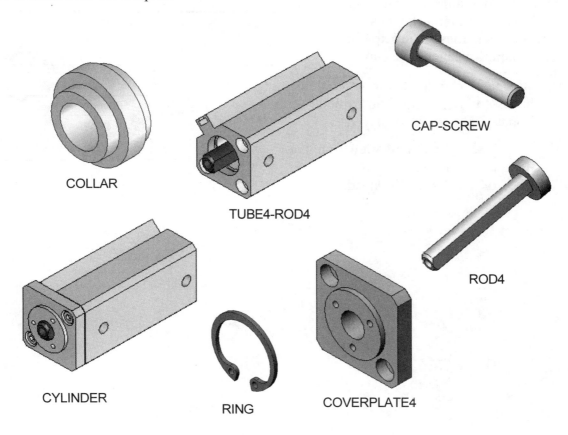

CYLINDER Assembly-Exploded View

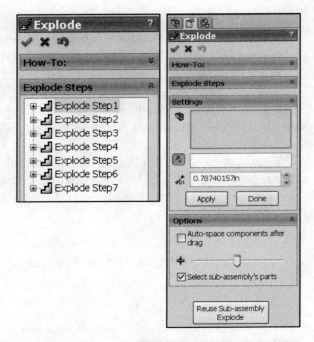

The Exploded view 🗗 tool utilizes the Explode PropertyManager.

An Exploded view illustrates how to assemble the components in an assembly.

Create an Exploded view in this section with seven steps. Click and drag components in the Graphics window.

The Manipulator icon ⊥ indicates the direction to explode. Select an alternate component edge for the Explode direction. Drag the component in the Graphics window or enter an exact value in the Explode distance box. Manipulate the top-level components in the assembly.

Access the Explode View 🗗 tool from the following locations:

- Click the **ConfigurationManager** tab. Right-click **Default**. Click **New Exploded View**. The Explode PropertyManager is displayed.

- Click the **Exploded View** 🗗 tool in the Assembly toolbar. The Explode PropertyManager is displayed.

- Click **Insert**, **Exploded View** from the Menu bar menu. The Explode PropertyManager is displayed.

Activity: CYLINDER Assembly-Exploded View

Open the CYLINDER assembly.
1) **Open** the CYLINDER assembly in the DRAWING-W-SOLIDWORKS-2010\Chapter 5 folder which you copied from the CD in the book.

Insert an Exploded view.

2) Click **Exploded View** from the Assembly toolbar. The Explode PropertyManager is displayed.

Create Explode Step1.
3) **Expand** the fly-out FeatureManager in the Graphics window.

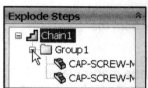

4) Click **CAP-SCREW-M3x16<1>** and **CAP-SCREW-M3x16<2>**.

5) Enter **180**mm in the Explode distance box or use the on-screen ruler with the control points.

6) Check the **Auto-space components after drag** box.

7) Check the **Select-sub-assembly's parts** box.

8) Click **Reverse direction**, if required.

9) Click **Apply**.

10) Click **Done**. Chain1/Group1 is created. View the illustration.

You can click and drag with the Manipulator icon to move the component in the assembly using the control points with on the on-screen ruler.

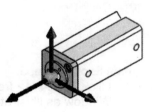

Fit the Model to the Graphics window.
11) Press the **f** key.

For a more realistic assembly animation, create the Explode Steps in the order to disassemble the physical components.

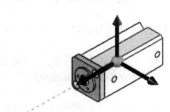

Create Explode Step2.
12) Click **COVERPLATE4<1>** from the FeatureManager.

13) Drag the **blue/orange manipulator handle** to the left approximately 100mms.

14) Click **Done**. Chain2 is created.

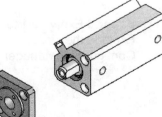

Create Explode Step3.

15) Click **RING<1>** from the FeatureManager.

16) Drag the **blue/orange manipulator handle** to the left approximately 50mms.

17) Click **Done**. Chain3 is created.

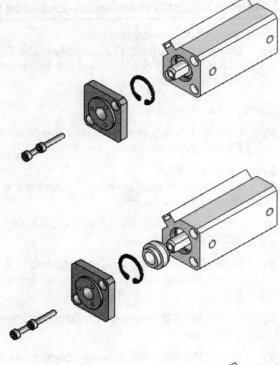

Create Explode Step4.

18) Click **COLLAR<1>** from the FeatureManager.

19) Drag the **blue/orange manipulator handle** to the left approximately 30mms.

20) Click **Done**.

Create Explode Step5.

21) Click **Tube4<1>** from the Graphics Window as illustrated.

22) Drag the **blue/orange manipulator handle** to the right approximately 70mms.

23) Click **Done**. View the results.

24) Click **OK** ✔ from the Explode PropertyManager.

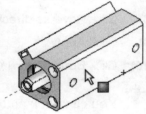

Display the Exploded view steps in the ConfigurationManager.

25) Click the

ConfigurationManager tab.

26) **Expand** Default.

27) **Expand** ExplView1 to display Explode the ConfigurationManager.

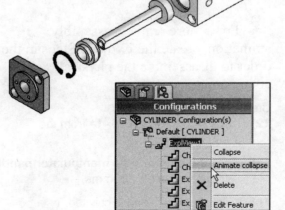

28) Right-click on **ExplView1**.

29) Click **Animate collapse**. View the animation.

30) Click **Close** ⊠ from the Animation Controller.

Return to the CYLINDER assembly.

31) Click the CYLINDER **FeatureManager** 🟦 tab.

Save the CYLINDER assembly.

32) Click **Save** 💾 .

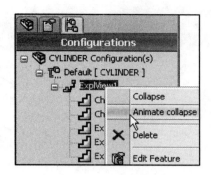

💡 When the Animation Controller is open, commands in SolidWorks are not accessible. Close the Animation Controller toolbar to return to SolidWorks.

💡 Click the **Animation1** tab/**MotionStudy1** tab at the bottom of the Graphics window to perform a MotionStudy on the assembly. Click the **Model** tab to return to a SolidWorks Graphics window.

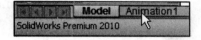

CYLINDER Assembly Drawing-Insert Balloons

The CYLINDER assembly drawing contains an Isometric Exploded view. Utilize View Properties to display the Exploded view. Use Balloon annotations to label components in an assembly. The Balloon contains the Item Number listed in the Bill of Materials. A Balloon displays different end conditions based on the arrowhead geometry reference.

Drag the endpoint of the arrowhead to modify the attachment and the end condition.

- Edge/vertex: - Arrowhead.

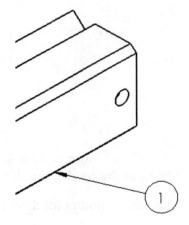

- Face/surface: - Dot.

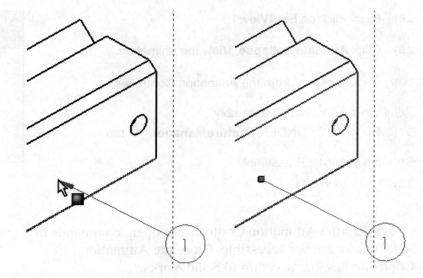

- Unattached: - Question mark.

🔆 Click the dimension, right-click the control point to select the correct arrow style.

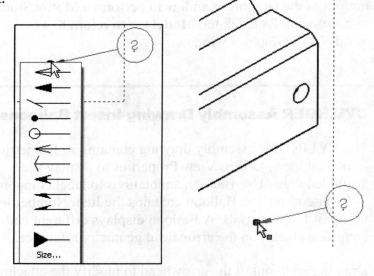

🔆 View mouse pointer feedback to distinguish between a vertex in the model and the attachment point in a Balloon.

The attachment point displays the Note icon for a Balloon and the Point icon for point geometry.

🔆 In SolidWorks 2010, when you right-click a component in an Assembly drawing, you can either open the component or the assembly. In previous versions, you could only open the part.

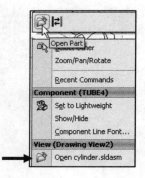

The Document Template, Drafting Standards, Balloons option defines the default arrow style and Balloons options.

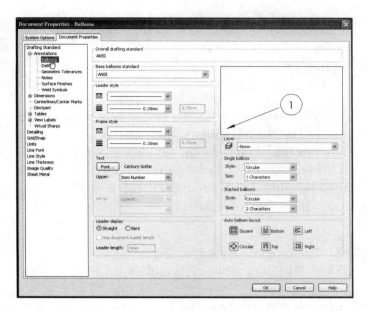

The Balloons option controls: *Single balloon*, *Stacked balloons*, *Balloon text*, *Bent leaders*, and *Auto Balloon Layout* options.

The Auto Balloon Layout option determines the display of the Balloons. Square Layout is the default. The Top Layout displays the Balloons horizontally aligned above the model. The Left Layout displays the Balloon vertically aligned to the left of the model.

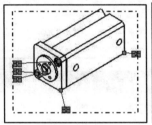
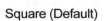
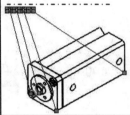
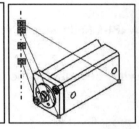

Square (Default)　　　Top Layout　　　Left Layout

Modify the selected Balloon with Balloon Properties. The Circular Split Line Style displays the Item Number in the Upper portion of the circle and the Quantity in the Lower portion of the Circle.

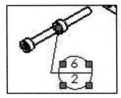

Select the Balloon option from the Annotation toolbar or Right-click Annotations in the Graphics window, or click Insert, Annotations from the Menu bar menu.

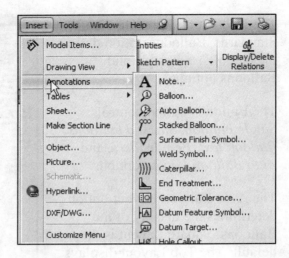

The Balloon option inserts a single item with a leader. The Auto Balloon option inserts Balloons based on the view boundary and the BOM type. The Stacked Balloon option contains multiple item numbers with a single leader from the Pop-up menu.

The Graphics window displays the CYLINDER assembly in the collapsed state.

Activity: CYLINDER Assembly Drawing-Insert Balloons

Create a drawing from the assembly.
33) Click **Make Drawing from Part/Assembly** from the Menu bar toolbar.

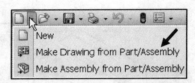

34) Double-click the **C-ANSI-MM** drawing template from the MY-TEMPLATES tab.

35) Drag the **Isometric view** boundary to the upper right corner of Sheet1.

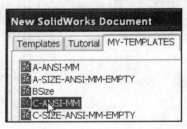

36) Click inside the **Top** predefined view.

37) Hold the **Ctrl** key down.

38) Click inside the **Front** and **Right** predefined views.

39) Release the **Ctrl** key. Press the **Delete** key.

40) Click **Yes to All**. If required, **deselect** the Origins.

Save the CYLINDER drawing.
41) Click **Save As** from the Menu bar toolbar.

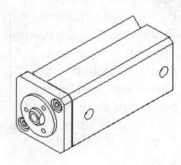

42) Enter **CYLINDER** for File name.

43) Click **Save**.

Display the Exploded view state.
44) Right-click inside the **Isometric view** boundary.

45) Click **Properties**. Check the **Show in exploded state** box.

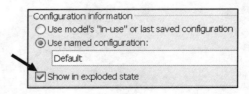

46) Click **OK** from the Drawing View Properties dialog box. The Isometric view displays the Exploded state.

Fit the Model to the Graphics window.
47) Press the **f** key.

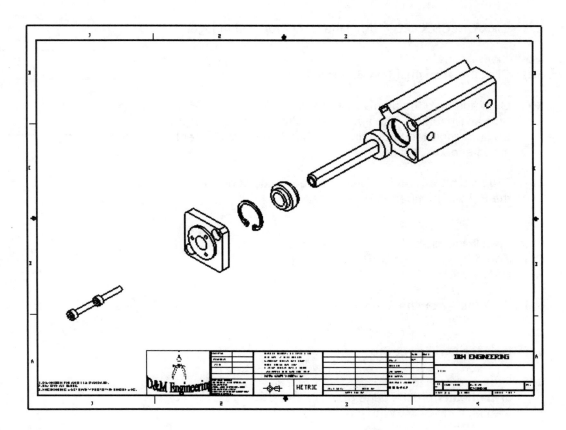

Insert Balloons to label each component.
48) Click inside the **Isometric view** boundary.

49) Click **AutoBalloon** from the Annotation toolbar. The Auto Balloon PropertyManager is displayed. Six balloons are displayed in the Isometric view.

50) Click **OK** from the Auto Balloon PropertyManager.

Modify the Balloons.
51) **Window-select** the six balloons in the Graphics window. The Balloon PropertyManager is displayed.

52) Click the **More Properties** button.

53) Click **Bent Leader** for Leader display.

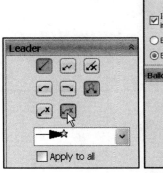

Modify the Font.
54) Uncheck the **Use document font** box.

55) Click the **Font** button. The Choose Font dialog box is displayed.

56) Enter **5**mm for font Height.

57) Click **OK**. Click **OK** ✔ from the Note PropertyManager.

Move the Balloons.
58) Click the **arrowhead** on **Balloon 1**.

59) Click and drag the **arrow head** to the middle of the TUBE face as illustrated. The arrow head changes shape per the Engineering Standard. The arrow head shape is different for an edge vs. a face.

60) Drag each **Balloon** into position. Leave space between the Balloon numbers.

Create two leader lines.
61) **Zoom in** on the two CAP-SCREWS.

62) Click the **Arrow head** on the CAP-SCREW.

63) Hold the **Ctrl** key down.

64) Drag and drop the **arrowhead** from the edge of the first CAP-SCREW to the edge of the second CAP-SCREW. Note: The Arrow head type for an edge vs. a surface.

65) Release the **Ctrl** key.

66) Click **OK** ✔ from the PropertyManager.

Save the CYLINDER drawing.
67) Click **Save** 💾 .

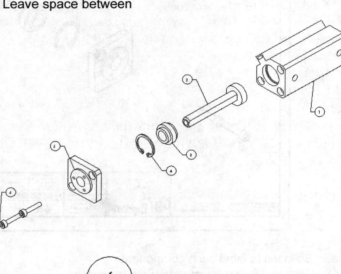

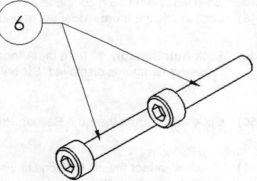

CYLINDER Assembly Drawing-Bill of Materials

The Bill of Materials (BOM) is a table that lists essential information on the components in an assembly. Insert a Bill of Materials (BOM) into the CYLINDER drawing. The BOM is linked to the Properties of the CYLINDER components. There are two options to create a BOM in the drawing:

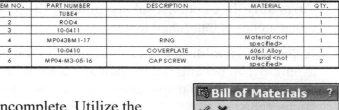

- Table option

- Excel spreadsheet option

ITEM NO.	PART NUMBER	DESCRIPTION	MATERIAL	QTY.
1	TUBE4			1
2	ROD4			1
3	10-0411			1
4	MP043BM1-17	RING	Material <not specified>	1
5	10-0410	COVERPLATE	6061 Alloy	1
6	MP04-M3-05-16	CAP SCREW	Material <not specified>	2

Investigate the Table option in this activity. The first BOM Table inserted into the CYLINDER drawing requires additional work. The information is incomplete. Utilize the Component Properties tool to define the majority of information located in the BOM.

The foundation for the BOM is the BOM template. The template contains the major column headings. The default BOM template, bom-standard.sldbomtbt contains the following column headings: ITEM NO., PART NUMBER, DESCRIPTION, QTY. (QUANTITY).

The SolidWorks\lang\<language> folder contains additional BOM templates:

- MATERIAL

- STOCK-SIZE

- VENDOR

- WEIGHT

The bom-all.sldbomtbt contains the default column headings. A BOM template also contains User Defined Custom headings. The User Defined Custom headings are linked to Custom Properties in the part or assembly. Define Custom Properties with the ConfigurationManager or a Design Table.

Create a Custom-BOM template. Start with a pre-defined BOM template. Insert additional headings. Right-click Save BOM template and select the MY-TEMPLATES folder. Open the Custom-BOM template through the Table Template option.

The BOM Table Anchor point locates the BOM at a corner of the drawing. The BOM Table moves when the Attach to anchor option is unchecked. The BOM Type contains three options:

- **Top level only**: List parts and sub-assemblies, but not sub-assembly components.

- **Parts only**: Does not list sub-assemblies. Lists sub-assembly components as individual items.

- **Indented assemblies**: Lists sub-assemblies. Indents sub-assembly components below their sub-assemblies. Select Show numbering to display item numbers for sub-assembly components.

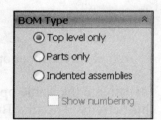

Summary Table:

Utilize the **Top level only** option (for assemblies that contain sub-assemblies) to display the highest level components in the FeatureManager.

ITEM NO.	PART NUMBER
1	TUBE4-ROD4
2	10-0411
3	MP04-3BM1-17
4	10-0410
5	MP04-M3-05-16

Utilize the **Parts only** option to display the parts in an assembly.

ITEM NO.	PART NUMBER
1	TUBE4
2	ROD4
3	10-0411
4	MP04-3BM1-17
5	10-0410
6	MP04-M3-05-16

Utilize the **Indented assemblies** option to display lower level components indented in the BOM.

ITEM NO.	PART NUMBER
1	TUBE4-ROD4
	TUBE4
	ROD4
2	10-0411
3	MP04-3BM1-17
4	10-0410
5	MP04-M3-05-16

By default, component order in the assembly determines their ITEM NO. in the BOM. The occurrence of the same component in an assembly defines the value in the QTY column.

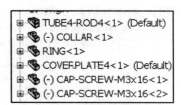

The PART NUMBER is the SolidWorks File name, Example: TUBE4.

DESCRIPTION is the text entered in the Description box. The Description box is blank.

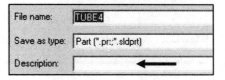

Define Description as a Custom Property in the next section. Create a Parts level only Bill of Materials with the SolidWorks BOM Template, bom-material.sldbomtbt for Sheet1. Create a Top level only Bill of Materials with the bom-standard.sldbomtbt for Sheet2.

Activity: CYLINDER Assembly Drawing-Bill of Materials

Insert the default Bill of Materials.
68) Click inside the **Isometric view** boundary.

69) Click **Bill of Materials** from the Consolidated Tables toolbar.

70) Double-click **bom-material.sldbomtbt** from the SolidWorks\lang\english folder.

71) Click the **Parts only** box.

72) Click **OK** from the Bill of Materials PropertyManager. The Bill of Materials is attached to the mouse pointer.

73) Click a **position** in the upper left corner of the sheet. View the results.

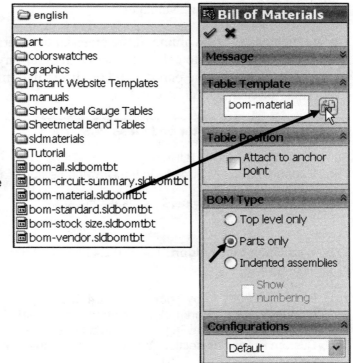

☼ Existing BOM tables can be modified after creation to include additional columns, formatting or changed settings.

74) **Zoom in** to enlarge the BOM. The RING and CAPSCREW components were taken from the SolidWorks Toolbox. Note the information in the Material column. The order in your BOM may differ than illustrated.

ITEM NO.	PART NUMBER	DESCRIPTION	MATERIAL	QTY.
1	TUBE4			1
2	ROD4			1
3	10-0411			1
4	MP043BM1-17	RING	Material<not specified>	1
5	10-0410	COVERPLATE	6061 Alloy	1
6	MP04-M3-05-16	CAPSCREW	Material<not specified>	2

Information in the current BOM is incomplete. The Custom Properties in the parts/components are linked to the PART NUMBER, DESCRIPTION, MATERIAL, and QTY. columns in the BOM. Create additional Custom Properties in the parts and in the BOM to complete the BOM in the drawing.

Materials Editor and Mass Properties

The BOM contains a Material column heading. The Materials Editor provides a list of predefined and user defined materials and their physical properties. Access the Materials Editor through the FeatureManager.

Utilize the density and volume of the material to determine the mass of the part. Select Tools, Mass Properties to calculate mass and other physical properties of the part. The physical properties of the part depend on different configuration. Review the Mass Properties for each part configuration.

Activity: Materials Editor and Mass Properties

Edit and Insert material for TUBE4.

75) **Expand** TUBE4-ROD4<1> in the Drawing FeatureManager.

76) Right-click the **TUBE4<1>** part in the Drawing FeatureManager.

77) Click **Open tube4.sldprt**. The TUBE4 FeatureManager is displayed

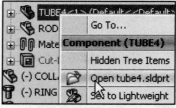

78) Right-click **6061 Alloy** from the TUBE4 (Default) FeatureManager. Part material information in the BOM is not transferred to the drawing – until you address it in the Custom Properties section. You will do this in the next section.

79) Click **Edit Material**. The Materials dialog box displayed. View the available information on the material.

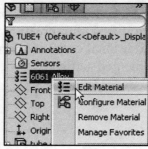

80)   Click **Apply**.

81)   Click **Close** from the
           Materials dialog box.

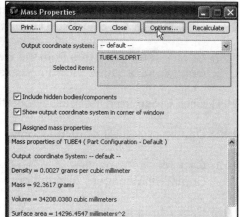

Display the Mass Properties.
82)   Click **Mass Properties**
           from the Evaluate tab in
           the CommandManager.
           The Mass Properties
           dialog box is displayed.

83)   Click the **Options** button.

84)   Enter **4** for Decimal
           Places.

85)   Click **OK**. The Mass
           92.3617g is display. The Density 0.0027g/mm³ is
           determined from the assigned material.

86)   Click **Close** from the Mass Properties dialog box.

Insert material for ROD4.
87)   **Open** the ROD4 part from the Chapter 5 folder.

88)   Right-click **Material** from the FeatureManager.

89)   Click **Edit Material**.

90)   **Expand** Steel.

91)   Select **AISI 304**.

92)   Click **Apply**. Click **Close** from the Material dialog box.

Calculate the Mass Properties for the ROD4 Default.
93)   Click **Mass Properties** from the Evaluate tab in the
           CommandManager. The Mass Properties dialog box is
           displayed.

94)   Click the **Options** button.

95)   Click **Use custom settings**.

96)   Enter **4** for Decimal Places.

97)   Click **OK**. View the mass
           properties.

98)   Click **Close** from the Mass
           Properties dialog box.

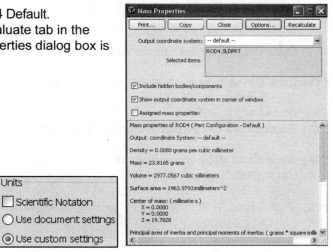

View the ShortRod and LongRod Mass Properties.
99)　Double-click the **ShortRod** Configuration.

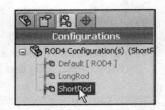

100) Click **Mass Properties** from the Evaluate tab in the CommandManager. View the mass properties.

101) Click **Close** from the Mass Properties dialog box.

102) Double-click the **LongRod** Configuration.

103) Click **Mass Properties** from the Evaluate tab in the CommandManager. View the properties.

104) Click **Close** from the Mass Properties dialog box.

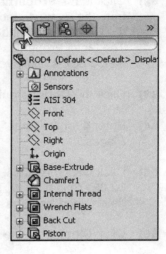

Return to the Default configuration.
105) Double-click **Default** from the ConfigurationManager.

106) Return to the FeatureManager.

Close the Mass Property dialog box before you switch to a different configuration. You cannot switch configurations when the Mass Properties dialog box is open. Select the new configuration and calculate the Mass Properties.

Review the material and mass for COVERPLATE4.
107) Open the COVERPLATE4 part from the Chapter 5 folder. The FeatureManager displays 6061 Alloy.

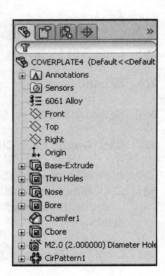

Calculate the Mass Properties for the COVERPLATE4 Default.
108) Click **Mass Properties** from the Evaluate tab in the CommandManager.

109) Click **Options**.

110) Enter **4** for Decimal Places.

111) Click **OK**. The Mass equals 10.8125 grams.

112) Click **Close** from the Mass Properties dialog box.

View the two configurations.
113) Double-click the **WithNoseHoles** Configuration.

114) Click **Mass Properties** from the Evaluate tab in the CommandManager. The Mass equals 10.8125 grams.

115) Click **Close** from the Mass Properties dialog box.

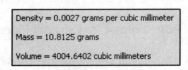

Density = 0.0027 grams per cubic millimeter

Mass = 10.8125 grams

Volume = 4004.6402 cubic millimeters

Density = 0.0027 grams per cubic millimeter

Mass = 10.8507 grams

Volume = 4018.7774 cubic millimeters

116) Double-click the **WithoutNoseHoles** Configuration.

117) Click **Mass Properties** from the Evaluate tab in the CommandManager. The Mass equals 10.8507 grams.

118) Click **Close** from the Mass Properties dialog box.

Return to the Default configuration.
119) Double-click **Default**.

Apply material to the COLLAR part.
120) Open the COLLAR part.

121) Right-click **Material**.

122) Click **Edit Material**.

123) Expand Steel.

124) Select **Alloy Steel**.

125) Click **Apply**.

126) Click **Close** from the Material dialog box. The FeatureManager displays the Material.

127) Repeat the above process for the **RING**. Select **Alloy Steel** for Material.

128) Repeat the above process for the **CAP-SCREW-M3x16**. Select **6061 Alloy** for Material.

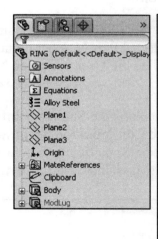

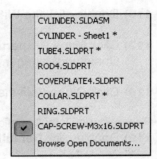

The TUBE4, ROD4, CAP-SCREW-M3x16, COLLAR, and COVERPLATE4 parts, CYLINDER assembly and CYLINDER drawing - Sheet1 remain open in the next activities. Properties modified in the part require a rebuild to update the drawing BOM.

Configuration Properties

In Chapter 2, you linked Custom Properties and SolidWorks Properties to Notes in the Sheet format. In this chapter, cell entries in the BOM are linked to Properties created in the part and assembly. Create Properties in the part with two techniques: **Configuration Properties** and **Design Table**.

Access the Configuration Properties through the ConfigurationManager. The BOM requires a part number. There are three options utilized to display the Part number in the BOM:

- **Document Name (file name)**. Note: Default setting.

- **Configuration Name**.

- **User Specified Name**.

Utilize two options in this section. The Document name is TUBE4. The current BOM Part Number column displays the Document Name. Utilize the User Specified Name to assign a numeric value.

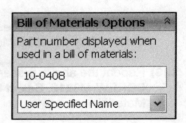

The Custom button contains the Summary Information, Custom Properties and Configuration Specific options. Utilize the Configuration Specific tab to control the Description, Material. Mass and Cost Properties.

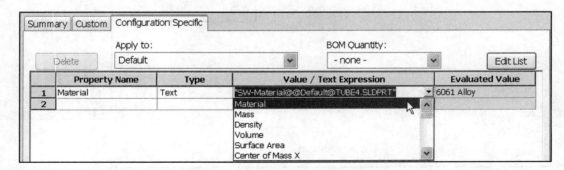

The Description Property links the BOM Description column heading. The TUBE 16MM Value corresponds to the Cell entry in the BOM.

Link the Material Property to the value; "SW-Material@@Default@TUBE4.SLDPRT". This value corresponds to the Material assigned with the Materials Editor. The parameter is in the form:

"SW-Material@@Default@TUBE4.SLDPRT".

Property Name@@Configuration Name@Part Name

Link the Mass Property to the value;"SW-Mass@@Default@TUBE4.SLDPRT". The value corresponds to the mass calculated through the Mass Properties tool. Enter values for the Custom Property Cost. Insert the Cost column into the BOM.

The Design Table is an Excel spreadsheet utilized to create multiple configurations of a part or assembly.

Utilize Custom Properties in the Design Table to save time in creating multiple configurations and their properties.

Activity: Configuration Properties

Add Custom Properties to TUBE4.

129) **Display** the TUBE4 part.

130) Click the **ConfigurationManager** 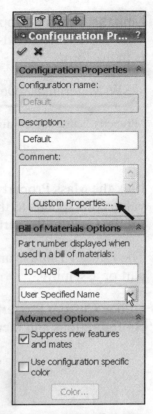 tab.

131) Right-click **Properties** on the Default [TUBE4] configuration.

Add a User Specified Part number.

132) Select the **User Specified Name** from the drop-down menu.

133) Enter **10-0408** for Part number displayed when used in bill of materials option.

Insert Custom Properties.

134) Click the **Custom Properties** button from the Configuration Properties dialog box.

Add the Material Property.

135) Click the **Configuration Specific** tab.

136) Select **Material** from the Property Name drop-down menu.

137) Select **Material** from the Value / Text Expression box. The "SW-Material@@Default@TUBE4.SLDPRT" value is added to the Value text box.

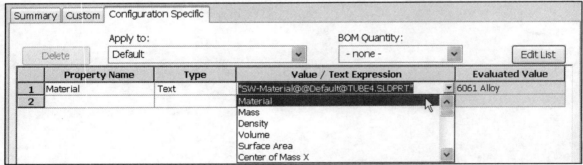

Add the Mass Property.

138) Enter **Mass** in the Property Name box.

139) Select **Mass** from the Value / Text Expression drop-down menu. The "SW-Mass@@Default@ TUBE4.SLDPRT" value is added to the Value text box.

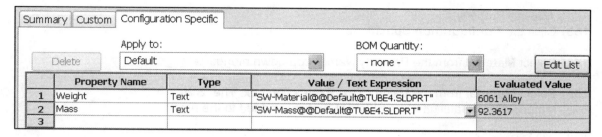

	Property Name	Type	Value / Text Expression	Evaluated Value
1	Weight	Text	"SW-Material@@Default@TUBE4.SLDPRT"	6061 Alloy
2	Mass	Text	"SW-Mass@@Default@TUBE4.SLDPRT"	92.3617
3				

Add a Description Property.
140) Select **Description** from the Property Name drop-down menu.

141) Enter **TUBE 16MM** in the Value / Text Expression box.

Add a Cost Property.
142) Select **Cost** from the Property Name drop-down menu.

143) Enter **200** in the Value / Text Expression box.

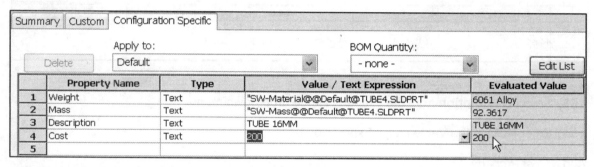

	Property Name	Type	Value / Text Expression	Evaluated Value
1	Weight	Text	"SW-Material@@Default@TUBE4.SLDPRT"	6061 Alloy
2	Mass	Text	"SW-Mass@@Default@TUBE4.SLDPRT"	92.3617
3	Description	Text	TUBE 16MM	TUBE 16MM
4	Cost	Text	200	200
5				

144) Click **OK** from the Summary Information dialog box.

145) Click **OK** from the Configuration Properties
PropertyManager. **Return** to the FeatureManager.

Save the TUBE4 part.
146) Click **Save** .

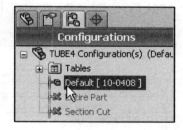

Add Custom Properties to the ROD4 part.
147) **Open** the ROD4 (Default) part.

148) Click the **ConfigurationManager** tab.

149) Right-click **Properties** on the Default configuration.

Add a User Specified Part number.
150) Select the **User Specified Name** from the drop-down menu.

151) Enter **10-0409** for Part number displayed when used in bill of
materials option.

152) Click the **Custom Properties** button.

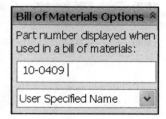

Add a Material Property.

153) Click the **Configuration Specific** tab.

154) Select **Material** from the Property Name drop-down menu.

155) Select **Material** from the Value / Text Expression box. The "SW-Material@@Default@ROD4.SLDPRT" value is added to the box.

Add a Mass Property.

156) Enter **Mass** in the Property Name box.

157) Select **Mass** from the Value / Text Expression box. The "SW-Mass@@Default@ROD4.SLDPRT" value is added to the Value text box.

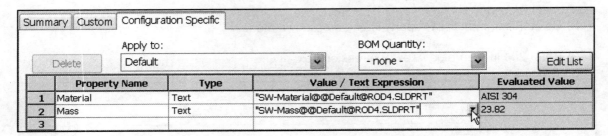

Add a Description Property.

158) Select **Description** from the Property Name drop-down menu.

159) Enter **ROD** in the Value / Text Expression box.

Add a Cost Property.

160) Select **Cost** from the Property Name drop-down menu.

161) Enter **50** in the Value / Text Expression box.

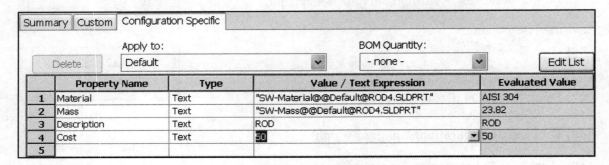

162) Click **OK** from the Summary Information dialog box.

163) Click **OK** ✔ from the Configuration Properties PropertyManager.

164) Click the **Part** FeatureManager icon.

Save the ROD4 part.
165) Click **Save** 🖫 .

Review Custom Properties for COVERPLATE4.
166) Open COVERPLATE4 (Default).

167) Click the **ConfigurationManager** 🔁 tab.

168) Right-click **Properties** on the Default configuration.

169) Click the **Custom Properties** button. View the Names
and Values for the Properties: Material, Mass,
Description and Cost.

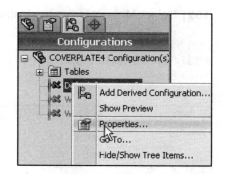

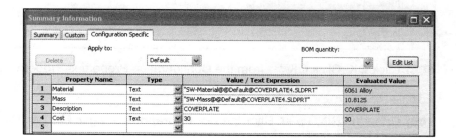

170) Click **OK** from the Summary Information dialog box.

171) Click **OK** ✔ from the Configuration Properties
PropertyManager.

172) Return to the FeatureManager.

Edit the COLLAR part.
173) Open the COLLAR part.

174) Click the **ConfigurationManager** 🔁 tab.

175) Right-click **Properties** on the Default configuration.

176) Select the **User Specified Name** from the drop-down menu.

177) Enter **10-0411**.

178) Click the **Custom Properties** button.

179) Select **Description** from the Property Name drop-down menu.

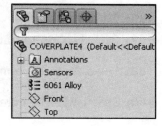

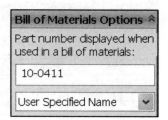

180) Enter **COLLAR** for Value / Text Expression.

Add a Material Property.
181) Select **Material** from the Property Name drop-down menu.

182) Select **Material** from the Value / Text Expression box.

Add a Cost Property.
183) Enter **Cost** in the Property Name drop-down menu. Enter **20** in the Value / Text Expression box.

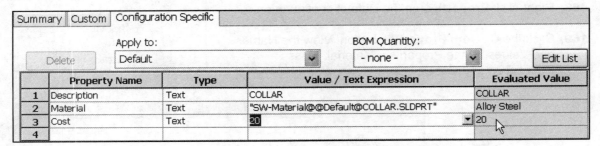

	Property Name	Type	Value / Text Expression	Evaluated Value
1	Description	Text	COLLAR	COLLAR
2	Material	Text	"SW-Material@@Default@COLLAR.SLDPRT"	Alloy Steel
3	Cost	Text	20	20
4				

184) Click **OK**. Click **OK** ✔ from the Configuration Properties PropertyManager.

Edit the Ring Part.
185) **Open** the RING part. Click the **ConfigurationManager** tab. Right-click **Properties** on the Default configuration.

186) Click the **Custom Properties** button.

Add a Material Property.
187) Click the **Configuration Specific** tab.

188) Select **Material** from the Property Name drop-down menu.

189) Select **Material** from the Value / Text Expression box.

Add a Cost Property.
190) Select **Cost** from the Property Name drop-down menu. Enter **5** in the Value / Text Expression box.

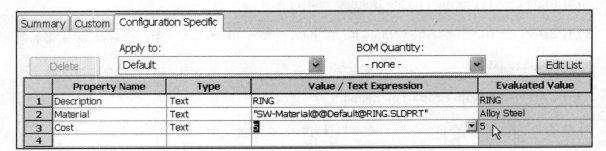

	Property Name	Type	Value / Text Expression	Evaluated Value
1	Description	Text	RING	RING
2	Material	Text	"SW-Material@@Default@RING.SLDPRT"	Alloy Steel
3	Cost	Text	5	5
4				

191) Click **OK**. Click **OK** ✔ from the Configuration Properties PropertyManager.

If needed, modify the CAP-SCREW-M3x16.

192) Open **CAP-SCREW-M3x16**. Click the
ConfigurationManager tab. Right-click **Properties** on the
Default configuration. Select the **User Specified Name** from the
drop-down menu. Enter **MP04-M3-05-16**. Click the **Custom
Properties** button. View the information.

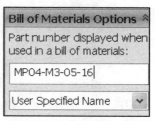

Bill of Materials Options

Part number displayed when used in a bill of materials:

MP04-M3-05-16|

User Specified Name

Summary	Custom	Configuration Specific			

	Apply to:			BOM Quantity:	
Delete	Default			- none -	Edit List

	Property Name	Type	Value / Text Expression	Evaluated Value
1	Description	Text	CAP SCREW	CAP SCREW
2	Material	Text	"SW-Material@@Default@CAP-SCREW-M3x16.SL	6061 Alloy
3	Cost	Text	5	5
4				

193) Click **OK**. Click **OK** ✓ from the Configuration Properties PropertyManager.

Design Table

A Design Table is an Excel spreadsheet utilized to create configurations and control
parameters in a part or assembly.

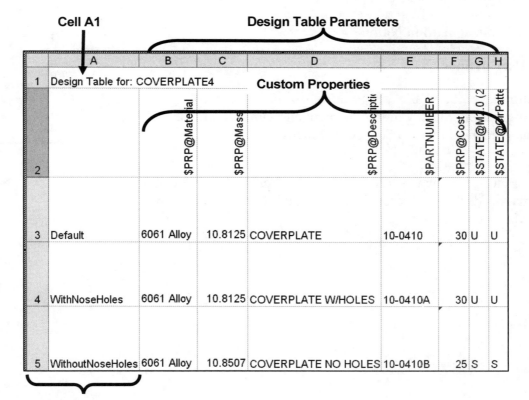

Cell A1   **Design Table Parameters**

	A	B	C	D	E	F	G	H
1	Design Table for: COVERPLATE4			**Custom Properties**				
2		$PRP@Material	$PRP@Mass	$PRP@Description	$PARTNUMBER	$PRP@Cost	$STATE@M?.0 (2	$STATE@?rPatte
3	Default	6061 Alloy	10.8125	COVERPLATE	10-0410	30	U	U
4	WithNoseHoles	6061 Alloy	10.8125	COVERPLATE W/HOLES	10-0410A	30	U	U
5	WithoutNoseHoles	6061 Alloy	10.8507	COVERPLATE NO HOLES	10-0410B	25	S	S

Configuration Names

The model name associated with the Design Table is located in Cell A1. Define the configuration names in the first column of an Excel spreadsheet. Define the parameters in the second row.

Enter values in the Cells that correspond to the configuration name and the parameter name. Leave Cell A2 blank.

Entering parameters into a Design Table is a cumbersome task. Utilize the Auto-create option to load all configured parameters and their associated values from a part or assembly. Utilize the Design Table to create multiple configurations for the ROD part and the CYLINDER assembly.

The current ROD Default Configuration contains Custom Properties: Mass, Material, Description and Cost. The Design Table with the Auto create option inserts the Custom Property parameters in Row 2.

Custom Properties begin with the prefix, $PRP@. Enter user defined values for the BOM Part Number in the Design Table. The Property, $PARTNUMBER displays three options in a Design Table:

- **$D Document Name (filename)**

- **$C Configuration Name**

- **User defined**

Additional part and assembly control parameters control Configuration, State, Color, Comment and Dimension. All parameters begin with a $, except Dimension.

Enter parameters carefully. The "$", "@" and "<>" symbol format needs to match exactly for the result to be correct in the BOM.

The Summary of Design Table Parameters is as follows:

Summary of Design Table Parameters:		
Parameter Syntax (header Cell)	Legal Values (body Cell)	Default if Value is Left Blank
Parts only:		
$configuration@part_name	configuration name	not evaluated
$configuration@<feature_name>	configuration name	not evaluated
Parts and Assemblies:		
$comment	any text string	empty
$part number	any text string	configuration name
$state@feature_name	Suppressed, S Unsuppressed, U	Unsuppressed
dimension @feature	any legal decimal value for the dimension	not evaluated
$parent	parent configuration name	property is undefined
$prp@ property	any text string	property is undefined
$state@equation_number@equations	Suppressed, S Unsuppressed, U	Unsuppressed
$state@lighting_name	Suppressed, S Unsuppressed, U	Unsuppressed
$state@sketch relation@sketch name	Suppressed, S Unsuppressed, U	Unsuppressed
$sw-mass	Any legal decimal value for mass of a component.	The calculated value of mass in the Mass Properties option
$sw-coq	Any legal decimal value for the center of gravity in x, y, z.	The calculated cog in the Mass Properties option.
$user_notes	any text string	not evaluated
$color	32-bit integer specifying RGB (red, green, blue) color. See Online Help, Color for more info	zero (black)
Assemblies only:		
$show@component<instance>	Yes, Y No, N	No
$state@component<instance>	Resolved, R, Suppressed, S	Resolved
$configuration@component<instance>	configuration name	Component's "in-use" or last saved configuration NOTE: If the component uses a derived configuration, and the value is left blank, the configuration used is linked to its parent.
$never_expand_in_BOM	Yes (never expand) No (allow to expand)	No

Perform two activities with Design Tables. In the first activity, review the Design Table for COVERPLATE4. Insert a Design Table into the ROD4.

Review the updates in the Bill of Materials. In the second activity, insert a Design Table into the CYLINDER assembly. Control multiple configurations in the CYLINDER drawing views.

Activity: Design Table

Review the COVERPLATE4 Design Table.

194) Open COVERPLATE4. Click the **ConfigurationManager** tab.

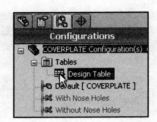

195) Right-click Design Table.

196) Click Edit Table. Review the Parameters for the Design Table.

Enlarge the Design Table.
197) Drag the **lower right corner** downward.

198) Click a **position** in the Graphics window to close the Design Table and to return to SolidWorks.

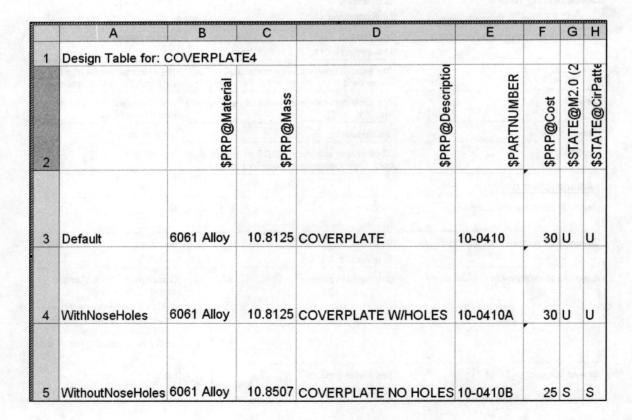

	A	B	C	D	E	F	G	H
1	Design Table for: COVERPLATE4							
2		$PRP@Material	$PRP@Mass		$PRP@Description	$PARTNUMBER	$PRP@Cost	$STATE@M2.0 (2	$STATE@CirPatte
3	Default	6061 Alloy	10.8125	COVERPLATE		10-0410	30	U	U
4	WithNoseHoles	6061 Alloy	10.8125	COVERPLATE W/HOLES		10-0410A	30	U	U
5	WithoutNoseHoles	6061 Alloy	10.8507	COVERPLATE NO HOLES		10-0410B	25	S	S

Insert a Design Table.
199) Open the ROD4 (Default) part.

200) Click **Insert, Tables, Design Table** from the Menu bar menu. The Design Table PropertyManager is displayed.

Select the parameters.
201) Check the **Auto-create** box.

202) Check the **New parameters** box.

203) Check the **New configurations** box.

204) Check **Warn when updating design table** in the Options box.

205) Click **OK** ✔ from the Design Table PropertyManager.

	A	B	C	D	E	F	G	H	I	J
1	Design Table for: ROD4									
2		$DESCRIPTION	$PARTNUMBER	$COLOR	$PRP@Material	$PRP@Mass	$PRP@Description	$PRP@Cost	D1@Base-Extrude	
3	Default	Default	10-0409	9871013	AISI 304	23.82	ROD	50	53.83	
4	ShortRod	ShortRod	$C		9871013	AISI 304			53.83	
5	LongRod	LongRod	$C		9871013	AISI 304			200	
6										

Copy the Material cell.
206) Copy **AISI 304** to Cell E4, and Cell E5.

 Click a position outside the Design Table to exit EXCEL and return to a SolidWorks session. To return to the Design Table, right-click Design Table in the ConfigurationManager. Select Edit Table.

Note: Your column numbers may vary per the illustration.

D	E	F
$COLOR	$PRP@Material	$PRP@Mass
9871013	AISI 304	23.82
9871013	AISI 304	
9871013	AISI 304	

Edit the Part number column.
207) Click Cell **C4**. Enter **10-0409S**.

208) Click Cell **C5**. Enter **10-0409L**.

Edit the Mass column.
209) Click Cell **F4**.

210) Enter **"SW-Mass@@ShortRod@ROD4.SLDPRT"**.

211) Click Cell **F5**.

212) Enter **"SW-Mass@@LongRod@ROD4.SLDPRT"**.

Edit the Description column.
213) Click Cell **G4**.

214) Enter **ROD 16MM SHORT**.

215) Click Cell **G5**.

216) Enter **ROD 16MM LONG**.

Edit the Cost column.
217) Click Cell **H4**.

218) Enter **50**.

219) Click Cell **H5**.

220) Enter **100**.

221) Click inside the **Graphics window**.

222) Rebuild the model.

223) Return to the Design Table to view the updates.

The parameter, SW-Mass is case sensitive. Your color cell numbers may vary slightly for the illustration.

	A	B	C	D	E	F	G	H
1	Design Table for: ROD4							
2		$PARTNUMBER	$COLOR	$PRP@Material	$PRP@Mass	$PRP@Description	$PRP@Cost	D1@Base-Extrude
3	Default	10-0409	9871013	AISI 304	23.82	ROD	50	53.83
4	ShortRod	10-0409S	11314333	AISI 304	23.82	ROD 16MM SHORT	50	53.83
5	LongRod	10-0409L	11314333	AISI 304	74.11	ROD 16MM LONG	100	200
6								

Bill of Materials - Part 2

The Custom Properties in the TUBE4, ROD4, and COVERPLATE4 parts produce changes to the BOM. Return to the CYLINDER Sheet1. Rebuild the drawing to update the BOM.

Editing Cells

The BOM requires additional changes. Double-click a cell brings up the Context toolbar with items specific to the

selected cell. The Context toolbar provides the ability to change the header, border, text and layer settings for the entire table.

Editing Columns

Hovering over a cell displays the Editing Table icon. Click a cell to display the Context toolbar. The toolbar's buttons reflect the available options for the type of table and selections, (rows, column, and cells).

To access a table's PropertyManager, click the move table icon in the upper left corner or Right-click the table, and click Properties from the Pop-up menu.

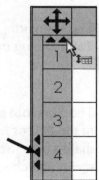

Click the vertical arrows as illustrated to insert a row. Click the Horizontal arrows as illustrated to insert a column.

The Table Properties option returns you to the BOM
PropertyManager.

The Insert tool provides the ability to insert a column to the
Right or Left side of the selected
column or a Row above or
below the selected row.

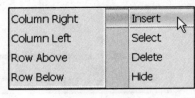

The Select tool provides the
ability to select a Table,
Column, or Row.

The Formatting tool provides the ability to format the width of
a column, the height of a row, or the entire table.

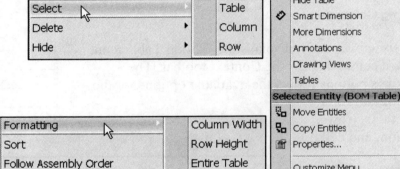

The Formatting Entire Table tool displayed the Entire
Table dialog box.

The Sort tool provides the ability to sort selected items
in the Bill of Materials. The Sort tool displays the Sort
dialog box. Select the sort by item from the drop-down
menu and check either ascending or descending order.

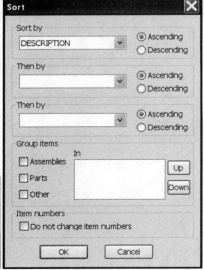

Activity: Bill of Materials-Part 2

Update to the CYLINDER-Sheet1 drawing.
224) Open the CYLINDER drawing-Sheet1. View the updated BOM.

Bill of Material - Insert Column

ITEM NO.	PART NUMBER	DESCRIPTION	MATERIAL	QTY.
1	10-0411	COLLAR	Alloy Steel	1
2	MP043BM1-17	RING	Alloy Steel	1
3	10-0410	COVERPLATE	6061 Alloy	1
4	MP04-M3-05-16	CAP SCREW	6061 Alloy	2
5	10-0408	TUBE 16MM	6061 Alloy	1
6	10-0409	ROD	AISI 304	1

Insert a column called COST.
225) Right-click inside the **MATERIAL** cell. The Pop-up toolbar is displayed.

226) Click **Insert**. Click **Column Right**.

227) Select **Column Properties**.

228) Select **Cost** from the Custom Property drop-down menu. Cost is inserted into the Bill of Materials.

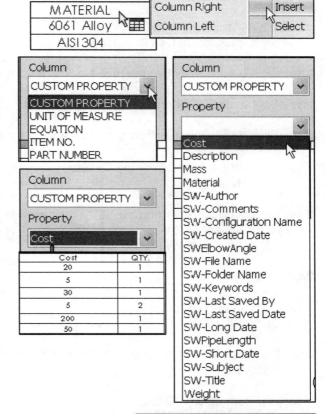

229) Position the **mouse point** on the column line between COST and QTY. Hovering over a column divider changes the mouse pointer.

230) Drag the **column divider line** to the left, to shrink the column by half as illustrated.

Bill of Materials - Header

Insert the BOM Title.
231) Click **inside** the ITEMS NO. cell

232) Click the **vertical up-arrows**. The Bill of Materials header is displayed. Note: BOM Table is displayed by default.

233) Enter **CYLINDER ASSEMBLY BILL OF MATERIALS** for Title in the Header box.

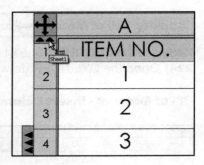

CYLINDER ASSEMBLY BILL OF MATERIALS

234) Click **outside** of the Bill of Materials.

Insert a bulk item in the BOM.
235) Right-click inside **Cell Item No 6**.

236) Click **Insert**, **Row Below**. Row No. 7 is displayed.

237) Double-click the **Cell** to the right of Item No 7.

238) Click **Yes** to the question; Continue editing the Cell?

239) Enter **DP01-1010-23** for the PART NUMBER.

240) Double-click inside the **Cell** to the right of DP01-1010-23.

241) Click **Yes**.

242) Enter **LOCTITE** for DESCRIPTION.

243) Click **outside** of the Bill of Materials.

Modify the Item Column Order.
244) Click inside the **ITEM NO. 1** Cell.

245) **Position** the mouse pointer on number 3 as illustrated.

246) Click and drag the **first column Cell** downward as illustrated.

247) Click **outside** of the Bill of Materials.

248) Press the **f** key to the drawing in Sheet1. The balloons displayed the updated Bill of Materials.

Return to the original Item No. order.
249) Click inside the **Items NO. 2** Cell. Position the mouse pointer on number 4.

250) Click and drag the **column Cell** upwards. The Bill of Materials returns to the original order.

251) Click **outside** of the Bill of Materials.

252) Press the **f** key to the drawing in Sheet1. The balloons displayed the updated Bill of Materials

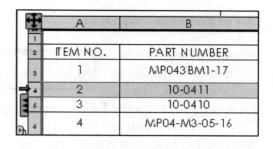

	A	B
1		
2	ITEM NO.	PART NUMBER
3	1	MP043 BM1-17
4	2	10-0411
5	3	10-0410
6	4	MP04-M3-05-16

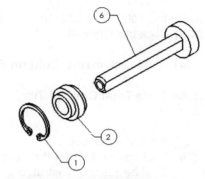

	A	B
1		
2	ITEM NO.	PART NUMBER
3	1	10-0411
4	2	MP043 BM1-17
5	3	10-0410
6	4	MP04-M3-05-16

Drawing View4

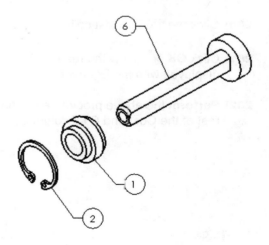

Bill of Materials - Equation

Apply an Equation to the Bill of Materials in a new Column. The Equation tool from the Edit Tables Context toolbar displays the Equation editor.

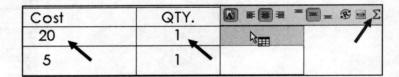

Insert the Total Cost Column.
253) Click the **Qty** cell.

254) Right-click **Insert, Column Right**.

255) Enter **Total Cost** for Title.

Apply the Equation tool.
256) Click the **cell** under the Total Cost header as illustrated.

257) Click the **Equation** Σ tool from the Context toolbar. The Equation editor is displayed.

Cost	QTY.
20	1
5	1

258) Click the **20** Cost cell.

259) Enter the multiplication * symbol

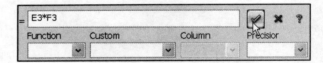

= E3*F3

260) Click the **1** QTY Cost cell.

261) Click **OK** ✔. View the results. 20 is displayed with the Equation icon.

262) **Perform** the above procedure for the rest of the Cost and QTY columns.

Cost	QTY.	Total Cost
20	1	20
5	1	
30	1	
5	2	
200	1	
50	1	

Enter Total Cost.

263) Click inside the illustrated **cell** to create the Total Cost sum.

264) Click the **Equation** Σ tool from the Context toolbar. The Equation editor is displayed.

265) Select the **SUM** Function from the drop-down menu.

266) Click **inside** cell G3. SUM(G3) is displayed.

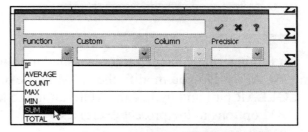

267) Enter: as illustrated.

268) Click **inside** cell G8. SUM(G3:G8) is displayed.

269) Click **OK** ✔. The value for Total Cost, 315 is calculated by the Equation.

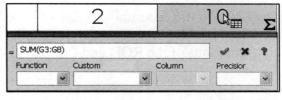

Modify the BOM Table Font size.

270) Click **CYLINDER ASSEMBLY BILL OF MATERIALS** in the Header box.

271) Modify the Font to **5**mm.

272) Select **Bold**.

Cost	QTY.	Total Cost
20	1	20
5	1	5
30	1	30
5	2	10
200	1	200
50	1	50
		315

273) Click **Inside** the Sheet. View the results.

Fit the drawing to the Graphics window.

274) Press the **f** key.

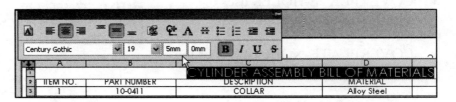

Save the CYLINDER drawing.

275) Click **Save** 💾 . Your order in the BOM may differ per the illustration.

🔅 You can double click in the PART, DESCRIPTION or Cost column to link directly back to modify the part.

		CYLINDER ASSEMBLY BILL OF MATERIALS				
ITEM NO.	PART NUMBER	DESCRIPTION	MATERIAL	Cost	QTY.	Total Cost
1	10-0411	COLLAR	Alloy Steel	20	1	20
2	MP043BM1-17	RING	Alloy Steel	5	1	5
3	10-0410	COVERPLATE	6061 Alloy	30	1	30
4	MP04-M3-05-16	CAP SCREW	6061 Alloy	5	2	10
5	10-0408	TUBE 16MM	6061 Alloy	200	1	200
6	10-0409	ROD	AISI 304	50	1	50
7	DP01-1010-23	LOCTITE				315

An Engineering Change Order is issued to modify the COLLAR from Alloy Steel to 6061 Alloy. Do you modify the BOM in the drawing? Answer: No. Return to the COLLAR part and update the Material in the Materials Editor. Investigate additional BOM options in the project exercises.

The CYLINDER assembly contains the default configuration for the TUBE, ROD and COVERPLATE parts. How do you modify the assembly to support multiple configurations of the ROD and COVERPLATE in a drawing? Answer: With a Design Table.

CYLINDER Assembly-Design Table

Design Tables control parameters in an assembly. Create a Design Table in the CYLINDER assembly with three different configurations of the COVERPLATE:

- NO-COVERPLATE (Suppressed COVERPLATE Component).

- COVERPLATE-HOLES uses the WithNoseHoles Configuration.

3	Default	Default
4	NO-COVERPLATE	Default
5	COVERPLATE-HOLES	WithNoseHoles
6	COVERPLATE-NOHOLES	WithoutNoseHoles

- COVERPLATE-NOHOLES uses the WithoutNoseHoles Configuration.

Insert three CYLINDER assembly configurations into a drawing. The TUBE, ROD, and COVERPLATE parts are set to their Default configurations. Utilize the configurations in the CYLINDER drawing views.

The TUBE4-ROD4 assembly contains two configurations:

- Default

- CutAway

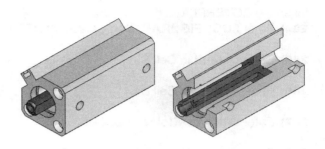

Utilize the CutAway configuration in the CYLINDER Design Table for Sheet2.

Activity: CYLINDER Assembly-Design Table

Create a Design Table in the CYLINDER assembly.
276) Open the CYLINDER assembly.

277) Click **Insert**, **Tables**, **Design Table** from the Menu bar menu. Accept the defaults. Note your options in the Design Table PropertyManager.

278) Click **OK** ✅ from the Design Table PropertyManager.

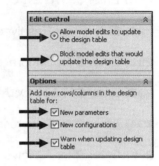

	A	B	C	D
1	Design Table for: CYLINDER			
2				
3	Default			

279) Enter **NO-COVERPLATE** in Cell A4.

280) Enter **COVERPLATE-HOLES** in Cell A5.

281) Enter **COVERPLATE-NOHOLES** in Cell A6.

282) Enter **NO-HARDWARE** in Cell A7.

283) Drag the **column bar** between Column A and Column B to the right until the full Configuration Names are displayed.

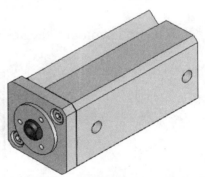

🔅 To avoid creating a Hyperlink in EXCEL, insert a single apostrophe 'before a parameter that contains the @ symbol. The COVERPLATE4<1> parameter is the same as the FeatureManager component name. The Component Name is case sensitive. Do not interchange upper and lower case letters. Use dashes and underscores, not spaces.

	A
1	Design Table for: CYLINDER
2	
3	Default
4	NO-COVERPLATE
5	COVERPLATE-HOLES
6	COVERPLATE-NOHOLES
7	NO-HARDWARE

Insert the COVERPLATE parameters
284) Enter **$CONFIGURATION@COVERPLATE4<1>** in Cell B2.

285) Enter **Default** in Cell B3.

286) Enter **Default** in Cell B4.

287) Enter **WithNoseHoles** in Cell B5.

288) Enter **WithoutNoseHoles** in Cell B6.

289) Enter **Default** in Cell B7.

290) Enter **$STATE@COVERPLATE4<1>** in Cell C2.

291) Enter **R** for Resolved in Cell C3, Cell C5, Cell C6 and C7.

292) Enter **S** for Suppress in Cell C4.

293) Enter **$STATE@CAP-SCREW-M3x16<*>** in Cell D2.

294) Enter **S** for Suppress in Cell D4 and Cell D7.

295) Enter **R** for Resolved in Cell D3, Cell D5 and Cell D6.

The <*> symbol indicates all instances for the CAP-SCREW-M3x16.

	A	B	C	D
1	Design Table for: CYLINDER			
2		$CONFIGURATION@COVERPLATE4<1>	$STATE@COVERPLATE4<1>	$STATE@CAP-SCREW-M3x16<*>
3	Default	Default	R	R
4	NO-COVERPLATE	Default	S	S
5	COVERPLATE-HOLES	WithNoseHoles	R	R
6	COVERPLATE-NOHOLES	WithoutNoseHoles	R	R
7	NO-HARDWARE	Default	R	S

Display the configurations.
296) Click a **position** outside the Design Table. Four
assembly CYLINDER configurations are created.

297) Click **OK**.

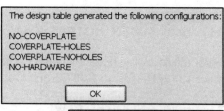

Verify the configurations.
298) Double-click on **NO-COVERPLATE**.

299) Double-click on **COVERPLATE-HOLES**.

300) Double-click on **COVERPLATE-NOHOLES**.

301) Double-click on **NO-HARDWARE**.

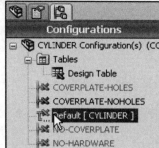

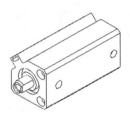 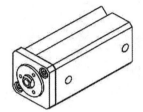 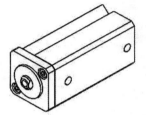 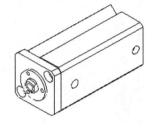

Return to the default configuration.
302) Double click the **Default** configuration.

Edit the Design Table.
303) Right-click **Design Table** in the ConfigurationManager.

304) Click **Edit Table**.

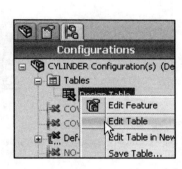

305) Click **Cancel** to the Add Rows and Columns dialog
box.

Enter the CUTAWAY configuration.
306) Enter **CUTAWAY** in Cell A8.

307) Enter **Default** in Cell B8. Enter **S** in Cell C8 and
Cell D8.

308) Enter **$CONFIGURATION@TUBE4-ROD4<1>** in
Cell E2.

309) Enter **Default** in Cell E3 - Cell E7.

310) Enter **CutAway** in Cell E8.

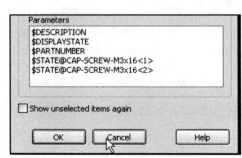

Add User_Notes.
311) Enter **$USER_NOTES** in Cell F2. SolidWorks does not calculate $USER_NOTES.

Enter the following notes displayed in Cells F3 through F8.
312) Enter **BASIC** in Cell F3 and Cell F4.

313) Enter **ANODIZED COVER** in Cell F5, Cell F6 and Cell F7.

314) Enter **SEE INTERNAL FEATURES** in Cell F8.

	A	B	C	D	E	F
1	Design Table for: CYLINDER					
2			$CONFIGURATION@COVERPLATE4<1>	$STATE@COVERPLATE4<1>	$STATE@CAP-SCREW-M3x16<*>	$CONFIGURATION@TUBE4-ROD4<1>	$USER_NOTES
3	Default	Default	R	R	Default	BASIC
4	NO-COVERPLATE	Default	S	S	Default	BASIC
5	COVERPLATE-HOLES	WithNoseHoles	R	R	Default	ANODIZED COVER
6	COVERPLATE-NOHOLES	WithoutNoseHoles	R	R	Default	ANODIZED COVER
7	NO-HARDWARE	Default	R	S	Default	ANODIZED COVER
8	CUTAWAY	Default	S	S	CutAway	SEE INTERNAL FEATURES

Update the configurations.
315) Click a **position** outside the Design Table.

316) Click **OK**.

Verify all CYLINDER configurations before creating additional
views in the CYLINDER drawing.
317) Double-click each CYLINDER **configuration**. View
      the results in the Graphics window.

318) Double-click the **Default** configuration.

☼ To delete a configuration, select the Configuration name in the ConfigurationManager. The Row entries are removed from the Design Table.

Save the CYLINDER assembly.
319) Click the **FeatureManager** tab.

320) Click **Save** 💾 .

The design table can include a column for configuration-specific colors. The value is a 32-bit integer that specifies RGB (red, green, blue). If no value is specified, zero (black) is applied.

If you know the 32-bit integer value of a color, you can type the number directly into the design table in a column with the **$COLOR parameter** as the header. If you do not know the 32-bit integer value, you can calculate it in the design table with the RGB component values.

☼ Color is an important property for visualization and machining purposes. One company provided the following colors as an example:

- Red - As Cast

- Blue - Machined Surface

- Orange - High Finish

The following table lists some typical colors, their components and the equivalent integer values.

Color	Red	Green	Blue	Integer
Black	0	0	0	0
Red	255	0	0	255
Orange	255	128	0	33023
Green	0	255	0	65280
Blue	0	0	255	16711680
Purple	255	128	255	16744703
Turquoise	0	255	255	16776960
White	255	255	255	16777215

CYLINDER Drawing-Multiple Configurations

Multiple configurations created in the CYLINDER Design Table allow you to insert various configurations into the drawing. Specify the configuration in the Properties of the current view. Modify the display options in the View Properties. Work between the three Sheets in the CYLINDER drawing.

Activity: CYLINDER Drawing-Multiple Configurations

Add Sheet2.

321) Open the CYLINDER drawing.

322) Click the **Add Sheet** icon at the bottom of the Graphics window. Sheet2 is displayed.

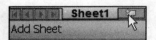

323) Click **No**.

Add Sheet3.

324) Click the **Add Sheet** icon at the bottom of the Graphics window.

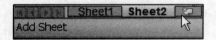

325) Click **No**. Sheet3 is displayed.

Copy the Sheet1 Drawing View to Sheet2.

326) Click the **Sheet1** tab.

327) Click inside the **Isometric Drawing view** boundary of Sheet1.

328) Click **Ctrl + C**.

329) Click the **Sheet2** tab.

330) Click a **position** in Sheet2.

331) Click **Ctrl + V**.

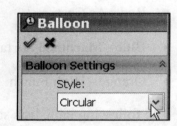

Hide the Balloons.

332) Window-select the **Balloons**. The Balloon PropertyManager is displayed.

333) Right-click **Hide**.

Drawing View #'s and Sheet Format #'s depend on the number of views you inserted and deleted. Your entries in the FeatureManager can vary to the illustrations in the next section.

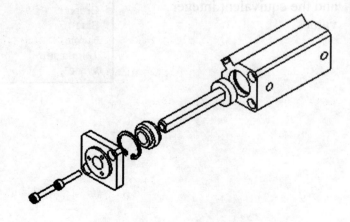

Modify View Properties.

334) Right-click **Properties** in the Isometric view boundary.

335) Uncheck **Show in exploded state**.

336) Select **NO-COVERPLATE** for the Use named configuration.

337) Un-check the **Link balloon text to specified table** box.

338) Click **OK** from the dialog box.

339) Hide all balloons if needed.

Insert a Bill of Material.

340) Click inside the **Isometric view** boundary.

Click **Bill of Materials** 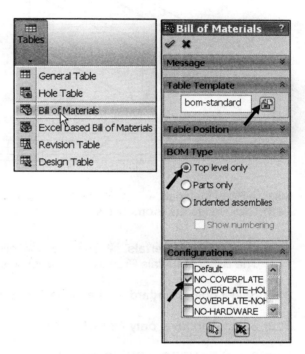 from the Consolidated Tables toolbar.

341) Select **bom-standard** for the Table Template.

342) Select **Top level only** for BOM Type.

343) Check **NO-COVERPLATE** for Configurations. Uncheck all other configurations.

344) Click **OK** ✓ from the Bill of Materials PropertyManager.

345) Click a **position** below the Isometric view. View the results.

Copy the NO-COVERPLATE view.

346) Click inside the **NO-COVERPLATE** view boundary.

347) Click **Ctrl + C**.

348) Click a **position** to the right of the view.

349) Click **Ctrl + V**.

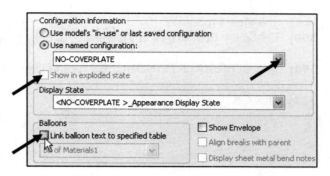

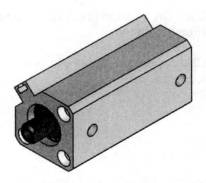

ITEM NO.	PART NUMBER	DESCRIPTION	NO-COVERPLATE/QTY.
1	99-1007-1	TUBE4_ROD4	1
2	10-0411	COLLAR	1
3	MP043BM1-17	RING	1

Modify the View Properties.
350) Right-click **Properties** in the view boundary of the new Isometric view.

351) Click **COVERPLATE-NOHOLES** for the Use named configuration.

352) Click **OK**.

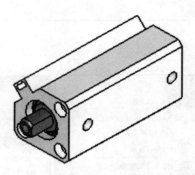
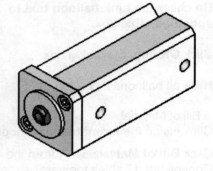

ITEM NO.	PART NUMBER	DESCRIPTION	NO COVERMATE/QTY
1	99-1007-1	TUBE4_ROD4	1
2	10-0411	COLLAR	1
3	MP043BM1-17	RING	1

Insert a Bill of Materials.
353) Click inside the **Isometric view** boundary.

354) Click **Bill of Materials** from the Consolidated Tables toolbar. The Bill of Materials PropertyManager is displayed.

355) Select **bom-standard** for the Table Template.

356) Select **Top level only** for BOM Type.

357) Select **COVERPLATE-NOHOLES**.

358) Click **OK** from the Bill of Materials PropertyManager.

359) Click a **position** below the second Isometric view.

⊞	Tables
⊞	General Table
🕳	Hole Table
📋	Bill of Materials
📋	Excel based Bill of Materials
📋	Revision Table

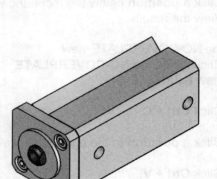

ITEM NO.	PART NUMBER	DESCRIPTION	COVERPLATE-NOHOLES/QTY.
1	99-1007-1	TUBE4_ROD4	1
2	10-0411	COLLAR	1
3	MP043BM1-17	RING	1
4	10-0410B	COVERPLATE NO HOLES	1
5	MP04-M3-05-16	CAP SCREW	2

Insert views into Sheet3.
360) Click the **Sheet3** tab.

361) Click **Model View** 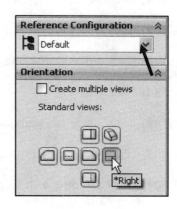 from the View Layout toolbar.

362) Click **Browse**.

363) Double-click the Default **CYLINDER** assembly configuration from the Open dialog box.

364) Select ***Right** from the View Orientation list.

365) Click a **position** on the upper left side of Sheet3.

366) Click **OK** ✔ from the Projected View PropertyManager.

367) Right-click **Properties** in the view boundary.

368) Click the **Show Hidden Edges** tab.

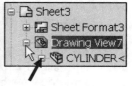

369) **Expand** CYLINDER in the drawing FeatureManager.

370) **Expand** Sheet 3 in the drawing FeatureManager.

371) **Expand** DrawingView7 (Right) in the FeatureManager.

372) **Expand** CYLINDER in the FeatureManager.

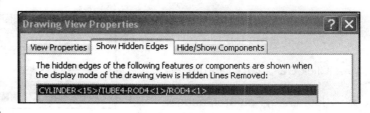

373) **Expand** TUBE4-ROD4<1> default in the FeatureManager.

374) Click **ROD4<1> Default** in the FeatureManager.

375) Click **Apply**.

376) Click **OK** from the Drawing View Properties dialog box.

377) Rename **Drawing View7** to **Drawing View7-Right**.

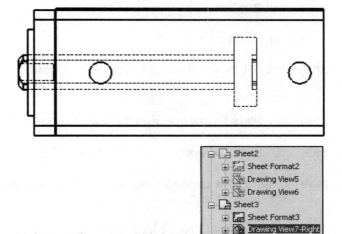

Copy the Right view.
378) Click inside the **Right** view boundary.

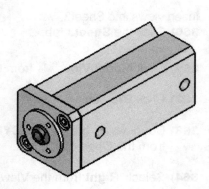

379) Click **Ctrl + C**.

380) Click a **position** to the right of the view.

381) Click **Ctrl + V**.

382) Click inside the **view** boundary.

383) Click ***Isometric** from the Model View PropertyManager.

384) Click **Shaded with Edges**.

385) Click **OK** ✓ from the PropertyManager.

386) Rename **Drawing View8** to **Drawing View8-Isometric**.

Modify the Properties.
387) Right-click **Properties** in the Isometric view boundary.

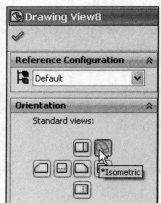

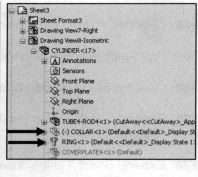

388) Select **CUTAWAY** for Use named configuration.

389) Click the **Hide/Show Components** tab.

390) Click **COLLAR<1>** from the Sheet 3, Drawing View8 (Isometric) FeatureManager.

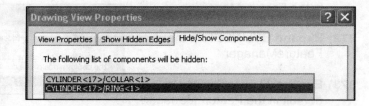

391) Click **RING<1>**.

392) Click **Apply**.

393) Click **OK** to hide the COLLAR and RING parts.

Insert COVERPLATE4 configurations.
394) Click **Model View** 🔲 from the View Layout toolbar.

395) Click **Browse**. Double-click **COVERPLATE4**.

396) Select ***Front** for View Orientation. Click a **position** on the left side of Sheet3.

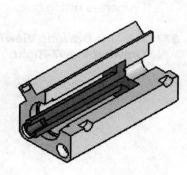

397) Click **OK** ✓ from the Projected View PropertyManager.

Modify the View Properties.
398) Right-click **Properties** in the Front view.

399) Click **WithNoseHoles** for Use named configuration.

400) Click **OK**.

Insert a Linked Note.
401) Click **Note** $\mathbf{A}$ from the Annotation toolbar.

402) Click a **position** below the profile, inside the view boundary.

403) Click **Link to Property** .

404) Check the **Model in view to which the annotation is attached** box.

405) Select **Description**.

406) Click **OK**. Click **OK** ✔ from the Note PropertyManager.

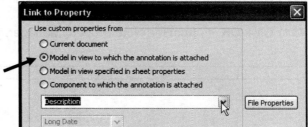

Utilize Lock View Focus to attach an Annotation to the selected view. For custom properties, the Model in view to which annotation is attached option displays when an Annotation references the view. When you move a view, the attached annotations move with the view.

Copy the Front view.
407) Click inside the **Front view** boundary.

408) Click **Ctrl + C**.

409) Click a **position** to the right of the view.

410) Click **Ctrl + V**. The Linked Note copies with the view.

Modify the View Properties.
411) Right-click **Properties** in the copied view.

412) Click **WithoutNoseHoles** for Use named configuration.

413) Click **OK**.

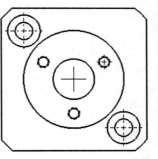
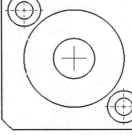

COVERPLATE W/HOLES   COVERPLATE NO HOLES

Align the Front view.
414) Right-click **Alignment** on the COVERPLATE W/HOLES view.

415) Select **Align Horizontal by Origin**.

416) Click **inside** the COVERPLATE NO HOLES view.

Align the Notes.
417) Click the **COVERPLATE W/HOLES** note.

418) Hold the **Ctrl** key down.

419) Click the **COVERPLATE NO HOLES** note.

420) Release the **Ctrl** key. Right-click **Align**. Click **Align Bottom**.

421) Click **OK** ✔ from the Note PropertyManager.

⧉	Align Left
⧈	Align Right
⊓	Align Top
⊔	Align Bottom
⊐⊃	Align Horizontal
𝟾	Align Vertical

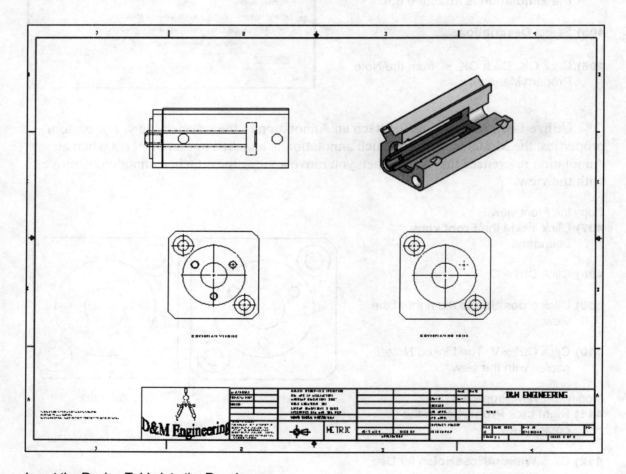

Insert the Design Table into the Drawing.
422) Click inside the **CutAway Isometric** view boundary.

423) Click **Insert**, **Tables**, **Design Table** from the Menu bar menu.

424) Click a **postion** in the left corner of Sheet3.

425) **Modify** the scale and position of the drawing views to fit the Sheet.

Design Table for: CYLINDER		\$CONFIGURATION@COVERPLATE4<1>	\$STATE@COVERPLATE4<1>	\$STATE@CAP-SCREW-M3x16<*>	\$CONFIGURATION@TUBE4-ROD4<1>	\$USER_NOTES
Default	Default	R	R	Default	BASIC	
NO-COVERPLATE	Default	S	S	Default	BASIC	
COVERPLATE-HOLES	WithNoseHoles	R	R	Default	ANODIZED COVER	
COVERPLATE-NOHOLES	WithoutNoseHoles	R	R	Default	ANODIZED COVER	
NO-HARDWARE	Default	R	S	Default	ANODIZED COVER	
CUTWAY	Default	S	S	CutAway	SEE INTERNAL FEATURES	

Save the Sheet1 BOM as a custom BOM Template.
426) Click the **Sheet1** tab.

427) Right-click the **BOM table** in Sheet1.

428) Click **Save as**.

429) Select the **MY-TEMPLATES** folder.

430) Enter **BOM-MATERIAL-COST** for BOM Template name.

431) Click **Save**.

Save the CYLINDER drawing and close all doucments.

432) Click **Save** .

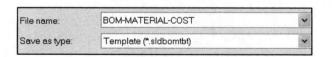

433) Click **Windows**, **Close All** from the Menu bar menu.

Review the following
additional tips on Bill of
Materials and Design Tables.

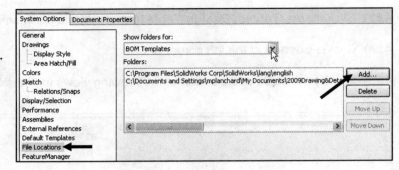

Locate a custom BOM
template quickly. Add the
MY-TEMPLATE folder to
the System Options, File
Locations, BOM Templates
for a default BOM Template folder location.

There are two options to create a Bill of Materials in an assembly drawing:

- SolidWorks table generated Bill of Materials.

- Excel generated Bill of Materials.

A drawing contains only one BOM creation option.

An Excel generated BOM utilizes Microsoft Excel 2000 or later.

Work quickly between the Design Table in the drawing and the Design Table in the
part or assembly. If you double-click the Design Table in the drawing, you return to the
Design Table in the part or assembly.

Modify the Design Table to display only the specific rows and columns of
information. Utilize the Excel Hide option. Modifying and formatting Design Tables is
explored in Chapter 6.

A goal of this book is to expose various SolidWorks design tools and features. The
most direct way may not be always shown.

Revision Table

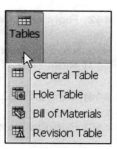

The Revision Table lists the Engineering Change Order (ECO) in the top right section of the drawing. An ECO documents changes that occur to a component. The Engineering department maintains each ECO with a unique document number. In this chapter, the ECO 8531 releases the drawing to manufacturing.

The current Revision block on the drawing was imported from AutoCAD. Delete the current Revision block lines and text. Utilize the Consolidated Tables toolbar to create a Revision Table. The default columns are as follows: Zone, Rev, Description, Date and Approved.

The Zone column utilizes the row letter and column number contained in the drawing border. Position the REV letter in the Zone area. Enter the Zone letter/number. Enter a Description that corresponds to the ECO number. Modify the date if required. Enter the initials/name of the engineering manager who approved the revision.

The REV. column in the Revision Table is a Sheet Property. Create a Linked Note in the Title block and utilize the Revision Sheet Property. The current Revision of the drawing corresponds to the letter in the last row of the Revision Table.

Activity: Revision Table

Create a new drawing.
434) Open the **COVERPLATE4** part.

435) Click **Make Drawing from Part/Assembly** from the Menu bar toolbar.

436) Double-click **A-ANSI-MM** from the MY-TEMPLATES folder.

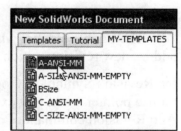

437) **Delete** the Right view and the Isometric view.

Edit the Sheet Format.
438) Right-click in the **Graphics window**.

439) Click **Edit Sheet Format**.

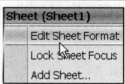

Delete the current Revision Table.
440) **Zoom in** on the upper right corner of the Sheet Format.

441) Window-select the **Revision Table**. The Revision Table is displayed in blue.

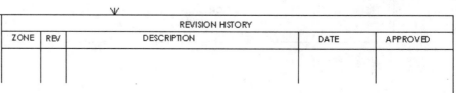

REVISION HISTORY					
ZONE	REV	DESCRIPTION		DATE	APPROVED

442) Right-click **Delete**.

Return to the drawing sheet.
443) Right-click in the **Graphics window**.

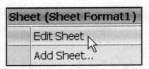

444) Click **Edit Sheet**.

445) **Rebuild** the drawing.

Fit the drawing to the Graphics window.
446) Press the **f** key.

Insert a Revision Table.
447) Click **Revision Table** from the Consolidated Tables toolbar. The Revision Table PropertyManager is displayed.

448) Select the **standard revision** Table Template

449) Click the **Circle Revision** Symbol Shape.

450) Check the **Enable symbol when adding new revision** option. Accept the default settings.

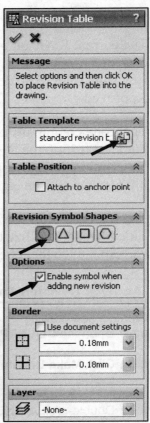

451) Click **OK** ✔ from the Revision Table PropertyManager. The Revision Table is displayed in the upper right corner.

452) Drag the **Revision Table** header downward to the inside upper right sheet boundary.

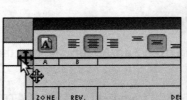

💡 The Enable symbol when adding new revision option displays the Revision Symbol 🗔 on the mouse pointer when you execute the Add Revision command. Position the revision symbol on the drawing that corresponds to the change.

REVISIONS					
ZONE	REV.	DESCRIPTION		DATE	APPROVED

Insert the first row.
453) Right-click the **Revision Table**.

454) Click **Revisions**, **Add Revision**.
The Revision letter, A and the
current date are displayed in the
Revision Table. The
Revision Symbol is displayed on the mouse pointer.

Position the Revision Symbol.
455) Click a **position** in the Front view.

456) Click **OK** ✔ from the Revision Symbol PropertyManager.

Edit the Revision Table.
457) Double-click the **text box** under the Description column.

458) Enter **ECO 8531 RELEASED TO MANUFACTURING**.

459) Click **outside** of the table.

460) Double-click the **text box** under the APPROVED column.

461) Enter Documentation Control Manager's Initials, Example: **DCP**.

462) Click **outside** of the table.

		REVISIONS		
ZONE	REV.	DESCRIPTION	DATE	APPROVED
	A	ECO 8531 RELEASED TO MANUFACTURING	2/24/2010	DCP

Edit the Sheet Format.
463) Right-click a **position** in the Sheet boundary.

464) Click **Edit Sheet Format**.

Insert a Linked Note for Revision.
465) Click **Note** A from the Annotation
toolbar.

466) Click a **position** below the REV text in
the Title block.

467) Click **Link to Property** 📋.

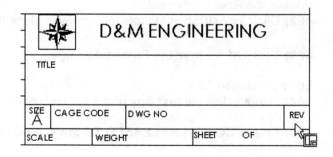

468) Select **Revision** from the drop-down list.

469) Click **OK**.

470) Click **OK** ✔ from the Note PropertyManager.

Return to the drawing sheet.
471) Right-click a **position** in the sheet boundary.

472) Right-click **Edit Sheet**.

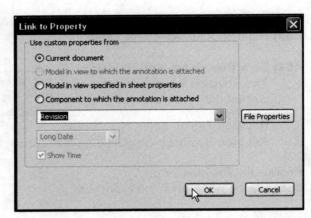

Save the COVERPLATE4 drawing.
473) Click **Save**.

474) Enter **COVERPLATE4** for File name.

Insert a Revision Table into the CYLINDER drawing.
475) Open the CYLINDER drawing.

476) Click the **Sheet1** tab.

Insert a Revision Table.
477) Click **Revision Table** from the Consolidated Tables toolbar. Accept the defaults.

478) Click **OK** ✔ from the Revision Table PropertyManager.

479) Drag the **Revision Table** header downward to the inside upper right sheet boundary.

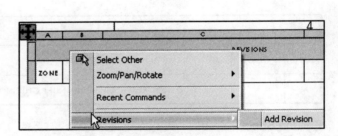

Insert the first row.
480) Right-click the **Revision Table**.

481) Click **Revisions**, **Add Revision**.

Position the Revision Symbol.
482) Click a **position** in the Isometric view to place the A Rev. letter.

483) Click **OK** ✔ from the PropertyManager.

Edit the Revision Table.
484) Double-click the **text box** under the Description column.

485) Enter **ECO 8531 RELEASED TO MANUFACTURING**.

486) Click a **position** outside of the table.

487) Double-click the **text box** under the APPROVED column. Enter Documentation Control Manager's Initials, Example: **DCP**.

		REVISIONS		
ZONE	REV.	DESCRIPTION	DATE	APPROVED
	A	ECO 8531 RELEASED TO MANUFACTURING	2/24/2010	DCP

488) Click a **position** outside of the table.

The C-ANSI-MM Drawing Template utilizes the $PRPSHEET:"Revision" property defined in the Sheet Properties. Utilize the $PRP:"Revision" property to link the REV letter in the Title block to the current REV letter in the Revision Table.

Edit the Sheet Format.
489) Right-click a **position** in the Sheet boundary.

490) Click **Edit Sheet Format**.

Modify the Linked Note for Revision.
491) Double-click the Note below the REV text in the Title block.

492) Click **Delete**.

493) Click **Link to Property** 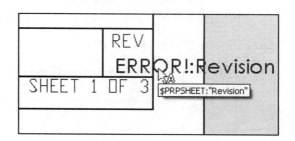.

494) Select **Revision** from the drop down list.

495) Click **OK**.

496) Click **OK** ✔ from the Note: PropertyManager.

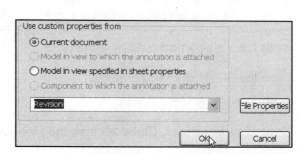

Return to the drawing sheet.
497) Right-click a **position** in the sheet boundary.

498) Click **Edit Sheet**.

Save the CYLINDER drawing.
499) Click **Save** 🖫 .

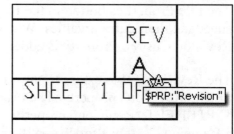

Return to the COVERPLATE4 drawing.
Insert the second row.
500) Open the **COVERPLATE4** drawing.

501) Right-click the **Revision Table**.

502) Click **Revisions**, **Add Revision**.

Position the Revision Symbol.
503) Click a **position** in the Front view to place the B Rev. letter.

504) Click **OK** ✔ from the Revision PropertyManager.

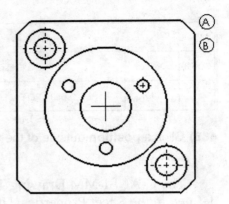

Note: The REV letter in the Title block displays the latest revision of the drawing.

Edit the Revision Table.
505) Double-click the **text box** under the Description column.

506) Enter **ECO 9932 ANODIZE BLACK** for DESCRIPTION.

507) Enter **DCP** for APPROVED.

		REVISIONS		
ZONE	REV.	DESCRIPTION	DATE	APPROVED
	A	ECO 8531 RELEASED TO MANUFACTURING	2/24/2010	DCP
	B	ECO 9932 ANODIZE BLACK	2/24/2010	DCP

508) Click a **position** outside of the table.

Save the COVERPLATE4 drawing.
509) Click **Save** 💾.

510) Click **Windows**, **Close All** from the Menu bar menu.

The File Properties button in the Link to Property box lists the Custom Properties of the sheet and their current values. When the Revision Table is inserted into the drawing, the Revision Custom Property is added to the list.

The Revision Table example shows how to control a REV. value through the $PRP:"Revision" property. The original C-ANSI-MM Template utilized $PRPSHEET:"Revision" property. Companies also control the REV. value by combining a Revision Custom Property in the part and a Linked Note in the drawing. Product Data Management systems, (PDM) control document revisions based on the Revision rules in your company's engineering documentation practices.

Only Sheet1 displays the current REV. You will have to update the Title block in every sheet. Is there a more efficient method to control notes in the Title block? Answer: Yes. Develop a Sheet Format with Drawing Specific SolidWorks Properties and Custom Properties. Insert the Revision Table into the Drawing Template.

For Revision A, the CYLINDER drawing and the COVERPLATE4 drawing utilized the same ECO 8531 number to release the documents to manufacturing. For Revision B, only the COVERPLATE4 drawing was modified. Does the COVERPLATE4 drawing require Revision B? Answer: This "up-rev" action depends on company policy for updating revisions on assemblies. In this case, since the form, fit and function of the CYLINDER assembly did not change, the drawing remained at Rev A.

The default A-size SolidWorks Sheet Format contains Custom Properties defined in the Title block. Set Drawing Specific System Properties: SW-Sheet Name, SW-Sheet Scale, SW-Sheet Format Size, and SW-Template Size in the Sheet Properties dialog box.

Additional Information

The following section explores additional tools and functions as they relate to assembly drawings. Explore these techniques in the chapter exercises. There are no step-by-step instructions.

Section View and Broken-out Section

The Section View and Broken-out Section View contains additional options for assemblies.

A Section View in the assembly starts similar to a Section View in the part. Sketch a line in the Parent view. Click Section View from the View Layout toolbar. The Section View dialog box displays the Section Scope option. Expand the FeatureManager that corresponds to the Sheet and Drawing View #. Select the components to exclude from the section cut. Example: COLLAR and RING.

The Auto hatching option creates alternate pattern hatching between components. The excluded components are not hatched.

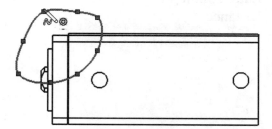

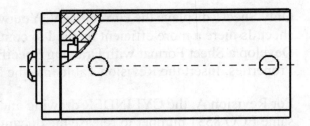

The Materials Editor determines the hatch pattern. A Broken-out Section in the assembly starts similar to a Broken-out Section View in the part. Sketch a Spline (Closed Profile) in the area of the Parent view to break away.

The Depth reference requires a value or an edge reference. The Preview check box displays a yellow cross arrow symbol indicating the Depth.

Hide Behind Plane

The Hide Behind Plane option hides components of an assembly drawing behind a plane. This option provides a quicker selection method than to select individual components.

Only the components that are completely behind the plane become hidden. Example: COVERPLATE, CAP-SCREW, COLLAR and RING.

Display an Isometric view in the drawing. Select the CYLINDER Front Plane from the FeatureManager. Right-click Hide Behind Plane. Enter 25mm for Distance.

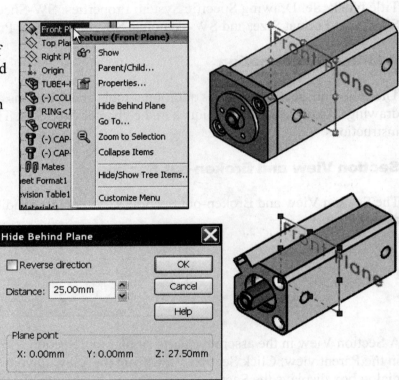

The X, Y and Z coordinates of the plane distance are shown in the Hide Behind Plane dialog box. The default offset distance is 0.

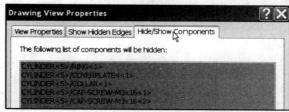

Show the hidden components. Right-click Properties in the current view. Select Hide/Show Components. Delete the component from the hidden list.

Large Assembly Drawing Performance

System Options, Drawings contains the settings for drawings that improve performance. Large assembly drawings are system memory intensive.

Check Automatically hide component on view creation. Review the available options, and uncheck any un-needed option to save system memory and time for large assembly drawings.

Set the default display style to Hidden lines removed and default display quality to Draft Quality.

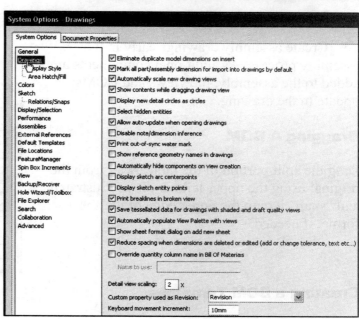

Splitting A BOM

The BOM can be split (Split options)into smaller tables by dividing horizontally or vertically. The split portion retains the column titles and can be dragged anywhere on the drawing. The Merge Table option brings a Split BOM back together.

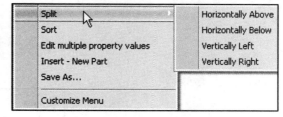

	A	B	C	D	E
1	ITEM NO.	PART NUMBER	DESCRIPTION	MATERIAL	QTY.
2	1	TUBE4			1
3	2	ROD4			1
4	3	10-0411			1

	A	B	C	D	E
	ITEM NO.	PART NUMBER	DESCRIPTION	MATERIAL	QTY.
5	4	MP043BM1-17		Material <not specified>	1
6	5	10-0410		6061 Alloy	1
7	6	MP04-M3-05-16		Material <not specified>	2

(Right-click menu overlay:)
- Zoom/Pan/Rotate ▶
- Recent Commands ▶
- Insert ▶
- Select ▶
- Delete ▶
- Hide ▶
- Formatting ▶
- Sort
- Merge Tables
- Edit Multiple property values

💡 Create assembly drawings early in the assembly process. As additional components are added to the assembly, the views and BOMs update in the drawing.

Dragging A BOM

Drag the split portion of the table away from the original using the upper left handle as illustrated and "snap" it onto the upper edge of the sheet format if needed.

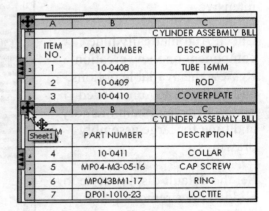

	A	B	C
			CYLINDER ASSEBMLY BILL
2	ITEM NO.	PART NUMBER	DESCRIPTION
3	1	10-0408	TUBE 16MM
4	2	10-0409	ROD
5	3	10-0410	COVERPLATE

	A	B	C
			CYLINDER ASSEBMLY BILL
	ITEM	PART NUMBER	DESCRIPTION
6	4	10-0411	COLLAR
7	5	MP04-M3-05-16	CAP SCREW
8	6	MP043BM1-17	RING
9	7	DP01-1010-23	LOCTITE

Creating a BOM Template

Customized BOM templates can be created by saving the current BOM to a file. Columns and formatting are saved in the template.

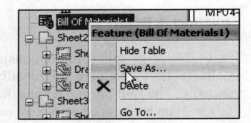

(Feature (Bill Of Materials1) menu:)
- Hide Table
- Save As...
- Delete
- Go To...

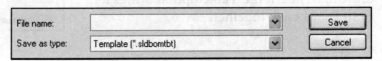

File name: _____ ▼   [Save]
Save as type: Template (*.sldbomtbt) ▼   [Cancel]

Tabulated Bill of Materials

A Tabulated Bill of Materials can be used when the assembly contains multiple configurations. The tabulation affects only the QTY.column. See SolidWorks Help for additional information.

eDrawings

An eDrawing is a compressed document of a SolidWorks part, assembly, or drawing. An eDrawing provides animation, view, measure, section and markup.

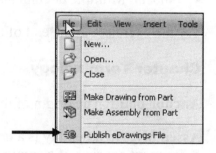

In a multi sheet drawing, select the sheets to create the eDrawing. An eDrawing can be sent via email to a vendor without the corresponding part, assembly or drawing documents.

Export

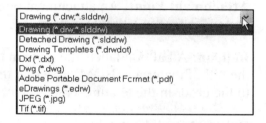

Export is the process to save a SolidWorks document in another format. Exported files are used in: other CAD/CAM, rapid prototyping, web, or graphics software applications. The Export options for SolidWorks drawings are: Dxf, Dwg, *.pdf, eDrawing, JPEG, and Tif.

Chapter Summary

You developed the following in this chapter: CYLINDER assembly with Custom Properties and a Design Table, CYLINDER drawing with multiple sheets and a Bill of Materials.

You inserted an Isometric Exploded view in the CYLINDER assembly and assigned Custom Properties to each part to describe: Material, Mass, Description and Cost parameters. The CYLINDER assembly consisted of the TUBE4, ROD4, COLLAR, RING, COVERPLATE4, and CAP-SCREW-M3x16 parts from the Chapter 5 folder on the CD.

You inserted a Design Table in the CYLINDER assembly to create six different configurations of the assembly. The Design Table contained the Custom Properties linked to the Bill of Materials.

Three sheets of the CYLINDER drawing was developed:

- Sheet1: Isometric Exploded view, Balloon labels, and a Bill of Materials.

- Sheet2: Various configurations of the CYLINDER assembly with corresponding Bill of Materials.

- Sheet3: Multiple documents and component display.

Try the exercises at the end of this project before going on to Project 6.

Chapter Terminology

Anchor point: The origin of the Bill of Material in a sheet format.

Assembly: An assembly is a document that consists of components and features. A component consists of a single part or an assembly. Components are mated together. The extension for a SolidWorks assembly file name is .SLDASM.

Attachment Point: An attachment point is the end of a leader that attaches to an edge, vertex, or face in a drawing sheet.

Balloon: A balloon labels the parts in the assembly and relates them to item numbers on the bill of materials (BOM) added in the drawing. The balloon item number corresponds to the order in the Feature Tree. The order controls the initial BOM Item Number.

Bill of Materials: A table inserted into a drawing to keep a record of the parts used in an assembly.

BOM: Abbreviation for Bill of Materials.

Broken-out Section: A broken-out section exposes inner details of a drawing view by removing material from a closed profile. In an assembly, the Broken-out Section displays multiple components.

Cell: Area to enter a value in an EXCEL spreadsheet, identified by a Row and Column.

CommandManager: The CommandManager is a Context-sensitive toolbar that dynamically updates based on the toolbar you want to access. By default, it has toolbars embedded in it based on the document type. When you click a tab below the Command Manager, it updates to display that toolbar. For example, if you click the **Sketches** tab, the Sketch toolbar is displayed.

Component: A part or sub-assembly within an assembly.

ConfigurationManager: The ConfigurationManager is located on the left side of the SolidWorks window and provides the means to create, select, and view multiple configurations of parts and assemblies in an active document. You can split the ConfigurationManager and either display two ConfigurationManager instances, or combine the ConfigurationManager with the FeatureManager design tree, PropertyManager, or third party applications that use the panel.

Configurations: Variations of a part or assembly that control dimensions, display and state of a model.

Copy and Paste: Utilize copy/paste to copy views from one sheet to another sheet in a drawing or between different drawings.

Datum Feature: An annotation that represents the primary, secondary and other reference planes of a model utilized in manufacturing.

Design Table: An Excel spreadsheet that is used to create multiple configurations in a part or assembly document.

Document: A file containing a part, assembly, or drawing.

Dimension: A value indicating the size of feature geometry.

Dimension Line: A line that references dimension text to extension lines indicating the feature being measured.

DimXpert for Parts: A set of tools that applies dimensions and tolerances to parts according to the requirements of the ASME Y.14.41-2003 standard.

Drawing: A 2D representation of a 3D part or assembly. The extension for a SolidWorks drawing file name is .SLDDRW.

Edit Sheet: The drawing sheet contains two modes. Utilize the Edit Sheet command to insert views and dimensions.

Edit Sheet Format: The drawing sheet contains two modes. Utilize the Edit Sheet Format command to add or modify notes and Title block information. Edit in the Edit Sheet Format mode.

Exploded view: A configuration in an assembly that displays its components separated from one another

Export: The process to save a SolidWorks document in another format for use in other CAD/CAM, rapid prototyping, web, or graphics software applications.

FeatureManager: The FeatureManager design tree located on the left side of the SolidWorks window provides an outline view of the active part, assembly, or drawing. This makes it easy to see how the model or assembly was constructed or to examine the various sheets and views in a drawing. The FeatureManager and the Graphics window are dynamically linked. You can select features, sketches, drawing views, and construction geometry in either pane.

First Angle Projection: Standard 3 Views are in either third angle or first angle projection. In first angle projection, the front view is displayed at the upper left and the other two views are the top and left views.

Fully defined: A sketch where all lines and curves in the sketch, and their positions, are described by dimensions or relations, or both, and cannot be moved. Fully defined sketch entities are displayed in black.

Geometric Tolerance: A set of standard symbols that specify the geometric characteristics and dimensional requirements of a feature.

Graphics window: The area in the SolidWorks window where the part, assembly, or drawing is displayed.

Heads-up View toolbar: A transparent toolbar located at the top of the Graphic window.

Hole Callouts: Hole callouts are available in drawings. If you modify a hole dimension in the model, the callout updates automatically in the drawing if you did not use DimXpert.

Leader: A solid line created from an annotation to the referenced feature.

Mass Properties: The physical properties of a model based upon geometry and material.

Model Item: Provides the ability to insert dimensions, annotations, and reference geometry from a model document (part or assembly) into a drawing.

Origin: The model origin is displayed in blue and represents the (0,0,0) coordinate of the model. When a sketch is active, a sketch origin is displayed in red and represents the (0,0,0) coordinate of the sketch. Dimensions and relations can be added to the model origin, but not to a sketch origin.

Parametric note: A Note that references a SolidWorks dimension or property.

Precision: Controls the number of decimal places displayed in a dimension.

Revision Table: The Revision Table lists the Engineering Change Orders (ECO), in a table form, issued over the life of the model and the drawing. The current Revision letter or number is placed in the Title block of the Drawing.

Section Scope: Specifies the components to be left uncut when you create an assembly drawing section view.

Sheet: A page in a drawing document.

Stacked Balloon: A group of balloons with only one leader. The balloons can be stacked vertically (up or down) or horizontally (left or right).

Task Pane: The Task Pane is displayed when you open the SolidWorks software. It contains the following tabs: SolidWorks Resources, Design Library, File Explorer, Search, View Palette, Document Recovery, and RealView/PhotoWorks.

Toolbars: The toolbars provide shortcuts enabling you to access the most frequently used commands. When you enable the Add-in application in SolidWorks, you can also display their associated toolbars.

Questions:

1. An assembly is comprised of _____.

2. True or False. Parts contained in an assembly cannot be opened from within that assembly.

3. Describe the procedure in a drawing to display an Exploded view and a Collapsed view.

4. True or False. A Design Table is used to create multiple configurations in an assembly.

5. True or False. A Design Table is used to create multiple configurations in a part.

6. True or False. A Design Table is used to create multiple configurations in a drawing.

7. Describe the types of Drawing views you can create from an assembly.

8. Describe the procedure to copy a drawing view from Sheet1 to Sheet2 utilizing the FeatureManager.

9. Identify the column that contains the configuration names in a Design Table.

10. True or False. The Materials Editor contains a library of materials and their properties.

11. Identify the location to create an Exploded view.

12. Describe the function of a Balloon annotation.

13. The Part Number column in the Bill of Materials displays the _____ name by default.

14. Describe the procedure to add the Material to the part and to the Bill of Materials.

15. Describe the procedure to add the Mass Property to the part and to the Bill of Materials.

16. Describe the procedure to add the Cost Property to the part and the Bill of Materials.

17. Describe the function of the $STATE variable in the part Design Table.

18. A drawing can contain multiple configurations of a _____ and an _____.

Exercises

Exercise 5.1:

Create an assembly drawing for the TUBE4-ROD4 assembly. The TUBE4-ROD4 assembly contains two configurations. Create a new configuration for the assembly that utilizes the LongRod configuration. The ShortRod Configuration Cost is $200 and the Long Rod is $250.

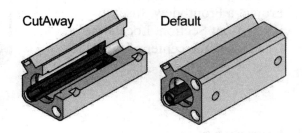

The drawing contains two sheets. Insert three Isometric views on Sheet1. Each view uses a different configuration. Add a Bill of Materials to each view. Add the Cost Column to the BOM.

Insert a Front view and Right view for the ROD part. Display the ShortRod and LongRod configuration on Sheet2.

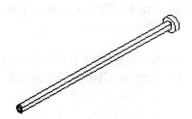

Exercise 5.2:

An Engineering Changer Order is issued to modify the COLLAR part from Alloy Steel to 7079 Alloy. Open the COLLAR part in the Chapter 5 folder on the CD in the book and update the Material in the Materials Editor. Open the CYLINDER drawing to update the BOM.

Exercise 5.3:

Insert a Sheet4 into the CYLINDER drawing. Insert a Right view and a Section view.

Hide the COLLAR and RING parts in the Section View Section Scope.

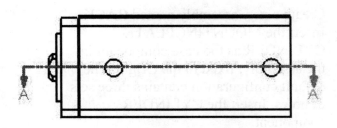

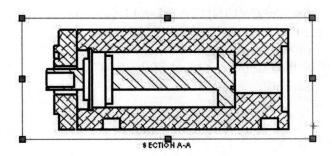

Exercise 5.4:

On Sheet4 in the CYLINDER drawing, create a Right view. Project a Front view. Insert a Broken-out Section. Locate the Distance at the center of the Bore hole.

Exercise 5.5:

An Engineering Change Order is issued to create a new configuration of the CYLINDER assembly. Create a new configuration of the CAP-SCREW-M3x16 that is 20mm in length.

Utilize the CYLINDER assembly Design Table to control the CAP-SCREW-M3x20 part. Update the Bill of Materials on Sheet1 to utilize the CAP-SCREW-M3x20.

Exercise 5.6:

Note: The RACK assembly project in Exercise 5.6 through 5.10 must be completed in order. Knowledge of assembly modeling Concentric and Coincident Mates is required. The chapter utilizes SW\Toolbox. If you do not have the Toolbox application, dimensions for the hardware utilize the dimensions in Exercise 5.7.

RACK Assembly Project.

Create a new assembly named RACK. Insert the MOUNTINGPLATE-CYLINDER as the base component in the assembly, fixed to the Origin. The default configuration contains three sets of holes. Insert the CYLINDER component.

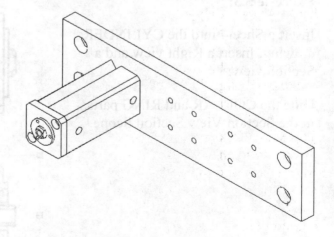

Open the CYLINDER assembly. Delete the two CAP-SCREW-M3x16 parts. You will insert new fasteners with Toolbox at the top level of the RACK assembly.

Mate the Cbore holes of the TUBE with the two diagonal holes of the
MOUNTINGPLATE-CYLINDER. Mate the back face of the TUBE and the front face of
the MOUNTINGPLATE-CYLINDER.

Create a Component Pattern in the RACK assembly. Click Insert, Component Pattern,
Use an Existing Feature Pattern (Derived). Select CYLINDER as the Seed Component
from the assembly FeatureManager. Select LPattern1 as the Pattern feature in the
MOUNTINGPLATE-CYLINDER.

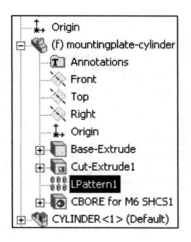
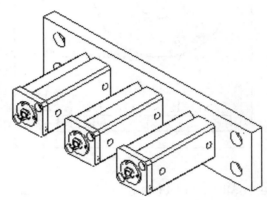

Exercise 5.7:

Add hardware to the RACK
assembly. Utilize the
SolidWorks Toolbox to obtain
hardware part files. The
SolidWorks Toolbox is a set of
industry standard bolts, screws,
nuts, pins, washers, structural
shapes, bearings, PEM inserts
and retaining rings.

The SolidWorks parts are
inserted into an assembly. An
M4x0.7x16 and M4x0.7x20
socket head cap screws and M4
washers complete the RACK
assembly.

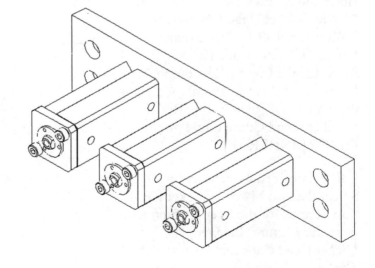

Note: Below are the part dimensions for the actual hex socket head cap screw and washer.

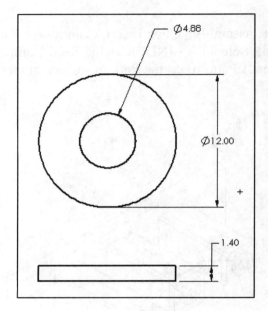
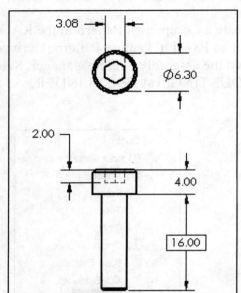

To utilize Toolbox, select Toolbox from the Add-Ins option. Insert an M4X0.7X16 Socket Head Cap Screw. Click the bottom left Cbore circle on the first CYLINDER. Select the Hardware option. Click the Bolts and Screws Tab. Select ANSI Metric, Socket Head Cap Screw, M4X0.7. Select 16 for Fastener Length. Click Create. The M4X0.7 Socket Head Cap Screw component is created and automatically mated to the CYLINDER assembly. Repeat for the second Cbore circle on the first CYLINDER.

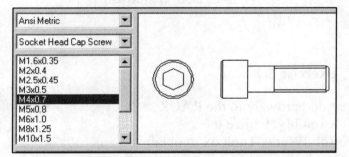

Edit the derived Component pattern. Select the two M4x0.7 Socket Head Cap Screws for the Seed Component from the FeatureManager. The Socket Head Caps Screws are displayed on the other components.

Insert a M4 Washer and an M4X0.7X20 Socket Head Cap Screw to the back face of the MOUNTINGPLATE-CLYLINDER.

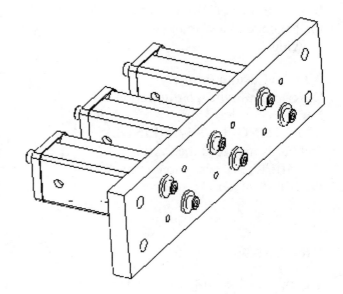

Before submitting the MOUNTINGPLATE-CYLINDER drawing to the machine shop, check material and hardware availability with the parts department. No metric size socket head cap screws are in the stock room. There are only ¼″ and ½″ flat plate stock available in the machine shop. What do you do? Modify your design to reflect inch components.

Exercise 5.8:

Create an Exploded view for the RACK assembly.

Create a new drawing, RACK. Add Balloons to the MOUNTINGPLATE-CYLINDER, CYLINDER and M4X0.7X16 Socket Head Cap Screw. Add a Stacked Balloon to the M4X0.7X20 Socket Head Cap Screw. Select the M4Washer.

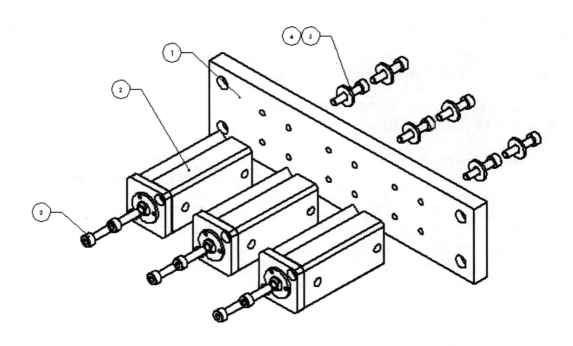

Insert a top level Bill of Materials to the Exploded view in the RACK drawing.

Add the Custom Property Description in the Configuration Manager for the MOUNTINGPLATE-CYLINDER and hardware. Add the PART NUMBERs necessary to complete the Bill of Materials.

RACK ASSEMBLY BILL OF MATERIALS			
ITEM NO.	PART NUMBER:	DESCRIPTION	QTY.
1	50-052-1	MOUNTING PLATE	1
2	99-0531	CYLINDER ASSEMBLY	1
3	5126-16	CAP SCREW 16MM	6
4	5126-20	CAP SCREW 20MM	6
5	5226-1	WASHER 4MM	6

Exercise 5.9:

The MOUNTINGPLATE-CYLINDER part has two configurations named:

2-PATTERN and 3-PATTERN. Review the configurations for the MOUNTING PLATE-CYLINDER part.

Design Table for: MOUNTINGPLATE-CYLINDER	
	D1@LPattern1
2-PATTERN	2
3-PATTERN	3

Control the configurations in the RACK assembly.

Create a Design Table for the RACK assembly. Add two RACK assembly configurations: 2-CYLINDER and 3-CYLINDER.

Enter $CONFIGURATION@MOUNTINGPLATE-CYLINDER<1>. Enter configuration names: 2-PATTERN and 3-PATTERN.

Design Table for: RACK	
	$CONFIGURATION@MOUNTINGPLATE-CYLINDER<1>
2-CYLINDER	2-PATTERN
3-CYLINDER	3-PATTERN

Sheet2 contains the MOUNTINGPLATE-CYLINDER, 2-PATTERN configuration.

Only one Exploded view can exist per assembly. Delete the Stacked Balloons. The hardware quantities are displayed in the Bill of Materials.

RACK ASSEMBLY BILL OF MATERIALS			
ITEM NO.	PART NUMBER	DESCRIPTION	QTY
1	50-052-2	2PATTERN	1
2	99-0531	CYLINDER ASSEMBLY	1
3	5126-16	CAP SCREW 16MM	4
4	5126-20	CAP SCREW 20MM	4
5	5226-1	WASHER 4MM	4

Add new Explode Steps to display the hardware in both a vertical and horizontal direction. Exploded view lines are 3D curves that are added to the Exploded view in the assembly.

Hint. Click Insert, Explode Line Sketch in the CYLINDER assembly. The Route Line PropertyManager is displayed. Click the circular edges of the corresponding cap screw and holes in order from left to right. Click OK. Repeat for the remaining hardware.

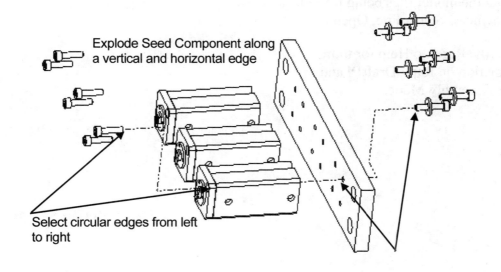

Explode Seed Component along a vertical and horizontal edge

Select circular edges from left to right

Add the Custom Property Description in the Configuration Manager for the MOUNTINGPLATE-CYLINDER and hardware. Add the PART NUMBER to the components necessary to complete the Bill of Materials for the 2PATTERN configuration.

Add the Property $Color. The 2PATTERN MOUNTINGPLATE-CYLINDER is Red. The 3PATTERN is Blue.

Exercise 5.10:

Create an eDrawing of the RACK assembly.

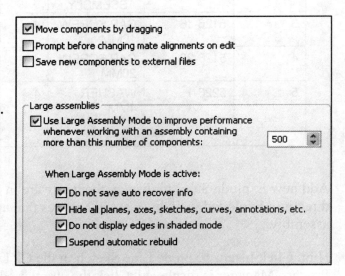

Set the Large Assembly Mode options. Assembly Drawings contain hundreds of components. Utilize Large Assembly Mode, drawing settings to optimize performance.

Work in the Shaded display mode for large assemblies to conserve drawing time.

Create a RapidDraft™ drawing of MOUTINGPLATE-CYLINDER part. RapidDraft™ drawings are designed to open and work in drawing files without the model files being loaded into memory. Select File, Open.

Check the Refer to Help for more information on RapidDraft™ and Large Assembly Mode.

Chapter 6

Datums, Feature Control Frames, Geometric Tolerancing and other Drawing Symbols

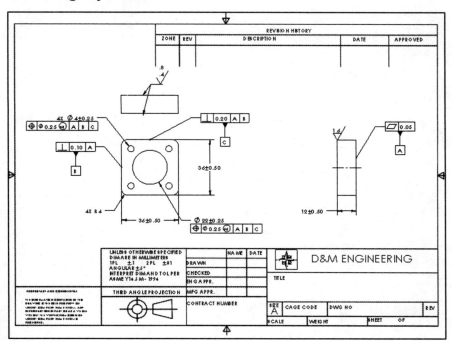

Below are the desired outcomes and usage competencies based on the completion of this Chapter.

Desired Outcomes:	Usage Competencies:
• VALVEPLATE1 drawing • VALVEPLATE1-GDT drawing	• Ability to insert and edit: Dimensions, Feature Control Frames, Datums, Geometric Tolerancing, Surface Finishes and Weld Symbols using DimXpert.
• VALVEPLATE1-GDT eDrawing • ASME14-41 drawing	• Ability to insert and edit: Dimensions, Features Control Frames, Datums, and Geometric Tolerancing manually in a drawing.
• PLATE-TUBE drawing • PLATE-CATALOG drawing	• Skill to develop and edit a Design Table in EXCEL. • Knowledge to create, apply, and save Blocks and Parametric Notes in a drawing.

Notes:

Chapter 6 - Geometric Tolerancing and other Symbols

Chapter Objective

Create five drawings: *VALVEPLATE1, VALVEPLATE1-GDT, VALVEPLATE1-GDT eDrawing, PLATE-TUBE, PLATE-CATALOG.* Modify the *ASME14-41* drawing.

On the completion of this chapter, you will be able to:

- Apply DimXpert and the DimXpertManager:
    - Plus and Minus option
    - Geometric option
- Knowledge of the DimXert toolbar.
- Knowledge of the View Palette.
- Modify dimensions to contain None, Bilateral, and Limit Tolerance.
- Insert Parametric notes.
- Insert Datums, Feature Control Frames, Geometric Tolerances, Surface Finishes, and Weld Symbols.
- Develop a Minimum Content Drawing.
- Insert a Weld Bead assembly feature.
- Format a Design Table in EXCEL.
- Create, Insert, and Save Blocks.
- Understand Fit types.

In Chapter 6, utilize the following SolidWorks tools and commands: *Smart Dimension, Model Items, Autodimension, Note, Balloon, AutoBalloon, Surface Finish, Weld Symbol, Geometric Tolerance, Datum Feature, Hole Callout, Area Hatch/Fill, Insert Block,* and *DimXpert.*

☼ DimXpert provides the ability to import dimensions and tolerances you created using The DimXpert tool for parts into drawings. DimXpert is not associative. DimXpert does not import annotations into an Isometric drawing view.

☼ TolAnalyst™ is a tolerance analysis tool used to study the effects tolerances and assembly methods have on dimensional stack-up between two features of an assembly. The result of each study is a minimum and maximum tolerance stack, a minimum and maximum root sum squared (RSS) tolerance stack, and a list of contributing features and tolerances.

TolAnalyst™ performs a tolerance analysis called a study, which you create using a four-step procedure. TolAnalyst is available only in SolidWorks Premium.

Chapter Overview

As a designer, you work on multiple projects. Each project involves a different type of drawing.

- **VALVEPLATE1 drawing**: Open the VALVEPLATE1 part. Apply DimXpert: Plus and Minus option. Insert dimensions and Geometric tolerances. Create the VALVEPLATE1 drawing. with the View Palette tool. Insert three drawing views. Hide the Top view. Insert a Centerline and Hide Tangent Edges in the Right view. Display None and Bilateral tolerance.

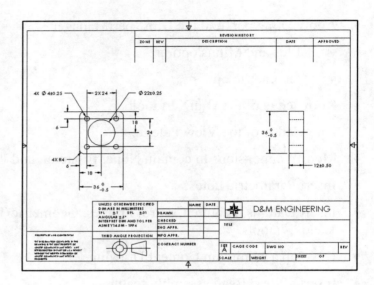

- **VALVEPLATE1-GDT drawing**: Open the VALVEPLATE1-GDT part. Apply DimXpert: Geometric option. Insert Datums, Feature Control Frames, and Geometric Tolerances. Edit Feature Control Frames. Create the VALVEPLATE1-GDT drawing using the View Palette tool. Insert three drawing views. Insert the Surface Finish symbol on the Top and Right view. Create multiple Leaders to the Surface Finish symbol. Insert Hide Tangent Edges in the Top and Right view.

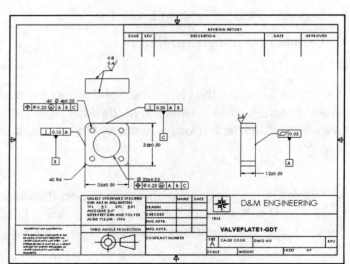

- **VALVEPLATE1-GDT eDrawing**: Send a SolidWorks eDrawing outside to a machine shop for quotation. The VALVEPLATE1-GDT eDrawing is a compressed stand alone document.

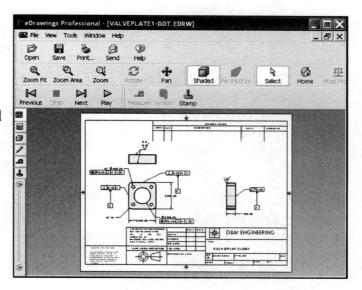

- **ASME14-41 drawing**: Open the ASME14-41-Rev-A part. Apply DimXpert: Geometric option. View the Inserted Datums, Feature Control Frames, and Geometric Tolerances. Modify the ASME14-41 drawing. Manually insert Datums, Feature Control Frames, Dimensions, and Geometric tolerances into an Isometric view on multiply drawing sheets. Note: DimXpert does not import annotations into an Isometric drawing view.

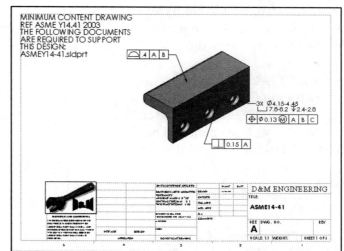

A goal of this book is to expose various SolidWorks design tools and features. The most direct way may not be shown.

- **PLATE-TUBE drawing**: Open the PLATE-TUBE assembly. Create the PLATE-TUBE drawing. The PLATE-TUBE drawing is a conceptual customer drawing. The customer is concerned about the cosmetic appearance of a weld.

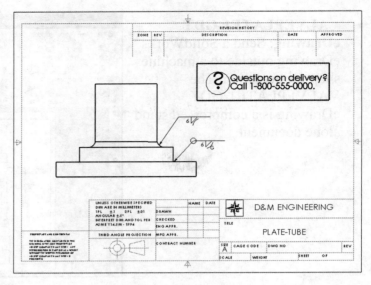

Insert the Weld Bead assembly feature between the TUBE and PLATE parts in the PLATE-TUBE assembly.

Add a second PLATE component to the PLATE-TUBE assembly. Create a Weld Symbol as a separate annotation in the PLATE-TUBE drawing.

- **PLATE-CATALOG drawing**: The PLATE-CATALOG drawing is used for the on-line catalog. The PLATE-CATALOG drawing utilizes a Design Table. Format the Design Table in EXCEL.

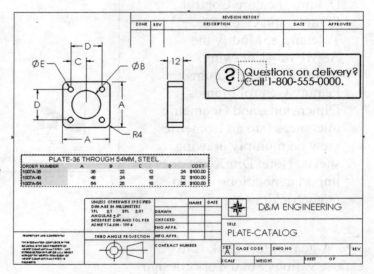

Each of the created drawing in this chapter displays examples of applying various types of symbols in SolidWorks.

This chapter requires you to work between multiple documents: Drawings, Parts, Assemblies and Design Tables.

Drawing Template

The PLATE-TUBE drawing and PLATE-CATALOG drawing utilize different model views. The current A-ANSI-MM Drawing template contains four views. Modify the font height for the Surface Finish Symbols and Weld Symbols. Create a new Drawing template from the A-ANSI-MM with no Predefined views.

Activity: Drawing Template

Open an existing Drawing template.

1)   Click **New** ⬚ from the Menu bar toolbar.

2)   Double-click the **A-ANSI-MM** template from the MY-TEMPLATES tab.

3)   Hold the **Ctrl** key down. Select **Drawing View 1** through **Drawing View 4** from the FeatureManager.

4)   Release the **Ctrl** key. Right-click **Delete**.

5)   Click **Yes to All**.

Set the Document Properties.

6)   Click **Options** 📋, **Document Properties** tab from the Menu bar toolbar.

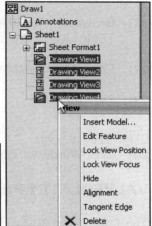

7)   Click the **Detailing** folder.

Clear the Auto insert on view creation box.
8)   Uncheck the **Center marks-holes** and **all other** options.

Set the Annotations Font Height.
9)   Expand the **Annotations** folder.

10)   Click the **Surface Finishes** folder.

11)   Click the **Font** button.

12)   Enter **3** mm for Height.

13)   Click **OK** from the Choose Font dialog box.

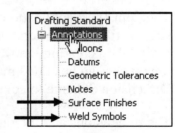

14)   Click the **Weld Symbols** folder.

15)   Click the **Font** button. The Choose Font dialog box is displayed.

16)   Enter **3**mm for Height.

17)   Click **OK** from the Choose Font dialog box.

18)   Click **OK** from the Document Properties – Weld Symbols dialog box.

Save the Drawing template.

19) Click **Save As** from the Menu bar toolbar.

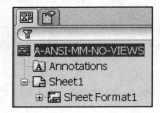

20) Select **Drawing Template** for Files of type.

21) **Browse** to the DRAWING-W-SOLIDWORKS-2010\MY-TEMPLATES folder.

22) Enter **A-ANSI-MM-NO-VIEWS** for file name.

23) Click **Save**.

Close all documents.

24) Click **Windows**, **Close All** from the Menu bar toolbar.

VALVEPLATE1 Part - DimXpert: Plus and Minus Option

The DimXpert application provides the ability to create a fully toleranced model with DimXpert features created from SolidWorks features and geometry. The model can be used with TolAnalyst stack analysis. The results can also be used for:

- Partner CAM applications

- Partner tolerance analysis applications

- Metrology (measurement) applications

- Creating dimensioned and annotated drawing views

The DimXpert application recognizes SolidWorks features such as fillets, chamfers, patterns, extrudes and hole wizard holes when creating DimXpert features. Dimensions and tolerances can be added manually or automatically using Auto Dimension Scheme to complete the process.

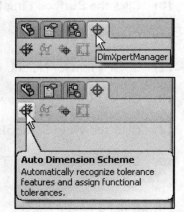

The dimensions and tolerances conform to the ASME Y14.41-2003 standard. The DimXpert application stores the features, dimensions and tolerances that comprise it in the DimXpertManager, a tree structure similar to the FeatureManager Design tree.

Colors are used to help visualize the status of the features, presented as fully, under or over defined like sketches.

Tolerance Types and Features

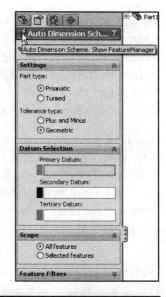

Using the Auto Dimension Scheme, the Tolerance types: Plus and Minus or Geometric can be created. The Geometric options includes Datums and Geometric Tolerances. See SolidWorks Help for additional information.

Settings for DimXpert

Settings exist for DimXpert at the part level. Three are size sub-topics that change the settings used by DimXpert - feature type:

- Size Dimension

- Location Dimension

- Chain Dimension

- Geometric Tolerance

- Chamfer Controls

- Display Options

Click **Tools, Options, Document Properties, DimXpert** to view the available settings.

Block Tolerance vs. General Tolerance

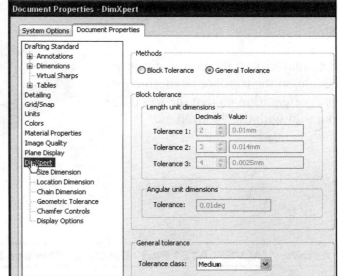

Under Tools, Options, Document Properties, DimXpert there are settings for Methods: Block Tolerance and General Tolerance. General Tolerance is selected by default. If Block Tolerance is selected, all of the feature types are set to these values. In General Tolerance, individual settings for each feature type is available.

Open the VALVEPLATE1 part from the CD. View the three
Extrude features, Linear Pattern feature, and the Fillet feature.
Modify the Sketch plane. Apply the DimXpert: Plus and Minus
option to the part. Apply View Palette to create the
VALVEPLATE1 drawing. Insert three drawing views with
annotations from DimXpert. Work between the part and drawing.

💡 DimXpert is not fully associative. Modify all DimXpert
dimensions before you insert the part and annotations into the
drawing. Care is required to apply DimXpert correctly on
complex surfaces or with some
existing models.

💡 Do not dimension the Mounting
Holes from the part edges. Dimension
the Mounting Hole from the Center
Hole axis.

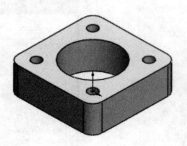
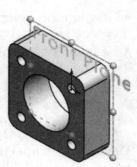

The majority of the part features
reside on the top face. Redefine the
part orientation so that the top face is
parallel with the Front Plane.

Activity: VALVEPLATE1 Part - DimXpert Plus and Minus Option

Open the part and modify the plane orientation.

25) Click **Open** 📂 from the Menu bar toolbar.

26) **Browse** to the DRAWING-W-SOLIDWORKS-2010 folder.

27) Double-click the **VALVEPLATE1** part. The VALVEPLATE1
FeatureManager is displayed.

Redefine the part orientation.
28) **Expand** Extrude1 from the FeatureManager.

29) Right-click **Sketch1**.

30) Click **Edit Sketch Plane** from the Context toolbar. The Sketch Plane PropertyManager is displayed. Top Plane is displayed.

Modify the Sketch Plane from Top Plane to Front Plane.
31) **Expand** VALVEPLATE1 from the Graphics window.

32) Click **Front Plane** from the Flyout FeatureManager. Front Plane is displayed in the Sketch Plane / Face box.

33) Click **OK** from the Sketch Plane PropertyManager. View the model in the Graphics window. The model is displayed on the Front Plane.

Access DimXpert from the DimXpertManager tab or from the DimXpert tab in the CommandManager. The DimXpertManager provides the ability to list the tolerance features defined by the DimXpert in chronological order and to display the available tools.

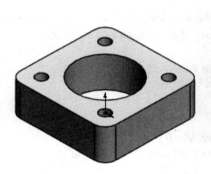
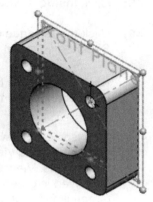

Apply DimXpert to the VALVEPLATE1 part.
34) Click the **DimXpertManager** tab.

35) Click the **Auto Dimension Scheme** tool from the DimXpertManager. The Auto Dimension PropertyManager is displayed. Prismatic, Plus and Minus, and Linear is selected by default. Note: Linear is a new option in SolidWorks 2010.

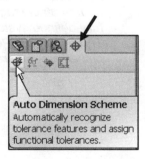

The Auto Dimension Scheme option is used to automate the process of recognizing features and adding functional tolerances. Starting with datum selection, features and planes can be added to define the scope of the scheme.

A key difference between the *Plus and Minus* option versus the *Geometric* option is how DimXpert controls the four-hole pattern, and how it applies tolerances to interrelate the datum features when in *Geometric* mode. You will apply both options in this chapter.

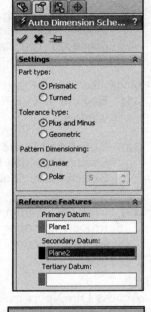

Select type of Scheme.
36) Check the **Prismatic** box.

Select the Primary Datum.
37) Click the **back face** of the model. Plane1 is displayed in the Primary Datum box. Note: Plus and Minus and Linear should be selected by default.

Select the Secondary Datum.
38) Click **inside** the Secondary Datum box.

39) Click the **left face** of the model. Plane2 is displayed in the Secondary Datum box. Two planes are selected.

40) Click **OK** ✔ from the Auto Dimension PropertyManager.

Display an Isometric view.
41) Click **Isometric view**. View the dimensions. View the features displayed in green and yellow. Green is fully constrained. Yellow is under constrained. *Note: Additional dimensions are required for manufacturing. This is NOT a fully defined system at this time. Three mutually Perpendicular planes are required.*

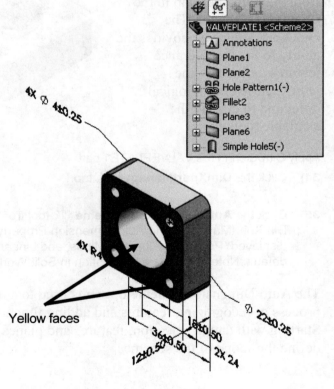

Yellow faces

The DimXpertManager displays either *no mark*, *(+)*, or a *(-)* sign next to the Plane or Feature.

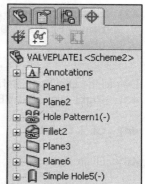

- Features with *no mark* after the name are fully constrained, as illustrated in the VALVEPLATE1 DimXpertManager and are displayed in green.

- Features with the *(+)* sign following the name are over constrained and are displayed in red in the Graphics window.

- Features with the *(-)* sign following the name are under constrained and are displayed in yellow in the Graphics window.

DimXpert dimensions and tolerances are magenta-colored by default.

For DimXpert - features means manufacturing features. For example, in the CAD world, you create a "shell" feature, which is a type of "pocket" feature in the manufacturing world.

When you apply DimXpert dimensions to manufacturing features, DimXpert uses the following two methods in this order to recognize features: *Model feature recognition*, and *Topology recognition*.

The Feature Selector is a floating, Context sensitive toolbar that you can use to distinguish between different DimXpert feature types. The available Feature Selector choices depend on the selected face and the active command.

The order of features in the Feature Selector is based on their complexity:

- Basic features like planes, cylinders, and cones are located on the left.

- Composite features like counterbore holes, notches, slots, and patterns are located in the middle.

- Compound features like compound holes and intersect points are located on the right. Compound features require additional selections.

Within DimXpert, a single face can typically define multiple manufacturing feature types that require different dimensions and tolerances.

42) Click each **Plane** and **feature** in the Show Tolerance Status FeatureManager. The selected item is displayed in blue.

Delete the DimXpert Scheme.
43) Right-click **VALVEPLATE1** from the DimXpertManager.

44) Click **Delete**.

45) Click **Yes**.

Create a New Scheme which is fully constrained.

46) Click the **Auto Dimension Scheme** tool from the DimXpertManager. The Auto Dimension PropertyManager is displayed. Prismatic, Plus and Minus, and Linear should be selected by default.

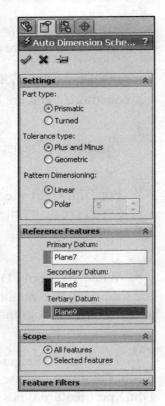

Select the Primary Datum.
47) Click the **back face** of the model. The selected plane is displayed in the Primary Datum box.

Select the Secondary Datum.
48) Click **inside** the Secondary Datum box.

49) Click the **left face** of the model. The selected plane is displayed in the Secondary Datum box.

Select the Tertiary Datum.
50) Click **inside** the Tertiary Datum box.

51) Click the **top face** of the model. The selected plane is displayed in the Tertiary Datum box.

52) Click **OK** from the Auto Dimension PropertyManager.

53) Click **Isometric view**. View the dimensions. All features are displayed in green.

54) **Drag** all dimensions off the model.

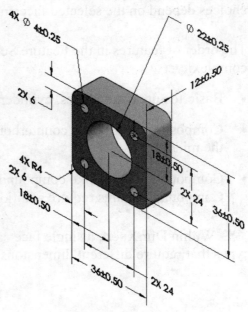

Modify Tolerance and dimensions in the part.

55) Click the **36 horizontal** dimension text. The DimXpert PropertyManager is displayed.

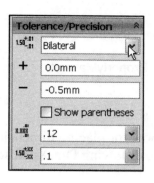

Create a Bilateral Tolerance.

56) Select **Bilateral** from the Tolerance Type drop-down menu.

57) Enter **0** for Maximum Variation.

58) Repeat the above procedure for the **36 vertical** dimension text.

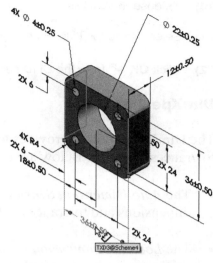

59) Click **OK** ✔ from the DimXpert PropertyManager. View the results.

Remove Instance Count from the part.

60) Click the **2X 6 vertical** dimension text.

61) Hold the **Ctrl** key down.

62) Click the **2X 6 horizontal** dimension text.

63) Click the **2X 24 vertical** dimension text.

64) Click the **2X 24 horizontal** dimension text.

65) Release the **Ctrl** key.

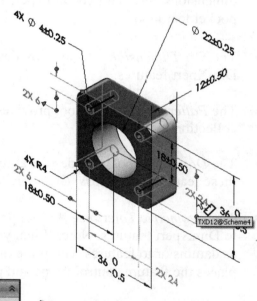

66) **Uncheck** the Instance Count box from the Dimension Text dialog box. View the results.

Remove a tolerance from the part.

67) Click the **18 vertical** dimension text.

68) Hold the **Ctrl** key down.

69) Click the **18 horizontal** dimension text.

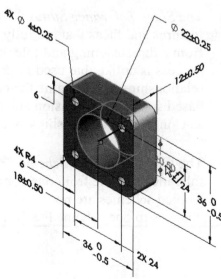

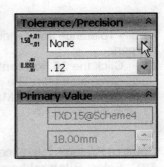

70)   Release the **Ctrl** key.

71)   Select **None** for Tolerance Type. View the results.

72)   Click **OK** ✔ from the DimXpert PropertyManager.

DimXpert toolbar

The DimXpert toolbar provides tools for placing dimensions and tolerances on a part. Below are the following DimXpert tools:

- The *Auto Dimension Scheme* ✦ tool provides the ability to automatically apply dimensions and tolerances to the manufacturing features of a part.

- The *Location Dimension* ▣ tool provides the ability to apply linear and angular dimensions between two DimXpert features, (excluding surface, fillet, chamfer, and pocket features).

- The *Size Dimension* ▣ tool provides the ability to place tolerance size dimensions on DimXpert features.

- The *Pattern Feature* ᴀᴀ tool provides the ability to create or edit pattern features and collection features.

- The *Datum* ᴴᴬ tool provides the ability to define datum features. The tool supports these feature types: *Boss*, *Cylinder*, *Notch*, *Plane*, *Simple Hole*, *Slot*, and *Width*.

- The *Geometric Tolerance* ▣ tool provides the ability to apply geometric tolerances to DimXpert features. Note: When you apply geometric tolerances to features defined as datums or to features with pre-existing size tolerances, DimXpert automatically places the feature control frame and pre-existing annotation in an annotation group.

- The *Show Tolerance Status* ⚭ tool provides the ability to identify the manufacturing features and faces that are fully constrained, under constrained, and over constrained from a dimensioning and tolerancing perspective. Note: The DimXpert identification process is unlike that used in sketches, which utilizes dimensional and geometrical relationships to determine the constraint status of the sketch entities. DimXpert is based solely on dimension and tolerance constraints. Geometrical relationships, such as Concentric relationships, are not considered.

- The *Copy Tolerance Scheme* ✦ tool provides the ability to copy a DimXpert tolerance scheme from one configuration of a part to another configuration. Note: Copied schemes are not synchronized with the Source configuration. Making changes to one scheme has no affect on the other.

- The *Delete All Tolerances* ✳ tool provides the ability to delete the entire DimXpert database. Note: To reinstate the DimXpert database, click **Undo** from the Menu bar toolbar.

☀ Various drawing standards display Tolerance zeros differently. The ASME Y14.5M standard states for millimeter dimensions, that there is no decimal point associated with a unilateral tolerance on a 0 value. There is no +/- sign associated with the unilateral tolerance on a 0 value.

A unilateral tolerance is similar to a SolidWorks bilateral tolerance; with one tolerance value set to 0. The other tolerance value contains a +/- sign. Select Bilateral Tolerance in SolidWorks when a unilateral tolerance is required.

$$\emptyset \ 22^{+0.4}_{0}$$

Decimal inch tolerance rules differ from millimeter rules. Explore decimal unilateral tolerance at the end of this chapter.

DimXpert Annotations and Drawings

The dimensions and annotations generated when dimensions schemes are created are considered DimXpert Annotations. These annotations, combined with the planes that hold them, are very useful which creating drawing views. In the next section, insert DimXpert annotations into a drawing.

Activity: VALVEPLATE1 Drawing - View Palette

73) Click the **FeatureManager** tab.

74) Right-click the **Annotations** folder from the FeatureManager.

75) **Uncheck** the Show DimXpert Annotations box. View the results in the Graphics window.

Display the DimXpert Annotations.
76) Right-click the **Annotations** folder from the FeatureManager.

77) **Check** the Show DimXpert Annotations box.

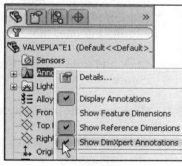

78) Click **Save**.

To modify the default DimXpert color, click **Options**, **Colors**. Under Color scheme settings, select **Annotations**, **DimXpert** and pick the new color.

Create a new VALVEPLATE1 drawing. Apply the DimXpert Annotations.

79) Click the **Make Drawing from Part/Assembly** from the Menu bar toolbar.

80) Click the **MY-TEMPLATES** tab.

81) Double-click the **A-ANSI-MM-NO-VIEWS** drawing template.

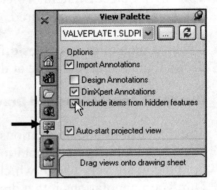

In the A-ANSI-MM-NO-VIEWS Template, there are no Pre-defined views and Auto insert on view creation Center Marks option is unchecked.

Insert three drawing views using the View Palette.

82) Click the **View Palette** ⊞ tab in the Task Pane. VALVEPLATE1 is displayed in the drop-down menu.

83) Check the **Import Annotations** box.

84) Check the **DimXpert Annotations** box.

85) To include all annotations that may be in annotation views other than the default Front, Top and Right, click **the Include items from hidden features** box. Note: The (A) next to the drawing view informs the user that DimXpert Annotations are present.

86) Click and drag the **(A) Front** view into Sheet1 in the lower left corner.

87) Click a **position** directly above the Front view.

88) Click a **position** directly to the right of the Front view. Three views are displayed.

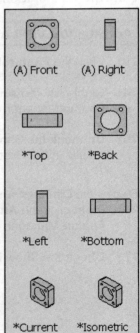

89) Click **OK** ✔ from the Project View PropertyManager.

Modify the Sheet Scale.
90) Right-click in the **sheet boundary**.

91) Click **Properties**. Enter **1:1** for Scale.

92) Click **OK** from the Sheet Properties dialog box.

93) If required, click **Options**, **Document Properties** tab from the Menu bar toolbar.

94) **Uncheck** the Dual dimensions display box from the Document Properties - Dimensions dialog box.

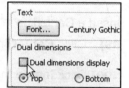

95) Click **OK**. Click and drag the **dimensions** off the model as illustrated. Move any dimensions if needed as illustrated.

💡 At this time, you can NOT insert extension line gaps when using DimXpert.

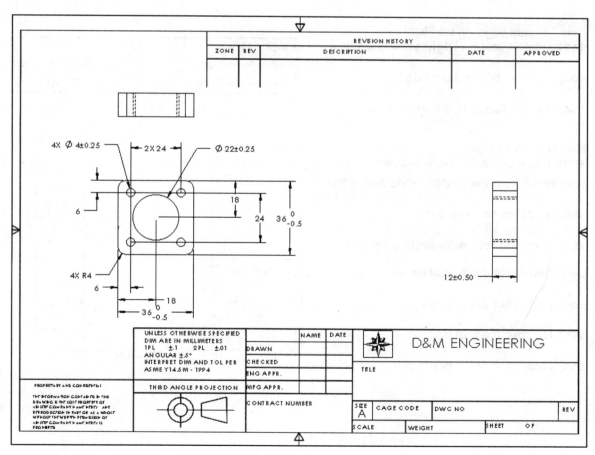

Hide the Top view.

96) Right-click **inside** the Top view boundary.

97) Click **Hide**.

98) Click **OK** ✔ from the Drawing View2 PropertyManager

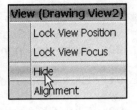

🔆 To displayed a hidden dimension, click View, Hide/Show Annotations. The Hidden Annotations are displayed in the drawing.

Insert a Centerline in the Right view.

99) Click **Centerline** 🔲 from the Annotation toolbar.

100) Click **inside** the Right view boundary.

101) Click **OK** ✔ from the Centerline PropertyManager. Note: The Right view is displayed with Hidden Lines Visible.

Hide Tangent edges in the Right view.

102) Click inside the **Right view** boundary.

103) Right-click **Tangent Edge**.

104) Check **Tangent Edges Removed**.

Hide small hole edges.

105) If needed, click **Hidden Lines Visible** ⬜ from the Display Style dialog box.

106) Hold the **Ctrl** key down.

107) Click the **four silhouette edges** as illustrated. Note the silhouette icon.

108) Right-click **Hide Edge**.

109) Release the **Ctrl** key.

110) **Hide** the Centerlines.

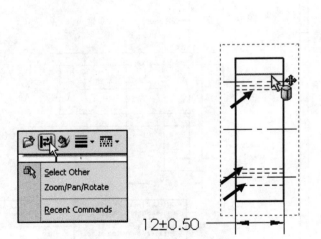

111) Click **Save** 💾 .

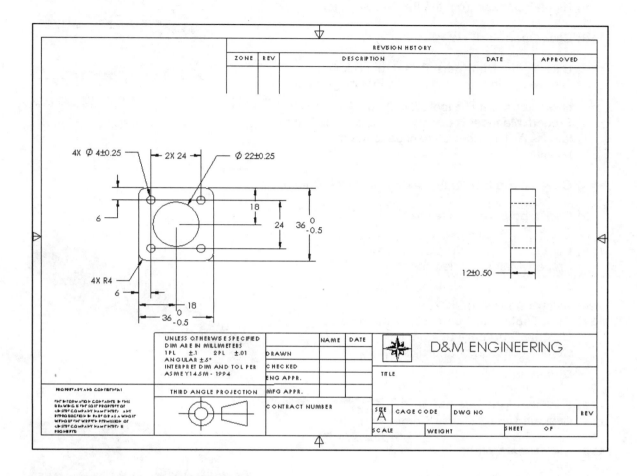

Using DimXpert Manually in a Part

SolidWorks provides the ability to apply DimXpert manually. In the next section, add datums, dimensions and geometric tolerance using the manual method.

Activity: Vise Assembly - DimXpert Manual Method in a Part

Open the assembly and apply the DimXpert Manual Method.

112) Click **Open** 📂 from the Menu bar toolbar.

113) Browse to the DRAWING-W-SOLIDWORKS-2010 folder.

114) Double-click the **Vise** assembly. The Vise FeatureManager is displayed.

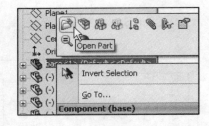

Add a Datum to the base component.

115) Right-click **base** from the FeatureManager.

116) Click **Open Part**.

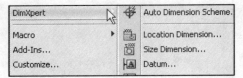

117) Click **Tools**, **DimXpert**, **Datum** or click the **DimXpert** tab from the CommandManager and click the **Datum** [A] tool. The Datum Feature PropertyManager is displayed. The default Datum label is A. The label is attached to the mouse pointer.

118) Click the **top face** of the part to locate the Datum.

119) Click a **position above** the datum.

120) Click **OK** ✔ from the Datum Feature PropertyManager. View the results.

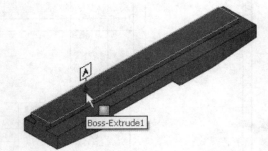

Insert a dimension using DimXpert.

121) Click **Tools**, **DimXpert**, **Size Dimension** or click the **DimXpert** tab from the CommandManager and click the Size **Dimension** ☐ tool.

122) Click the **right face** as illustrated.

123) Click **Create Width Feature**.

124) Click the **opposite face** as illustrated.

125) Click **OK** ✔ from the Pop-up menu.

126) Place the **dimension** off the model. The DimXpert PropertyManager is displayed.

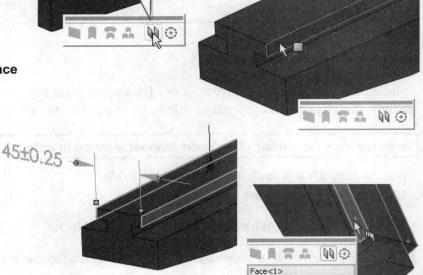

Set the Tolerance of the dimension.
127) Set Tolerance/Precision to **limit**.

128) Enter Maximum Variation: **-0.12**mm.

129) Enter Minimum Variation: **-0.20**mm.

130) Set **Tolerance Precision** as illustrated.

131) Click **OK** from the DimXpert
PropertyManager.

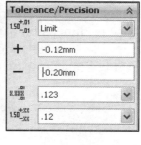

132) **Save** and **close** the part. The Vise
assembly is displayed.

133) Open the **jaw1 part** from the vise
assembly. The jaw1 FeatureManager is
displayed.

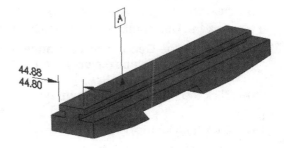

134) Insert **datums A, B and C** as shown using
DimXpert. Follow the above procedure.

Insert a dimension using DimXpert.
135) Click **Tools**, **DimXpert**, **Size Dimension** or
click the **DimXpert** tab from the
CommandManager and click the Size
Dimension tool.

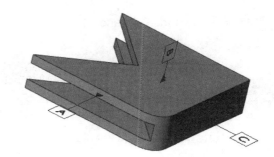

136) Add a **size dimension between the inner
faces** as illustrated.

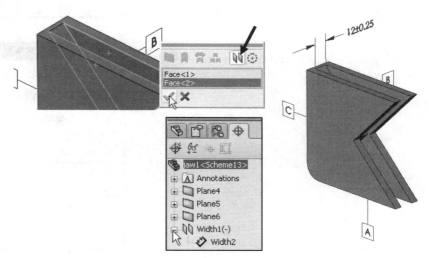

The Geometric Tolerance symbol can be added to a face or dimension of the model. It is created in the same way as the annotation geometric tolerance symbol in a drawing.

💡 The Primary, Secondary and Tertiary datum names must exist before adding them to the geometric tolerance symbol.

Insert Geometric Tolerance to the part.
137) Click the **size dimension.**

138) Click **Tools**, **DimXpert**, **Geometric Tolerance** or click the **DimXpert** tab from the CommandManager and click the **Geometric Tolerance** tool. The Properties dialog box is displayed.

139) Click the **Symbol drop-down** arrow.

140) Click the **Position** ⊕ symbol.

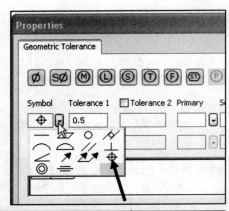

141) Enter **0.0** for Tolerance 1.

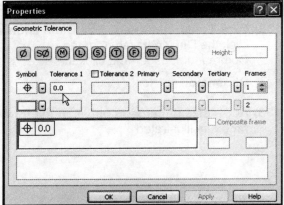

142) Click the **Max Material Condition** Ⓜ **symbol**.

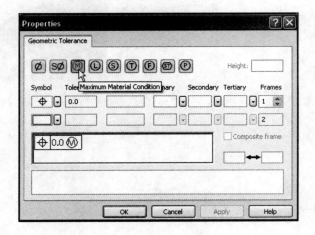

143) Click the **Primary datum** drop-down menu.

144) Enter **A**.

145) Click **OK** ✓.

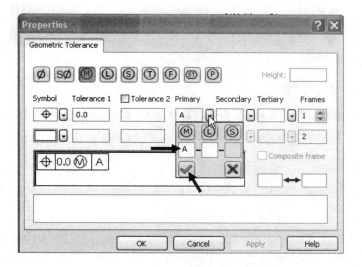

146) Click the **Secondary datum** drop-down menu.

147) Enter **B**.

148) Click **OK** ✓.

149) Click **OK** from the Properties dialog box. View the results.

150) **Save** and **Close** all models.

🔆 Double-click the Feature Control frame as illustrated to displayed the Properties dialog box.

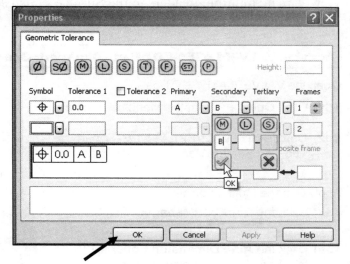

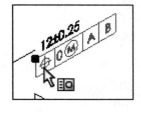

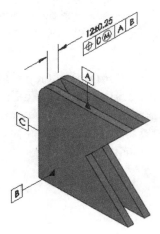

The Annotation PropertyManager is displayed each time you add new DimXpert dimensions. If you do not update the annotations at that time, you must click View, Hide/Show Annotations from the Menu bar menu to display the updated annotations.

VALVEPLATE1-GDT Part - Datums, Feature Control Frames, Geometric Tolerances, and Surface Finish

Open the VALVEPLATE1-GDT part from the CD. View the three Extrude features, Linear Pattern feature, and Fillet feature. Apply the DimXpert: Geometric option to the part. View the inserted Datums, Feature Control Frames, and Geometric tolances.

Edit the Feature Control Frames. Create the VALVEPLATE1-GDT drawing using the View Palette. Insert three drawing views. Insert Surface Finish on the Top and Right view. Create multiple Leaders to the Surface Finish symbol in the Top view. Insert Hide Tangent Edges in the Top and Right view.

Activity: VALVEPLATE1-GDT Part - DimXpert: Geometric option

Open the VALVEPLATE1-GDT part.

151) Click **Open** from the Menu bar toolbar.

152) Double-click **VALVEPLATE1-GDT** part. The Part FeatureManager is displayed.

Apply DimXpert to the part.

153) Click the **DimXpertManager** tab.

154) Click the **Auto Dimension Scheme** tool from the DimXpertManager. The Auto Dimension PropertyManager is displayed. Prismatic and Plus and Minus is selected by default. In this section, select the Geometric option.

DimXpert: Geometric option provides the ability to locate axial features with position and circular run out tolerances. Pockets and surfaces are located with surface profiles.

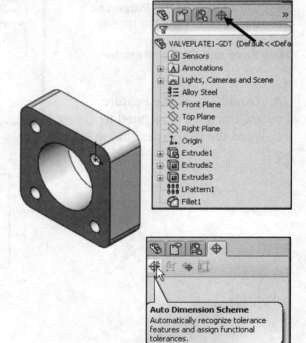

155) Check the **Geometric** box as illustrated. Prismatic is selected by default.

Select the three Datums.
156) Click the **back face** of the model. Plane1 is displayed in the Primary Datum box.

157) Click **inside** the Secondary Datum box.

158) Click the **left face** of the model. Plane2 is displayed in the Secondary Datum box.

159) Click **inside** the Tertiary Datum box.

160) Click the **top face** of the model. Plane3 is displayed in the Tertiary Datum box.

161) Click **OK** ✓ from the Auto Dimension PropertyManager.

162) Click **Isometric view**. View the Datum's, Feature Control Frames, and Geometric tolerances. All features are displayed in green.

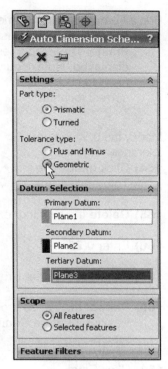

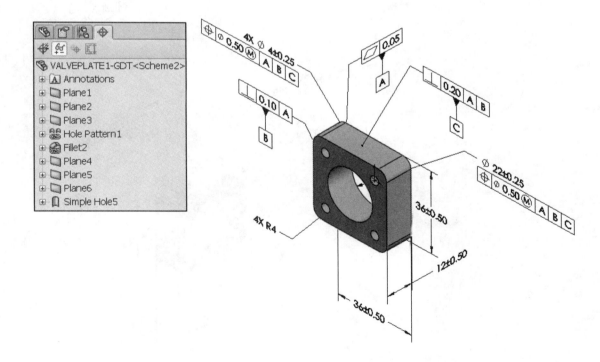

Edit a Feature Control Frame in the part.

163) Double-click the illustrated Feature Control Frame. The Properties dialog box is displayed. Note: You need to click in the correct location.

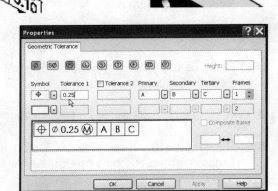

Modify the 0.50 feature tolerance.

164) Click **inside** the Tolerance 1 box.

165) Delete the existing text.

166) Enter **0.25**.

167) Click **OK** from the Properties dialog box.

168) Repeat the above procedure for the second Position Feature Control Frame. View the results.

169) Click **Save**.

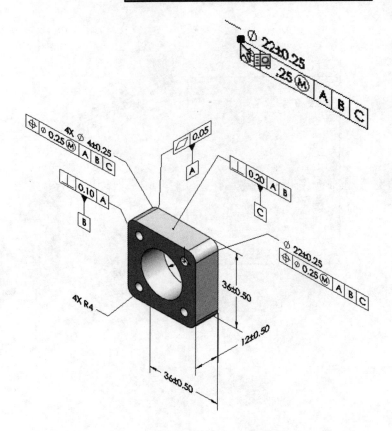

Activity: VALVEPLATE1-GDT Drawing - View Palette

Create the VALVEPLATE1-GDT drawing.

170) Click the **Make Drawing from Part/Assembly** in the Menu bar toolbar.

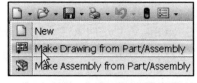

171) Click the **MY-TEMPLATES** tab.

172) Double-click the **A-ANSI-MM-NO-VIEWS** drawing template.

In the A-ANSI-MM-NO-VIEWS Template, there are no Pre-defined views and Auto insert on view creation Center Marks option is unchecked.

Insert three views from the View Palette.

173) Click the **View Palette** tab in the Task Pane. VALVEPLATE1-GDT is displayed in the drop-down menu.

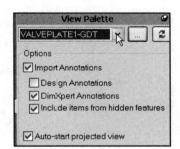

174) Check the **Import Annotations** box.

175) Check the **DimXpertAnnotations** box.

176) Check the **Include items from hidden features** box. Note: The (A) next to the drawing view informs the user that DimXpert Annotations are present.

177) Click and drag the **(A) Front** view into Sheet1 in the lower left corner.

178) Click a **position** directly above the Front view.

179) Click a **position** directly to the right of the Front view. Three views are displayed.

180) Click **OK** from the Projected View PropertyManager.

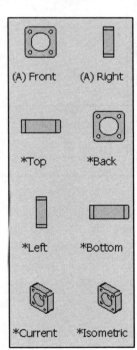

Modify the Sheet Scale.

181) Right-click in the **sheet boundary**.

182) Click **Properties**.

183) Enter **1:1** for Scale.

184) Click **OK** from the Sheet Properties dialog box.

185) Uncheck the Dual dimensions display box.

186) Click and drag the **dimensions** off the model as illustrated.

Save the VALVEPLATE1-GDT drawing.

187) Click **Save** 💾 . Accept the default name.

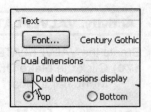

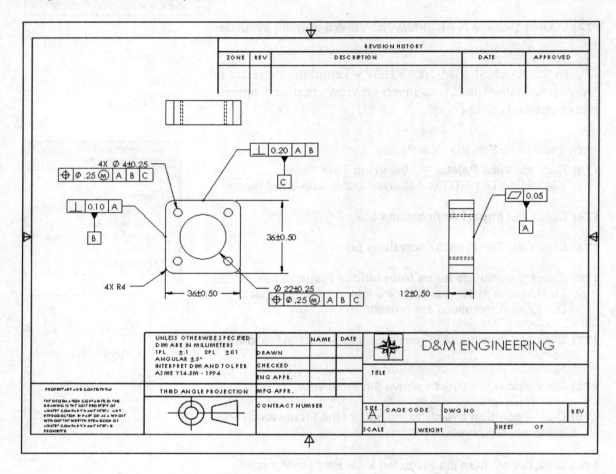

Activity: VALVEPLATE1-GDT Drawing- Surface Finish

Insert the Surface Finish symbol with a Bent Leader into the Top View.
188) Zoom in on the Top view.

189) Click **Surface Finish** ⩗ from the Annotation toolbar.

190) Click **Basic** for Symbol.

191) Enter **0.8** micrometers for Maximum Roughness.

192) Enter **0.4** micrometers for Minimum Roughness.

193) Click **Leader**.

194) Click **Bent Leader**.

195) Click the **top horizontal edge** of the Top view for the arrowhead attachment.

196) Click a **position** for the Surface Finish symbol

197) Click **OK** ✔ from the Surface Finish PropertyManager.

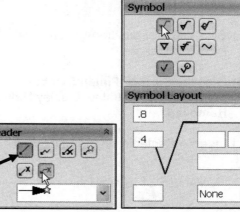
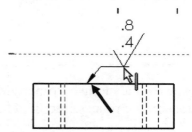

Create multiple Leaders to the Surface Finish symbol.
198) Hold the **Ctrl** key down.

199) Click the tip of the **arrowhead**.

200) Drag the **arrowhead** to the bottom edge of the Top view.

201) Release the **Ctrl** key. **Release** the mouse button.

Remove the Tangent Edge in the Top view.
202) Click inside the **Top view**.

203) Right-click **Tangent Edge**.

204) Check **Tangent Edges Removed**.

205) Display **Hidden Edges Removed** in the Top View.

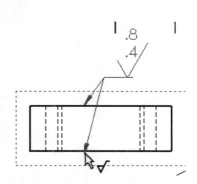

Insert Surface Finish symbol in the Right View.
206) Display **Hidden Edges Removed** in the Right view.

207) Click the **top horizontal edge** in the Right view.

208) Click **Surface Finish** √ from the Annotation toolbar.

209) Select the **Machining Required** option for Symbol.

210) Enter **1.6** micrometer for Maximum Roughness.

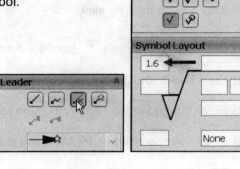

211) Click **No Leader** .

212) Click the **top horizontal edge** of the Right view.

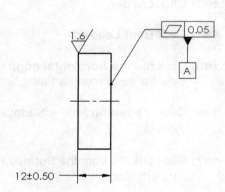

213) Click **OK** ✔ from the Surface Finish PropertyManager.

214) Drag the **Surface Finish Symbol** to the left of the profile line as illustrated. Display **Hidden Edges Removed**.

215) **Insert** a Centerline in the Right view.

Save the VALVEPLATE drawing.

216) Click **Save** .

The Surface Finish PropertyManager contains additional options that refer to the machining process required to complete the part.

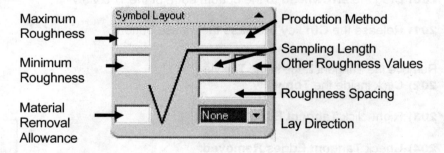

To utilize a specific Finish in the Title Block, add the Custom Property, Finish in the Part. Link the Finish box in the Title Block to the Finish Property. The Greek Letter, m, is obtained from the SWGrekc Font.

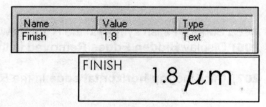

Name	Value	Type
Finish	1.8	Text

FINISH $1.8\,\mu m$

eDrawing

An outside machine shop will manufacture the VALVEPLATE1-GDT. Send a SolidWorks eDrawing of the VALVEPLATE1-GDT to the machine shop for a price quotation. Create a SolidWorks eDrawing.

Activity: eDrawing

Create an eDrawing.
217) Click **File**, **Publish eDrawing 2010 File** from the Menu bar menu.

 The Mark-up options are available in eDrawings Professional software application.

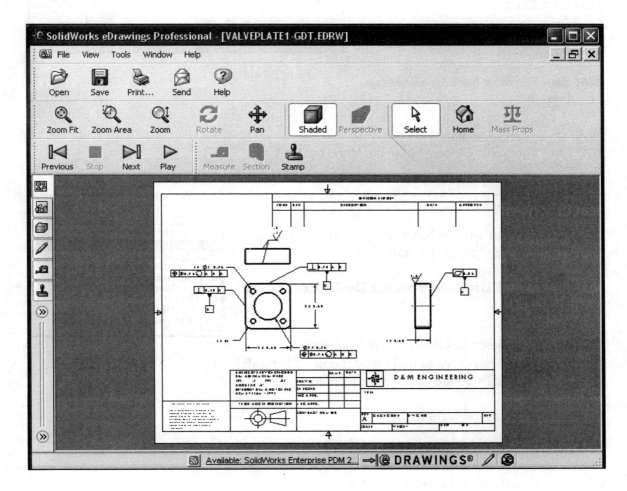

Display the views.
218) Click the **Play** button. View the three views.

219) Click **Stop**.

View the Full Sheet.
220) Click **Home**.

Save the eDrawing.
221) Click **Save**.

222) Accept the default file name.

223) Click **Save**.

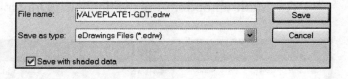

Exit the eDrawing module. Return to SolidWorks.

224) Click **File**, **Exit** from the eDrawings Main menu.

Close all parts and drawings.
225) Click **Windows**, **Close** All from the Menu bar toolbar.

💡 Additional eDrawing Save As type options include: *.zip, *htm, *exe, *bmp, *tif, and *jpg.

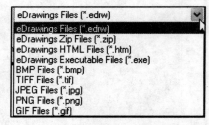

ASME Y14.41 Digital Product Definition Data Practices

ASME Y14.41 describes the rules for applying dimensions and tolerances to a 3D model and a 3D model and 2D drawing. There are two digital formats:

• Model only digital format.

• Model and drawing digital format.

Why does this standard become important in SolidWorks? Answer: The SolidWorks designer requires a standard to control parts, assemblies, and drawings in electronic form.

Example for Model only digital format: An engineer supplies a 3D model file electronically to a manufacturing prototype vendor in Mexico. The part requires a key tolerance within a specified range. The engineer inserts Geometric tolerances into the 3D model file and emails the file to the vendor.

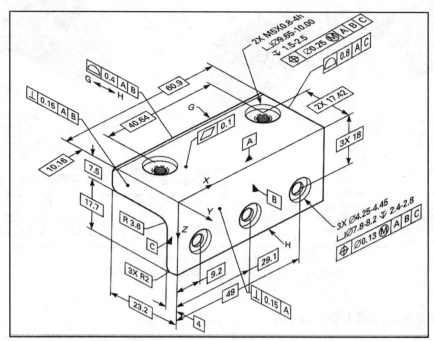

Y14.41 Digital Product and Data Definition Practices
Reprinted from ASME Y14.41-2003, by permission of
The American Society of Mechanical Engineers. All rights reserved.

Example for Model and drawing digital format: A design engineer supplies a 2D eDrawing to the local machine shop to create a tooling drawing. Mating parts contain critical dimensions.

The designer creates all geometric tolerances in the part and inserts model items into the drawing. Part configurations control the Section views. View orientation controls named views. The drawing references the model filename.

A drawing (electronic, eDrawing, or paper) combined with a corresponding electronic model file becomes a Minimum Content Drawing (MCD). The MCD contains key dimensions, tolerances and annotations required to manufacture the part. The MCD usually is not fully detailed.

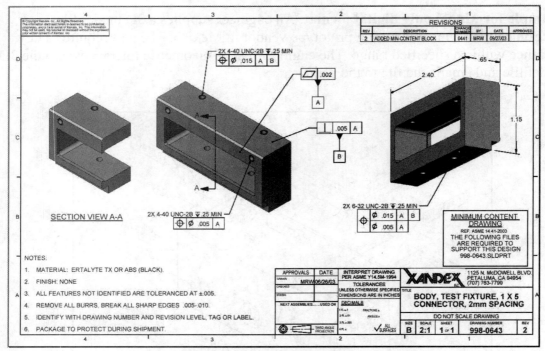

Tooling Drawing (Minimum Content Drawing)
Courtesy of XANDEX, Inc. Petaluma, CA, USA

Modify a ASME14-41 Drawing

Utilize the Y14.41 standard to modify the ASME14-41 drawing. Open the ASME14-41-Rev-A part. Apply DimXpert: Geometric option. View the Inserted Datums, Feature Control Frames, and Geometric Tolerances. Open the ASME14-41 drawing. Insert Datums, Feature Control Frames, Dimensions and Geometric Tolerances into an Isometric drawing view on multiple drawing sheets. Note: A this time, DimXpert does not import annotations into an Isometric drawing view.

Activity: Open the ASME14-41 Part - Modify the ASME14-41 Drawing

Open the ASME14-41 part.
226) Open the ASME14-41-Rev-A part in the DRAWING-W-SOLIDWORKS-2010 folder. The model is displayed in the Graphics window.

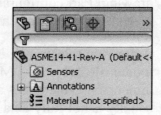

Set Dimensioning standard to **ANSI** under **Tools, Options, Document Properties, Detailing** to display annotations according to the ASME standard. Standards other than ANSI are not yet supported in DimXpert.

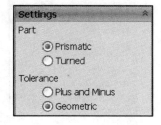

Apply DimXpert to the part.

227) Click the **DimXpertManager** ⊕ tab.

228) Click the **Auto Dimension Scheme** ⚛ icon from the DimXpertManager. The Auto Dimension PropertyManager is displayed.

229) Check the **Prismatic** box.

230) Check the **Geometric** box.

⚲ Three mutually Perpendicular planes are required.

231) Click the **Top face** of the model. Plane1 is displayed in the Primary Datum box.

232) Click **inside** the Secondary Datum box.

233) Click the **Right face** of the model. Plane2 is displayed in the Secondary Datum box.

234) Click **inside** the Tertiary Datum box.

235) Click the **Front face** of the model. Plane 3 is displayed in the Tertiary Datum box.

236) Click **OK** ✔ from the Auto Dimension PropertyManager. View the results. The model is displayed in green and is fully constrained.

237) Click and drag the **annotation** off the model.

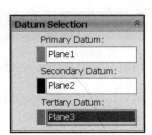

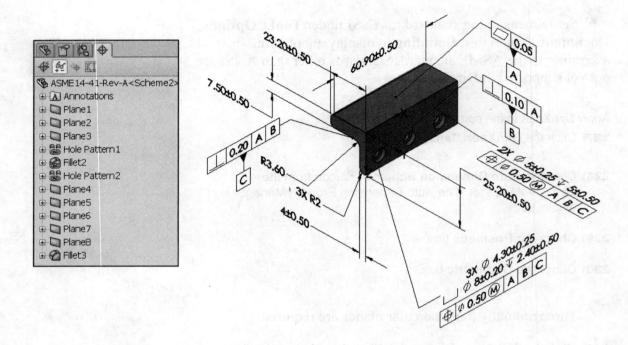

ASME Y14.41 requires a Coordinate System X, Y, Z symbol. Utilize Insert, Reference Geometry, Coordinate System.

ASME Y14.41 requires a Section Plane in the drawing. The Section Plane configuration contains a rectangular sketch with a line indicating the cut direction.

Modify the ASME14-41 drawing.
238) Open the ASME14-41drawing from the DRAWING-W-SOLIDWORKS-2010 folder.

Insert Geometric Tolerances and Notes.
239) Click **Model Items** ✏ from the Annotation toolbar.

240) Select **Entire model** from the Source/Destination box.

241) Click the **Notes** box from the Annotations dialog box.

242) Click the **Geometric tolerances** box from the Annotations dialog box.

243) Click **OK** ✔ from the Model Items PropertyManager.

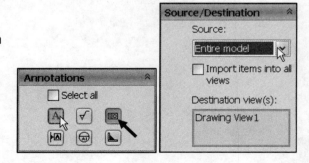

244) Position the **annotations** in the view as illustrated.

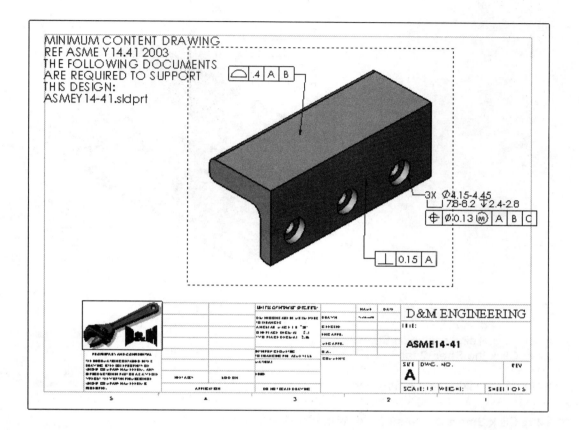

Modify the arrowhead to a dot for the annotations that references a top face.

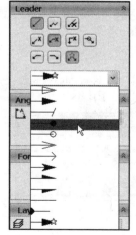

245) Click the **arrowhead tip** as illustrated on the top face. The Geometric Tolerance PropertyManager is displayed.

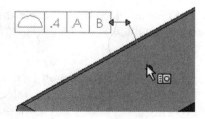

246) Right-click and select the **dot arrowhead**.

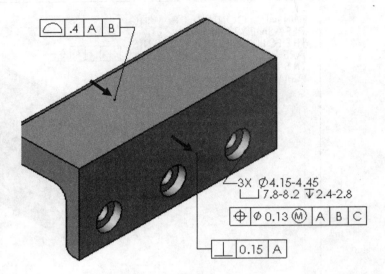

Insert overall dimensions on Sheet2.
247) Click the **Sheet2** tab.

248) Click inside the **Isometric view** boundary.

249) Click **Smart Dimension** ✐ from the Annotation toolbar.

250) Check the **Smart dimensioning** box.

251) Insert three overall **dimensions** for width, height, and depth as illustrated.

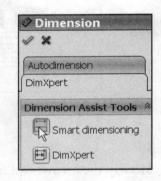

🔆 To dimension in an Isometric view, select edges not vertices. Avoid selecting fillets and chamfers.

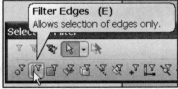

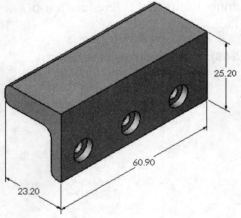

Insert Geometric Tolerances and Datum Features.
252) Click the **Sheet3** tab.

253) Click **Datum Feature** from the Annotation toolbar.

254) Click the **top face** in the Isometric view for Datum A.

255) Click a **position** above the top face.

256) Click the **Perpendicular** Feature Control Frame for Datum B. Click a **position** below the Feature Control Frame as illustrated.

257) Click **OK** from the Datum Feature PropertyManager.

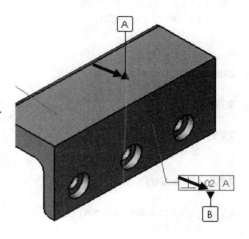

Review Sheet4.
258) Click the **Sheet4** tab. Click inside the **Isometric view** boundary.

259) Right-click **Properties**.

260) Select **large-100mm** for Use name configuration.

261) Click **OK** from the Drawing Views Properties box.

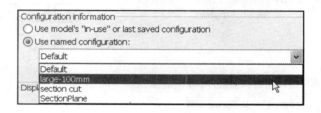

Review Sheet 5.
262) Click the **Sheet 5** tab.

263) Click inside the **Isometric** view boundary.

264) Click **Model Items** from the Annotation toolbar.

265) Select **Entire model** from the Source/Destination box.

266) Click the **Notes** box from the Annotations dialog box.

267) Click the **Geometric tolerances** box from the Annotations dialog box.

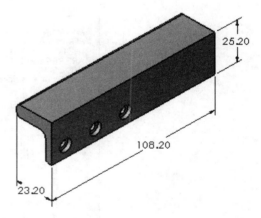

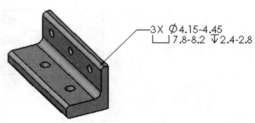

268) Click **OK** ✔ from the PropertyManager.

Copy the Annotation.
269) Click the **Note**.

270) Click **Ctrl + C**.

271) Click a **position** to the top left of the profile.

272) Click **Ctrl + V**.

273) Drag the **arrowhead** to the back hole edge.

274) **Hide** the first Note.

275) **Hide** the other annotations as illustrated.

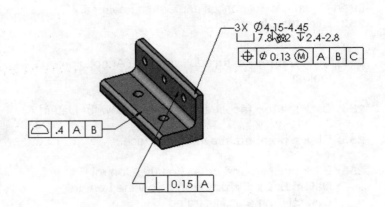

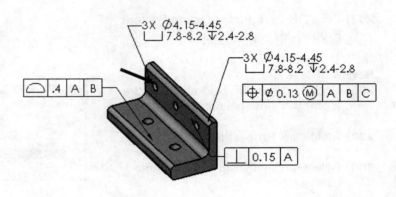

Save the ASME14-41 drawing.
276) Click **Save** 💾 .

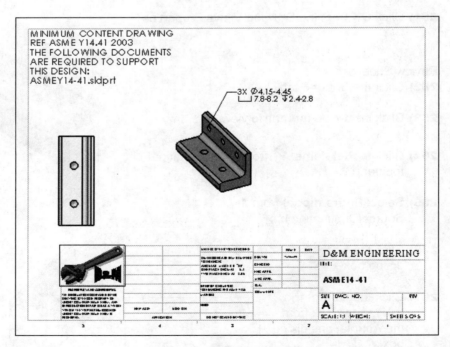

Review the notes created in the 3D part and inserted into the Isometric view in the drawing. Modify the note attachment point to reference the appropriate geometry.

PLATE-TUBE Assembly Drawing and Weld Symbols

Open the PLATE-TUBE assembly from the DRAWING-W-SOLIDWORKS-2010 folder. The customer requires a concept drawing of the PLATE-TUBE assembly. The TUBE part is welded to the PLATE part. Explore the procedures to create Weld Symbols:

- Weld Bead Assembly Feature

- Weld Symbol Annotation

Insert the Weld Bead Assembly feature between the TUBE and PLATE parts in the PLATE-TUBE assembly. A Weld Symbol automatically attaches to the Weld Bead. Utilize the Model Items tool to insert the Weld Symbol into the Left drawing view.

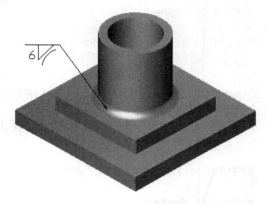

Add a second PLATE component to the PLATE-TUBE assembly. Create a Weld Symbol as a separate annotation in the PLATE-TUBE drawing.

The PLATE-TUBE assembly is created with three components:

- PLATE1-W<1> (Default)

- TUBE1-W<1>

- PLATE1-W<2> (Large Plate)

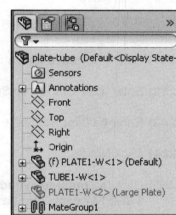

PLATE1-W<2> (Large Plate) is suppressed for the first portion of this activity.

Activity: PLATE-TUBE Assembly Drawing and Weld Symbols

Create a Weld Bead in the PLATE-TUBE assembly.

277) Open the PLATE-TUBE assembly from the DRAWING-W-SOLIDWORKS-2010 folder.

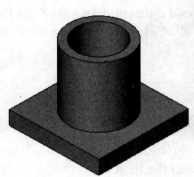

Create a Weld Bead between the PLATE1-W<1> and TUBE1-W<1> components.

278) Click **Insert**, **Assembly Feature**, **Weld Bead** from the Menu bar menu.

279) Select **Fillet** for Weld Type.

280) Click **Next>**.

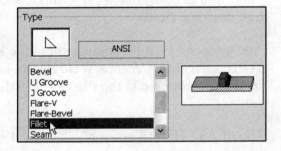

281) Select **Concave** for Surface Shape.

282) Enter **1.00** for the Top Surface Delta.

283) Enter **6.00** for Radius.

284) Click **Next>**.

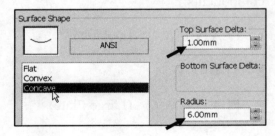

285) Click the **outside cylindrical face** of the TUBE1-W component as illustrated.

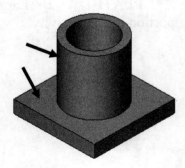

286) Click the **top face** of the PLATE1-W<1> component.

287) Click **Next>**.

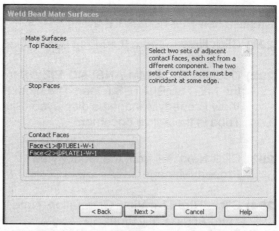

288) Click **Finish**. Note: The default Weld Bead part name is bead1.SLDPRT.

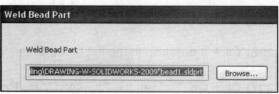

289) Drag the **Weld Symbol** off the profile as illustrated.

Save the PLATE-TUBE assembly.
290) Click **Save** .

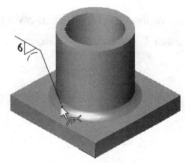

☀ Save time searching for suppliers and manufacturers. Use 3D ContentCentral in the Design Library.

☀ Company: MicroGroup, Inc., Medway, MA. Web site: (www.microgroup.com) MicroGroup, Inc. manufactures high precision tubing and handles fabrication.

Create a new PLATE-TUBE drawing.

291) Click **New** ▢ from the Menu bar toolbar.

292) Double-click **A-MM-ANSI-NO-VIEWS** from the MY-TEMPLATES folder. The Model View PropertyManager is displayed. Plate-Tube is the active document.

293) Click **Next** ⊙ from the Model View PropertyManager.

294) Click ***Right** for View Orientation. Note: Third Angle Projection!

295) Enter **.75:1** for Scale.

296) Click a **position** to the left of the Sheet.

297) Click **OK** ✔ from the Projected View PropertyManager.

Save the PLATE-TUBE drawing.

298) Click **Save** 💾 . Accept the default name.

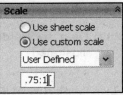

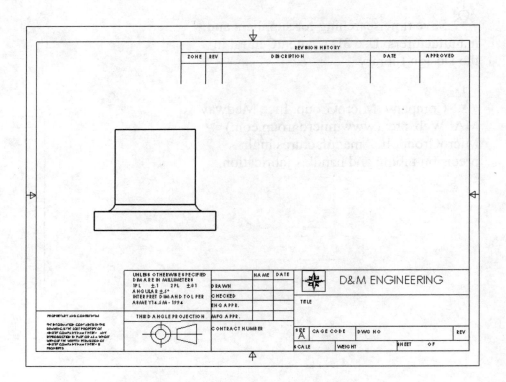

Insert the Model Items Weld Symbols.
299) Click **inside** the drawing view.

300) Click **Model Items**  from the Annotation toolbar.

301) Select **Entire model** from the Source/Destination box.

302) **Uncheck** the Dimensions, Marked for Drawing option. Note: No Dimensions are inserted.

303) Click **Welds** from the Annotations box.

304) **Uncheck** any other options.

305) Click **OK** ✔ from the Model Items PropertyManager.

306) Drag the **Weld Symbol** off the profile.

The Weld attachment point inserted from a Weld Assembly feature cannot be modified.

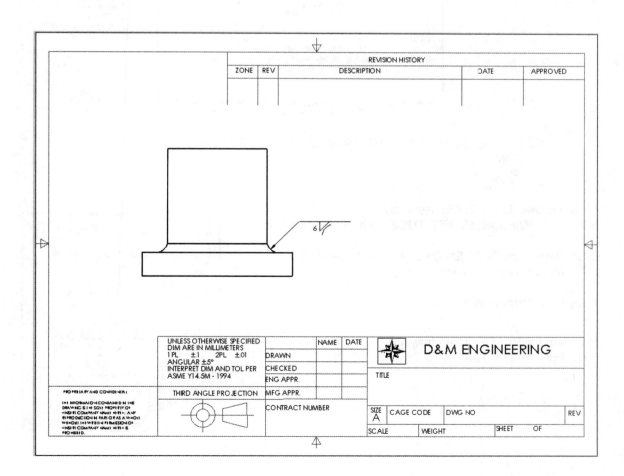

The Weld Symbol dialog box corresponds to the standard location of elements, a welding symbol as defined by AWS A2.4:1997.

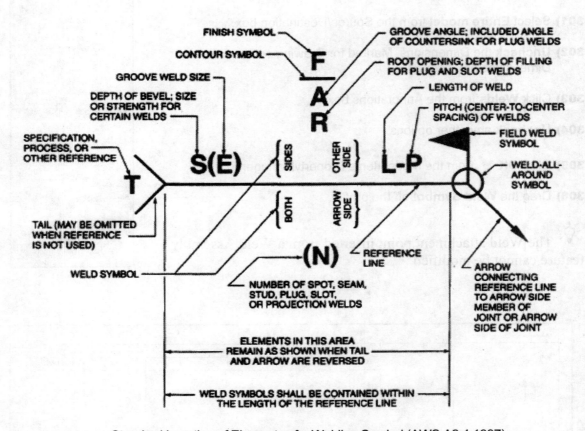

Standard Location of Elements of a Welding Symbol (AWS A2.4:1997)

Return to the PLATE-TUBE assembly.
307) Click **Window**, **PLATE-TUBE** from the Menu bar menu.

308) Right-click **PLATE1-W<2> (Large Plate)** in the assembly FeatureManager.

309) Click **Unsuppress**.

Return to the PLATE-TUBE drawing.
310) Press **Ctrl + Tab**.

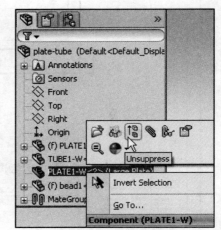

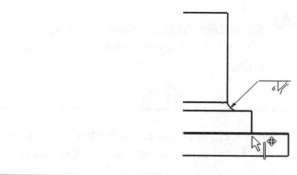

311) Click the **right intersection** as
illustrated.

312) Click **Weld Symbol** /ᵖᵏ from the
Annotation toolbar.

313) Click the **Around** check box to
indicate that the weld extends
completely around the joint.

314) Click the second Weld **Symbol**
button.

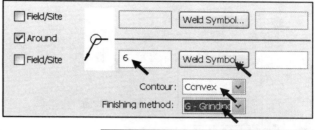

315) Select **Fillet**. Click **OK**.

316) Enter **6** for Radius.

317) Select **Convex** for Contour.

318) Select **G-Grinding** for Finish Method.

319) Click **OK** from the Properties dialog
box.

320) Drag the **Weld Symbol** off the profile
line as illustrated.

Save the PLATE-TUBE drawing.
321) Click **Save** 🖫.

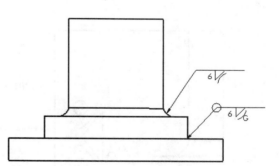

The ANSI Weld Properties dialog box
contains Weld Symbols, Contour options, and
Finishing method options:

- Weld Symbol options: *Square, Scarf, V
  Groove, Bevel, U Groove, J Groove,
  Flare-V, Flare-Bevel, Fillet, Seam,
  Flange-Edge, Flange-Corner.*

- Contour options: *None, Flat, Convex,* or *Concave.*

- Finishing method: *None, Chipping, Grinding, Hammering, Machining, Rolling,* or
  Unspecified.

🔆 Additional Weld options are available for ISO and GOST standards.

☼ Save Rebuild time. Save Weld Symbols created in the drawing onto a Weld layer.
Turn off the Weld layer when not required. Suppress Weld Beads created in the
assembly.

When a weld is required on both sides, select the Arrow Side option and the Other Side
option. Enter all weld options for the Arrow Side. Enter all options for the Other Side.

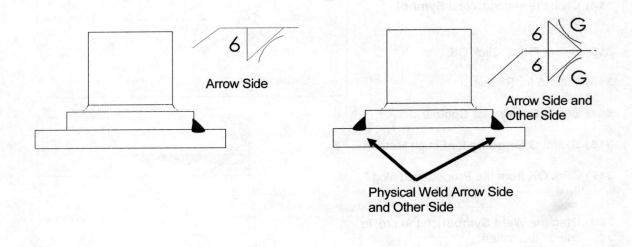

Arrow Side

Arrow Side and
Other Side

Physical Weld Arrow Side
and Other Side

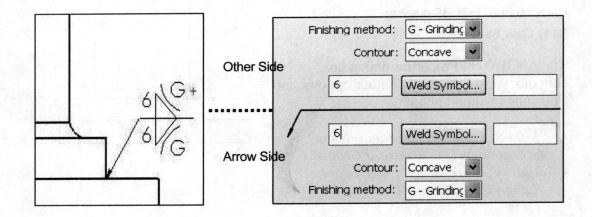

Other Side

Arrow Side

Finishing method: G - Grinding

Contour: Concave

6   Weld Symbol...

6   Weld Symbol...

Contour: Concave

Finishing method: G - Grinding

Example: Weld Arrow Side and Other Side

PLATE-CATALOG Drawing, Design Table, and EXCEL Formatting

Create the PLATE-CATALOG drawing for the company's online catalog. The PLATE-CATALOG drawing utilizes a Design Table. Review the PLATE-CATALOG configurations. The PLATE-CATALOG part contains three configurations:

- 1007A-36

- 1007A-48

- 1007A-54

The configurations names represent the family part number (1007A -). The last two digits represent the square plate size: 36mm squared, 48mm squared and 54mm squared.

Create the PLATE-CATALOG drawing. Insert dimensions from the PLATE-CATALOG Default part. Modify the PLATE-CATALOG drawing to contain symbolic representations of the dimensions. Utilize EXCEL tools to format the Design Tables. Example: The letter A replaces the dimension 36. Insert the Design Table into the drawing. Modify the Design Table to represent the various configurations as a family of parts.

Activity: PLATE-CATALOG Drawing, Design Table and EXCEL Formatting

Open the PLATE-CATALOG part.
322) Open the PLATE-CATALOG part from the DRAWING-W-SOLIDWORKS-2010 folder.

Review the PLATE-CATALOG configurations.
323) Click the **ConfigurationManager** tab.

324) Double click **1007A-54**.

325) Double click **1007A-48**.

326) Double-click **1007A-36**.

Edit the Design Table.
327) Right-click **Design Table**.

328) Click **Edit Table**. The Design Table PropertyManager is displayed.

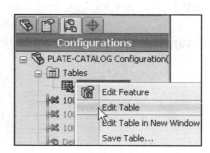

View the table.

	A	B	C	D	E	F	G
1	Design Table for: PLATE-CATALOG						
2		D1@Sketch1	D1@Sketch2	D2@Sketch3	D3@LPattern1	D4@LPattern1	
3	1007A-36	36	22	12	24	24	
4	1007A-48	48	24	16	32	32	
5	1007A-54	54	26	18	36	36	

⏮ ◀ ▶ ⏭ \ Sheet1 /

329) Click a **position** in the sheet boundary to exit the Design Table.

Create a PLATE-CATALOG drawing.

330) Click **New** ⬜ from the Menu bar toolbar.

331) Double-click **A-MM-ANSI-NO-VIEWS** from the MY-TEMPLATES folder.

332) Click **Cancel** ✖ from the Model View PropertyManager.

333) Click **Model View** 🗔 from the View Layout toolbar.

334) Select **PLATE-CATALOG**.

335) Click **Next** ➡.

336) Click ***Top**.

337) Click a **position** on the left of the sheet as illustrated.

338) Click a **position** to the right of the first view as illustrated.

339) Enter **1:1** for Custom Scale.

340) Click **OK** ✔ from the Drawing View PropertyManager.

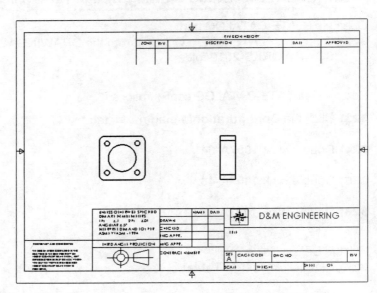

Save the PLATE-CATALOG drawing.
341) Click **Save As** from the Menu bar toolbar. Accept the default name.

342) Click **Save**.

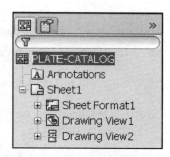

Modify the configuration.
343) Right-click **Properties** in Drawing View1. Note: The Top view is the Front view in the drawing.

344) Select **1007A-36** for the current Used named configuration. Click **OK**.

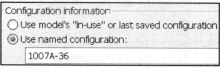

Increase the dimension height.
345) Click **Options** 🗒, **Document Properties** tab from the Menu bar toolbar.

346) Click the **Dimensions** folder. Click the **Font** button.

347) Enter **5**mm for Height in the Units text box.

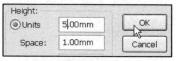

348) Click **OK** from the dialog box.

349) Click **OK**.

Insert Model dimensions.
350) Click a **position** inside Sheet1.

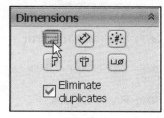

351) Click **Model Items** ✑ from the Annotation toolbar.

352) Select **Entire model** from the Source/Destination box.

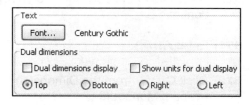

353) Click **OK** ✔ from the Model Items PropertyManager.

354) Drag the **dimensions** approximately 10mm away from the profile as illustrated.

355) If required, uncheck the **Dual dimensions display** box.

Hide all superficial dimensions.
356) Hide the 36 dimension text in the right view.

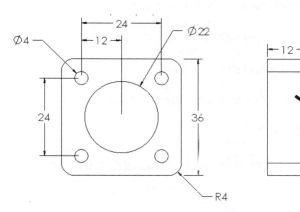

Add an overall horizontal dimension in Drawing View1.

357) Click **Smart Dimension**.

358) Click the **left** and **right vertical lines**.

359) Click a **position** below the profile for the 36 horizontal dimension text.

360) Drag the **extension lines** off the profile.

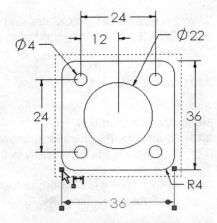

Modify dimensions to text symbols.

361) Click the **36 horizontal** dimension text.

362) Select the **<DIM>** text.

363) Press **Delete**.

364) Click **Yes** to the question, Do you want to continue?

365) Enter **A**.

366) Click **OK** from the Dimension PropertyManager.

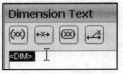

367) Click the **36 vertical** dimension text.

368) Select the **<DIM>** text.

369) Press **Delete**.

370) Click **Yes** to the question, Do you want to continue?

371) Enter **A**.

372) Click **OK** from the Dimension PropertyManager.

373) Click the **∅22** dimension text.

374) Select the **<DIM>** text.

375) Press **Delete**.

376) Click **Yes** to the question, Do you want to continue?

377) Enter **B**.

378) Click **OK** from the Dimension PropertyManager.

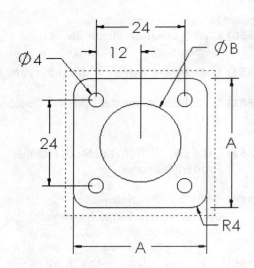

379) Click the **12** dimension text in the Front view.

380) Select the **<DIM>** text.

381) Press **Delete**.

382) Click **Yes** to the question, Do you want to continue?

383) Enter **C**.

384) Click **OK** ✓ from the Dimension PropertyManager.

385) Click the **24 horizontal** dimension text.

386) Select the **<DIM>** text.

387) Press **Delete**. Click **Yes** to the question, Do you want to continue?

388) Enter **D**. Click **OK** ✓ from the Dimension PropertyManager.

389) Click the **24 vertical** dimension text.

390) Select the **<DIM>** text. Press **Delete**.

391) Click **Yes** to the question, Do you want to continue?

392) Enter **D**.

393) Click **OK** ✓ from the Dimension PropertyManager.

394) Click the Ø**4** dimension text.

395) Select the **<DIM>** text.

396) Press **Delete**.

397) Click **Yes** to the question, Do you want to continue?

398) Enter **E**.

399) Click **OK** ✓ from the Dimension PropertyManager.

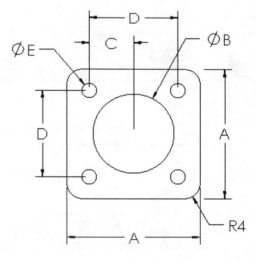

☀ When letters replace the <DIM> placeholder, the part dimensions update to reflect both the letter and the dimension value. Example: 36 is replaced with A36.

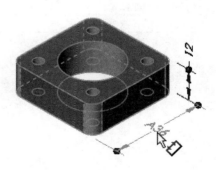

Return to the part. Note: You need Microsoft Excel to perform the following steps.
400) Press **Ctrl + Tab** to display the PLATE-CATALOG part.

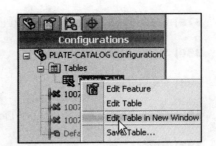

Edit the Design Table in an EXCEL window.
401) Right-click **Design Table** in the ConfigurationManager.

402) Click **Edit Table in New Window**. The Microsoft Excel dialog box is displayed.

Format the Design Table in Excel. Utilize Microsoft Excel functions, Excel Main menu, Toolbars, and Pop-up menus.

Expand the Design Table.
403) Click and drag the **lower right corner** of the Design Table to display all entries.

Hide Row 1 and Row 2.
404) Click **Row 1**.

405) Drag the mouse pointer to **Row 2** in the Row frame. Both Row 1 and Row 2 are selected.

A1	▼	*fx*	Design Table for: PLATE-CATALOG		
	A	B	C	D	E	F
1	Design Table for: PLATE-CATALOG					
2		D1@Sketch1	D1@Sketch2	D2@Sketch3	D3@LPattern1	D4@LPattern1
3	1007A-36	36	22	12	24	24
4	1007A-48	48	24	16	32	32
5	1007A-54	54	26	18	36	36
6						

406) Right-click **Hide**. Row 3 is now displayed as the first row.

A1	▼	*fx*	Design Table for: PLATE-CATALOG		
	A	B	C	D	E	F
3	1007A-36	36	22	12	24	24
4	1007A-48	48	24	16	32	32
5	1007A-54	54	26	18	36	36
6						

Insert 2 Rows.
407) Click **Row 3** in the Row frame.

408) Right-click **Insert**. Row 3 is the new row.

409) **Repeat** the same steps for a second row.

	A	B	C	D	E	F
3						
4						
5	1007A-36	36	22	12	24	24
6	1007A-48	48	24	16	32	32
7	1007A-54	54	26	18	36	36

Hide Column F.
410) Click **Column F**.

411) Right-click **Hide**. Column G is displayed to the right of Column E.

Modify the Hyperlink option.
412) Click **Tools**, **AutoCorrect Options** from the Microsoft Excel Main menu.

413) Click the **Autoformat As You Type** tab.

414) Uncheck **Internet and network paths with hyperlinks**.

415) Click **OK** from the AutoCorrect dialog box.

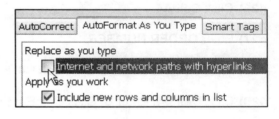

The "@" symbol creates a hyperlink in the Design Table if the AutoFormat option remains checked.

Add Title and Headers.

416) Click **Cell A3.**

417) Hold the left mouse button down.

418) Drag the mouse pointer to **Cell G3**

419) Release the left mouse button.

420) Right-click **Format Cells**
Format Cells...

421) Click the **Alignment** tab.

422) Click the **Merge cells** check box.

423) Select **Center** for Horizontal.

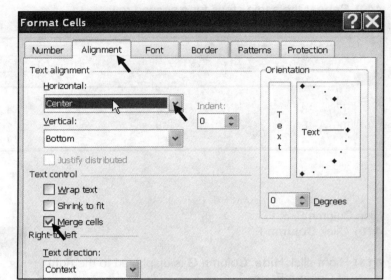

424) Click **OK** from the Format Cells dialog box.

425) Enter **PLATE – 36 THROUGH 54 MM, STEEL** for the title.

426) Click **Cell A4.**

427) Enter **ORDER NUMBER**.

428) Click **Cell B4**. Enter **A**. Click **Cell C4**. Enter **B**.

429) Click **Cell D4**. Enter **C**. Click **Cell E4**. Enter **D**. Note: D3@LPattern1 appears.

430) Delete and enter **D**.

Increase the Column A width.
431) Click the **vertical line** between Column A and Column B in the Column frame.

432) Drag the **vertical line** to the right until ORDER NUMBER is completely displayed.

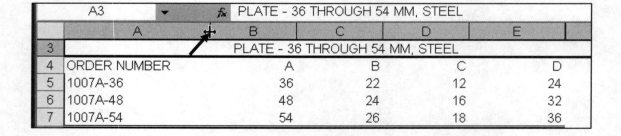

A3	f_x	PLATE - 36 THROUGH 54 MM, STEEL			
	A	B	C	D	E
3	PLATE - 36 THROUGH 54 MM, STEEL				
4	ORDER NUMBER	A	B	C	D
5	1007A-36	36	22	12	24
6	1007A-48	48	24	16	32
7	1007A-54	54	26	18	36

Format the A, B, C, and D Column text.
433) Click **Cell B4**.

434) Hold the left mouse button down.

435) Drag the mouse pointer to **Cell E7**.

436) Release the left mouse button.

437) Right-click **Format Cells**.

438) Click the **Alignment** tab.

439) Click **Center** from the Horizontal drop down list.

440) Click **OK**.

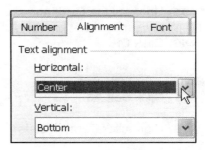

Format Column G for COST.
441) Click **Cell G4**. Enter **COST**.

442) Drag the mouse pointer to **Cell G7**.

443) Right-click **Format Cells**.

444) Click the **Number** tab.

445) Click **Currency** from the Category list. The default Decimal place is 2.

446) Click **OK**.

447) Click **Cell G5**.

448) Enter **100**. The currency value $100.00 is displayed.

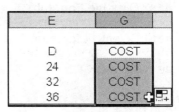

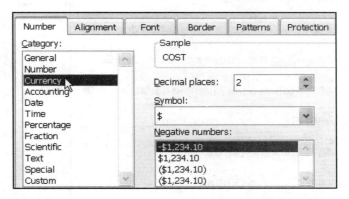

449) Click **Cell G5**. The Fill handle is located in the bottom right corner of the cell.

450) Position the **mouse pointer** over the small black square. The mouse pointer displays a black cross.

451) Click the **left mouse button**.

452) Drag the **mouse pointer** downward to **Cell G7**. The value $100.00 is displayed in Cell G6 and Cell G7.

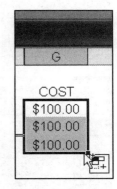

Remove Gridlines.
453) Click **Tools**, **Options** from the Microsoft Excel Main menu.

454) Click the **View** tab.

455) Uncheck the **Gridlines** check box.

456) Click **OK**.

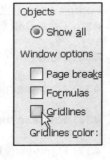

Increase the title size.
457) Click **Cell A3**.

458) Right-click **Format Cells**.

459) Click the **Font** tab.

460) Select **14** for Size.

461) Click **OK**.

Add Borders.
462) Click **Cell A3**.

463) **Hold** the left mouse button down.

464) Drag the mouse pointer to **Cell G7**

465) **Release** the left mouse button.

466) Right-click **Format Cells**.

467) Click the **Border** tab.

468) Click the **Outline** button.

469) Select the **double line border** Style.

470) Click **OK**.

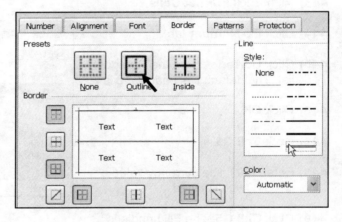

A3		fx	PLATE - 36 THROUGH 54 MM, STEEL			
	A	B	C	D	E	G
3	PLATE - 36 THROUGH 54 MM, STEEL					
4	ORDER NUMBER	A	B	C	D	COST
5	1007A-36	36	22	12	24	$100.00
6	1007A-48	48	24	16	32	$100.00
7	1007A-54	54	26	18	36	$100.00
8						

Add pattern color.
471) Click **Cell A4**. **Hold** the left mouse button down.

472) Drag the mouse pointer to **Cell G4**.

473) Release the left mouse button.

474) Right-click **Format Cells**.

475) Click the **Patterns** tab.

476) Select a **light blue color** for shading.

477) Click **OK**.

478) Click **Cell A4**. **Hold** the left mouse button down.

479) Drag the mouse pointer to **Cell A7**.

480) Release the left mouse button.

481) Right-click **Format Cells**.

482) Click **Patterns**.

483) Select a **light blue color** for shading.

484) Click **OK**.

	A	B	C	D	E	G
	A4		fx	ORDER NUMBER		
3	PLATE - 36 THROUGH 54 MM, STEEL					
4	ORDER NUMBER	A	B	C	D	COST
5	1007A-36	36	22	12	24	$100.00
6	1007A-48	48	24	16	32	$100.00
7	1007A-54	54	26	18	36	$100.00
8						

The Family Cell indicates the start of the SolidWorks parameters.

Create comment rows above and columns to the right of the Family Cell. The Family Cell displays the word, Family in the Name box. The text Family does not display in the Cell or Formula area.

	A	B
	Family	fx
3		PLATE - 36
4	ORDER NUMBER	A
5	1007A-36	36
6	1007A-48	48
7	1007A-54	54
8		

You inserted comments into Row 3 and Row 4. Move Family Cell Row 2 below Row 4 for the Design Table to work properly.

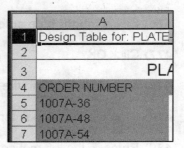

Unhide Row 1 and Row 2.
485) Right-click on the **Row 3 top line** in the Row frame.

486) Click **Unhide**.

487) **Perform** the same procedure for Row 2.

Cut/Insert Row 2.
488) Select **Row 2** in the Row frame.

489) Right-click **Cut**.

490) Select **Row 5** in the Row frame.

491) Right-click **Insert Cut Cells**. The dimension parameters row is below the ORDER NUMBER row.

Insert the Cost Custom Property.
492) Click **Cell G4**. Enter **$prp@cost**.

	A	B	C	D	E	G
1	Design Table for: PLATE-CATALOG					
2	PLATE - 36 THROUGH 54 MM, STEEL					
3	ORDER NUMBER	A	B	C	D	COST
4		D1@Sketch1	D1@Sketch2	D2@Sketch3	D3@LPattern1	$prp@cost
5	1007A-36	36	22	12	24	$100.00
6	1007A-48	48	24	16	32	$100.00
7	1007A-54	54	26	18	36	$100.00
8						

💡 Column Custom Properties in the Design Table are accessible as Linked Notes in the Drawing.

Insert a new Column.
493) Select **Column A** in the Column frame.

494) Right-click **Insert**.

495) Enter **Catalog Title** in Cell A2 for comment.

496) Enter **Catalog Values** in Cell A3.

497) Double-click the **Column A – Column B** frame to resize the column width.

	A
1	
2	Catalog Title
3	Catalog Values
4	

Verify the B4 Family Cell.
498) Click **Cell B4**. The word, Family appears in the Name box.

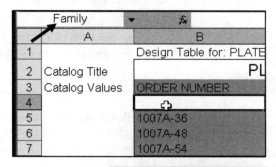

⛭ Enter the text, Family in the Name Box for the Cell name if required.

Hide Rows and Columns.
499) Select **Row1**.

500) Right-click **Hide**.

501) Select **Row4**.

502) Right-click **Hide**.

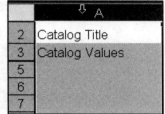

503) Select **Column A** in the Column frame.

504) Right-click **Hide**.

	B	C	D	E	F	H	I
2	PLATE - 36 THROUGH 54 MM, STEEL						
3	ORDER NUMBER	A	B	C	D	COST	
5	1007A-36	36	22	12	24	$100.00	
6	1007A-48	48	24	16	32	$100.00	
7	1007A-54	54	26	18	36	$100.00	
8							

Save and Update EXCEL.
505) Click **File**, **Save Copy As** from the EXCEL Main menu.

506) Browse and **select** the DRAWING-W-SOLIDWORKS 2010 folder.

507) Enter **TABLE-PLATE-CATALOG** to save a copy in EXCEL format.

508) Click **Save**.

Update the linked Design Table in SolidWorks.
509) Click **File**, **Update** from the EXCEL Main menu.

510) Click **File**, **Exit** from the EXCEL Main menu.

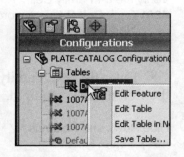

Return to SolidWorks and the PLATE-CATALOG part.
511) Right-click **Design Table** from the FeatureManager.

512) Click **Edit Table**.

513) **Resize** the EXCEL window to display Cell B2 through H7. The Design Table window in the part determines the Design Table display in the drawing.

	B	C	D	E	F	H
2	PLATE - 36 THROUGH 54 MM, STEEL					
3	ORDER NUMBER	A	B	C	D	COST
5	1007A-36	36	22	12	24	$100.00
6	1007A-48	48	24	16	32	$100.00
7	1007A-54	54	26	18	36	$100.00
8						
9						

Insert a Design Table into the drawing.
514) Press **Ctrl-Tab** to display the PLATE-CATALOG drawing.

515) Click inside the **Drawing View1** boundary.

516) Click **Design Table** from the Annotate toolbar.

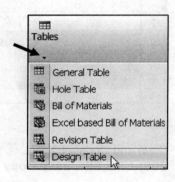

517) Drag the **Design Table** below the Front view.

Enlarge the Design Table.
518) Right-click the **Design Table**.

519) Click **Reset Size**.

520) Drag the **corner handle** to the right.

521) Click **inside** the sheet.

As an exercise, add Center Marks and Centerlines to complete the PLATE-CATALOG drawing.

Save the PLATE-CATALOG drawing.

522) Click **Save** 💾 .

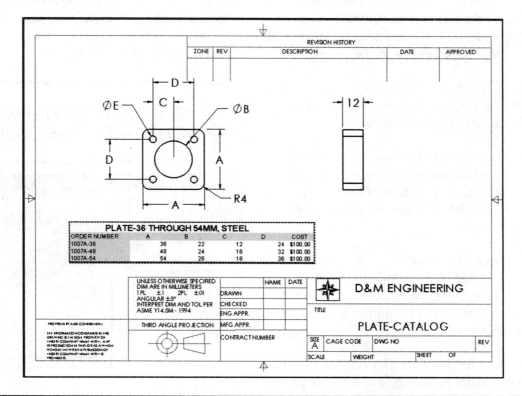

PLATE-36 THROUGH 54MM, STEEL					
ORDER NUMBER	A	B	C	D	COST
1007A-36	36	22	12	24	$100.00
1007A-48	48	24	16	32	$100.00
1007A-54	54	26	18	36	$100.00

🔅 Save Time, Reuse Design Tables and their parameters. You saved the Design Table, TABLE-PLATE-CATALOG.XLS as an Excel Spread Sheet. Insert Excel Spread Sheets into other part and assembly documents. Utilize Insert, Design Table, From File option.

Utilize consistent names in Design Tables. Example: $PRP:Material is the variable name for Material in all Design Tables. Utilize the comment entry "ORDER NUMBER" in the same Cell location for all Catalog drawings. Insert Comments above and to the left of the Family Name Cell.

Plan your Catalog drawings. Identify the comments and the parameters to display in the drawing. Insert additional comments, formulas and values not required in a Design Table by leaving a blank column or row. The Design Table does not evaluate Cell entries placed after the column space.

E	G	H	I
EL			
D	COST		MY COMMENTS HERE
D3@LPattern1	$prp@cost		
24	$100.00		
32	$100.00		

Blocks

Blocks can be used to create standard notes, labels and any other custom symbols that SolidWorks does not provide. Blocks consist of the following elements: *text*, *sketched entities*, *Area Hatch* and *Single Balloon*. Blocks are symbols that exist on one or more drawings. Save Blocks in the current file folder or create a symbol library.

Set the Block file folder location in Tools, Options, System Options, File Locations when creating symbol libraries.

In the next example, make a new Block. Combine text and a rectangle. Save the Block to the current file folder. Insert the new Block. Modify the Properties of the Block.

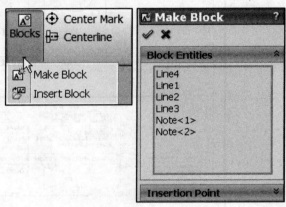

The Block PropertyManager controls the Source Name of the Block to insert. Specify Location by selecting a position with the mouse pointer or entering the exact X, Y coordinates.

Scale and Rotate a Block in Block Display. Select Leader arrow style and Layer for the Block.

Insert an Empty View. Insert sketch geometry and annotations. The new geometry references the Empty View.

An Empty View is not required to create a Block. Block geometry can reference the sheet.

The Design Library, Add File Location option, creates a reference to a folder that contains Blocks. Position the mouse pointer on the Block icon to display a preview.

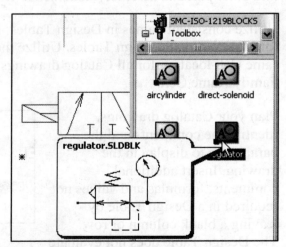

Blocks can be created from sketch geometry and notes and be used locally (within a drawing) or be saved to a file for use in any drawing.

Activity: Blocks

Insert an Empty View.
523) Click **Insert**, **Drawing View**, **Empty** from the Menu bar menu.

524) Click a **position** to the right of the PLATE-CATALOG Right view.

525) Right-click the **Empty view boundary**.

526) Click **Lock View Focus**. The blue view boundary, with filled corners indicates a locked view. Added geometry will reference the Empty view.

Add Notes.
527) Click **Note** A from the Annotation toolbar.

528) Click a **position** inside the Empty view; Drawing View3.

529) Click the **No Leader** box.

530) Enter **Questions on delivery?**

531) Press the **enter** key.

532) Enter **Call 1-800-555-0000** on the second line.

533) Select the **text**.

534) Modify the Font height to **5**mm.

Questions on Delivery?
Call 1-800-555-0000

535) Click **OK** from the Note Property Manager.

536) Click **Note** A from the Annotation toolbar.

537) Click a **position** to the left of the Note.

538) Click **No Leader**.

539) Enter **?**.

Question on delivery?
Call 1-800-555-0000

540) Click **OK** from the Note Property Manager.

541) Click the **?** mark. The Note PropertyManager is displayed.

542) **Expand** the Border dialog box.

543) Select **Circular** from the drop-down menu. Tight Fit is selected by default.

544) **Uncheck** the Use document font box.

545) Click the **Font** button.

546) Select **14**mm for Font height.

547) Click **OK** from the Choose Font dialog box.

548) Click **OK**  from the Note PropertyManager.

Sketch a rectangle around the two Notes.

549) Click **Corner Rectangle**  from the Sketch toolbar.

550) Sketch a **rectangle** around the two notes as illustrated.

551) Click **OK**  from the Rectangle PropertyManager.

Display the Line Format toolbar. Modify the Line color and thickness.

552) Click **View**, **Toolbars**, **Line Format** from the Menu bar menu. The Line Format toolbar is displayed.

553) Click the **Line Color** 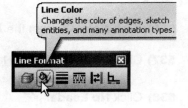 tool from the Line Format toolbar.

554) Select a **Blue Color Swatch**.

555) Click **OK**.

556) Click the **Line Thickness** ≡ tool from the Line Format toolbar.

557) Select **Medium** Thickness.

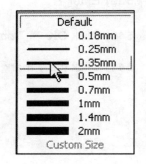

Create a new Block.

558) Click inside the **Sheet** boundary.

559) Hold the **Ctrl** key down.

560) Select the two **Notes** and the **Rectangle**.

561) Release the **Ctrl** key.

562) Click **Make Block** from the consolidated Blocks toolbar. The selected block entities are displayed in the Block Entities dialog box.

563) Click **OK** ✔ from the Make Block PropertyManager. Blocks is displayed in the drawing FeatureManager.

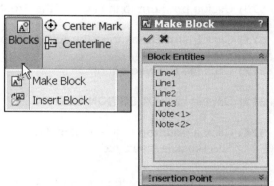

Save the Block.

564) Click **Tools**, **Block**, **Save** from the Menu bar menu.

565) Enter **QUESTION-BLOCK** for File name.

566) Click **Save**. Note: Blocks contain the file extension .sldblk.

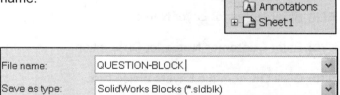

Position the Block.

567) Drag the **Empty view** to the right side of the sheet boundary. The QUESTION-BLOCK moves with the Empty view.

Save the PLATE-CATALOG drawing.

568) Click **Save** 💾 .

The Block contains one insertion point. Insert the Block into the
PLATE-TUBE drawing. Modify the scale and layer for the
QUESTION-BLOCK.

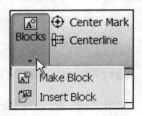

Insert a Block.
569) Open the PLATE-TUBE drawing.

570) Click a **position** to the right of the Front view.

571) Click **Insert Block** from the Annotate toolbar.

572) Click the **Browse** button.

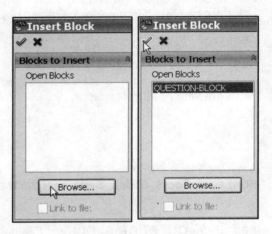

573) Double-click **QUESTION-BLOCK**.

574) Click a **position** to the right of the Front view.
The Block is displayed.

575) Click **OK** ✔ from the Insert Block
PropertyManager.

Create a new layer.
576) Click **Layer Properties** from the Layer toolbar.

577) Click the **New** button.

578) Enter **Notes** for Layer Name.

579) Enter **Customer Notes** for Description.

580) Click **OK** from the Layers dialog box.

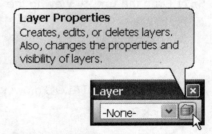

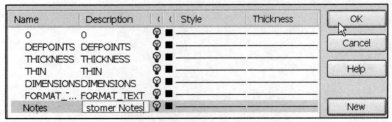

Modify the Properties of the block.

581) Click **QUESTION-BLOCK** in the Sheet. The QUESTION-BLOCK PropertyManager is displayed.

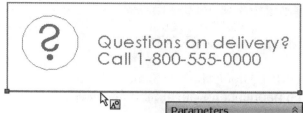

582) Enter **0.9** for Block Scaling.

583) Select **Notes** from the Layer drop-down menu.

584) Click **OK** ✓ from the QUESTION-BLOCK PropertyManager.

Save the PLATE-TUBE drawing.
585) Click **Save** 🖫 .

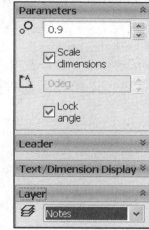

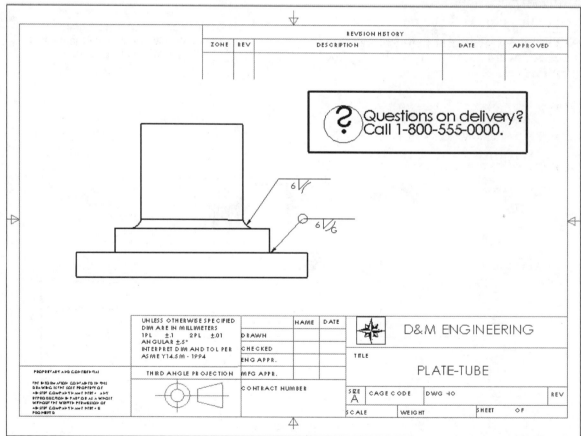

Additional Information

Blocks

Utilize Blocks in a drawing to represent components for pneumatic, mechanical and HVAC systems.

Example: Import the .dxf file ISO-1219 pneumatic symbols. Select the drawing option on Import. Create individual Blocks in SolidWorks.

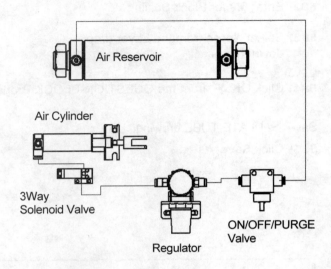

Pneumatic Components Diagram
Courtesy of SMC Corporation of America and
Gears Educational Systems.

Utilize Blocks in the exercises at the end of this project. Each pneumatic symbol is a separate Block. Sketch lines connect the symbols to display the airflow.

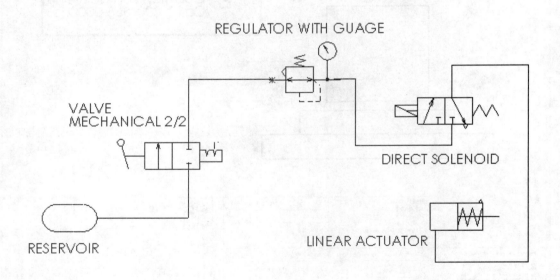

ISO-1219 Symbols – Blocks
Courtesy of SMC Corporation of America

DWGEditor

The SolidWorks DWGEditor is a software application that provides the ability to create and modify two-dimensional and three-dimensional drawings and designs. The DWGEditor reads, writes and displays DWG files without conversion. Utilize the DWG files in the DRAWING-W-SOLIDWORKS 2010\Exercises\Autocad-dwg folder. As an exercise, utilize the Line tool and sketch a new Deck Area for the existing Floor-Plan. Save the Floor-Plan.dwg. The document remains in DWG format.

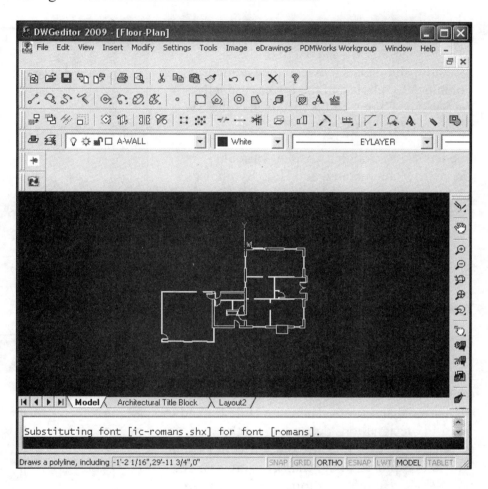

DXF/DWG Import

Dxf and Dwg format files are read during File, Open. Select Dwg or Dxf for Files of type.

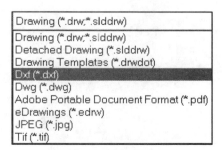

The files are imported in the
SolidWorks DWGEditor, SolidWorks
drawing or part sketch. Additional
exercises are found in the Appendix.

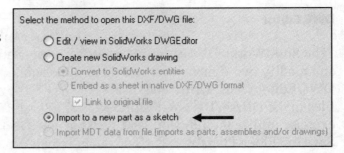

Geometric Tolerance Symbols

A relationship exists between the Geometric
Tolerance Symbols and the lower case letters in
the SW-GDT Font. In EXCEL, select the SW-
GDT Font type for Column H.

The letters, a through z, display various
Geometric Tolerancing, and Hole Symbols.

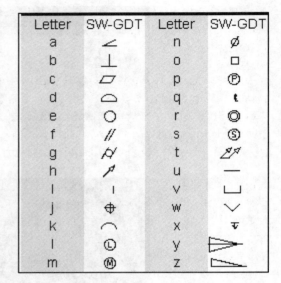

Types of Fits

Utilize Fit tolerances for dimensions for shafts
and holes. The Tolerance options are Fit, Fit
with tolerance, Fit (tolerance only). The
Classification options User Defined, Clearance,
Transitional and Press. There are Hole Fit and
Shaft Fit designations depending on the
geometry. An example utilizing Fit with Design
Tables is explored in the chapter exercises. See
SolidWorks Help for additional information.

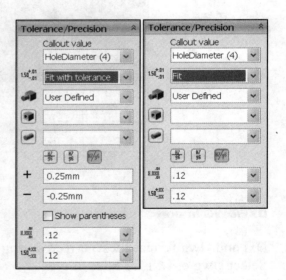

The SolidWorks 2010 Reference Guide is available online in .pdf format. The .pdf document contains additional tools and options.

The project exercises explore additional techniques with symbols, Hole Tables, Types of Fits in the drawing. The Appendix explores 2D-3D conversion and layout sketches.

Chapter Summary

You created five drawings: VALVEPLATE1, VALVEPLATE1-GDT, VALVEPLATE1-GDT eDrawing, PLATE-TUBE, PLATE-CATALOG. You modified the ASME14-41 drawing.

You created the VALVEPLATE1 drawing. You opened the VALVEPLATE1 part. Applied the DimXpert tool using the Plus and Minus option. Inserted dimensions and Geometric tolerances. Created the VALVEPLATE1 drawing using the View Palette tool. Inserted three drawing views. Inserted a Centerline and Hide Tangent Edges in the Right view. Displayed None and Bilateral tolerance.

You created the VALVEPLATE1-GDT drawing. You opened the VALVEPLATE1-GDT part. Apply the DimXpert tool using the Geometric option. Inserted Datums, Feature Control Frames, and Geometric Tolerances. Edited the Feature Control Frames. Created the VALVEPLATE1-GDT drawing with the View Palette tool. Inserted three drawing views. Inserted the Surface Finish symbol on the Top and Right view. Created multiple Leaders to the Surface Finish symbol. Inserted Hide Tangent Edges in the Top and Right view.

You created the VALVEPLATE1-GDT eDrawing. The VALVEPLATE1-GDT eDrawing is a compressed stand alone document.

You modified the ASME14-41 drawing. Manually inserted Datums, Feature Control Frames, Dimensions, and Geometric tolerances into an Isometric view on multiply drawing sheets. The ASME14-41 drawing consisted of five sheets.

You created the PLATE-TUBE drawing. Inserted the Weld Bead assembly feature between the TUBE and PLATE parts in the PLATE-TUBE assembly.

Added a second PLATE component to the PLATE-TUBE assembly. Created a Weld Symbol as a separate annotation in the PLATE-TUBE drawing.

You created the PLATE-CATALOG drawing. The PLATE-CATALOG drawing utilized a Design Table.

Chapter Terminology

ASME: American Society of Mechanical Engineering, publisher of ASME Y14 Engineering Drawing and Documentation Practices that controls drawing, dimensioning and tolerancing.

AWS: American Welding Society, publisher of AWS A2.4, Standard Location of Elements of a Welding Symbol.

Block: A symbol in the drawing that combines geometry into a single entity.

Cell: Area to enter a value in an EXCEL spreadsheet, identified by a Row and Column.

Component: A part or sub-assembly within an assembly.

Configurations: Variations of a part or assembly that control dimensions, display and state of a model.

CommandManager: The CommandManager is a Context-sensitive toolbar that dynamically updates based on the toolbar you want to access. By default, it has toolbars embedded in it based on the document type. When you click a tab below the Command Manager, it updates to display that toolbar. For example, if you click the **Sketches** tab, the Sketch toolbar is displayed.

ConfigurationManager: The ConfigurationManager is located on the left side of the SolidWorks window and provides the means to create, select, and view multiple configurations of parts and assemblies in an active document. You can split the ConfigurationManager and either display two ConfigurationManager instances, or combine the ConfigurationManager with the FeatureManager design tree, PropertyManager, or third party applications that use the panel.

Copy and Paste: Utilize copy/paste to copy views from one sheet to another sheet in a drawing or between different drawings.

Datum Feature: An annotation that represents the primary, secondary and other reference planes of a model utilized in manufacturing.

Design Table: An Excel spreadsheet that is used to create multiple configurations in a part or assembly document.

Dimension: A value indicating the size of feature geometry.

Dimension Line: A line that references dimension text to extension lines indicating the feature being measured.

Dimension Tolerance: Controls the dimension tolerance values and the display of non-integer dimensions. The tolerance types are *None, Basic, Bilateral, Limit, Symmetric, MIN, MAX, Fit, Fit with tolerance*, or *Fit (tolerance only)*.

DimXpert for Parts: A set of tools that applies dimensions and tolerances to parts according to the requirements of the ASME Y.14.41-2003 standard.

Document: A file containing a part, assembly, or drawing.

Drawing: A 2D representation of a 3D part or assembly.

Edit Sheet Format: The drawing sheet contains two modes. Utilize the Edit Sheet Format command to add or modify notes and Title block information. Edit in the Edit Sheet Format mode.

eDrawing: A compressed document that does not require the referenced part or assembly. eDrawings are animated to display multiple views in a drawing.

Exploded view: A configuration in an assembly that displays its components separated from one another

Export: The process to save a SolidWorks document in another format for use in other CAD/CAM, rapid prototyping, web, or graphics software applications.

Family Cell: A named empty cell in a Design Table that determines indicates the start of the evaluated parameters and configuration names. Locate Comments in a Design Table to the left or above the Family Cell.

FeatureManager: The FeatureManager design tree located on the left side of the SolidWorks window provides an outline view of the active part, assembly, or drawing. This makes it easy to see how the model or assembly was constructed or to examine the various sheets and views in a drawing. The FeatureManager and the Graphics window are dynamically linked. You can select features, sketches, drawing views, and construction geometry in either pane.

First Angle Projection: Standard 3 Views are in either third angle or first angle projection. In first angle projection, the front view is displayed at the upper left and the other two views are the top and left views.

Fully defined: A sketch where all lines and curves in the sketch, and their positions, are described by dimensions or relations, or both, and cannot be moved. Fully defined sketch entities are displayed in black.

Geometric Tolerance Symbol: Set of standard symbols that specify the geometric characteristics and dimensional requirements of a feature.

Hole Table: A table in a drawing document that displays the positions of selected holes from a specified origin datum. The tool labels each hole with a tag. The tag corresponds to a row in the table.

Line Format: A series of tools that controls Line Thickness, Line Style, Color, Layer and other properties.

Parametric Note: A Note annotation that links text to a feature dimension or property value.

Precision: The number of decimal places displayed for a dimension value.

Revision Table: The Revision Table lists the Engineering Change Orders (ECO), in a table form, issued over the life of the model and the drawing. The current Revision letter or number is placed in the Title block of the Drawing.

Sheet: A page in a drawing document.

Surface Finish: An annotation that represents the texture of a part.

Weld Bead: An assembly feature that represents a weld between multiple parts.

Weld Symbol: An annotation in the part or drawing that represents the parameters of the weld.

Questions:

1. Datum Feature, Geometric Tolerance, Surface Finish and Weld Symbols are located in the _____ Toolbar.

2. True or False. A SolidWorks part file is a required attachment to email a SolidWorks eDrawing.

3. Describe the procedure to create a Basic dimension.

4. Dimensions on the drawing are displayed with three decimal places. You require two decimal places on all dimensions except for one diameter dimension. Identify the correct Document Property options.

5. Describe the procedure to create a Unilateral Tolerance.

6. Datum Symbols A, B and C in the VALVEPLATE1 drawing represent the _____, _____, and _____ reference planes.

7. Describe the procedure to attach a Feature Control Frame to a dimension.

8. Surface Finish symbols are applied in the _____ and in the _____.

9. Describe the procedure to create multiple leader lines that attach to the same symbol.

10. A Weld Bead is created in the _____. A Weld Symbol is created in the _____.

11. _____ combine text and sketched entities, Area Hatch and single Balloons to create symbols in a drawing document.

12. Format Design Tables using _____.

13. True or False. In a Minimum Content Drawing, the designer adds every dimension in the drawing in order to manufacture the part.

14. Describe the purpose of a Family Cell in a Design Table.

15. Identify the annotations created in the part and inserted into the drawing.

16. In your opinion, why would a Rapid Prototype manufacturer accept a Minimum Content Drawing or an eDrawing from a designer?

Exercises:

Exercise 6.1:

Create a new drawing for the part, ANGLEPLATE2 located in the DRAWING-W-SOLIDWORKS 2010\Exercise file folder.

Insert a Front view, Bottom view,gand Auxiliary view. Use Geometric relations when constructing centerlines. The centerline drawn between the Front view and the Auxiliary view is perpendicular to the angled edge.

Insert the Feature Control Frame before applying Datum Reference Symbols, (Example Datum E).

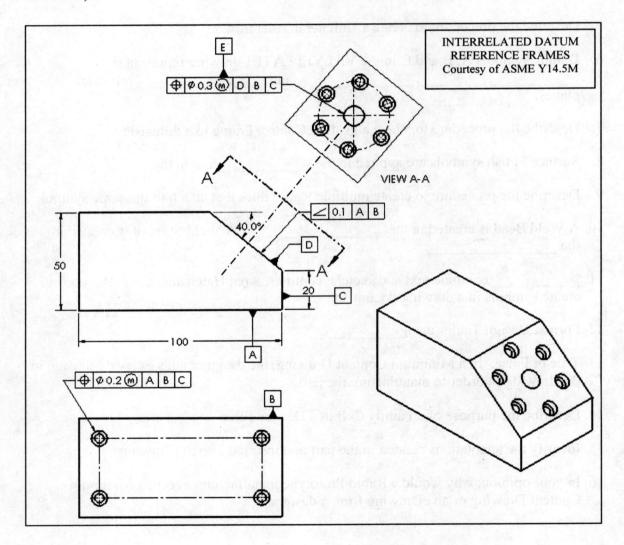

Exercise 6.2:

Create a new drawing for the part, FIG5-28 located in the DRAWING-W-SOLIDWORKS-2010\Exercises file folder. View A is created with an Auxiliary view from the angled edge in the Right view. Crop the Auxiliary view.

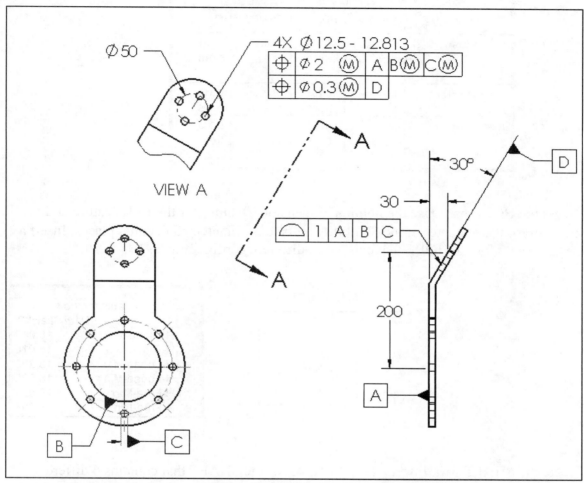

MULTIPLE POSITIONAL TOLERANCING FOR A PATTERN OF FEATURES
COURTESY ASME Y14.5M

Use spaces to align Feature Control Frames 1 and 2.

Insert Datum Feature Symbols to circular pattern features. Utilize a Linear Diameter Dimension.

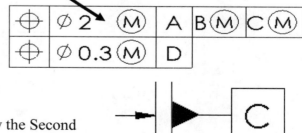

Modify the Display options to display only the Second Dimension line.

Exercise 6.3:

Investigate three different fits for a 16mm shaft and a 16mm hole using the HOLE part, SHAFT part and HOLE-SHAFT assembly configurations, Table 6.1.

TabLE 6.1 TYPE of FIT (MILLIMETERS ASME B4.2)				
Type of Fit	MAX/MIN	HOLE	SHAFT	FIT
Close Running Fit	MAX	16.043	16.000	0.061
	MIN	16.016	15.982	0.016
Loose Running Fit	MAX	16.205	16.000	0.315
	MIN	16.095	15.890	0.095
Free Sliding Fit	MAX	16.024	16.000	0.035
	MIN	16.006	15.989	0.006

Create the HOLE part. Use the nominal dimension ∅16mm for the Hole feature and ∅16mm for the diameter of the Shaft. Set units to millimeters, 3 decimal places. Insert a Design Table for the HOLE that contains 6 different configurations.

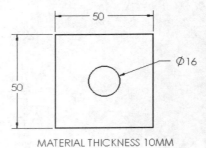

MATERIAL THICKNESS 10MM

	A	B
1	Design Table for: hole	
2		D1@Sketch2
3	H-Close-Max	16.043
4	H-Close-Min	16.016
5	H-Loose-Max	16.205
6	H-Loose-Min	16.095
7	H-Free-Max	16.024
8	H-Free-Min	16.006

Create the SHAFT part. Insert a Design Table for the SHAFT that contains 6 different configurations. The Min value is before the Max value. Format the columns in Excel to three decimal places.

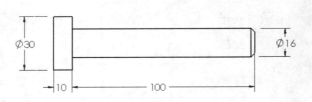

	A	B
1	Design Table for: shaft	
2		D1@Sketch1
3	S-Close-Min	15.982
4	S-Close-Max	16.000
5	S-Loose-Min	15.890
6	S-Loose-Max	16.000
7	S-Free-Min	15.989
8	S-Free-Max	16.000

Create the HOLE-SHAFT assembly. Insert a new Design Table into the assembly that contains 6 configurations

	A	B	C	D	E
1	Design Table for: HOLE-SHAFT				
2		$CONFIGURATION@HOLE<1>	$STATE@HOLE<1>	$CONFIGURATION@SHAFT<1>	$STATE@SHAFT<1>
3	CLOSE-MAX	H-CLOSE-MAX	R	S-CLOSE-MIN	R
4	CLOSE-MIN	H-CLOSE-MIN	R	S-CLOSE-MAX	R
5	LOOSE-MAX	H-LOOSE-MAX	R	S-LOOSE-MIN	R
6	LOOSE-MIN	H-LOOSE-MIN	R	S-LOOSE-MAX	R
7	FREE-MAX	H-FREE-MAX	R	S-FREE-MIN	R
8	FREE-MIN	H-FREE-MIN	R	S-FREE-MAX	R

Create a new Excel document, HOLE-SHAFT-COMBINED.XLS. Copy cells A3 through A8 in the Design Table HOLE-SHAFT to column A. Copy cells B3 through B8 in the Design Table HOLE to column B. Copy cells B3 through B8 in the Design Table SHAFT to column C. Insert the formula =B2-C2 in column D to calculate the Fit.

HOLD-SHAFT-COMBINED

	A	B	C	D
1		HOLE	SHAFT	FIT
2	CLOSE-MAX	16.043	15.982	0.061
3	CLOSE-MIN	16.016	16.000	0.016
4	LOOSE-MAX	16.205	15.890	0.315
5	LOOSE-MIN	16.095	16.000	0.095
6	FREE-MAX	16.024	15.989	0.035
7	FREE-MIN	16.006	16.000	0.006

Create a new drawing that contains the HOLE-SHAFT assembly, the SHAFT part and the HOLE part. Insert Balloons for the two components in the assembly. Modify the Ballon Property from Item Number to Custom. Enter H for the HOLE and S for the SHAFT.

Insert the Excel Worksheet, HOLE-SHAFT-COMBINED. Click Insert, Object, Microsoft Excel. Add dimensions.

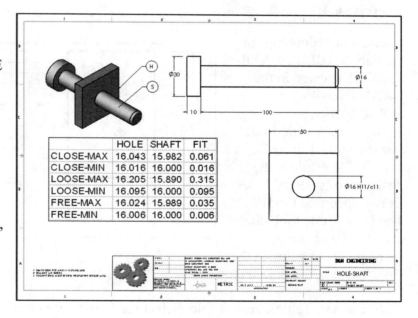

Open the Hole part. Select the LOOSE-MAX configuration. Select Clearance for Type of Fit for ∅16. Select H11 for Hole Fit. Select c11 for Shaft Fit.

HOLE/SHAFT Metric Fit (ASME B4.2)		
Clearance Fit	**Hole**	**Shaft**
Loose running	H11/c11	C11/h11
Free running	H9/d9	D9/h9
Close running	H8/f7	F8/h7

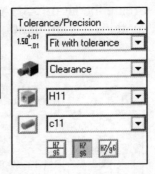

Create a HOLE drawing. Select the HOLE, default configuration for the Front view. Copy the view two times. Select the LOOSE-MAX configuration. The ISO symbol Hole/Shaft Classification is displayed on the Hole diameter dimension. Modify the dimensions in the other two views to create a Free Running and Close Running Clearance Fit.

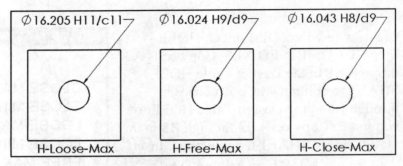

Exercise 6.4:

Create a new drawing for the part, TABLE-PLATE-LABELS located in the DRAWING-W-SOLIDWORKS 2010\Exercises file folder. Insert a Hole Table. A Hole Table displays the positions of selected holes from a specified Origin. The Hole Table tool labels each hole with a tag, which corresponds to a row in the Hole Table in the drawing.

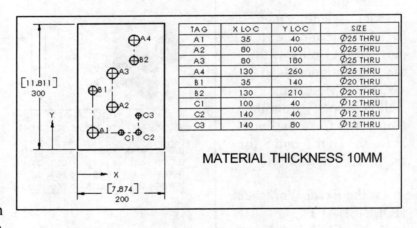

TAG	X LOC	Y LOC	SIZE
A1	35	40	∅25 THRU
A2	80	100	∅25 THRU
A3	80	180	∅25 THRU
A4	130	260	∅25 THRU
B1	35	140	∅20 THRU
B2	130	210	∅20 THRU
C1	100	40	∅12 THRU
C2	140	40	∅12 THRU
C3	140	80	∅12 THRU

MATERIAL THICKNESS 10MM

Utilize Insert, Tables, Hole Table. Select the lower left vertex for Hole Origin. Select the front face of the Front view for Holes. Insert Center Marks, overall dimensions and a Parametric note for Material Thickness. The Parametric note links to the depth dimension.

Exercise 6.5:

A U.S. company designs components and specifies basic welding joints in inch units. Two ½ inch plates are welded together with an intermittent fillet weld to form a T shape. The BASE PLATE is 19.00in x 6.00in.

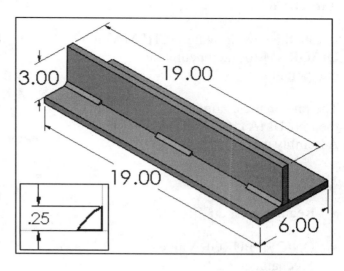

The SECOND PLATE is 19.00in x 3.00in. The .25in Radius weld is placed on both sides of the SECOND PLATE. The weld bead is placed at 8.00in intervals. Parts, assembly and drawings are in inch units, 2 decimal places.

Create the BASE PLATE and SECOND PLATE parts. Create the T-PLATE assembly. A SolidWorks Weld Bead Assembly Feature creates a continuous bead.

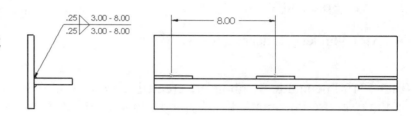

Create the Weld Bead part with a .25in Radius. Insert a Component Pattern, Linear Pattern in the assembly.

Create a T-PLATE drawing. Insert a Weld Symbol on the Arrow side option and the Other side option. Add dimensions to complete the drawing.

Exercise 6.6:

Import the DRAWING-WITH-SOLIDWORKS 2010\EXERCISES\AUTOCAD-DWG\LOGIC-GATES.dwg file as a SolidWorks drawing.

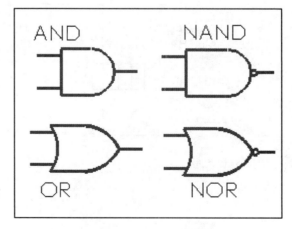

Explode the blocks and increase the line thickness.

Create a new block for each logic gate. Save the blocks. Utilize their logic name for file name.

Exercise 6.7:

Create the new drawing, SCHEMATIC DIAGRAM for the pneumatic components.

The pneumatic components utilized in the PNEUMATIC TEST MODULE Assembly are:

- Air Reservoir

- Regulator

- ON/OFF/PURGE Valve – Mechanical 2/2

- 3Way Solenoid Valve

- Air Cylinder – Linear Actuator

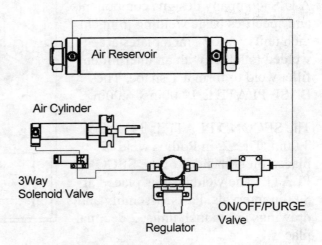

Pneumatic Components Diagram
Courtesy of SMC Corporation of America and
Gears Educational Systems.

ISO-1219 Pneumatic Symbols are created as SolidWorks Blocks. The Blocks are stored in the Exercise Pneumatic ISO Symbols folder. Utilize the Design Library and create a new folder location for the ISO-Symbols.

Utilize Insert, Block. Insert the Blocks into a B-size drawing. Enter 0.1 for Scale. Label each symbol. Utilize the Line tool to connect the pneumatic symbols.

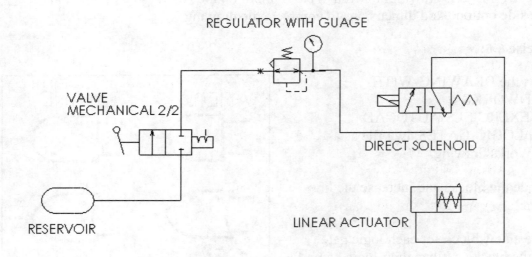

ISO-1219 Symbols
Courtesy of SMC Corporation of America

Chapter 7

Introduction to the Certified SolidWorks Associate Exam

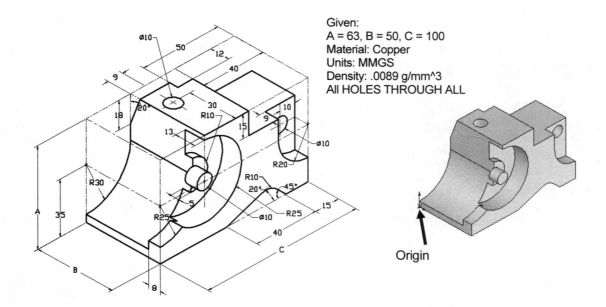

Given:
A = 63, B = 50, C = 100
Material: Copper
Units: MMGS
Density: .0089 g/mm^3
All HOLES THROUGH ALL

Origin

Below are the desired outcomes and usage competencies based on the completion of Chapter 7.

Desired Outcomes:	Usage Competencies:
• Procedure and process knowledge. • Exam categories: o Basic Theory and Drawing Theory, Part Modeling, Advanced Part Modeling, Assembly Modeling and Advanced Modeling Theory and Analysis	• Familiarity of the CSWA exam. • Comprehension of the skill sets to past the CSWA exam. • Awareness of the question types. • Capability to locate additional CSWA exam information.

Notes:

Chapter 7 - Certified SolidWorks Associate CSWA Exam

Chapter Objective

Provide a basic introduction into the curriculum and categories of the Certified SolidWorks Associate CSWA exam. Awareness to the exam procedure, process, and required model knowledge needed to take and past the CSWA exam. The five exam categories are:

- Basic Theory and Drawing Theory

- Part Modeling

- Advanced Part Modeling

- Assembly Modeling

- Advanced Modeling Theory and Analysis (SimulationXpress)

Introduction

SolidWorks Corporation offers two levels of certification representing increasing levels of expertise in 3D CAD design as it applies to engineering: *Certified SolidWorks Associate CSWA* and the *Certified SolidWorks Professional CSWP*.

The CSWA certification indicates a foundation in and apprentice knowledge of 3D CAD design and engineering practices and principles. The main requirement for obtaining the CSWA certification is to take and pass the 3 hour, seven question on-line proctored exam at a Certified SolidWorks CSWA Provider, "university, college, technical, vocational, or secondary educational institution" and to sign the SolidWorks Confidentiality Agreement.

Passing this exam provides students the chance to prove their knowledge and expertise and to be part of a World-wide industry Certification standard.

Intended Audience

The intended audience for the CSWA exam is anyone with a minimum of 6 - 9 months of SolidWorks experience and basic knowledge of engineering fundamentals and practices. SolidWorks recommends that you review their SolidWorks Tutorials on Parts, Assemblies, Drawings, and SolidWorks SimulationXpress as a prerequisite and have at least 45 hours of classroom time learning SolidWorks or using SolidWorks with basic engineering design principles and practices.

To prepare for the CSWA exam, it is recommended that you first perform the following:

- Take a CSWA exam preparation class or review a text book written for the CSWA exam.

- Complete the SolidWorks Tutorials

- Practice creating models from the isometric working drawings sections of any Technical Drawing or Engineering Drawing Documentation text books.

- Complete the sample CSWA exam in a timed environment, available at www.solidworks.com.

Additional references to help you prepare are as follows:

- **SolidWorks Users Guide**, SolidWorks Corporation, 2010.

- **Official Certified SolidWorks® Associate (CSWA) Examination Guide**, Planchard & Planchard, SDC Publications, Mission, KS 2009.

- **Fundamentals of Graphics Communication**, Bertoline, Wiebe, Miller, Irwin, 1995.

- **Engineering Design Graphics**, Earle, Addison Wesley, 1999.

- **Engineering Mechanics Statics and Dynamics**, Hibbler, 8th ed, Prentice Hall, Saddle River, NJ.

- **Graphics for Engineers**, Hoelscher & Dobrovolny, John Wiley, 1968.

- **Interpreting Engineering Drawings**, Jensen, Cecil, Glencoe, 2002.

- **Engineering Drawing and Design**, Jensen & Helsel, Glencoe, 1990.

- **Visualization, Modeling, and Graphics for Engineering**, Lieu, Sorby, Delmar Thomson, 2007.

- **Engineering Drawing and Design**, Madsen, Delmar Thomson, 2007.

- **Drawing and Detailing with SolidWorks**, Planchard & Planchard, SDC Pub., Mission, KS 2010.

🔅 View the Certified SolidWorks Associate CSWA exam pdf file on the enclosed CD for a sample exam!

CSWA Exam Content

The CSWA exam is divided into five key categories. Questions on the timed exam are provided in a random manor. The following information provides general guidelines for the content likely to be included on the exam. However, other related topics may also appear on any specific delivery of the exam. In order to better reflect the contents of the exam and for clarity purposes, the guidelines below may change at any time without notice.

Basic Theory and Drawing Theory (2 Questions - Total 10 Points)

- Recognize 3D modeling techniques:

  - How parts, assemblies, and drawings are related, identify the feature type icon, identify parameters, and dimensions, identify the correct standard reference planes: Top, Right, and Front, and determine the design intent for a model

- Identify and understand the procedure for the following:

  - Assign and edit material to a part, apply the Measure tool to a part or an assembly, locate the Center of mass, and Principal moments of inertia relative to the default coordinate location, and Origin.

- Calculate the overall mass and volume of a part

- Identify the process of creating a simple drawing from a part or an assembly

- Recognize various drawing name view types by their icons

- Identify the procedure to create a named drawing view

- Specify Document Properties: Select Unit System, and Set Precision

Part Modeling (1 Question - Total 30 Points)

- Read and understand an Engineering document:

- Identify the Sketch plane, part Origin location, part dimensions, geometric relations, and design intent of the sketch and feature

- Build a part from a detailed dimensioned illustration using the following SolidWorks tools and features:

- 2D & 3D sketch tools, Extruded Boss/Base, Extruded Cut, Fillet, Mirror, Revolved Base, Chamfer, Reference geometry, Plane, Axis, calculate the overall mass and volume of the created part, and locate the Center of mass for the created part relative to the Origin

Advanced Part Modeling (1 Question -Total 20 Points)

- Specify Document Properties

- Interpret engineering terminology:

- Create and manipulate a coordinate system

- Build an advanced part from a detailed dimensioned illustration using the following tools and features:

- 2D & 3D Sketch tools, Extruded Boss/Base, Extruded Cut, Fillet, Mirror, Revolved Boss/Base, Linear & Circular Pattern, Chamfer and Revolved Cut

- Locate the Center of mass relative to the part Origin

- Create a coordinate system location

- Locate the Center of mass relative to a created coordinate system

Assembly Modeling (1 Question - Total 30 Points)

- Specify Document Properties

- Identify and build the components to construct the assembly from a detailed illustration using the following features:

- Extruded Boss/Base, Extruded Cut, Fillet, Mirror, Revolved Cut, Revolved Boss/Base, Linear Pattern, Chamfer and Hole Wizard

- Identify the first fixed component in an assembly

- Build a bottom-up assembly with the following Standard mates:

- Coincident, Concentric, Perpendicular, Parallel, Tangent, Distance, Angle, and Aligned, Anti-Aligned options

- Apply the Mirror Component tool

- Locate the Center of mass relative to the assembly Origin

- Create a coordinate system location

- Locate the Center of mass relative to a created coordinate system

- Calculate the overall mass and volume for the created assembly

- Mate the first component with respect to the assembly reference planes

Advanced Modeling Theory and Analysis (2 Questions - Total 10 Points)

- Comprehend basic Engineering analysis definitions

- Wisdom of the SimulationXpress Wizard interface

- Skill to apply SimulationXpress to a simple part

☀ In the Part Modeling, Advanced Part Modeling and Assembly Modeling categories, you will be required to read and interpret all types of drawing views.

About the CSWA exam?

Most CAD professionals today recognize the need to become certified to prove their skills, prepare for new job searches, and to learn new skill, while at their existing jobs.

Specifying a CSWA or CSWP certification on your resume is a great way to increase your chances of landing a new job, getting a promotion, or looking more qualified when representing your company on a consulting job.

CSWA Certification

For Educational customers, SolidWorks Corporation requires that you take and pass (minimum of 70% correct) a three hour (3) on-line exam in a secure environment at an designated CSWA Provider and to sign the SolidWorks Confidentiality Agreement. A CSWA Provider can be a university, college, technical, vocational, or secondary educational institution. Contact your local SolidWorks Value Added Reseller (VAR) or instructor for information on CSWA Providers.

☀ Commercial customers can obtain information on taking the CSWA exam through the SolidWorks Customer Portal.

There are five key categories in the CSWA exam. The minimum passing grade is 70 out of 100 points. There are two questions in both the Basic Theory and Drawing, and Advanced Modeling Theory and Analysis Categories, (multiple choice, single answer format) and one question in each of the Part modeling, Advanced Part Modeling and Analysis, and the Assembly Modeling categories. The single questions are on an in-depth illustrated dimension model. All questions are in a multiple choice single answer format. There is no partial credit on exam questions.

Exam Day

You will need:

- A computer with SolidWorks installed on it in a secure environment.

- An internet connection.

- A valid email address.

- A voucher ID code
  (Provided by the
  CSWA Provider).

- ID: Student, ID,
  drivers license, etc.

Log into the
Tangix_TesterPRO site
(http://www.virtualtester.
com/solidworks) and
click the Download
TesterPRO Client link to
start the exam process.

Click the Run button.

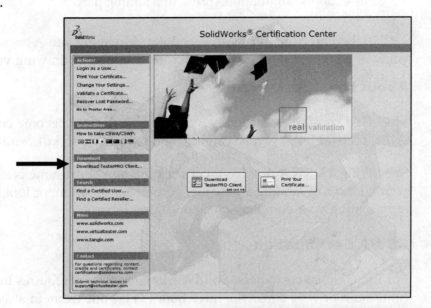

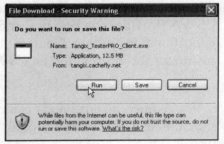

To run the exam engine software. Click the Run button.

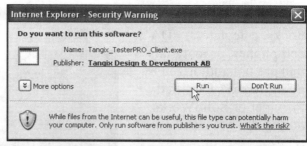

Candidates must agree to the Tangix_TesterPRO_Client engine software license agreement. If the candidate does not agree, you will not be able to proceed with the exam and a refund for the exam will not provided.

Click the I Agree button to proceed with the exam.

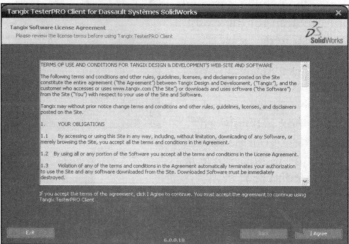

Select a language for the exam engine. The CSWA exam at this time is provided in the following languages: English, Brazilian Portuguese, Chinese-S, Chinese-T, French, German, Italian, Japanese, Spanish and Korean.

Click the Continue key. The system connects to the internet to continue and download the exam engine and exam in the selected language. This may take a minute or so.

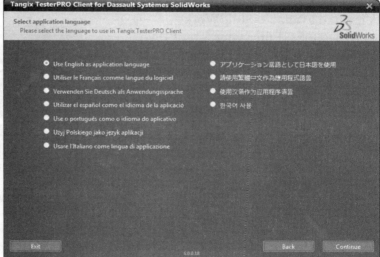

Students can not use notes, books, calculators, PDA's, cell phones, or materials that are not authorized by a SolidWorks Certified Provider or SolidWorks during the exam period.

Enter the needed personal information for the exam as illustrated.

Press the Continue button.

A Save your password dialog box is displayed. Document your password for future logins. *Write it down* and save it in a secure location.

Click the Yes, I have written my password down button.

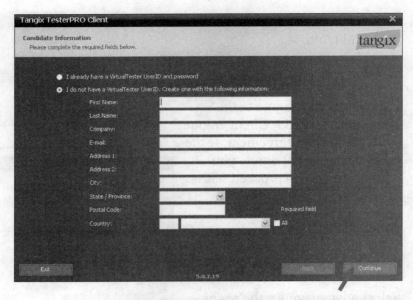

View the available SolidWorks Certifications. Enter your Event ID/ Voucher in the box as illustrated. This is the number that your Provider gave you at the beginning of this session.

Click the Submit button.

Click the Continue button as illustrated to start the three (3) hour CSWA exam process.

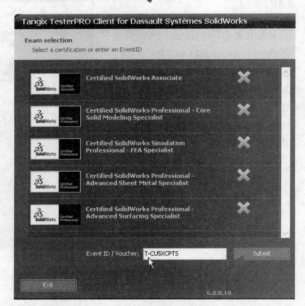

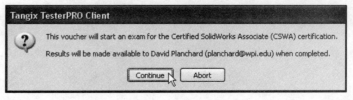

Select the exam Language.

Click the Start Examination button.

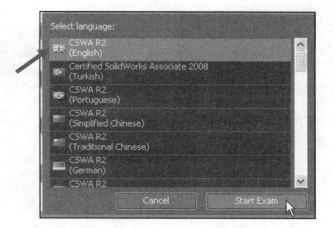

Click the I Agree button to proceed with the exam. Note: This is the SolidWorks usage Agreement for the exam.

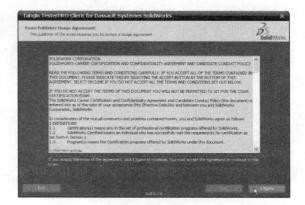

Click the Start Examination button. You have 180 minutes (3 hours) to complete the exam. Good luck!

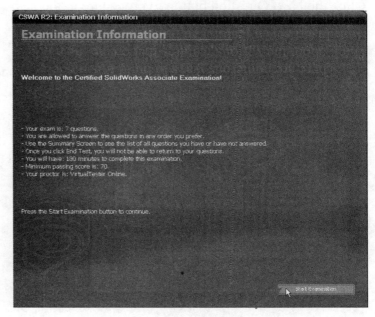

The exam generates unique questions for each student.

Click on different images to display additional views as illustrated.

Read the questions slowly, view the additional views, model your part or assembly and then select the correct answer.

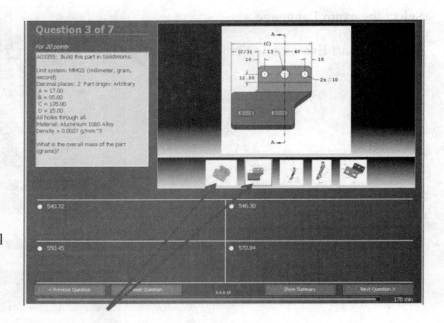

 The exam uses a multi-question single answer format.

 In the Part Modeling, Advanced Part Modeling and Assembly Modeling categories, you will be required to read and interpret all types of drawing views.

Click the Next Question button to procedure to the next question in the exam.

You can also click in the image itself to zoom in on that area.

Below are examples for a part and an assembly screen shot in the CSWA exam.

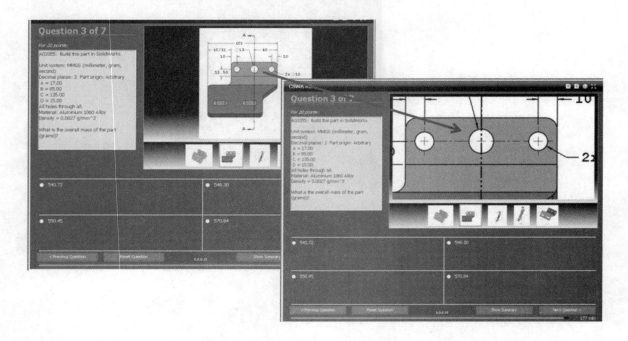

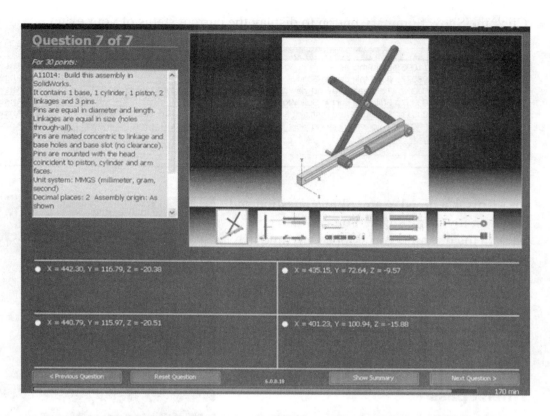

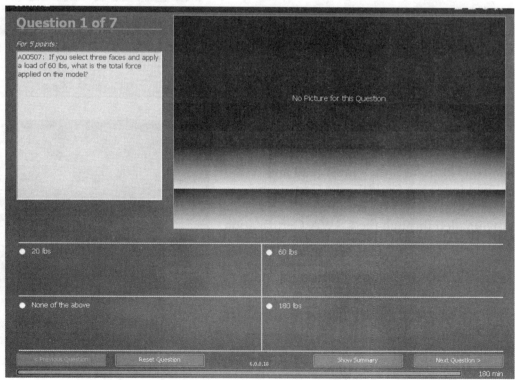

Click the Show Summary button to display the current status of your exam.

1	A00507: If you select three faces and apply a load of 60 lbs, what is the total f...	5	Answered
2	A11006: Build this assembly in SolidWorks.	30	Not Answered
3	A08077: Build this part in SolidWorks.	30	Not Answered
4	A00003: To create drawing view 'B' from drawing view 'A' insert which SolidW...	5	Not Answered
5	A03357: Build this part in SolidWorks.	20	Not Answered
6	A00511: When a Fixed restraint is applied on a face, what happens to the face?	5	Not Answered
7	A00005: To create drawing view 'B' it is necessary to sketch a spline (as show...	5	Not Answered

This is a timed exam. Skip a question and move on it you are stuck. You can also go back to the question you skipped anytime in the exam.

At the completion of the exam, Click the End Examination button. Click Yes to confirm.

Candidates receive a score report along with a score breakout by exam section.

When I pass

After a candidate passes the CSWA exam and signs the required agreements an email is sent to you to visit the following website: www.virtualtester.com/solidworks.

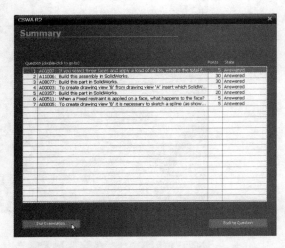

Certified candidates are authorized to use the appropriate CSWA SolidWorks certification logo indicating certification status. Prior to use, they must read and acknowledge the SolidWorks Certification Logo Agreement. Logos can be downloaded through the CSWA Certification Tracking System.

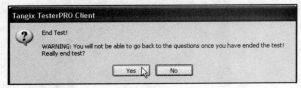

The CSWA Certification Tracking System provides a record of both exam and certification status. Candidates and certification holders *are expected* to keep contact information up to date for receiving notifications from SolidWorks.

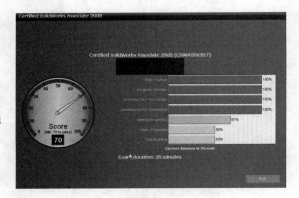

VirtualTester is a system for delivering and managing multiple choice tests over the internet. The system consists of a web service complete with company and user database, question editor and a client.

The VirtualTester website: www.virtualtester.com/solid works provides the following menu options:

The following dialog box with *Actions*, *Downloads*, *Search* and *More* are displayed.

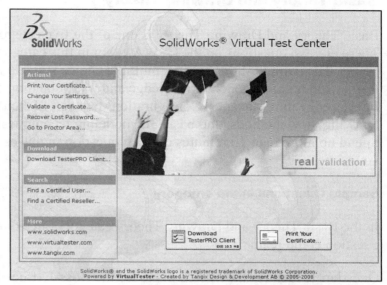

Use the login credentials sent by email from virtualtester.com. If you do not receive the email, check your spam filters, junk email filters, etc. to receive the email.

A certificate suitable for framing is provided with your name and CSWA Certification ID.

View the Certified SolidWorks Associate CSWA exam pdf file on the enclosed CD for a sample exam!

Basic Theory and Drawing Theory

Basic Theory and Drawing Theory is one of the five categories on the CSWA exam. There are two questions on the CSWA exam in this category. Each question is worth five points. The two questions are in a multiple choice single answer or fill in the blank format and requires general knowledge and understanding of the SolidWorks User Interface, FeatureManager, ConfigurationManager, Sketch toolbar, Feature toolbar, Drawing view methods, and basic 3D modeling techniques and engineering principles. Spend no more than 10 minutes on each question in this category for the exam. Manage your time.

Sample Questions in the category

In the Basic Theory and Drawing Theory category, an exam question could read:

Question 1: Identify the Sketch plane for the Boss-Extrude1 feature. Simplify the number of features!

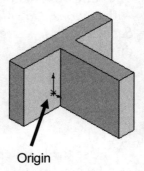

Origin

A: Top Plane

B: Front Plane

C: Right Plane

D: Left Plane

The correct answer is A.

Question 2: Identify the Sketch plane for the Boss-Extrude1 feature. Simplify the number of features!

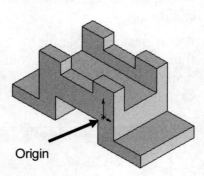

Origin

A: Top Plane

B: Front Plane

C: Right Plane

D: Left Plane

The correct answer is B.

Question 3: Identify the Sketch plane for the Boss-Extrude1 feature. Simplify the number of features!

A: Top Plane

B: Front Plane

C: Right Plane

D: Left Plane

The correct answer is B.

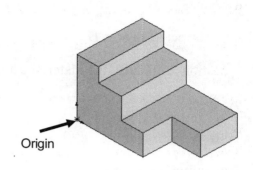

Origin

Question 4: Identify the Sketch plane for the Boss-Extrude1 feature. Simplify the number of features!

A: Top Plane

B: Front Plane

C: Right Plane

D: Left Plane

The correct answer is A and C.

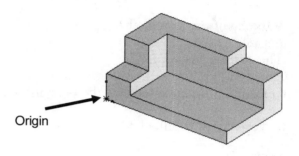

Origin

Question 5: Identify the number of instances in the illustrated model.

A: 7

B: 5

C: 8

D: None

The correct answer is B.

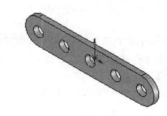

Question 6: Identify the number of instances in the illustrated model.

A: 7

B: 4

C: 8

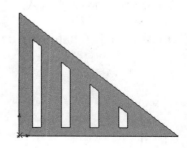

D: None

The correct answer is B.

Question 7: Identify the material category for 6061 Alloy.

A: Steel

B: Iron

C: Aluminum Alloys

D: Other Alloys

E: None of the provided

The correct answer is C.

Question 8: In an assembly, the (-) symbol means?

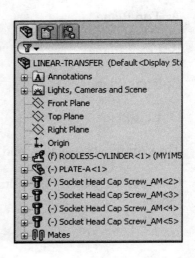

A: Reference is unlocked

B: The reference is broken

C: A floating component

D: A fixed component

The correct answer is C.

Question 9: In an assembly, the symbol before a component <1> indicates?

A: First inserted instance of the component

B: First inserted instance of a drawing

C: Nothing

D: External reference broken

The correct answer is A.

Question 10: What is the default part file format in SolidWorks?

A: *.sldfop

B: *.sldprt

C: *.hjyy

D: *.pprt

The correct answer is B.

Question 11: Which is a valid assembly format in SolidWorks?

A: *.tiffe

B: *.jpgg

C: * .assmy

D: * .stl

The correct answer is D.

Question 12: Identify the view procedure. To create the following view, you need to insert a:

- A: Open Spline
- B: Closed Spline
- C: 3 Point Arc
- D: None of the above

The correct answer is B.

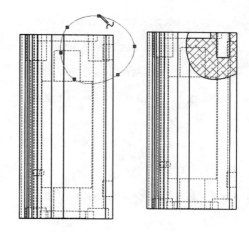

Question 13: Identify the illustrated view type.

- A: Crop view
- B: Section view
- C: Projected view
- D: None of the above

The correct answer is A.

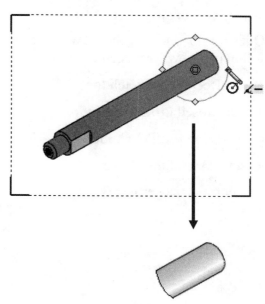

Question 14: Identify the illustrated Drawing view.

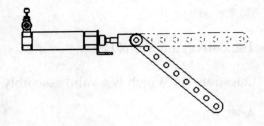

- A: Projected View

- B: Alternative Position View

- C: Extended View

- D: Aligned Section View

The correct answer is B.

Question 15: Identify the illustrated Drawing view.

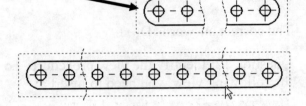

- A: Crop View

- B: Break View

- C: Broken-out Section View

- D: Aligned Section View

The correct answer is B.

Question 16: Identify the illustrated Drawing view.

- A: Section View

- B: Crop View

- C: Broken-out Section View

- D: Aligned Section View

The correct answer is A.

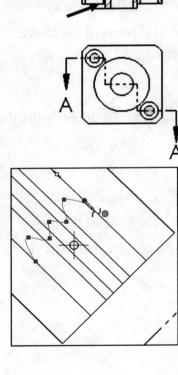

Question 17: Identify the view procedure. To create the following view, you need to insert a:

- A: Rectangle Sketch tool

- B: Closed Profile: Spline

- C: Open Profile: Circle

- D: None of the above

The correct answer is a B.

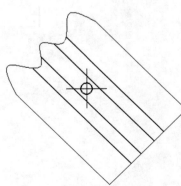

Part Modeling

Part Modeling is one of the five categories on the CSWA exam. This category covers the knowledge to identify the part Origin, design intent, and key features to build a simple part from a detailed dimensioned illustration.

There is one question on the CSWA exam in this category. The question is in a multiple choice single answer or fill in the blank format. The question is worth thirty points. You are required to build a model, with six or more features and to answer a question either on the overall mass, volume, or the location of the Center of mass relative to the default part Origin. Spend no more than 40 minutes on the question in this category. This is a timed exam. Manage your time.

The main difference between the Part Modeling category and the Advanced Part modeling category is the complexity of the sketches and the number of dimensions and geometric relations along with an increase in the number of features.

Sample Questions in the category

In the Part Modeling category, an exam question could read:

Question 1: Build the illustrated from the provided information. Calculate the Center of mass to the part Origin with the provided information.

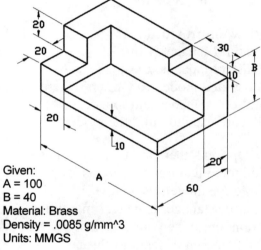

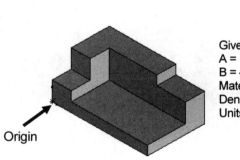

Origin

Given:
A = 100
B = 40
Material: Brass
Density = .0085 g/mm^3
Units: MMGS

Think about the steps that are required to build this model. There are numerous ways to build models. The CSWA is a three hour timed exam. Work efficiently.

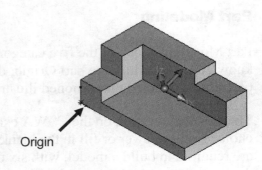

Origin

- A: X = 43.36 millimeters, Y = 15.00 millimeters, Z = -37.69 millimeters

- B: X = 1.63 inches, Y = 1.01 inches, Z = -0.04 inches

- C: X = 44.44 millimeters, Y = -15.00millimeters, Z = -37.02 millimeters

- D: X = 1.66 inches, Y = 1.04 inches, Z = -1.04 inches

The correct answer is A.

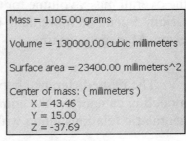

Mass = 1105.00 grams

Volume = 130000.00 cubic millimeters

Surface area = 23400.00 millimeters^2

Center of mass: (millimeters)
    X = 43.46
    Y = 15.00
    Z = -37.69

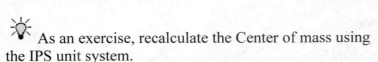 As an exercise, recalculate the Center of mass using the IPS unit system.

View the provided Part FeatureManager. Both FeatureManagers create the same illustrated model. In Option1, there are four sketches and four features that are used to build the model.

In Option2, there are three sketches and three features that are used to build the model. Which FeatureManager is better? In a timed exam, optimize your time and use the least amount of features through mirror, pattern, symmetry, etc.

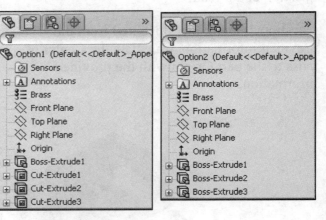

All models for this Chapter are located on the CD in the book.

Question 2: Build the illustrated model from the provided information. Locate the Center of mass relative to the default coordinate system, Origin.

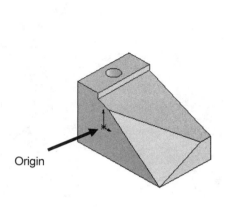

Origin

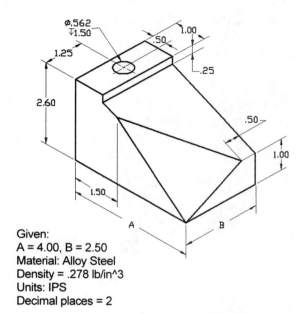

Given:
A = 4.00, B = 2.50
Material: Alloy Steel
Density = .278 lb/in^3
Units: IPS
Decimal places = 2

- A: X = -1.63 inches, Y = 1.48 inches, Z = -1.09 inches

- B: X = 1.63 inches, Y = 1.01 inches, Z = -0.04 inches

- C: X = 43.49 inches, Y = -0.86 inches, Z = -0.02 inches

- D: X = 1.63 inches, Y = 1.01 inches, Z = -0.04 inches

The correct answer is B.

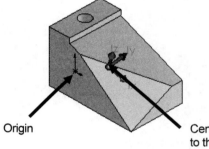

Origin

Center of mass relative to the part Origin

In the Part Modeling category of the exam; you are required to read and understand an engineering document, set document properties, identify the correct Sketch planes, apply the correct Sketch and Feature tools, and apply material to build a simple part.

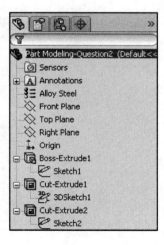

☀ Note the Depth/Deep ⊤ symbol with a 1.50 dimension associated with the hole. The hole Ø.562 has a three decimal place precision. Hint: Insert three features to build this model: Extruded Base, and two Extruded Cuts. Insert a 3D sketch for the first Extruded Cut feature. You are required to have knowledge in 3D sketching for the exam.

Question 3: Build the illustrated model from the provided information. What is the volume of the part?

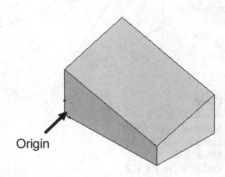

Origin

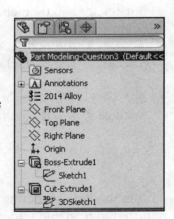

1.50

4.00   B

Given:
A = .75, B = 2.50
Material: 2014 Alloy
Density = .10 lb/in^3
Units: IPS
Decimal places = 2

A: 18.88 cubic inches

B: 19.55 cubic inches

C: 17.99 cubic inches

D: 16.25 cubic inches

The correct answer is D.

☀ To build this model, insert two features: Extruded Base, Extruded Cut. Apply a closed four point 3D sketch as the profile for the Extruded Cut feature. The part Origin is located in the lower left front corner of the model.

☀ All models for this Chapter are located on the CD in the book.

Question 4: Build the illustrated model
from the provided information. Locate
the Center of mass of the part?

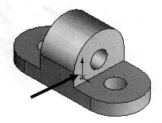

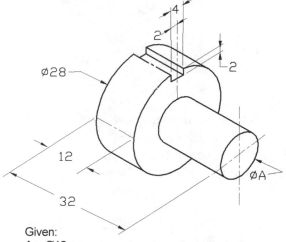

Given:
A = 40, B = 20
All Thru Holes
Material: Copper
Density = .0089 g/mm^3
Units: MMGS

- A: X = 0.00 millimeters, Y = 19.79
  millimeters, Z = 0.00 millimeters

- B: X = 0.00 inches, Y = 19.79 inches, Z = 0.04 inches

- C: X = 19.79 millimeters, Y = 0.00 millimeters, Z = 0.00
  millimeters

- D: X = 0.00 millimeters, Y = 19.49 millimeters, Z = 0.00
  millimeters

The correct answer is A.

Question 5: Build the illustrated model
from the provided information. Locate the
Center of mass of the part.

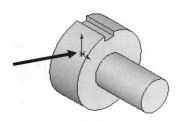

Given:
A = Ø12
Material: Cast Alloy Steel
Density = .0073 g/mm^3
Units: MMGS

- A: X = 10.00 millimeters, Y = -79.79 millimeters, Z: = 0.00 millimeters

- B: X = 9.79 millimeters, Y = -0.13 millimeters, Z = 0.00 millimeters

- C: X = 9.77 millimeters, Y = -0.10 millimeters, Z = -0.02 millimeters

- D: X = 10.00 millimeters, Y = 19.49 millimeters, Z = 0.00 millimeters

The correct answer is B.

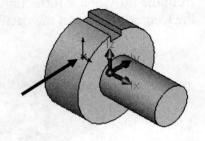

Question 6: Build the illustrated model from the provided information. Locate the Center of mass of the part.

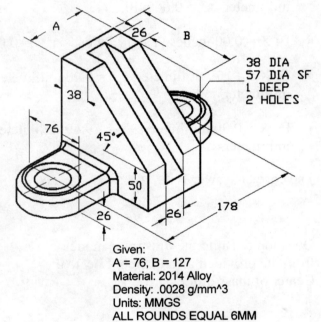

38 DIA
57 DIA SF
1 DEEP
2 HOLES

Given:
A = 76, B = 127
Material: 2014 Alloy
Density: .0028 g/mm^3
Units: MMGS
ALL ROUNDS EQUAL 6MM

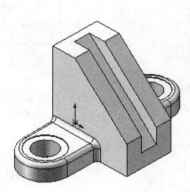

There are numerous ways to build this model.
Think about the various features that create the model.
Hint: Insert seven features to build this model: Extruded Base, Extruded Cut, Extruded Boss, Fillet, Extruded Cut, Mirror, and a second Fillet. Apply symmetry.

In the exam, create the left half of the model first, and then apply the Mirror feature. This is a timed exam.

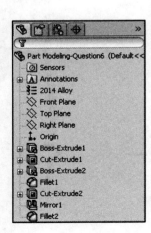

- A: X = 49.00 millimeters, Y = 45.79 millimeters, Z = 0.00 millimeters

- B: X = 0.00 millimeters, Y = 19.79 millimeters, Z = 0.04 millimeters

- C: X = 49.21 millimeters, Y = 46.88 millimeters, Z = 0.00 millimeters

- D: X = 48.00 millimeters, Y = 46.49 millimeters, Z = 0.00 millimeters

The correct answer is C.

Question 7: Build the illustrated model from the provided information. Locate the Center of mass of the part.

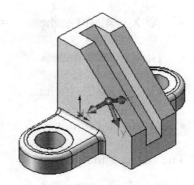

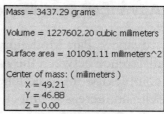

Mass = 3437.29 grams

Volume = 1227602.20 cubic millimeters

Surface area = 101091.11 millimeters^2

Center of mass: (millimeters)
  X = 49.21
  Y = 46.88
  Z = 0.00

Think about the various features that create this model. Hint: Insert five features to build this part: Extruded Base, two Extruded Bosses, Extruded Cut, and Rib. Insert a Reference plane to create the Extruded Boss feature.

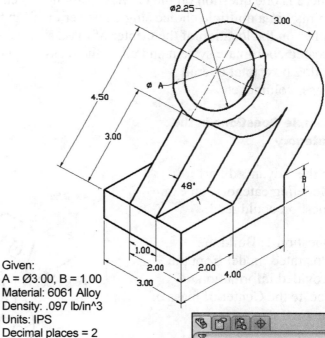

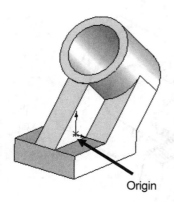

Origin

Given:
A = Ø3.00, B = 1.00
Material: 6061 Alloy
Density: .097 lb/in^3
Units: IPS
Decimal places = 2

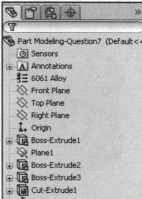

- A: X = 49.00 inches, Y = 45.79 inches, Z = 0.00 inches

- B: X = 0.00 inches, Y = 19.79 inches, Z = 0.04 inches

- C: X = 49.21 inches, Y = 46.88 inches, Z = 0.00 inches

- D: X = 0.00 inches, Y = 0.73 inches, Z = -0.86 inches

Density = 0.10 pounds per cubic inch
Mass = 2.99 pounds
Volume = 30.65 cubic inches
Surface area = 100.96 inches^2
Center of mass: (inches)
  X = 0.00
  Y = 0.73
  Z = -0.86

The correct answer is D.

Advanced Part Modeling

Advanced Part Modeling is one of the five categories on the CSWA exam. The main difference between the Advanced Part modeling and the Part Modeling category is the complexity of the sketches and the number of dimensions and geometric relations along with an increase number of features.

There is one question on the CSWA exam in this category. The question is worth twenty points - in a multiple choice single answer or fill in the blank format. The question is either on the location of the Center of mass relative to the default part Origin or to a new created coordinate system and all of the mass properties located in the Mass Properties dialog box: total overall mass, volume, etc.

Sample Questions in the category

In the Advanced Part Modeling category, an exam question could read:

Question 1: Build the illustrated model from the provided information. Locate the Center of mass of the part.

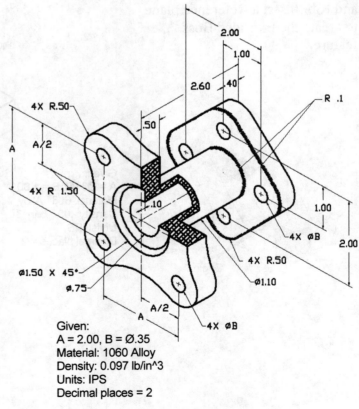

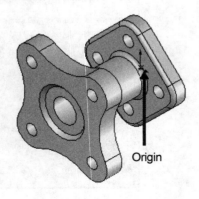

Origin

Given:
A = 2.00, B = Ø.35
Material: 1060 Alloy
Density: 0.097 lb/in^3
Units: IPS
Decimal places = 2

🔆 Built the model with seven features: Extruded Base, two Extruded Bosses, two Extruded Cuts, Chamfer, and Fillet. Think about the steps that you would take to build the illustrated part. Identify the location of the part Origin. Start with the back base flange. Review the provided dimensions and annotations in the part illustration.

🔆 The key difference between the Advanced Part Modeling and the Part Modeling category is the complexity of the sketches and the number of features, dimensions, and geometric relations. You may also need to locate the Center of mass relative to a created coordinate system location.

- A: X = 1.00 inches, Y = 0.79 inches, Z = 0.00 inches

- B: X = 0.00 inches, Y = 0.00 inches, Z = 1.04 inches

- C: X = 0.00 inches, Y = 1.18 inches, Z = 0.00 inches

- D: X = 0.00 inches, Y = 0.00 inches, Z = 1.51 inches

The correct answer is D.

🔆 All models for this Chapter are located on the CD in the book.

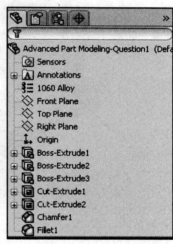

```
Mass = 0.59 pounds

Volume = 6.01 cubic inches

Surface area = 46.61 inches^2

Center of mass: ( inches )
    X = 0.00
    Y = 0.00
    Z = 1.51
```

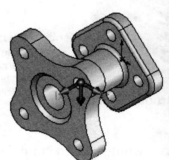

```
Advanced Part Modeling-Question1 (Defa
    Sensors
    Annotations
    1060 Alloy
    Front Plane
    Top Plane
    Right Plane
    Origin
    Boss-Extrude1
    Boss-Extrude2
    Boss-Extrude3
    Cut-Extrude1
    Cut-Extrude2
    Chamfer1
    Fillet1
```

Question 2: Build the illustrated model from the provided information. Locate the Center of mass of the part.

Hint: Create the part with eleven features and a Reference plane:
Extruded Base, Plane1, two Extruded Bosses, two Extruded Cuts, Extruded Boss, Extruded Cut,

Extruded-Thin, Mirror, Extruded Cut, and Extruded Boss.

Given:
A = 3.500, B = 4.200, C = 2.000,
D =1.750, E = 1.000
Material: 6061 Alloy
Density: 0.097 lb/in^3
Units: IPS
Decimal places = 3

Think about the steps that you would take to build the illustrated part. Create the rectangular Base feature. Create Sketch2 for Plane1. Insert Plane1 to create the Extruded Boss feature: Extrude2. Plane1 is the Sketch plane for Sketch3. Sketch3 is the sketch profile for Extrude2.

- A: X = 1.59 inches, Y = 1.19 inches, Z = 0.00 inches
- B: X = -1.59 inches, Y = 1.19 inches, Z = 0.04 inches
- C: X = 1.00 inches, Y = 1.18 inches, Z = 0.10 inches
- D: X = 0.00 inches, Y = 0.00 inches, Z = 1.61 inches

The correct answer is A.

Density = 0.10 pounds per cubic inch
Mass = 1.37 pounds
Volume = 14.05 cubic inches
Surface area = 79.45 inches^2
Center of mass: (inches)
X = 1.59
Y = 1.19
Z = 0.00

Question 3: Build the illustrated model from the provided information. Locate the Center of mass of the part. Note the coordinate system location of the model as illustrated.

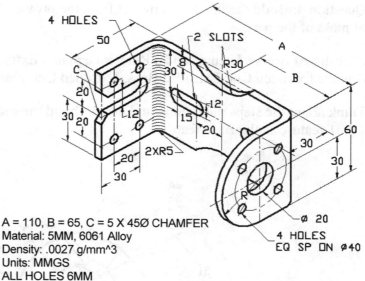

A = 110, B = 65, C = 5 X 45Ø CHAMFER
Material: 5MM, 6061 Alloy
Density: .0027 g/mm^3
Units: MMGS
ALL HOLES 6MM

Where do you start? Build the model. Insert thirteen features: Extruded-Thin1, Fillet, two Extruded Cuts, Circular Pattern, two Extruded Cuts, Mirror, Chamfer, Extruded Cut, Mirror, Extruded Cut, and Mirror.

Think about the steps that you would take to build the illustrated part. Review the provided information. The depth of the left side is 50mm. The depth of the right side is 60mm

Create Coordinate System1 to locate the Center of mass.

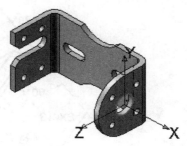

Coordinate system: +X, +Y. +Z

The SolidWorks software displays positive values for (X, Y, Z) coordinates for a reference coordinate system. The CSWA exam displays either a positive or negative sign in front of the (X, Y, Z) coordinates to indicate direction as illustrated, (-X, +Y, -Z).

- A: X = -53.30 millimeters, Y = -0.27 millimeters, Z = -15.54 millimeters

- B: X = 53.30 millimeters, Y = 0.27 millimeters, Z = 15.54 millimeters

- C: X = 49.21 millimeters, Y = 46.88 millimeters, Z = 0.00 millimeters

- D: X = 45.00 millimeters, Y = -46.49 millimeters, Z = 10.00 millimeters

The correct answer is A.

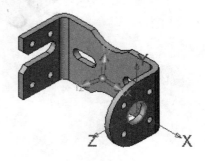

Question 4: Build the illustrated model from the provided information. Locate the Center of mass of the part.

Hint: Insert twelve features and a Reference plane: Extruded-Thin1, two Extruded Bosses, Extruded Cut, Extruded Boss, Extruded Cut, Plane1, Mirror, five Extruded Cuts.

Think about the steps that you would take to build the illustrated part. Create an Extrude-Thin1 feature as the Base feature.

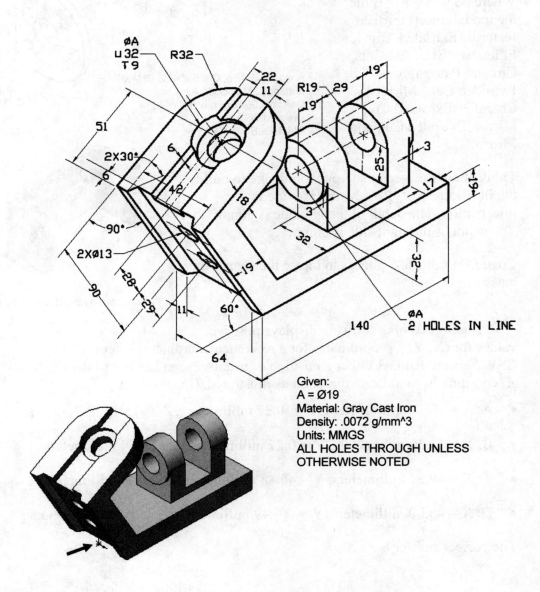

Given:
A = Ø19
Material: Gray Cast Iron
Density: .0072 g/mm^3
Units: MMGS
ALL HOLES THROUGH UNLESS
OTHERWISE NOTED

- A: X = -53.30 millimeters, Y = -0.27 millimeters, Z = -15.54 millimeters

- B: X = 53.30 millimeters, Y = 1.27 millimeters, Z = -15.54 millimeters

- C: X = 0.00 millimeters, Y = 34.97 millimeters, Z = 46.67 millimeters

- D: X = 0.00 millimeters, Y = 34.97 millimeters, Z = -46.67 millimeters

The correct answer is D.

🔆 Due to software rounding, you may view a negative -0.00 coordinate location in the Mass Properties dialog box.

Question 5: Build the illustrated model from the provided information. Locate the Center of mass of the part.

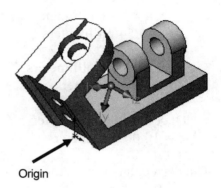

```
Mass = 2536.59 grams

Volume = 352304.50 cubic millimeters

Surface area = 61252.90 millimeters^2

Center of mass: ( millimeters )
   X = 0.00
   Y = 34.97
   Z = -46.67
```

Origin

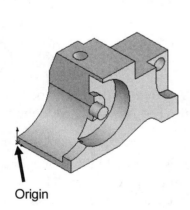

Origin

Given:
A = 63, B=50, C=100
Material: Copper
Units: MMGS
Density: .0089 g/mm^3
ALL HOLES THROUGH ALL

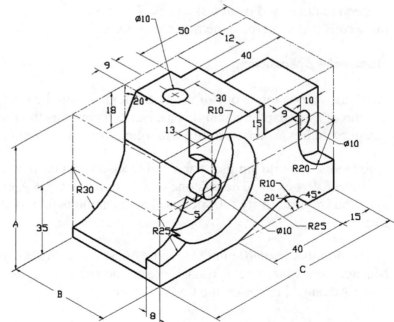

Hint: Insert thirteen features to build this model: Extruded Base, nine Extruded Cuts, two Extruded Bosses, and a Chamfer. Note: The center point of the top hole is located 30mm from the top right edge.

Think about the steps that you would take to build the illustrated part. Review the centerlines that outline the overall size of the part.

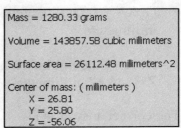

- A: X = 26.81 millimeters, Y = 25.80 millimeters, Z = -56.06 millimeters

- B: X = 43.30 millimeters, Y = 25.27 millimeters, Z = -15.54 millimeters

- C: X = 26.81 millimeters, Y = -25.75 millimeters, Z = 0.00 millimeters

- D: X = 46.00 millimeters, Y = -46.49 millimeters, Z = 10.00 millimeters

The correct answer is A.

This example was taken from the SolidWorks website, **www.solidworks.com/cswa** as an example of an Advanced Part on the CSWA exam. This model has thirteen features and twelve sketches. There are numerous ways to create the models in this chapter.

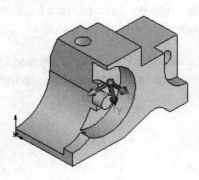

Assembly Modeling

Assembly Modeling is one of the five categories on the CSWA exam. In the last two section of this chapter, a simple or advanced part was the focus. The Assembly Modeling category addresses an assembly with numerous sub-components.

Knowledge to build simples parts and to insert Standard mates is required in this category for the CSWA exam. There is one question on the CSWA exam in this category. The question is worth thirty (30) points. The question is in a multiple choice single answer format.

Spend no more than 40 minutes on the question in this category. This is a timed exam. Manage your time. At this time, there are no sheet metal assembly questions or question using Advanced mates on the CSWA exam.

Sample Questions in the category

In the Assembly Modeling category, an exam question could read:

Question 1: Build this assembly. Locate the Center of mass of the model with respect to the illustrated coordinate system.

The assembly contains the following: One Clevis component, three Axle components, two 5 Hole Link components, two 3 Hole Link components, and six Collar components. All holes Ø.190 THRU unless otherwise noted. Angle A = 150deg. Angle B = 120deg. Note: The location of the illustrated coordinate system: (+X, +Y, +Z).

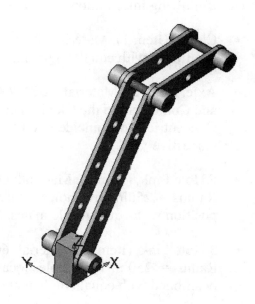

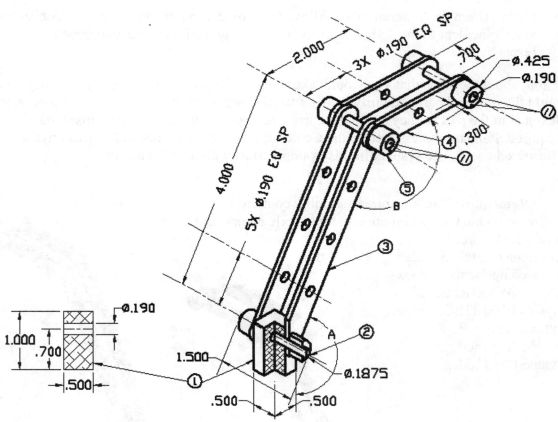

The following information is provided:

- Clevis, (Item 1): Material: 6061 Alloy. The two 5 Hole Link components are positioned with equal Angle mates, (150deg) to the Clevis component.

- Axle, (Item 2): Material: AISI 304. The first Axle component is mated Concentric and Coincident to the Clevis. The second and third Axle components are mated Concentric and Coincident to the 5 Hole Link and the 3 Hole Link components respectively.

- 5 Hole Link, (Item 3): Material: 6061 Alloy. Material thickness = .100in. Radius = .250in. Five holes located 1in. on center. The 5 Hole Link components are position with equal Angle mates, (120deg) to the 3 Hole Link components.

- 3 Hole Link, (Item 4): Material: 6061 Alloy. Material thickness = .100in. Radius = .250in. Three holes located 1in. on center. The 3 Hole Link components are positioned with equal Angle mates, (120deg) to the 5 Hole Link components.

- Collar, (Item 5): Material: 6061 Alloy. The Collar components are mated Concentric and Coincident to the Axle and the 5 Hole Link and 3 Hole Link components respectively.

Think about the steps that you would take to build the illustrated assembly. Identify and build the required parts. Identify the first fixed component. Position the Base component features in the part so they are in the correct orientation in the assembly. Insert the required Standard mates. Locate the Center of mass of the model with respect to the illustrated coordinate system. In this example, start with the Clevis part.

Remember: The illustrated assembly contains the following: One Clevis component, three Axle components, two 5 Hole Link components, two 3 Hole Link components, and six Collar components. All holes Ø.190 THRU unless otherwise noted.
Angle A = 150deg.
Angle B = 120deg.

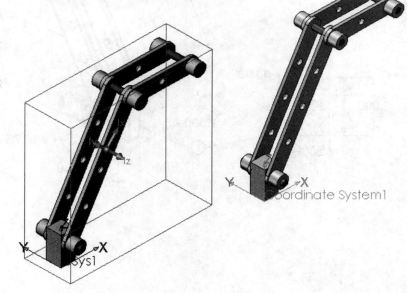

- A: X = 1.59 inches, Y = 1.19 inches, Z = 0.00 inches

- B: X = -1.59 inches, Y = 1.19 inches, Z = 0.04 inches

- C: X = 1.00 inches, Y = 1.18 inches, Z = 0.10 inches

- D: X = 1.79 inches, Y = 0.25 inches, Z = 2.61 inches

The correct answer is A.

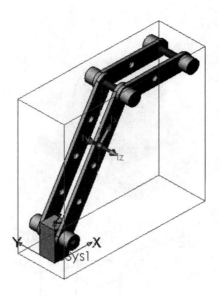

Question 2: Build this assembly. Locate the Center of mass using the illustrated coordinate system.

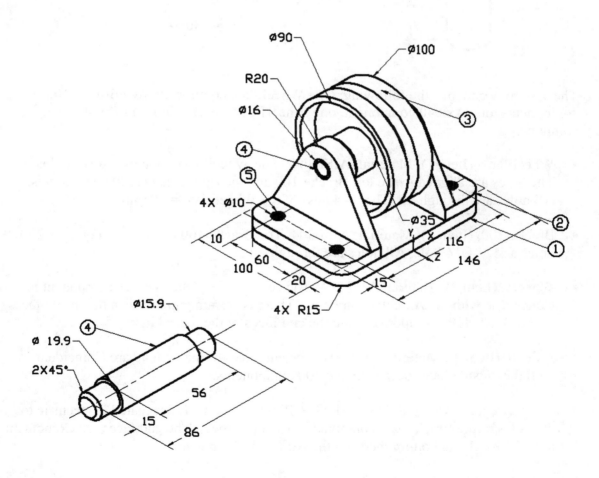

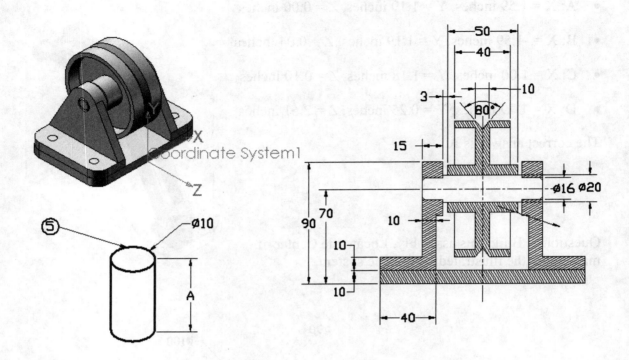

The assembly contains the following: One WheelPlate component, two Bracket100 components, one Axle40 component, one Wheel1 component, and four Pin-4 components.

- WheelPlate, (Item 1): Material: AISI 304. The WheelPlate contains 4-Ø10 holes. The holes are aligned to the left Bracket100 and the right Bracket100 components. All holes are through-all. The thickness of the WheelPlate = 10 mm.

- Bracket100, (Item 2): Material: AISI 304. The Bracket100 component contains 2-Ø10 holes and 1- Ø16 hole. All holes are through-all.

- Wheel1, (Item 3): Material AISI 304: The center hole of the Wheel1 component is Concentric with the Axle40 component. There is a 3mm gap between the inside faces of the Bracket100 components and the end faces of the Wheel hub.

- Axle40, (Item 4): Material AISI 304: The end faces of the Axle40 are Coincident with the outside faces of the Bracket100 components.

- Pin-4, (Item 5): Material AISI 304: The Pin-4 components are mated Concentric to the holes of the Bracket100 components, (no clearance). The end faces are Coincident to the WheelPlate bottom face and the Bracket100 top face.

Identify and build the required parts. Identify the first fixed component. This is the Base component of the assembly. Position the Base component features in the part so they are in the correct orientation in the assembly. Insert the required Standard mates. Locate the Center of mass of the illustrated model with respect to the referenced coordinate system. The referenced coordinate system is located at the bottom, right, midpoint of the Wheelplate. In this example, start with the WheelPlate part.

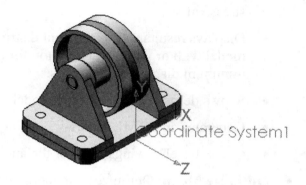

- A: X = 26.81 millimeters, Y = 25.80 millimeters, Z = -56.06 millimeters

- B: X = 0.00 millimeters, Y = 25.27 millimeters, Z = -15.54 millimeters

- C: X = 0.00 millimeters, Y = 37.14 millimeters, Z = -50.00 millimeters

- D: X = 0.00 millimeters, Y = -46.49 millimeters, Z = -50.00 millimeters

The correct answer is C.

 All models are located on the CD in the book.

Advanced Modeling Theory and Analysis

Advanced Modeling Theory and Analysis is one of the five categories on the CSWA exam. There are two questions on the CSWA exam in this category. Each question is worth five (5) points. The two questions are in a multiple choice single answer format.

As in the Part Modeling category of the exam, you are not required to perform an analysis on a part or assembly, but are required to understand general engineering analysis terminology and how SolidWorks SimulationXpress works.

SolidWorks Simulation Interface

SimulationXpress guides you through various default steps to define fixtures, loads, material properties, analyze the model, view the results and the optional Optimization process.

The SimulationXpress interface consists of the following options:

- **Welcome Menu**: Allows you to set the default units and to specify a folder for saving the analysis results.

- **Fixture Menu**: Applies fixtures / restraints to faces of the part.

- **Loads Menu**: Applies forces and pressures to faces of the part.

- **Material Menu**: Applies material properties to the part. The material can be assigned from the material library or you can input the material properties.

- **Run Menu**: Provides the ability to either display the analysis with the default settings or to change the settings.

- **Results Menu**: Displays the analysis results in the following ways:

  - Shows critical areas where the factor of safety is less than a specified value.

  - Displays the stress distribution in the model with or without annotation for the maximum and minimum stress values.

  - Displays resultant displacement distribution in the model with or without annotation for the maximum and minimum displacement values.

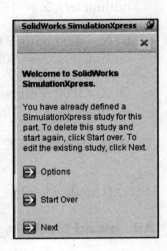

  - Shows deformed shape of the model.

  - Generates an HTML report.

  - Generates eDrawings files for the analysis results.

- **Optimize Menu**: Optimizes a model dimension based on a specified criterion.

- **Start Over button**: Deletes existing analysis data and results and starts a new analysis session.

Sample Questions in the category

In the Advanced Modeling Theory and Analysis category, an exam question could read:

Question 1: Under what SimulationXpress menu do you set System units?

- A = Material

- B = Fixture

- C = Welcome

- D = Load

The correct answer is C. Either SI or the IPS system units.

Question 2: Under what SimulationXpress menu can you modify the Mesh period of the part?

- A = Fixture

- B = Material

- C = Run

- D = Welcome

The correct answer is C = Run

Question 3: Yield strength is typically determined at _____ strain.

- A = 0.1%
- B = 0.2%
- C = 0.02%
- D = 0.002%

The correct answer is B.

Question 4: There are four key assumptions made in Linear Static Analysis: 1: Effects of inertia and damping is neglected, 2. The response of the system is directly proportional to the applied loads, 3: Loads are applied slowly and gradually, and_____ .

- A = Displacements are very small. The highest stress is in the linear range of the stress-strain curve.

- B = There are no loads.

- C = Material is not elastic.

- D = Loads are applied quickly.

The correct answer is A.

Question 5: How many degrees of freedom does a physical structure have?

- A = Zero.

- B = Three – Rotations only.

- C = Three – Translations only.

- D = Six – Three translations and three rotations.

The correct answer is D.

Question 6: Brittle materials has little tendency to deform (or strain) before fracture and does not have a specific yield point. It is not recommended to apply the yield strength analysis as a failure criterion on brittle material. Which of the following failure theories is appropriate for brittle materials?

- A = Mohr-Columb stress criterion.

- B = Maximum shear stress criterion.

- C = Maximum von Mises stress criterion.

- D = Minimum shear stress criterion.

The correct answer is A.

Question 7: You are performing an analysis on your model. You select three faces and apply a 40lb load. What is the total force applied to the model?

- A = 40lbs

- B = 20lbs

- C = 120lbs

- D: Additional information is required.

The correct answer is C.

Question 8: In an engineering analysis, you select a face to restrain. What is the affect?

- A = The face will not translate but can rotate.

- B = The face will rotate but can not translate.

- C = You can not apply a restraint to a face.

- D = The face will not rotate and will not translate.

The correction answer is D.

Question 9: A material is orthotropic if its mechanical or thermal properties are not unique and independent in three mutually perpendicular directions.

- A = True

- B = False

The correction answer is B.

Definition Review

Buckling:

Is a failure mode characterized by a sudden failure of a structural member subjected to high compressive stresses, where the actual compressive stresses at failure are smaller than the ultimate compressive stresses that the material is capable of withstanding. This mode of failure is also described as failure due to elastic instability.

Coefficient of Thermal Expansion:

Defined as the change in length per unit length per one degree change in temperature (change in normal strain per unit temperature).

Creep:

Term used to describe the tendency of a solid material to slowly move or deform permanently under the influence of stresses. It occurs as a result of long term exposure to levels of stress that are below the yield strength or ultimate strength of the material. Creep is more severe in materials that are subjected to heat for long periods, and near the melting point.

Degrees of Freedom:

The set of independent displacements and/or rotations that specify completely the displaced or deformed position and orientation of the body or system. This is a fundamental concept relating to systems of moving bodies in mechanical engineering, aeronautical engineering, robotics, structural engineering, etc. There are six degrees of freedom: Three translations and three rotations.

Density:

Mass per unit volume. Density units are lb/in^3 in the English system, and kg/m^3 in the SI system.

Density is used in static, nonlinear, frequency, dynamic, buckling, and thermal analyses. Static and buckling analyses use this property only if you define body forces (gravity and/or centrifugal).

Ductile:

Mechanical property which describes how able the material lends itself to be formed into rod-like shapes before fracture occurs. Examples of highly ductile metals are silver, gold, copper, and aluminum. The ductility of steel varies depending on the alloying constituents. Increasing levels of carbon decreases ductility, i.e. the steel becomes more brittle.

Elastic Modulus:

For a linear elastic material, the elastic modulus is the stress required to cause a unit strain in the material. In other words stress divided by the associated strain. The modulus of elasticity was first introduced by Young and is often called the Young's Modulus.

Fatigue:

Progressive and localized structural damage that occurs when a material is subjected to cyclic loading. The maximum stress values are less than the ultimate tensile stress limit, and may be below the yield stress limit of the material.

Fixed Restraint /Fixture:

For solids this restraint type sets all translational degrees of freedom to zero. For shells and beams, it sets the translational and the rotational degrees of freedom to zero. For truss joints, it sets the translational degrees of freedom to zero. When using this restraint type, no reference geometry is needed.

Force:

Is a push or pull upon an object resulting from the object's interaction with another object. Whenever there is an interaction between two objects, there is a force upon each of the objects. When the interaction ceases, the two objects no longer experience the force. Forces only exist as a result of an interaction.

For example, if you select 3 faces and specify a 50 lb force, COSMOSXpress applies a total force of 150 lbs (50 lbs on each face).

Knowing how a design will perform under different conditions allows engineers to make changes prior to physical prototyping, thus saving both time and money.

Linear Static Analysis:

Linear static analysis allows engineers to test different load conditions and their resulting stresses and deformation. What is stress? Stress is a measure of the average amount of force exerted per unit area. It is a measure of the intensity of the total internal forces acting within a body across imaginary internal surfaces, as a reaction to external applied forces and body forces.

Deformation is a change in shape due to an applied force. This can be a result of tensile (pulling) forces, compressive (pushing) forces, shear, bending or torsion (twisting). Deformation is often described in terms of strain.

When loads are applied to a body, the body deforms and the effect of loads is transmitted throughout the body. The external loads induce internal forces and reactions to render the body into a state of equilibrium.

Linear Static analysis calculates *displacements*, *strains*, *stresses*, and *reaction forces* under the effect of applied loads. Linear static analysis makes the following assumptions:

1. The induced response is directly proportional to the applied loads.

2. The highest stress is in the linear range of the stress-strain curve characterized by a straight line starting from the origin.

3. The maximum calculated displacement is considerably smaller than the characteristic dimension of the part. For example, the maximum displacement of a plate must be considerably smaller than its thickness and the maximum displacement of a beam must be considerably smaller than the smallest dimension of its cross-section. Inertia is neglected.

4. Loads are applied slowly and gradually until they reach their full magnitudes. Suddenly applied loads cause additional displacements, strains, and stresses.

Below are three simple graphics of Stress vs. Strain:

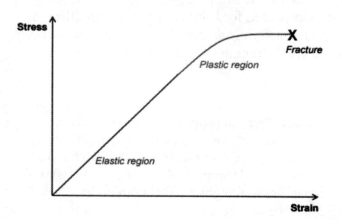

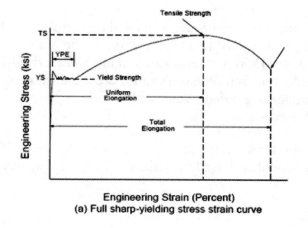

(a) Full sharp-yielding stress strain curve

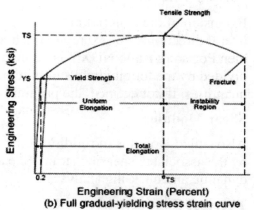

(b) Full gradual-yielding stress strain curve

Inertia:

Describes the motion of matter and how it is affected by applied forces. The principle of inertia as described by Newton in Newton's First Law of Motion states: "An object that is not subject to any outside forces moves at a constant velocity, covering equal distances in equal times along a straight-line path." In even simpler terms, inertia means "A body in motion tends to remain in motion, a body at rest tends to remain at rest."

Material Strength:

In materials science, the strength of a material refers to the material's ability to resist an applied force.

Mohr-Columb Stress Criterion:

The Mohr-Columb stress criterion is based on the Mohr- Columb theory also known as the Internal Friction theory. This criterion is used for brittle materials with different tensile and compressive properties. Brittle materials do not have a specific yield point and hence it is not recommended to use the yield strength to define the limit stress for this criterion.

Orthotropic Material:

A material is orthotropic if its mechanical or thermal properties are unique and independent in three mutually perpendicular directions. Examples of orthotropic materials are wood, many crystals, and rolled metals. For example, the mechanical properties of wood at a point are described in the longitudinal, radial, and tangential directions. The longitudinal axis (1) is parallel to the grain (fiber) direction; the radial axis (2) is normal to the growth rings; and the tangential axis (3) is tangent to the growth rings.

Poisson's Ratio:

Extension of the material in the longitudinal direction is accompanied by shrinking in the lateral directions. For example, if a body is subjected to a tensile stress in the X-direction, then Poisson's Ratio NUXY is defined as the ratio of lateral strain in the Y-direction divided by the longitudinal strain in the X-direction. Poisson's ratios are dimensionless quantities. If not defined, the program assumes a default value of 0.

Shear Modulus:

Also called modulus of rigidity, is the ratio between the shearing stress in a plane divided by the associated shearing strain. Shear Moduli are used in static, nonlinear, frequency, dynamic and buckling analyses.

Thermal Conductivity:

Indicates the effectiveness of a material in transferring heat energy by conduction. It is defined as the rate of heat transfer through a unit thickness of the material per unit temperature difference. The units of thermal conductivity are Btu/in sec $^\circ$F in the English system and W/m $^\circ$K in the SI system.

Thermal conductivity is used in steady state and transient thermal analyses.

Tensile Strength:

Tensile strength is the maximum load sustained by the specimen in the tension test, divided by the original cross sectional area.

von Mises yield Criterion:

A scalar stress value that can be computed from the stress. In this case, a material is said to start yielding when its von Mises stress reaches a critical value known as the yield strength. The von Mises stress is used to predict yielding of materials under any loading condition from results of simple uniaxial tensile tests. The von Mises stress satisfies the property that two stress states with equal distortion energy have equal von Mises stress.

Yield Strength:

The stress at which the metal yields or becomes permanently deformed is an important design parameter. This stress is the elastic limit below which no permanent shape changes will occur.

The elastic limit is approximated by the yield strength of the material, and the strain that occurs before the elastic limit is reached is called the elastic strain. The yield strength is defined in three ways, depending on the stress-strain characteristics of the steel as it begins to yield. The procedures in SAE J416, ASTM E8, and ASTM A370.

SimulationXpress uses this material property to calculate the factor of safety distribution. SimulationXpress assumes that the material starts yielding when the equivalent (von Mises) stress reaches this value.

Notes:

Appendix

Engineering Changer Order (ECO)

<table>
<tr><td colspan="2">D&M</td><td colspan="3">Engineering Change Order</td><td colspan="2">ECO # _____
Page 1 of __</td></tr>
<tr><td rowspan="2"></td><td>☐ Hardware
☐ Software</td><td colspan="3"></td><td colspan="2">Author
Date</td></tr>
<tr><td>Product Line</td><td>☐ Quality
☐ Tech Pubs</td><td colspan="3"></td><td colspan="2">Authorized Mgr.
Date</td></tr>
<tr><td colspan="7">Change Tested By</td></tr>
<tr><td colspan="7">Reason for ECO(Describe the existing problem, symptom and impact on field)</td></tr>
<tr><td>D&M Part No.</td><td colspan="2">Rev From/To</td><td>Part Description</td><td>Description</td><td colspan="2">Owner</td></tr>
</table>

ECO Implementation/Class		Departments	Approvals	Date	
All in Field	☐	Engineering			
All in Test	☐	Manufacturing			
All in Assembly	☐	Technical Support			
All in Stock	☐	Marketing			
All on Order	☐	DOC Control			
All Future	☐				
Material Disposition		ECO Cost			
Rework	☐	DO NOT WRITE BELOW THIS LINE (ECO BOARD ONLY)			
Scrap	☐	Effective Date			
Use as is	☐	Incorporated Date			
None	☐	Board Approval			
See Attached	☐	Board Date			

This text follows the ASME Y14 Engineering Drawing and Related Documentation Practices for drawings. Display of dimensions and tolerances are as follows:

TYPES of DECIMAL DIMENSIONS (ASME Y14.5M)			
Description:	**UNITS: MM**	**Description:**	**UNITS: INCH**
Dimension is less than 1mm. Zero precedes the decimal point.	0.9 0.95	Dimension is less than 1 inch. Zero is not used before the decimal point.	.5 .56
Dimension is a whole number. Display no decimal point. Display no zero after decimal point.	19	Express dimension to the same number of decimal places as its tolerance. Add zeros to the right of the decimal point. If the tolerance is expressed to 3 places, then the dimension contains 3 places to the right of the decimal point.	1.750
Dimension exceeds a whole number by a decimal fraction of a millimeter. Display no zero to the right of the decimal.	11.5 11.51		

TABLE 1		
TOLERANCE DISPLAY FOR INCH AND METRIC DIMENSIONS (ASME Y14.5M)		
DISPLAY:	**UNITS: INCH:**	**UNITS: METRIC:**
Dimensions less than 1	.5	0.5
Unilateral Tolerance	$1.417^{+.005}_{-.000}$	$36^{0}_{-0.5}$
Bilateral Tolerance	$1.417^{+.010}_{-.020}$	$36^{+0.25}_{-0.50}$
Limit Tolerance	.571 .463	14.50 11.50

SolidWorks Keyboard Shortcuts

Listed below are some of the pre-defined keyboard shortcuts in SolidWorks:

Action:	Key Combination:
Model Views	
Rotate the model horizontally or vertically:	**Arrow** keys
Rotate the model horizontally or vertically 90 degrees.	**Shift + Arrow** keys
Rotate the model clockwise or counterclockwise	**Alt** + left of right **Arrow** keys
Pan the model	**Ctrl + Arrow** keys
Magnifying glass	**g**
Zoom in	**Shift + z**
Zoom out	**z**
Zoom to fit	**f**
Previous view	**Ctrl + Shift + z**
View Orientation	
View Orientation menu	**Spacebar**
Front view	**Ctrl + 1**
Back view	**Ctrl + 2**
Left view	**Ctrl + 3**
Right view	**Ctrl + 4**
Top view	**Ctrl + 5**
Bottom view	**Ctrl + 6**
Isometric view	**Ctrl + 7**
Normal To view	**Ctrl + 8**
Selection Filters	
Filter edges	**e**
Filter vertices	**v**
Filter faces	**x**
Toggle Selection Filter toolbar	**F5**
Toggle selection filters on/off	**F6**
File menu items	
New SolidWorks document	**Ctrl + n**
Open document	**Ctrl + o**
Open From Web Folder	**Ctrl + w**
Make Drawing from Part	**Ctrl + d**
Make Assembly from Part	**Ctrl + a**
Save	**Ctrl +s**
Print	**Ctrl + p**
Additional shortcuts	
Access online help inside of PropertyManager or dialog box	**F1**
Rename an item in the FeatureManager design tree	**F2**
Rebuild the model	**Ctrl + b**
Force rebuild – Rebuild the model and all its features	**Ctrl + q**
Redraw the screen	**Ctrl + r**

Cycle between open SolidWorks document	**Ctrl + Tab**
Line to arc/arc to line in the Sketch	**a**
Undo	**Ctrl + z**
Redo	**Ctrl + y**
Cut	**Ctrl + x**
Copy	**Ctrl + c**
Additional shortcuts	
Paste	**Ctrl + v**
Delete	**Delete**
Next window	**Ctrl + F6**
Close window	**Ctrl + F4**
View previous tools	**s**
Selects all text inside an Annotations text box	**Ctrl + a**

 In a sketch, the **Esc** key un-selects geometry items currently selected in the Properties box and Add Relations box. In the model, the **Esc** key closes the PropertyManager and cancels the selections.

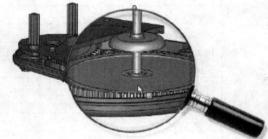

Use the **g** key to activate the Magnifying glass tool. Use the Magnifying glass tool to inspect a model and make selections without changing the overall view.

Use the **s** key to view/access previous command tools in the Graphics window.

Windows Shortcuts

Listed below are some of the pre-defined keyboard shortcuts in Microsoft Windows:

Action:	**Keyboard Combination:**
Open the Start menu	Windows Logo key
Open Windows Explorer	Windows Logo key + E
Minimize all open windows	Windows Logo key + M
Open a Search window	Windows Logo key + F
Open Windows Help	Windows Logo key + F1
Select multiple geometry items in a SolidWorks document	Ctrl key (Hold the Ctrl key down. Select items.) Release the Ctrl key.

Helpful On-Line Information

The SolidWorks URL: http://www.solidworks.com contains information on Local Resellers, Solution Partners, Certifications, SolidWorks users groups, and more.

Access 3D ContentCentral using the Task Pane to obtain engineering electronic catalog model and part information.

Use the SolidWorks Resources tab in the Task Pane to obtain access to Customer Portals, Discussion Forums, User Groups, Manufacturers, Solution Partners, Labs, and more.

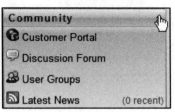

Helpful on-line SolidWorks information is available from the following URLs:

- http://www.dmeducation.net

    Information on the CSWA Certification, software updates, design tips and new book releases.

- http://www.mechengineer.com/snug/

    News group access and local user group information.

- http://www.nhcad.com

    Configuration information and other tips and tricks.

- http://www.solidworktips.com

    Helpful tips, tricks on SolidWorks and API.

- http://www.topica.com/lists/SW

    Independent News Group for SolidWorks discussions, questions and answers.

Certified SolidWorks Professionals (CSWP) URLs provide additional helpful on-line information.

- http://www.scottjbaugh.com   Scott J. Baugh

- http://www.3-ddesignsolutions.com   Devon Sowell

- http://www.zxys.com   Paul Salvador

- http://www.mikejwilson.com   Mike J. Wilson

- http://www.dimontegroup.com   Gene Dimonte & Ed Eaton

*On-line tutorials are for educational purposes only. Tutorials are copyrighted by their respective owners.

Notes:

INDEX

*.drwdot - 2-46
*slddrt - 2-16
.dwg - 2-49
3D Drawing view tool - 1-9, 3-70

A
A (ANSI) Size Drawing template - 2-76
A-ANSI-MM - 2-77, 3-17, 3-41
A-ANSI-MM Drawing template - 2-2
Accelerator keys - 1-15
Add a Datumn - 6-22
Add a New Sheet - 4-53
Add a Note - 3-28
Add Parentheses - 2-40, 4-41
Add Revision tool - 5-64
Add Sheet - 3-26, 5-50
Add Sheet tab - 3-21
Add Symbol tool - 4-34
Add-Ins - 1-16
Advanced mode - 1-21
a-format - 2-77
A-Landscape - 2-76
Align a Note - 5-56
Align Dimension text - 4-22
Align Dimensions - 4-39
Align Text - 2-54
Align views - 3-30
Aligned Section view tool - 3-64
Alignment tool - 3-30
Alternative Position view tool - 3-73
A-MM-ANSI-NO-VIEWS - 6-46
AMSE Y14.3M Principle View Names -
    3-9
Angular Dimension - 4-54
Annotation Link Errors - 2-66
Annotation toolbar - 4-75
    Area Hatch/Fill Tool - 3-54
    AutoBalloon tool - 5-15
    Bill of Materials tool - 5-19, 5-50
    Center Mark tool - 4-34, 4-41
    Centerline tool - 4-24, 4-50, 6-20
    Datum Feature - 6-41
    Hole Callout tool - 4-32, 4-39
    Insert Block tool - 6-70
    Model Items tool - 4-14
    Note tool - 3-28, 4-34
    Revision Table tool - 5-60
    Surface Finish tool - 6-31, 6-32
    Weld Symbol tool - 6-49
ANSI Dimension standard - 2-33
Appearances/Scenes - 1-18

Apply Scene tool - 1-9
Area Hatch/Fill tool - 3-54
ASME 14-41 Part: DimXpert - 6-36
ASME Y14 Engineering Drawing and
    Related Practices - 2-5
ASME Y14 Standards - 2-5
ASME Y14.1 Drawing Sheet Size and
    Format - 2-10
ASME14-41 Drawing - 6-36
ASME14-41 Drawing - Datum Feature -
    6-41
Auto Balloon PropertyManager - 5-13
Auto Dimension Scheme tool - 6-11, 6-12
AutoBalloon tool - 5-15
AutoCAD Drawing - 2-52
Auxiliary view - 3-26
Auxiliary view tool - 3-48

B
Base Line Dimensioning - 4-73
Base Sketch - 1-20
Bent Leader option - 5-15
Bent Leader tool - 6-31
Bill of Materials PropertyManager - 5-17
Bill of Materials tool - 5-19, 5-51
Block PropertyManager - 6-66
Blocks - 6-66
BOM Template - 5-58
Break view tool - 3-23
Broken view PropertyManager - 3-23
Broken-out Section view tool - 3-46
Build Checks tool - 2-8

C
C (ANSI) Landscape - 2-11
C-ANSI-MM - 2-75
Center Dimension text - 4-21
Center Mark tool - 4-34, 4-41
Center Marks in a Drawing view - 3-59
Center/Min/Max Arc Condition - 4-70
Centerline Sketch tool - 3-60, 3-64
Centerline tool - 4-24, 4-50, 6-20
C-FORMAT - 2-74
Chamfer dimension - 4-51
CHAPTER2-TEMPLATES folder - 2-7
Check Active Document tool - 2-8
Child View - 3-18, 3-28
Close All - 1-26, 2-46, 2-47
Closed Spline - 3-33
Coincident relation - 3-61
Collapse Items - 1-14

Collinear relation - 3-51
Color Display Mode tool - 2-13
CommandManager - 1-10
    Assembly document - 1-12
    Drawing document - 1-11
    Part document - 1-10
Configuration Properties - 5-25
Configuration tab - 3-15
ConfigurationManager tab - 1-13
Confirmation Corner - 1-8
Consolidated Tables toolbar - 5-17
Consolidated toolbar - 1-7
Context-sensitive toolbar - 1-10
Copy a Drawing view - 3-22
Copy a Note - 4-36
Copy Tolerance Scheme tool - 6-16
Copy/Paste Custom Properties - 2-65
Corner Rectangle Sketch tool - 3-51, 6-68
Cosmetic Thread - 4-55, 4-58
COVERPLATE Drawing - 3-56
COVERPLATE Drawing - Detailing - 4-46
COVERPLATE Drawing: Offset Section
    view, and Aligned Section view - 3-60
Create a New Drawing - 2-11
Create two Leader Lines - 5-16
Crop view tool - 3-49
C-SIZE-ANSI-MM-EMPTY - 2-46, 2-47
Cursor Feedback - Drawing Views - 2-15
Custom Properties - 2-58, 2-59
Custom Properties in Parts and
    Assemblies - 2-67
Custom Properties in the Design Table -
    5-24
Customize CommandManager - 2-13
Customize Keyboard - 2-14
Cut-Away view - 3-50
CYLINDER Assembly Drawing - Insert
    Balloons - 5-11
CYLINDER Assembly Drawing - Bill of
    Materials - 5-17
CYLINDER Assembly Exploded view - 5-8
CYLINDER Assembly - Design Table -
    5-44
CYLINDER Drawing: Multiple
    Configurations - 5-50

D

Datum Feature tool - 6-41
Datum Planes - 3-8
Datum tool - 6-16
Deactivated the Origins - 3-18
Default Drawing Template - 2-7
Default Sheet Format - 2-7
Default Sheet Size - 2-7
Delete All Tolerances tool - 6-17
Design Checker tool - 2-8

Design Library - 1-16
Design Table - 3-52, 5-31
    Insert Column - 5-39
    Insert Equation - 5-42
    Insert Header - 5-40
    Insert Row - 5-40
    Modify Font size - 5-43
    Modify Item Order - 5-40
Design Table Parameters - 5-33
Design Table PropertyManager - 5-32
Detached drawing - 2-3
Detail view tool - 3-33, 3-34, 3-44
Detailing tips - 4-43
Dimension Precision - 2-40
Dimension PropertyManager - 4-60
    Leader tab - 4-64
    Other tab - 4-66
    Value tab - 4-60
DimXpert - 4-17
    Dimension - 6-22, 6-23
    Edit Feature Control Frame - 6-28
    Geometric Option - 6-27
    Geometric Tolerance - 6-24
    Max Material Condition - 6-24
    Plus and Minus Option - 6-8
    Tolerance - 6-23
Dimxpert Manager tab - 6-26
DimXpert Manually in a Part - 6-21
DimXpert Scheme - 6-12
DimXpert toolbar - 6-16
    Auto Dimension Scheme Tool - 6-16
    Copy Tolerance Scheme tool - 6-16
    Datum tool - 6-16
    Delete All Tolerances tool - 6-17
    Geometric Tolerance tool - 6-16
    Location Dimension tool - 6-16
    Pattern Feature tool - 6-16
    Show Tolerance Status tool - 6-16
    Size Dimension tool - 6-16
DimXpertManager - 1-13, 6-11
    AutoDimension Scheme tab - 1-15
    Copy Scheme tab - 1-15
    Show Tolerance Status tab - 1-15
    TolAnalyst Study tab - 1-15
Display modes - 2-20
    Hidden Lines Removed - 2-20
    Hidden Lines Visible - 2-20
    Shaded - 2-20
    Tangent Edges Removed - 2-20
    Tangent Edges Visible - 2-20
    Tangent Edges With Font - 2-20
    Wireframe - 2-20
Display Origins - 3-60
Display Style tool - 1-8
Display styles - 2-20
Display Temporary Axes - 3-60

Document Properties - Alternative Section Display Option - 2-29
Document Properties - Annotations Arrow Font - 2-36
Document Properties - Arrowheads - 2-24
Document Properties - Arrows - 2-42
Document Properties - Arrows Option - 2-39
Document Properties - Auto Insert on View Creation Option - 2-30
Document Properties - Automatic Update on BOM Options - 2-31
Document Properties - Auxiliary view / Auxiliary view Label Font - 2-35
Document Properties - Balloons - 5-12
Document Properties - Bend Leader Length Option - 2-39
Document Properties - Break Dimension / Extension Option - 2-39
Document Properties - Break Line Option - 2-31
Document Properties - Centerline Extension and Center Marks Option - 2-29
Document Properties - Cosmetic Thread Display Option - 2-31, 2-32
Document Properties - Datum Feature Option - 2-31
Document Properties - Detail view / Detail view Label Font - 2-35
Document Properties - Detailing - 2-33
Document Properties - Dimensioning Standard - 2-27
Document Properties - Dimensions Options - 2-38
Document Properties - Display Datums per 1982 Option - 2-29
Document Properties - Document Properties, Annotations Font - 2-34
Document Properties - Drafting Standard Options - 2-28
Document Properties - Dual Dimensions Display Options - 2-28
Document Properties - Extension Lines Option - 2-30
Document Properties - Fixed Size Weld Symbols Option - 2-28
Document Properties - Font - 2-23
Document Properties - General - 2-22
Document Properties - Leading Zeros and Trailing Zeroes Option - 2-29
Document Properties - Line Font - 2-26, 2-43
Document Properties - Line Widths - 2-25
Document Properties - Note Font - 2-34

Document Properties - Notes and Balloons Option - 2-40, 2-41
Document Properties - Offset Distance Option - 2-38, 2-40
Document Properties - Section view / Section view Label Font - 2-36, 2-37
Document Properties - Surface Finish Symbols - 2-31
Document Properties - Surface Finish, Weld Symbol, and Balloon Font - 2-36
Document Properties - View Arrow Font - 2-36
Document Recovery - 1-18
Drafting Standard - 2-34
Drawing Logo - 2-63, 2-64
Drawing Scale Properties - 2-61
Drawing Sheet - 2-61
Drawing Size - 2-51
Drawing View Boundary Properties - 3-20
Drop-down menu - 1-6
Dual dimension display - 2-33
DWGEditor - 6-73
DXF/DWG Import - 6-73

E
Edit a Note - 4-37
Edit Appearance tool - 1-9
Edit Design Table - 3-53, 5-34
Edit Dimension text - 4-28
Edit Feature Control Frame - 6-28
Edit Material - 3-55
Edit Sheet Format - 5-61
Edit Sheet Format mode - 2-49, 2-51
Edit Sheet mode - 2-49, 2-51
Edit Sketch Plane - 6-11
Edit Table tool - 6-51
Edit the Revision Table - 5-62
Edit Title Block - 2-53
Editing Design Table - 5-37
Editing Design Table Cells - 5-37
eDrawing - 5-69, 6-33
Empty view - 3-73
Equation tool - 5-42
Exploded view state - 5-14
Exploded view tool - 5-9
Export - 5-69
Extruded Cut feature - 3-52

F
Family Cell - 6-61
Feature - 1-20
Feature Control Frame - 6-28
FeatureManager Design Tree - 1-13
    ConfigurationManager tab - 1-13
    DimXpertManager - 1-13
    PropertyManager tab - 1-13

File Explorer - 1-17
File Management - 2-6
Filter FeatureManager - 1-14
First Angle Projection - 2-16, 2-17, 2-19,
    3-9
Flyout / Consolidated menus - 1-6
Fly-out FeatureManager - 1-15
Foreshortened Radii - 4-69
Format Cells - 6-62
Format-C-ACAD - 2-52
Front Plane - 1-22

G
General Notes - 2-69
Geometric Tolerance Symbols - 6-74
Geometric Tolerance tool - 6-16
Glass Box method - 2-17
Grid/Snap - 4-73
Grid/Snaps tool - 1-9

H
Heads-up View toolbar - 1-8
    3D Drawing view - 1-9
    Apply Scene - 1-9
    Display Style - 1-8
    Edit Appearance - 1-9
    Hide/Show Items - 1-8
    Previous View - 1-8
    Rotate - 1-9
    Section view, 1-8
    View Orientation - 1-8
    View Setting - 1-9
    Zoom to Area - 1-8
    Zoom to Fit - 1-8
Help - 1-24
Hidden Lines Removed mode - 2-16
Hidden Lines Visible - 2-20, 3-14, 6-20
Hide Behind Plane tool - 5-66
Hide Dimension - 4-26, 4-32
Hide Drawing view - 6-20
Hide Edge - 6-20
Hide FeatureManager Tree area - 1-14
Hide Show edges tool - 2-13
Hide Superficial Dimensions - 6-53
Hide tool - 4-15
Hide view - 3-20
Hide/Show Annotations - 4-50
HideDims layer - 4-19
HideDims Layer off - 4-37
Hole Callout tool - 4-32, 4-39

I
Import From AutoCAD - 2-52
Insert a Bill of Materials - 5-51
Insert a Break - 4-26
Insert a Centerline - 4-24, 4-33, 4-34

Insert a Design Table - 3-52
Insert a Note - 4-34
Insert a Relative view - 4-53
Insert a Revision Table - 5-60
Insert Area Hatch - 3-54
Insert Block tool - 6-71
Insert Center Marks - 4-37
Insert Custom Properties - 5-25
Insert Drawing dimensions - 4-14
Insert Drawing view dimensions - 4-32
Insert Hole Wizard dimension - 4-54
Internal Gap - 4-20

J-K-L
Keyboard Shortcut key - 2-13, 2-14
Large Assembly Drawing Performance -
    5-67
Layer Properties - 2-54
Layer Properties tool - 2-13, 2-60, 3-35
Layers dialog box - 2-54
Layers toolbar - 2-54, 3-18
Leader tab - 4-23
Line Color Properties tool - 2-13
Line Format toolbar - 2-13, 6-68
    Color Display Mode - 2-13
    Hide Show edges- 2-13
    Layer Properties - 2-13
    Line Color Properties - 2-13
    Line Style Properties - 2-13
    Line Thickness - 2-13
Line Sketch tool - 3-35
Line Style Properties tool - 2-13
Line Thickness tool - 2-13
Link to Property tool - 2-58, 2-59, 2-60,
    2-61, 2-62, 5-61, 5-63
Linked Notes - 2-58, 2-60
Location Dimension tool - 6-16
Lock view command - 2-15
Lock view options - 3-20
Lock view position - 3-35
Lock view tool - 2-15

M
Magnifying glass - 1-9
Mass Properties - 5-20
Material Editor - 5-20
Menu bar menu - 1-5
Menu bar toolbar - 1-5
    New tool - 1-5
    Open tool - 1-4
    Options tool - 1-5
    Print tool - 1-5
    Rebuild tool - 1-5
    Save tool - 1-5
    Select tool - 1-5
    Undo tool - 1-5

MMGS (millimeter, grams, second) - 2-34
Model Items PropertyManager - 4-12
Model Items tool - 4-14
Model View PropertyManager - 2-11
Model view tool - 3-32, 5-54
Modify Annotations - 3-27
Modify Drawing view Properties - 4-51
Modify Drawing view scale - 3-23
Modify Extension line value - 2-33
Modify Precision - 4-33
Modify Sheet Properties - 3-42
Modify Sheet Scale - 6-18, 6-24
Modify Sketch Plane - 6-11
Modify the Properties of a Block - 6-71
Modify the Sheet Order - 4-53
Modify View Dimensions - 6-54
Modify View Properties - 5-51, 5-52
Modifying Features - 4-58
Motion Study tab - 1-19
MotionManager - 1-19
    Animation tab - 1-19
    Basic Motion tab - 1-19
Mouse gesture wheel - 1-14
Move a Balloon - 5-16
Move Drawing View Dimensions - 4-22
MY-SHEETFORMATS folder - 2-7, 3-12
MY-TEMPLATE tab - 3-17
MY-TEMPLATES folder - 2-7

N
Named Model views - 3-16
Named view - 1-9
New Drawing - 2-11
New Drawing command - 2-46
New folder - 2-6
New Layer - 6-70
New Motion Study - 1-20
New Part - 1-21
New Scheme - 6-12
New SolidWorks Document dialog box - 2-8
New tool - 1-5
New view tool - 1-9
No Leader tool - 6-32
Note tool - 2-58, 2-60, 2-61, 3-28, 4-34
Novice mode - 1-21

O
Offset Dimension text - 4-24
Open a Part document - 1-21, 3-13
Open tool - 1-5
Options tool - 1-5
Ordinate Dimension - 4-74
Origin - 1-22
Orthographic Projection - 2-18, 2-44, 3-8

P
Parent view - 3-18, 3-28
Partially Rounded Ends - 4-70
Paste a Drawing view - 3-22
Paste a Note - 4-37
Paste view - 3-27, 3-29
Pattern Feature tool - 6-16
Perspective view tool - 3-72
Pin tool - 1-6
PLATE-CATALOG Drawing - 6-53, 6-54
PLATE-CATALOG Part - 6-51
PLATE-TUBE Assembly Drawing - 6-41, 6-42
Point Sketch tool - 3-61, 3-64
Precision - 2-40
Predefined and Projected Views - 2-44
Predefined views - 3-16, 3-18
Previous view tool - 1-8
Primary Datum Plane - 3-8
Print tool - 1-5
Projected Back view - 3-42
Projected Right view - 3-63
Projected view tool - 2-45, 3-22
PropertyManager tab - 1-13

Q-R
Quadrants - 2-18
Rebuild tool - 1-5
Reference Planes - 1-22
    Front Plane - 1-22
    Right Plane - 1-22
    Top Plane - 1-22
Relative view - 4-53
Removed view - 3-26
Rename tool - 3-22
Revision - 5-62
Revision Symbol - 5-60
Revision Table - 5-59
Revision Table - Anchor Point - 2-70
Revision Table - Insert Row - 5-61
Revision Table tool - 5-60
Right Plane - 1-22
Right-click Pop-up menus - 1-6
ROD Drawing - Sheet1 - 3-17
ROD Drawing - Broken Isomeric view - 3-32
ROD Drawing - Revolved Section - 3-29
ROD Drawing - Sheet1-Short Rod Configuration - 3-16
ROD Drawing - Sheet2-Long Rod Configuration - 3-21
ROD Drawing - Sheet3 - Long Rod Configuration - 3-25
ROD Part - 3-11
ROD Part - Configurations - 3-15
Rollback Bar - 3-14

Rotate Drawing view - 3-70
Rotate view tool - 1-9
Rotated view tool - 3-71

S
Save As - 2-12, 2-37
Save Drawing template - 2-74
Save Sheet Format - 2-74
Save the Block - 6-70
Save tool - 1-5
Search - 1-17
Secondary Datum Plane - 3-8
Section view tool - 3-30, 3-43
Select Configuration - 3-54
Select tool - 1-5
Sensor tool - 1-13
Shaded mode - 2-20
Shaded With Edges - 3-19
Sheet Boundary - 2-16
Sheet Format - 2-46
Sheet Format/Size dialog box - 2-9
Sheet formats - 2-4
Sheet Properties - 2-15, 2-16, 3-19
Sheet Scale - 6-18, 6-24
Shortcut keys - 1-15
Show Dimensions - 4-16
Show Layer - 4-33
Show Tolerance Status tool - 6-16
Show tool - 4-32
Silhouette edges - 6-10
Size Dimension tool - 6-16
Size Principal views - 2-17
Slotted Holes - 4-71
Smart Dimension Sketch tool - 4-19, 4-39
SolidWorks Design Checker tool - 2-8
SolidWorks Graphics window - 1-22
SolidWorks Help - 1-24
SolidWorks Installation - 1-9
SolidWorks Resources - 1-16
SolidWorks Tutorials - 1-25
SolidWorks User Interface - 1-5, 1-20
Spline Sketch tool - 3-33, 3-45
Split FeatureManager - 1-14
Standard Sheet formats - 2-9
Standard Views toolbar - 1-8
Start a SolidWorks Session - 1-3
Suppress - 3-52
Surface Finish tool - 6-31, 6-32
SW Prefix - 2-56
System feedback icons - 1-7
    Dimension - 1-7
    Edge - 1-7
    Face - 1-6
    Vertex - 1-7
System Options - 2-16
System Options - Display Style - 2-21

System Options - File Locations - 2-21
System Options - General - 2-21
System Properties - 2-56, 2-57

T
Tables - 2-70
Tables Font - 2-37
Tags - 1-14, 1-22
Tangent Edge - 6-20
Tangent Edges Removed - 2-20, 6-20
Tangent Edges Visible - 2-20
Tangent Edges With Font - 2-20
Task Pane - 1-16
    Appearances/Scenes - 1-18
    Custom Properties - 1-18
    Design Library - 1-16
    Document Recovery - 1-18
    File Explorer - 1-17
    Search - 1-17
    SolidWorks Resources - 1-16
    View Palette - 1-17
Templates tab - 1-21
Tertiary Datum Plane - 3-8
Third Angle Projection - 2-16, 2-17, 2-18,
    3-9
Tip of the Day - 1-4
Title Block Notes and Properties - 2-56
TolAnalyst - 6-3
Tolerance Type - 4-11
    Basic - 4-11
    Bilateral - 4-11
    Limit - 4-11
    Max - 4-11
    Min - 4-11
    Symmetric - 4-11
Tolerance/Precision box - 4-8, 4-9
Top Plane - 1-22
Trailing zeroes - 4-9
TUBE Drawing - 3-41
TUBE Drawing - Add Dimensions - 4-38
TUBE Drawing - Broken-out Section view,
    Auxiliary view, and Crop view - 3-45
TUBE Drawing - Detailing - 4-12
TUBE Drawing - Detailing Detail view, and
    Front view - 4-25
TUBE Drawing - Detailing Right view,
    Back view, and Holes - 4-29
TUBE Drawing - Half Section Isometric
    view - 3-50
TUBE Drawing - Section view and Detail
    view - 3-43
TUBE Drawing - Section view, Top view,
    and Detail view - 4-17
TUBE Part - 3-37
Tutorial tab - 1-21
Tutorials - 1-25

Type of Projection - 2-16, 2-17
Types of Decimal Dimensions (ASME
    Y14.5M) - 4-7
Types of Fits - 6-74

U
Un-Break view tool - 3-23
Undo tool - 1-5
UnHide - 6-62
Units - 2-34
Unsuppress tool - 6-48
Use Custom scale - 3-26, 3-31
User Defined - 3-31
User Defined Custom Property - 2-65
User Defined Properties - 2-58
User Specified Part Number - 5-25

V
VALVEPLATE1 Drawing - View Palette -
    6-17
VALVEPLATE1 Part - DimXpert: Plus and
    Minus Option - 6-8
VALVEPLATE1-GDT Drawing - view
    Palette - 6-29
VALVEPLATE1-GDT Drawing - Surface
    Finish - 6-31
VALVEPLATE1-GDT Part - 6-26
View Layout tab - 2-45
View Layout toolbar - 3-67, 4-75
    Aligned Section view tool - 3-64, 3-67

Alternative Position view tool - 3-68
Auxiliary view tool - 3-26, 3-48, 3-67
Break view tool - 3-23, 3-68
Broken-out Section view tool - 3-46,
    3-68
Crop view tool - 3-49, 3-68
Detail view tool - 3-33, 3-34, 3-67
Model view tool - 3-32, 3-67
Projection view tool - 3-67
Section view tool - 3-30, 3-33, 3-67
Standard 3 view tool -3-67
View Orientation tool - 1-8
View Origins - 1-23
View Palette - 1-17, 3-25
View Palette tab - 6-18
View scale - 3-57
View Setting tool - 1-9
View toolbar - 1-8
Vise Assembly - 6-21

W-X-Y-Z
Weld Bead - 6-43
Weld Symbol tool - 6-49
Weld Symbols - 6-43, 6-46, 6-48, 6-49
Window - Select - 3-49, 5-15
Wireframe - 2-20, 3-15
Zoom out - 3-15
Zoom to Area tool - 1-8
Zoom to Fit tool - 1-8

Notes:

Notes:

Notes:

Notes:

Notes:

Notes:

Notes:

Notes:

Notes:

Notes:

Notes:

Notes:

Notes: